THE SHAPING
OF A LIFE

OTHER BOOKS BY THE AUTHOR

NONFICTION
The Divine Hours (Volumes 1, 2, and 3)
God-Talk in America
My Father's Prayer
Re-Discovering the Sacred—Spirituality in America
The Tickle Papers
Ordinary Time
Final Sanity
What the Heart Already Knows
The City Essays

LITURGICAL DRAMA
Tobias and the Angel
Children of Her Name
Figs and Fury

GENERAL EDITOR
HomeWorks—A Book of Tennessee Writers
Confessing Conscience—Churched Women on Abortion

PHYLLIS TICKLE

IMAGE BOOKS
DOUBLEDAY
New York   London   Toronto   Sydney   Auckland

THE SHAPING
OF A LIFE

A Spiritual Landscape

An Image Book
PUBLISHED BY DOUBLEDAY
a division of Random House, Inc.

IMAGE, DOUBLEDAY, and the portrayal of a deer drinking
from a stream are trademarks of Doubleday, a division of
Random House, Inc.

The Library of Congress has cataloged the Doubleday
hardcover edition as follows:
Tickle, Phyllis.
    The shaping of a life : a spiritual landscape / by Phyllis Tickle.
        p. cm.
    1. Tickle, Phyllis.   2. Episcopalians—Tennessee—
Biography.   I. title.

BX5995.T53 A3 2001
283'.092—dc21
[B]   2001017283

ISBN 0-385-49756-3

PRINTED IN THE UNITED STATES OF AMERICA

February 2003

First Hardcover Edition May 2001

Book design by Jennifer Ann Daddio

10   9   8   7   6   5   4   3   2   1

AUTHOR'S NOTE

There are times in any autobiography when the lives and privacy of others must be protected. For that reason, some of the names in this one have been changed and/or an occasional telltale circumstance modified slightly to make the participants less immediately identifiable.

Jeb and Tina's story has appeared in print once before—in *Homewords—A Book of Tennessee Writers,* edited by Doug Paschall and published by the University of Tennessee Press in 1986.

For my daughters and daughters-in-law
Nora Katherine Cannon
Mary Gammon Ballard
Laura Lee Palermo
Rebecca Rutledge Howell
Patricia Rose Tickle
Mary Gore Tickle

Because of them I walk each day
in the company of good women.

Let not those who hope in you be put to
shame through me, Lord God of hosts;
let not those who seek you be disgraced
because of me, O God of Israel.

—PSALM 69:7
PSALTER, THE BOOK OF
COMMON PRAYER

THE SHAPING
OF A LIFE

PART ONE

My Mother's House,
My Father's Garden

1.

MY FATHER taught me to love words, and my mother taught me to pray. In his case, it was patient and intentional. In hers, quite the opposite.

The house in which I grew up and in which my first subjective instruction was played out was a determinant in those lessons. Or if not a determinant, then at least a kind of text upon which my memory and understanding have recorded them and to which I have attached their intricacies. This is not to say that the old house was in any way a thing of beauty or even that it could lay claim to any pretensions. It most assuredly was not that kind of house.

Built in the 1920s just before the Great Depression wrought havoc on everybody including the house's original owner/builder, the poor thing was still not entirely finished when my father bought it fifteen years later from the man's widow. The roughed-in, but unfinished, portions of the upstairs that looked out through broad dormer windows onto a line of silver maple trees and then to the street beyond became mine within a few days of our moving in.

"Phyllis's playroom" was the way my mother came to refer to that near-sixth of her new house that yawned, dusty and inviting, at the end of the upstairs hall and just beyond my bedroom door. It was a phrasing that, once she had invented it, allowed Mother to live more comfortably with the notion that her only child was setting up shop on a loose-planked floor and sitting on cross braces nailed to open studs. With or without such euphemisms, however, my mother and I both knew that that unfinished space was my soul's home, just as my father and I knew that so long as I lived as a child among them, the space was to remain unfinished except by my imagination or my own juvenile carpentry. It was a kind of gentlemen's agreement amongst the three of us.

Almost as a result of that agreement, I came in time, subtly but surely, to divide the old house into "theirs" (the downstairs) and "mine" (the upstairs.) I found theirs considerably less interesting than mine for adventures, but rivetingly more absorbing for its revelations about adults and adult ways of living. I spent whole afternoons, in fact, just sitting on the upstairs steps and contemplating the complexities of what was going on below me and what, presumably, I was to become in time. But the house was so laid out that no one seat, not even my favored one on the stairs, was totally satisfactory as an observatory. No, ours was a house that required an inquisitive child to move about a lot.

The floor plan of the downstairs was hardly more imaginative or less phlegmatic than was the house itself. A huge (the most odious chore of my late childhood was having to sweep the whole thing every Saturday morning for the perfectionist who masqueraded as my mother) . . . a huge porch ran the entire front of the house. At the porch's western end was the front door. Made of heavy oak, the door groaned its way into an entrance room the size of most people's bedrooms and that, as a result, no one could ever figure out how to either appoint or use. Ultimately it became a kind of parlor-anteroom that just sat there and, according to my father, used up space and heat. The unruly parlor did serve one good purpose, however; it opened into a living room that was almost the size of the porch and many times more pleasing to me.

The living room ran from east to west paralleling the porch. On its south wall, which it shared with the porch, a bank of broad-paned windows looked across the front yard to the maples trees that, when one was downstairs, totally obscured the street beyond. On its north wall, the room was interrupted in two places. At its western end was the door to the downstairs hall and at its eastern, the double french doors that led into the dining room. The hall, which was far and away the house's greatest impediment to easy living, was a long narrow affair whose only purpose was to connect other necessary spaces in as narrow and dark a manner as possible. It had, I always suspected, been the builder's attempt to conserve the heat and floor footage he had squandered in the entrance hall parlor.

But for whatever reason, the downstairs hall was and remained a domestic bottleneck that led, straight as an arrow, north from the living room to the back of the house. On the way, it opened first onto my father's study—onto that sunny, book-lined room where, as a college professor, he spent so many hours at his desk and where he taught me how poetry could give body to the soul and how the voice speaking words aloud could give life to the printed page.

Just beyond the study door, the hallway accessed on one's left what has to have been the world's largest linen closet and on one's right the landing of the steps to my upstairs world. Beyond the closet and landing, the hall squeezed past my parents' bedroom door, pretended to terminate in their bathroom, and then abruptly bent around the corner past the basement door to actually terminate in Mother's industrial-sized, white-and-red kitchen.

If one wished to come at the kitchen from the other direction, one had to pass through the living room and then through the dining room doors, or more correctly, through the open doorway where they were. (I never remember the doors themselves being shut except on Christmas Day when they hid the coming feast, the better to tease my excitement.) Directly across the dining room from the french doors, positioned in its own kind of arrow-straight alignment, was our breakfast room. While there was no door at all, only a doorway, between the kitchen and that breakfast room, there was most definitely a door between the breakfast and the dining rooms. It was one of those somewhat antique, heavy swinging doors that allow the cook to move easily from kitchen to table while carrying hot dishes and full trays. It was a rule of the house that this door, unlike the glass double ones across from it, was always closed. Always, that is, except from about three-thirty until about four-thirty in the afternoon. That was when my mother prayed.

If we had, as a family, early reached the accommodation of splitting the house by layers between parents and child, so likewise had my mother and father managed early to split it by rooms between his and hers. The study was his, the living room hers. This is not to say that their division was as complete as was theirs with me.

My mother rarely if ever came above stairs except to clean or to deliberately visit for a while. Visiting was a great skill with her, in fact. She was a brilliant and widely read woman as well as a gifted conversationalist, and I remember those times in her company with quiet pleasure to this day. But when Mother came up, it was always purposeful rather than coincidental; and her presence was never actively enough a part of my upstairs life for me to feel her rhythms after she had left or to discover the faint traces of her perfume in my quarters a day later.

My father came upstairs only by my insistent invitation, frequently because I lacked some skill of carpentry that I needed and he possessed or because, almost as often, I needed his sheer strength to accomplish some construction or other. Many of those command visits, of course, were also close to trumped-up excuses; all too frequently I just wanted to show off something I had done and had assumed, in my naïveté, that my petite and very feminine mother could never fully appreciate.

In much the same way, below stairs there was a similar kind of arrangement. My mother cleaned and straightened the study very respectfully each morning, and every evening she sat in the rocker beside my father's desk and read or talked or listened as the case might be; but one never thought, even then, that the study was her room. It was his and, while she was clearly the life of his life and his most honored guest, she was still nonetheless in his space. The living room was an almost exact reversal of this pattern.

Though we all shared with laughter and gossip and deeply sensual pleasure the kitchen and the breakfast and dining rooms as well as the gardens and porch and even the cool basement where we dried produce and repaired everything from tricycles to chairs—even though we shared all of this seamlessly and unselfconsciously, it was understood that the parental bedroom was theirs, though I could visit if need be, and that the shaded living room with its cool, papered walls and its wine-dark drapes was Mother's.

Admittedly, when my father came in from the university just at dusk each afternoon, he as a rule came directly from the back door through the kitchen, breakfast and dining rooms to the living room, which by that hour was always empty. His favorite easy chair was there in the corner; and he liked to read the afternoon paper, listen to the early evening news on the Zenith radio, doze for a few minutes in the room's quiet before he began his evening. But even snoring lightly in his own chair, he looked to me, when I would slip in to watch him, as if he were there only in passing, so strongly impressed upon her living room was Mother's aura, her imprint, her perfume.

Just under the porch windows and parallel to the living room's south wall was a long sofa that my mother referred to during all my growing-up years as "a long bench." I always found the term singularly appropriate in attitude if not in absolute accuracy. The piece really was a sofa—velvet-covered with seat cushions, substantial curved arms, and a tripartite design. It was also the most uncomfortable and unforgiving contrivance I have ever tried to sit on. Originally my grandmother's, the long bench must have had some associative or sentimental value for Mother, or maybe it just eased her constantly painful lower back. For the rest of us and for most of our friends and guests, it not only lacked emotional connectedness, but also positively discouraged any lingering. Not so for Mother.

Every afternoon at three-thirty and with little waffling on either side of that appointed time, Mother left the kitchen, went to the bedroom for her Bible, her current magazine, and her manicure kit. The process was so without variation that I knew without looking the exact order in which she would collect these three things and the exact gestures with which she would carry them to the front of the house, set the magazine and Bible on the long bench's middle cushion, the manicure set on its right arm, arrange the throw pillow for her back, turn on her reading lamp, and then move quite purposefully across the dining room to the swinging oak door. This she would push fully open, often even setting a doorstop under it lest the door should accidentally close and thereby disturb her. She then went back to her place on the long bench and sat down. There she would remain for an hour, impervious to every possible interruption or distraction short of an emergency.

She read her magazine first. Never more than one article or story or, should one prove too long, never more than ten minutes. She next did the most astonishing thing of her day . . . or so it was for me as a child, hiding in the kitchen and watching her. She who was indeed a martinet of cleanliness and domestic order opened her manicure kit and began to trim the cuticles and file the nails that had somehow managed to escape the configurations she had laid on them the day before.

That Mother should daily attend to her nails was not unusual, and it certainly wasn't out of character. Not only was she fastidious; she was also inordinately proud of her hands. No, what was so disturbingly out of character was the fact that she daily laid down all around her and on the wine velvet of the long bench a circle of filings and clippings that, before my father's return, she would feel compelled to tidy up with the same Bissell sweeper that, in its pushing, further inflamed her back. Yet even this prospect in no way deterred her from her regimen.

Mother filed and scissored and buffed away for another ten minutes or until she ran out of material on which to work. She then put the instruments back in their case, set the whole on top of the closed magazine beside her, and opened the Bible where, for another ten minutes, she read and pondered the words she was reading. Once, long after I was grown, I heard her say to one of my children that she had managed "when your mother was a girl growing up" to read through the Bible "just in the afternoons" once every ten months. It was, so far as I know, the only time she ever made any explicit mention of what happened on all those afternoons in the living room. Certainly she never spoke of, would never, ever have spoken of, what followed next.

Just as the hall clock struck four, Mother closed the Bible, setting it, too, on the sofa's middle cushion. She turned off the lamp, she crossed her short legs at the ankles, and she went somewhere.

This was to me the most curious of my mother's feats. It was also the thing I would on many an afternoon sneak into the kitchen to wait to see. Her eyes were as frequently open as shut, and I am very sure that had I opened a cupboard for one of my father's knives or even tried to spirit away a pair of kitchen shears, she would have "seen" me, but she was not in the business of seeing her house at that time in her afternoon. She was otherwise occupied.

After I had children of my own, of course, I understood that the swinging door was opened not to monitor my mischief so much as to assure my safety and her comforting presence if needed. Even as a young adult still at home, I understood that her choice of the living room for her afternoons had been dictated by the fact that from there she could hear me if I were upstairs and that only from there and with the doors opened did she have any chance of watching over me if I were downstairs.

I honestly don't know at what age it was, however, that I first began to wonder if my mother were praying on that long bench in the living room; but I do know the morning on which that suspicion was confirmed for me. It was the winter shortly before I was to turn nine.

Just after dawn on a bitterly cold and snowy mountain morning, I was suddenly, acutely and wretchedly sick. The snow outside was so bright that I made my way down the steps and through the narrow hallway without even bothering to turn on the lights. Too sick to care about domestic rules, I opened the bedroom door and went straight to my mother's bed. The covers were pulled almost completely over her head, and though only her eyes and forehead showed, she obviously had heard me enter for her eyes were open. When she did not stir at my approach, I shook her gently. Instead of speaking, she brought her right hand up from the mound of covers and just for an instant held it up, palm-side out, as one does who is trying to stop traffic or signal "Wait."

In no more than half a breath later, though, she came out from the covers, her usual maternal self and filled with concern about my health. But all her attention and subsequent care—I was coming down with the measles—could not obliterate the memory for me of those few seconds and the raised hand. They were exactly like the thirty minutes each afternoon on the sofa; and my mother with the upturned hand was the same mother who sat on the sofa. I understood in some dumb way that wherever she was in the afternoons, she had been on the morning of my incipient measles. When I got to feeling better, I asked her about that morning.

"When I came into your room to get you last week when I first got sick, what were you doing?"

She was making biscuits—always a good time to talk together for she was a gifted cook—and turned her head just slightly away from the rolling pin to look me in the eye. "I was saying my prayers."

"In bed?" I was amazed and my voice must have betrayed me.

"It is too cold in the winter to say them anywhere else," she said, returning her full attention now to the flattened dough, as if she had settled the matter by sheer logic.

"Do you do that every morning?" Logic is not known to be effective with almost–nine-year-olds.

"Every morning."

"Is that why your clock goes off so long before you get up?"

"Yes."

It was that simple.

What my mother had just taught me, of course, was the first two basic principles of prayer: It requires a disciplined routine and it is an art best practiced by a composed mind and spirit: for that, I came to understand, was what the magazine and manicure kit and Bible were all about. They were not the purposes of Mother's afternoon, only her preparation for it.

And one last thing . . . I shall believe for as long as I live that my mother had neither the requisite self-awareness nor the desire to articulate the details of her spiritual life; but she was, nonetheless, an accomplished traveler in those lands. As a result, her greatest gift to me was not some principle or other characterizing prayer, but the implicit suggestion that those lands were there to be entered into. I was to spend the rest of my life in their discovery.

2 .

THE YEARS OF MY CHILDHOOD were the years of the playroom in the old house, but they were also years of outdoor play and across-the-alley play and of "Can Marshall please, please, please, come over?" play. There were children everywhere, a good, solid baker's dozen of us just on our end of the block alone. Because of some strange twist of fate, all the boys except one lived across the street from us and all the girls (plus the one beleaguered male straggler) lived on my side of it.

As children in that classically mid-century neighborhood, our favorite occupations were paper dolls for the girls, bikes and war games with toy soldiers for the boys, and hide-and-seek and kick-the-can for everybody. Paper dolls, or soldiers and bikes as the case might be, were for the morning and early afternoon hours. Paper dolls, for some reason I can't remember now, were usually played out at my house under Mother's huge dining room table. Hide-and-seek was an afternoon game for all of us, boys and girls alike, even in the hottest days of summer. And kick-the-can began after supper ("Please, can I go now? I've finished everything on my plate.")

Kick-the-can was my favorite. Only an elaboration actually on hide-and-seek, it involved one child's being "It" and closing his or her eyes while the rest of us hid before It's count to one hundred could end. As one by one It would discover us in our various hiding places, she or he would haul us as captives back to base, base being an upended, no. 10 can in the middle of our side driveway. The rules said that those of us who had been caught really did have to act like prisoners and stay put at base, wordless and impotent, until everyone else was caught. Or, of course, until a still-free playmate could liberate us.

The trick in this was for some member of the not-yet-caught to sneak into base while It was out on patrol, kick the can so hard that it would go clattering and sailing down the driveway, and then holler, "Go free!" At that point the game would start all over again. Under such rules, of course, even a gifted player could end up being "It" for whole evenings at a time. And God knows, there certainly was no end to the inventiveness we exercised in our bids to escape. As prisoners, we routinely used extravagant charades and even complicated birdcalls to inform our fellows in hiding about where It was and whether or not one could safely change locations or—best yet—even attempt a raid on base to kick the can.

I think now that I loved kick-the-can so much because I was fairly good at it. For an awkward and definitely not athletically inclined child like me, physical games that require quick wittedness and audacity as much as, or more than, prowess are precious things and much to be encouraged among one's playfellows. The happiness of my April-through-September evenings depended in no small way on my ability to hide near enough to base to be able to kick that dratted can with some degree of regularity. Playmates left too long in captivity, I had learned, tend to become restive and eventually to demand a change of activity. Thus I was always on the search for new coverts that were nearer and nearer to the driveway where base was. And for one brief, enchanted fortnight in the August of my ninth year, I had the *sine qua non* of hiding places.

My father was a consummate grower of things. His vegetables, grown on some abandoned acreage belonging to the university, sustained not only us but also helped sustain half of our near-neighbors during World War II. (Gasoline rationing made the commercial distribution of fresh produce essentially impossible during those years while, ironically, the rationing of meat had rendered produce more and more necessary.) But food was one thing to my father, and flowers were quite another. Next to my mother and the joy I always assumed he had in me, the only nonprofessional passion in my father's life was his flowers and the backyard in which he grew them.

Running deep and narrow from the back wall of the house north to an alley that was more a private street than an access lane, the yard was defined on the east by our garage and broad, paved driveway and on the west by a dense hedge of tall evergreens that shielded us from view and, alas, from late summer breezes as well. Within that clearly scribed space, my father created a world. One went out the kitchen door, down five wooden steps to a small brick landing, turned left around a giant boxwood and entered . . . actually, one just entered.

It was beautiful—at some seasons breathtaking, in fact. Controlled in the rife way of an English country garden, his yard always had some plant or other in colorful bloom even if, as in winter, that meant only the hawthorns and the Japanese lanterns that burned orange upon their ungainly stalks. We children hated it, of course; for the end result of such perfected creation was that children, especially rowdy ones shrieking through the half-light of dusk, were not welcome to race about, much less to hide among its summer flowers and beds. In fact, we were rather emphatically forbidden to do so.

Paradoxically, the yard was the safest place to hide just simply because we were forbidden the use of it in our play. "It" could not afford to go on a search-and-destroy in that one place; the price was too great. I gave many a summer hour to the study of this situation during my sixth year, which probably means that I was born devious. It also meant that despite all my best efforts, I could find no safe way to secrete myself inside that backyard. But within the matter of three growing seasons thereafter, my father was to inadvertently solve the problem for me.

The north end of our yard, which bounded and was bounded by the alley, had been a problem for him right from the first day we bought the old house and for weeks before we actually moved into it. He fretted with it constantly. There were suppertime conversations before we moved about "the problem with that alley." And once we had moved in and settled down a bit, there were genuinely serious ones with the neighbors about the various ways in which each of them had solved "the alley problem" before our coming.

In all fairness, I should say immediately that the "problem" truly was one. Not only was an uninterrupted view of the alley's cinder-paved and well-rutted roadbed less than aesthetically pleasing, the thing itself was a bit of a hazard. It opened right into our yard and, as alleys go, it was so well trafficked by every sort and condition of humankind as to be a positive thoroughfare at some hours of every day. Many of the traffickers were those whom we would regard today as the homeless or the mildly deranged. In those less politically correct times, we called them bums or hoboes or gypsies. By whatever label, they afflicted the neighborhood with a kind of constant, though low-grade, thieving and, in winter, with a constant threat of fire in garages and outbuildings. They were also notorious

for engaging us children in conversation whenever possible, mostly as I remember it, trying to commandeer us into stealing food for them from our
mothers' kitchens.

The alley, in short, was a problem that had to be solved, and sooner
rather than later, especially since ours was the only yard that had not yet
erected some kind of fence or gate or outbuildings to prevent vagrant access. Yet all those obvious solutions seemed to my father to be likely to de-
tract from the natural integrity of his yard. He simply was loath to diminish
the beauty of his landscaped flowers with any of them.

While he was busy being frustrated with the open stretch of alley that
bounded our yard, he did manage to seal off the small section of equally
open boundary that ran between our garage and that of our next door
neighbors. He simply hung a gate between the two buildings, a resolution
that was without offense because the garage was not in the yard and the
gate in no way visible from it. None of this addressed the real problem,
however. Then, in March of our second year in the old house and just as
I was turning seven, my father solved it.

On a still-cool Saturday morning, he came home from the campus
with a university truck, six male undergraduates, and twelve huge bushes
of mountain forsythia. Looking at that season of the year less like bushes
and more like mutilated willow trees that had had their trunks excised, the
poor forsythias each had a burlap-bundled rootball that was bigger than it
itself was. Within a matter of that one Saturday, though, the balls of root
and university dirt with their spindly, truncated tops were planted deep and
evenly along the back width of our yard. One could still see the alley, of
course, but clearly one had to trespass now to leave it for our yard.

The high hill country of upper East Tennessee is Mother Nature's own
garden spot. That, combined with my father's native genius for horticul-
ture, meant that in less than a full year the forsythias had grown enough to
touch one another. By the end of the next summer when I was fully eight
and already bored with most forms of agronomy, they had begun to fill in
their own interiors. And by late August of the next year, just at the peak
of the kick-the-can season, the forsythias were an impenetrable bank of
heavily leafed fronds that rose lithely up from their centers toward the sun
and then cascaded over and down to the earth below in one long, continuous curtain of whispering green. The end result of all of this was not just

an effective but pleasing alley wall. It was also (and more significantly) a tunnel that was about four feet across from frond tips to frond tips and as dry as our basement in a summer storm.

I cannot even imagine now what audacious flight of imagination first prodded me to try the tunnel as a hiding place for kick-the-can. I certainly don't remember on what August twilight I first dared it. I do remember very, very well, however, that I was shrewd enough to slip through the new gate between the garages, sneak down the alley, and then crawl in from the alley side rather than from that of the forbidden yard. The advantages to be gained by this derring-do were immediately apparent. Not only had I found a spot where even the archangel could not have found me, but I had also accidentally stumbled onto the one place from which I could actually see base for myself without being in any danger of detection. Simply by crawling to the center of the tunnel's length. I could sight through the forsythia branches straight to the gleam of the can's tin surface in the dusky twilight.

My increased performance record after this discovery turned me rather quickly into a neighborhood wonder woman, though I wasn't about to share the secret of my sudden success with anyone. It was at about that point—that is, at about the end of the first week of my unfair advantage—that it dawned on me that if the tunnel were good for kick-the-can, it would also most surely be good for hide-and-seek, even though the latter was considerably less of a challenge.

Thus there came the day, also forgotten in terms of the exact date, when for the first time I wiggled into the forsythia tunnel in the middle of a sunny August afternoon. I crawled easily through its now-familiar thickness, entered the shady tunnel, and made my way to my new observatory near the center of the long row of bushes. Then I lay down on the cool earth of the tunnel floor to wait for that satisfying moment when, in hide-and-seek, It has to say, "I give up. Come out, I can't find you."

I was lying there contemplating this delicious inevitability when I decided I owed it to the game and my playmates to at least act like I was playing. I decided I would sit up and see if I could see It anywhere near the driveway. So I did. I sat up, turned toward my father's yard, and looked out not on a yard, though it was certainly still there, but upon an experience.

Forsythia blooms early in the calendar year, so early that it can almost not be called a spring bush at all. For us in East Tennessee, its lushest bloom often came in January during that first hesitation of winter which people in the mountains call, somewhat erroneously, "the spring thaw." The misnomer is that there's no thaw to it, just two or three days when the sun shines lemon, but not yet orange, and everybody takes the gesture seriously. The most gullible of Nature's creatures, the one most susceptible to this blink of winter's, traditionally is mountain forsythia, which sends dozens of small, yellow, trumpet-shaped blooms up, over, and down dozens of leafless fronds in celebration.

Forsythia in bloom is hardly as thick and impenetrable as the forsythia that will come later when the bushes are in foliage; but the yellow of those myriad January blooms is so creamy and intense against a winter landscape as to obscure everything else from view. It is as if the forsythia in bloom compels the eye to total loyalty, and all else lies beyond one's visual ken. The petals, while hardy, do drop off in the due course of things, and the lanceolate leaves come in equal profusion. Being larger, they of course are also thicker. But there is a strange thing about those leaves. While they appear at a distance to be regulation green, they are actually a kind of yellow-green when one looks through them, almost as if they, too, remember, and are reluctant to let go of, their powerful January glow.

I knew all of this already, after having lived with the bushes for two and a half years. So it was no particular surprise to discover that my father's flower beds, seen through a scrim of forsythia leaves, glowed more or less golden in the mid-afternoon sunshine above them. The surprise was the perfectness of, simultaneously, both my presence within and my safe removal from those beds and that yard. The light with its goldenness certainly must have exaggerated the effect, but it did not cause it. I had unwittingly stumbled into what the Celts call a thin place and Alice called a looking glass.

I was totally of the world I was watching. In fact, I was so intimately engaged in it as to make "watching" a poor choice of words. "I was and I was watching" comes much closer to the truth of the thing. Through the windows I could see the faint shape of my mother bent over her kitchen sink and then could follow her shadow as she left there and went into their bedroom. I could see the outline of Mrs. Thomas, our next-door neighbor, as she came out onto her back porch and then her whole form as she shook her dust mop out the door. I could see the hummingbirds gathering seeds from the poppy pods and the bugs crawling up the scored bark of the apple tree. I could even see the skink that was sunning on a protected rock within two yards of me. What I couldn't see was any space or separation between me and all these things. The forsythia leaves' natural yellow blended so completely into the natural yellow of the sun that there were no stopping and starting places for either, only one continuous spectrum of being . . . which was what I had stumbled into: a "being" place.

The playroom was a doing place. It was a space made almost holy and certainly personally sacred for me because it protected from interruption my active absorptions of building and enacting. It allowed me to move into them with complete impunity. But the playroom was that perfect concentration of activity which in adults goes under the guise of entertainment or rest and recreation or hobbying. I "did" in the playroom.

In the tunnel there was nothing to do. Yet the experience of being alive in a world that I was invisible to was an absorption beyond any I had ever known before, even in the playroom. My amazement was ended only by hearing all my playmates and my mother begin to cry, "Phyllis! Phyllis! Where are you?" Apparently I had failed to hear It declare the end to our afternoon game.

After that, I never used the forsythia as a hiding place, for it seemed to me to be a kind of sacrilege to do so, though I hardly had the words for that decision or even the thought processes to grasp the concept itself. Instead, I returned to my former hiding places, got caught just as frequently as I had in the past, and suffered terribly from my diminished status of being just an ordinary player again. But I went often to the forsythia tunnel. I went, in fact, as often as I thought I could safely absent myself from parents and playmates, though usually I dared not stay there for more than ten or fifteen minutes on any one occasion. But on each of those stolen visits, the sensation of being alive in the womb of the world held. It was not as intense as the weeks and then the summers passed, but it was as constant and unvaried. Nor did the tunnel ever degenerate into a "dreaming" place. It kept, instead, its edge of vitality, of active, involved engagement in stillness.

Cradled as gently still by the unities of childhood as by the gold of the forsythias, I was two or three years away from the rush of hormones that casts all of us out of Eden. More to the point, I was at least seven or eight from the academic lectures and assigned readings that would furnish me with tools for articulating the life of the self to myself. It was sufficient instead, in those last years in my father's garden, that I experienced beyond all forgetting life in a being place and that I learned to know it as distinct from life in the doing place of my playroom. Of the three great gifts of my childhood, the second was this naïve discovery that doing was one place and being an entirely different and other place. As a talisman, a locative understanding of the spirit would serve me well; for soon I would stumble across, or into, other places of the interior. Soon I would begin to feel that, like Balboa, I was no longer a visitor in pleasant spaces but a voyager on strange seas.

3.

WHEN I WAS GROWING UP in the mountains of East Tennessee, the folklore surrounding me was a sympathetic mixture of two cultures—the Native American tradition of the Cherokee nation who were indigenous to those primeval hills and the Celtic one of the Scotch-Irish who had begun to settle the Appalachian and Great Smoky ranges in the early eighteenth century. By the time of my coming, the two traditions had blended into a number of shared conventions. Not the least among these was the belief that for every child there was an appointed narrative, a story that would unlock life for him or her. Like a totem, the story would be for one's whole life an identity, an explanation, and an enduring tool. Without such a narrative, one would be forever confined to a stumbling confusion and a wearying poverty of spirit. The work of childhood was to discern one's narrative, and the work of the adult community was to provide an abundance of possibilities from which each of us might choose.

The process was, admittedly, far less formal and explicit than my retelling makes it sound here. Rather, the quest of the totem-story was so suffused into the culture as to be a daily, but inconspicuous, part of our rearing. Cherokee and Celt were both storied people, their mysticism and earthbound theologies naturally compatible not only with each other but also with the environment of the hazy, cloud-wet hilltops in which we all lived. No child could possibly have grown up there in the 1930s without understanding the role of story, and no adult could have parented there without storying. There were always a few of us, of course, who never found our narratives or our lives; but most of us, me included, were more fortunate.

Some of us met our futures in family anecdotes that combined the old Celtic values with those of hardtack endurance in America's hill country. We learned young "to see out of the corner of the eye." Others of us found our definitions in the sagas of Appalachia's woodsmen-heroes or Cherokee stories of the Corn Mother and in the nimbus of the Great Spirit. Most of us, being as we all were the products of unending hours of public but still classical education, stumbled unwittingly into other paradigms. There was, for the greatest number of us, that one snippet of German fairy tale or that one bit of Norse or Greek mythology that would come out of nowhere to grab the world by the hair of its head and then turn it just enough to put the whole, emerging concept of patterns into register. Unfortunately, or perhaps fortunately, I was not of so romantic a disposition even in those days of innocence. Nor was my totem to be a gift from the mountains or my parents or even from my education, at least not directly.

The year I was six and going on seven, I managed to contract in uninterrupted progression every childhood disease known to humankind, save one. The German measles were to come later. Otherwise, I endured in order: chicken pox, mumps, inflamed ears, strep throat, red measles, and whooping cough. During this last affliction, I whooped so hard that I ruptured a vessel in my eye and spent another month in dark confinement waiting for it to heal. While none of this comedy of sorrows seems to have been life-threatening, it was a distinct nuisance, especially for me. There were, however, two advantages. Except for an occasional cold and the German measles of my ninth year, I was never sick again (there was simply nothing left to catch). And before the whole miserable winter was over, I had received my story.

My parents were Presbyterians in those days, that communion being the compromise they had struck when they married. My urban-Baptist mother deplored the ecclesial ways of my country-Methodist father, while he deplored the idiosyncrasies of her theology. He deplored even more vigorously, however, the incensed and chasubled Catholicism of some of the rest of his own family. So Presbyterianism it was, a bargain made and kept, but not always an easy fit. Fortunately, the Presbyterian minister during those years of my innocence was a rather accomplished theolog as well as a shrewd interpreter of people. Consequently, he spent a good deal of time either discussing Calvinism with my father or pastorally visiting with my theologically more carefree mother. As a result, I think I was comfortable with, but probably had never been alone with, the man until that winter of unremitting illness.

As one disease process followed hard on the heels of another, Dr. King began coming in to my sickroom to chat a minute at the end of each parental visit. Over the months I honestly began to look forward to his coming. For one thing, he was the only other human being besides my parents and the doctor who was allowed in, and for another he had a kind of huge gentleness and curious intelligence that appealed to me. We became friends of a sort; and thus it was that on my seventh birthday in the midst of a precedent-setting case of red measles, I received my first Bible story book—that is, my first "real" one.

My previous Bible story collections had been just that, collections. They were heavy on pictures, scarce on text, and highly selective, their stories having no discernible connection one to another. Dr. King's, on the other hand! Dr. King had given me a copy of *Story of the Bible for Young and Old* by Dr. Hurlburt. *Hurlburt's*, as my father called it, was long on words and no more than modestly generous with its pictures. Those pictures, moreover, were adult engravings, not silly drawings. And the stories! The stories began at the beginning and marched in lockstep straight through three hundred pages to the Apocalypse.

I might have been sick, but I was not too far gone to know my first rush of pride in ownership. The text was considerably beyond my reading skills, at least at first, and the level of vocabulary and diction were certainly not those of a seven-year-old, but none of that mattered. I had a book, an honest-to-john book book that was mine and mine alone. I pored over the pictures, struggled with the words, and demanded that my father read only from the *Hurlburt's* each night for my story time. It was during this process, some six or seven weeks into it, that I stumbled into the presence of my totem.

Mine obviously was and remains a story, at least more or less, about the Children of Israel. It concerns an event that took place in the thirty-seventh year of the Exodus, only months before that journey's trials and hardships were over. But like most good stories, mine has its roots firmly planted in earlier events.

The story of the Exodus is one of apostasy and human doubt as well as of impatience and despair on the part of both God and the Children of Israel. That was not how things had started out, however. In the beginning, *Hurlburt's* said, men and women who had known slavery and oppression in Egypt had followed a man named Moses out into the desert with hope in their hearts. A people who had felt the lash and known the shame of it had come to know as well the glory of the Red Sea's parting, of their own safe passage through it, and of Pharaoh's watery death in it. With a cloud before them by day and a pillar of fire behind them at night, they had trekked with their herds and their stolen Egyptian jewelry and their little ones across the Sinai Peninsula until they had come, within a matter of a few months of their leaving, to the borders of the Promised Land, the land flowing with milk and honey. With the dust of Egypt still upon them, they had moved under Moses' leadership from the northern borders of Goshen to the western ones of Canaan.

Once encamped there on the eastern side of the Jordan River, they appointed twelve wise and able men, one from each of the twelve tribes of Israel, to slip across the river by night and spy out the land. For forty days, the Children waited in their tents and for forty days the twelve spies searched out the land across Jordan. But when at last the twelve returned, they brought both samples of the rich, lush produce of the land and frightening words. The land, they said, was inhabited by giants too large, too organized, and too well armed for the untrained clans of Israel. To attack, they said, would be death. Surely Moses had misunderstood or Yahweh had changed His intent for them. The situation was without remedy and the Children of Israel must withdraw from Jordan's banks, not crossing it but traveling instead below its fords and finding another place through which to enter . . . or perhaps even another promised land?

Of the twelve, two spies—Joshua and Caleb—disagreed, protesting that the hand of Yahweh was greater than all the hands of the Canaanites. Joshua argued that what Yahweh had led them to, Yahweh would also deliver. The tribes must, he said, move forward or risk apostasy and disobedience. With the Children, however, as with all humanity, the voices of the ten overrode the counsel of the two. The Children of Israel refused to follow Moses into Canaan and turned south instead.

Then it was that God spoke to Moses and, through him, to the people. Because of their rebellious act of distrust and defiance, the Israelites would wander homeless in the wilderness for forty years, one year of exile for every day that their scouts had spent in spying out the Promised Land. They were to wander, Yahweh decreed, until every adult man and woman who had known Pharaoh's hand was dead, buried in the shallow sands of the alien desert. Only when those who had not known the curse of slavery were adult in Israel; only when those who had not seen the Angel of Death pass over Egypt's homes or watched while the Red Sea parted; only when those who had never known anything other than life in the trackless waste had come to their own adulthood; then and only then would Yahweh fulfill His promise. He would begin again with a new generation, with the Children's children, and take them safely to the land He had promised to Abraham, Isaac, and Jacob.

So it happened, my story begins, that it was the thirty-seventh year of their pilgrimage through waterless places and purposeless corridors of scrub growth, and the time of deliverance was approaching. Those who wandered now were those who had grown up in the wilderness. They had buried in its arid graves and half-scooped caves the bones of the apostate. Thus it was the Children's children who came in those fateful weeks to gather one last time at the foot of Mount Horeb and wait out the remaining months in its shadow. But as one day of dreary waiting led inexorably to another and that day to yet another, the Children's children wearied of too much wandering and too little accomplishment. Like their parents and grandparents, they, too, rebelled.

Protesting to Moses that Yahweh was no longer interested in them or their plight, that the desert was hard and that the tales of life in Egypt were poignantly sweet, the Children's children, like their fathers and mothers before them, tempted God's anger. And there came upon them there in the camps of their protest huge snakes, serpents such as live in the desert. And the snakes came in droves, so that there were serpents in the manna baskets and serpents in the bedrolls and serpents in the babies' hammocks. Everywhere serpents, and everywhere men and women and children screaming out their terror and their pain as well as their endings, for the snakes were killing the people.

Hearing the cries, Moses went running out into the camp; and seeing him, the people cried out. "We have sinned! We have sinned! Beg Yahweh's mercy for us!"

Moses, the story says, went quickly to the Tent of Meeting to implore God's deliverance for His repentant people. God, accepting the cries of sorrow as an offering of repentance, instructed Moses to fashion quickly from the braziers of the sanctuary a bronze serpent in every way like those that were afflicting and killing the people. Moses was then to take the serpent he had made, place it upon a cross pole with its body twined in the way of snakes around a tree branch, and march through the camp of Israel with the serpent-draped pole held high before him. Whoever looked up at the bronze serpent, Yahweh said, would be saved from death—not from being bitten, just from death as a result of being bitten.

Moses, doing as he had been told, quickly hammered a brazier into a serpent, entwined it upon a cross pole, and went through the corridors of tents crying, "Look up! Look up!" Those men and women and children who believed him and believed in Yahweh's message through him looked up at the pole with its burnished snake and not down at the desert vipers who were besieging them. They elected by a combined act of will and faith to look, not down where the agony was and where the snakes might still be pulled from their bodies and their children's bodies, but up where the mercy was promised. They elected to be bitten in order that by faith they might live. And, the story says, some eighteen months later those who had made that choice were those who entered by way of Jericho and its tumbling walls into the Promised Land, the land flowing with milk and honey.

It is a horrendous story, replete with all the elements that fire a child's imagination and outrage an adult's sensibilities. I no longer remember exactly when I first began to sense in the bronze serpent something more than a child's delight in a scary story, of course; but I do know that by the time I was twelve or thirteen, I had come to recognize this as the narrative that would unlock life for me, that would be an enduring tool, that would become my explanation.

Later, in college, I discovered sympathetic medicine in anthropology classes; and I was as enthralled as only a late adolescent can be by long lectures on shamanistic magic. I was charmed by the notion of using the thing that is afflicting to cure the affliction. I was intellectually intrigued by human similarities and the world's habit of interesecting connections; and predictably, my reverent and proprietary respect for totem stories was confirmed by these further evidences of their historic efficacies in other times and among other peoples.

More to the point, however, is the fact that by the time I hit sympathetic shamanism, I had already hit several other, far less ethereal things. By the semester of my sophomore anthropology lectures, I had already lived long enough to know for a hard, enduring fact that life is full of snakes; that they bite fiercely; that they will kill you if you look down and wrestle them; and that, peculiarly enough, the very act of being wrestled with often is what gives them their potency. I had also learned that, just as the story teaches, looking up doesn't stop the pain immediately, but it does prevent death from it. By the time I hit anthropology, in fact, I had already recognized a score of life's swirling circumstances as snakes in poor disguise.

It was at about this same time that I made another discovery. Among my own contemporaries, and probably among adult Americans even today, the most clichéd and abused bit of Christian scripture was the famous "For God so loved the world, that he gave his only begotten Son, that whosoever believes in him should not perish, but have everlasting life" of John 3:16, but . . . But, truth told, it is the immediately preceding two verses that tell the story. Those sentences, labeled so innocuously as John 3:14–15, say simply, "And as Moses lifted up the serpent in the wilderness, even so must the Son of man be lifted up: That whosoever believes in Him should not perish, but have eternal life. For God so loved the world," etc. In terms of their content, those two were, and still are, far more horrific to me than Moses and his cross pole ever could be.

An insult to both orderliness and reason, they position the Nazarene firmly in the middle of an intention at which only the gods could play. They are also undeniable, at least for confessing Christians, for they constitute one of only the four or five times that Jesus even mentions a story from the Hebrew Bible at all in His teaching, and one of only two or three times that He ever likens Himself or His actions to any of His antecedents in those scriptures. By the time I was nineteen and had blundered my way into this wonderment quite by accident one early Sunday morning, I had already stumbled as well across the fact that the invading snakes of the Sinai massacre were called in Hebrew by the same word as was the snake of Eden, an enticing association that has winked and teased at me for all the years since.

Actually, the burden of the words, as I would in time come to understand, seems to have been more than an association; it would seem to have been a predictive assessment. Moses' bronze snake (we are told in the

Bible, though not in *Hurlburt's*) was taken by the Israelites as a kind of holy mascot into Canaan when they entered Jericho. In time, the snake on the cross pole became not the symbol of God, but the god itself and an idolatrous statue the people worshiped. One of the righteous acts of good King Hezekiah when he ascended to the throne of Judah generations later in the eighth century B.C.E. was to "break into fine pieces" Moses' serpent, whom he named Nehustan in contemptuous disgust. And almost a millennium later, St. Paul was to caution the young Christian church at Corinth to "tempt not the spirit of Christ as some of our fathers did and were destroyed of serpents."

And so over the years, the story of the snake has done as a good totem story must. It has grown and morphed and then morphed again, expanding as I have grown and evolving its possibilities as I myself have evolved and as my need of its recondite mysteries has matured. What I have discovered in the process, of course, is religion—messy, sometimes repugnant, always earthy, constantly greater than morality, religion. In that suspended time of my seventh winter I had received, almost without my knowing it, my own beginning. Reverence may be the road to the sacred and wisdom may be the natural song of the spirit, but story is the text of God and the groundskeeper of prayer. Its coming was the third and final of childhood's three great gifts to my soul's education.

4.

NOVELISTS ARE AN ENVIABLE LOT, or so they have always seemed to me. When they sit down to uncover and expose the processes of life, they can use the whole inventory of their own autobiographical experience with impunity while, at one and the same time, shamelessly filling in all its deficits by the exercise of fictive imagination. Not so for poor fools like me who, unable to escape the call of the writing life, spend all our careers laboring in the fields of nonfiction.

A bit of business in a novel's plot may be parsed by the critics as identical to events in the life of its creator, or a shard of expertise may be easily attributed by reviewers to some prior experience in its narrator's own life; and we may all enjoy those clever, if small, discoveries. Even so, however, all but the most academic of us are reluctant to corrupt the pleasures of good fiction with too much rooting around in its personal sources. In literary nonfiction quite the opposite is true. I know, because my own fifty-plus years of labor have included whole decades in almost every sub-category of that major one.

For poets, which is how I began my professional life, and especially for poets writing in the twentieth century in America, every line was as-sumed—even expected—to reek with the autobiographical. It was the century of the confessional in every way; and if I failed as a poet because of having no more than a modest talent for it, I most certainly did not fail for any lack of trying. I left behind me, as a matter of fact, a whole trail of poetry, every line of it, so far as I can remember, true to its times as fully confessional.

For essayists, the matter is less clear-cut. The reading public expects, correctly, that the good essayist has both some personal expertise in his or her subject and some emotional intimacy with it as well. In the case of the personal essayist, the name itself tells all. My husband has observed for all the years I have written in the genre that the personal essay is what poets do when they grow up. He may well be right, for the border between the confessional poem and the memoirist essay is often as much a matter of how the typesetter has broken the lines as of the euphony and type of craft em-ployed. I can say this without hesitation, for goodness knows I have left small libraries of such material in my own wake.

Over the years of my writing life, I have also decided that there is at least some defensible basis for finding the autobiographical even in objec-tive nonfiction. While I gave up writing poetry years ago (except for my own continuing joy in its luxuriant music), I have continued to this very day to write literary nonfiction and, within the last decade or so, have come to spend a good bit of time in writing straight reportage and com-mentary within the field of religion. Even here (and with all due respect to the god of journalistic objectivity) I suspect the lurking presence of the autobiographical, for we human beings see what we have been prepared by prior experience to see, barring, of course, divine interruption of that principle. This book is, to a large extent, about both those phenomena—the preparation to see and the process of interruption; but it has another agenda as well.

Anyone who has ever written in literary nonfiction, and especially the personal essay, knows that very, very often the needs of a deadline or the unwieldiness of a recalcitrant point requires a slight adjustment of things as they really were to things as they need to be if one is to complete a piece of writing on schedule and on point. Most of us working within the restraints of those difficulties pass such adaptations off as necessities of the trade. Rarely, if ever, do we spend time castigating ourselves as liars or even as fibbers. We do what we have to do; I have often done what I had to do.

Autobiography, however, does not suffer either liars or fibbers gladly. Autobiography lays claims to itself as what it is. It has no materials beyond its own subject and no plot beyond its own already lived one. These very limitations are sometimes attractive to those who, having lived public lives, feel some yearning to set the record straight. Sometimes the singularly fixed focus of autobiography is appealing to those who, having simply lived long lives, want to use its literary restrictions as a way to organize and impose pattern upon their experience. I am no different, I suspect. At least I certainly feel the pull of these two things. But my major reason for setting myself the task at hand is other than either of them.

I have spent my life as a pray-er. It has been, from the beginning, my vocation within the religious life, albeit one followed as a member of the unvowed laity rather than as a religious. And if I wore that vocation lightly as a child and saw it but dimly in my early maturity, I certainly have had a lifetime of ever-increasing instruction in its disciplines, its often harsh labors, its ferocious potency, and its addictive glories. What I have also discovered in the course of my vocation is that nothing so harms it as religiosity or the smallest suggestion of overt devoutness. I have come to fear spiritual conspicuousness, in fact, about as much as the angels are said to fear the hierarchies of Hell and, presumably, for the same reasons. As a result, for a lot of years it seemed best to do the work of my vocation as unobtrusively and privately as possible. In a life as public as mine has sometimes been, carrying out that purpose was frequently awkward at best and many times downright impossible without offering some bit of explanation.

Over the years of awkwardness and explanations, the business involved in my sealing off fixed times for prayer inevitably became more and more obvious to those working around me. In all honesty, it probably could not even have been effected in many situations without their toleration. The notion, in other words, that I was following my vocation in any kind of secrecy had to give way not too many years ago to the realization that what I was really doing was making a conspicuous exercise out of my own piety. I had, in the ironic way of things, created a kind of religiosity out of elaborate attempts to avoid it. Those attempts, I now realize, were also very useful as shields for keeping me and my way of life unexamined by anyone else. They were safety barriers against the kind of criticism and leveling cynicism that rear their corrective heads when those who claim religion fail to live out their claim in any humble or significant detail.

What follows hereafter, then, is the story of the shaping of my vocation toward a life of prayer. If that story is told, albeit rather belatedly, in terms of how vocation came to be for me, it is also most assuredly told out of the fear that, as with the angels and the lords of Hell, so with me. I have no other choice than the breaking of silence. I have no choice, in other words, except to lay out the gifts that were the stuff of my soul's formation, and then leave it to others to determine how I may have spent or misspent them over the years since they were given.

PART TWO

Alma Mater

5.

THE BUSINESS of defining childhood has not been an easy one in recent years. Authorities, both academic and popular, have drawn and then redrawn its borders, slicing and dicing babyhood and infancy and toddlerdom and early childhood off of one end and prepubescence, pubescence, early adolescence, and young adulthood off at the other. While the beginning of childhood was, in my own case, never either very clear or very significant to me, its ending was. My childhood ended on an early September day in my seventeenth year when I got into the family Chevrolet beside my mother and chattered as she drove the three hundred miles that lay between our driveway and my life as a college freshman.

In the careless and often cruel directness of the young, I could not have been happier or more outspoken about that fact. If there were an appreciative comment or even a maudlin and sentimental moment in that day-long ride, I don't remember it. What I can remember is the excruciating tension, once we had arrived at my new dormitory, of thinking that my mother would never go away. We unloaded, and then she wanted to help unpack. I demurred. She wanted to meet my new friends-to-be. I demurred again, noting that since we had come in a day early, few if any of them were even around yet. She insisted that she take me to supper in as much as the cafeteria would not open until the next day. I countered that the college bookstore was open and would have everything I might want. Finally she ran out of ideas, or maybe just out of enthusiasm, and headed off to her hotel. I think I kissed her good-bye, but I cannot even be sure of that. I did stand at my window and watch the car move off down the hill toward the campus gates. As it faded from view, I let out a whoop that resounded beyond my room and out into the whole suite of which it was a part. I was free!

"Free" always implies "nonfree," and that was not exactly what I felt or remember. There were things I had to do, a person I had to become; and I couldn't accomplish either of those things with my mother watching. Why I couldn't is a mystery as old as mothers and daughters, and even at seventeen I was astute enough to know not to wrestle with it. Instead, within seconds of my window whoop, I changed my self-perception from "free" to "new." I realized, watching the empty landscape through which the Chevrolet had vanished, that what I really had just become was a person. In effect, my childhood had just been abruptly, cleanly ended, and I had passed from my parents' house to the world's keeping.

What happened next was to affect my soul for the rest of my temporal life, and presumably beyond it. I turned from the window and the room filled with boxes and valises, got out the campus map Student Affairs had sent me for orientation, located the campus bookstore, and headed out my new door to begin my new life. Despite what I had said to Mother, I was less than faintly hungry. It was not food, but a different purchase I had in mind. I wanted that parentally forbidden sign of true adulthood, cigarettes.

Like most American kids, I had snuck puffs from the time I was old enough to beg them from errant older friends and naughty cousins. I had even, of late, managed to beg a whole cigarette or two from slightly older chums at parties or sleepovers. The problem was not, therefore, whether or not I liked smoking. I already knew the answer to that: I did. The problem was that I not only liked the nicotine of smoking, but I liked the image as well. I liked the sophisticate-at-large cachet of the elegant hand holding a long cigarette against a petulant chin while smoke curled up around a slightly tilted head. Yes, that was what I most wanted to be, a sophisticate at large. It most certainly was how I intended to present myself to the new friends whom my mother had not contrived to meet.

To accomplish this new image, I had to learn first how to inhale without coughing and, also central to my plan, how to hold a cigarette in a glamorous pose without having my eyes smart and water. The only possible way to do that—and it was why I had insisted so vehemently on our taking advantage of the earliest arrival date permitted by the college—was to practice. It seemed reasonable that if I could buy a carton of cigarettes before anyone else in my suite arrived, I could hide them for a few days while I practiced learning to smoke gracefully. Once I had learned that, I could just gradually meld into the public exercise of my skills . . . leave a pack out a day or two for my new roommate to see, but so casually that at first, I hoped, she wouldn't even notice . . . arrange to be "caught" smoking one just as she came into the room from some class or errand, so she would think I had been smoking all along, but had been just too considerate to do so when she was at home . . . or one night when we were studying, just pull one out and light up so easily that she would not even notice that I had not been smoking all along. My plan was thorough and elaborate in direct proportion to the daydreaming hours that had gone into plotting it.

Twenty minutes after my mother had left, as I left the college store with my carton safely under my arm, the only thing I lacked was a place in which to practice. Somehow, in all my anticipation and strategizing, I had failed to provide for that rather integral part of my scheme. To make matters even more complex, smoking was not allowed on campus except in the dorm rooms, on the outside grounds, or, with permission, in faculty offices. Offices were out of the question; I didn't even know where they were yet. My dorm room ran entirely counter to all my surreptitious intentions. And outdoors was of no use at all, for I obviously had to have a mirror in which to watch myself learn my sensuous holding routine. As I rolled this new frustration around in my mind, I somehow took a wrong turn at the end of a corridor and ended up at the far, rather than the near, end of my dormitory; and the resolution of my quandary fell as easily into my lap as the problem itself had.

What I encountered, as I was making my way back toward my new room and considering the problem of a private, practicing space, was a half-floor of empty suites on the lower, far level of my dormitory. Never mind that there were signs on the doors forbidding access. Never mind that there were really remarkable penalties in those days for freshmen who violated "No Pass" signs. Never mind that this was my first day on campus and that I was virtually alone in a huge old building. Never mind any of it.

I walked in rather gingerly. I'm not sure what I thought I might see, but what I actually saw was nothing. The suite I had entered was the exact duplicate of my own three floors up—two bedrooms connected by a common room with one bathroom, two sinks, six windows, and three outside doors. That was it. Nothing else.

I opened the door to the bathroom. Perfect! A regulation-issue bathroom mirror was affixed to the wall over the sink, but far more pertinent to my needs, a full-length one was screwed to the inside of the bathroom door. Almost as fortuitously, there was a pull-out, half window or transom

over the bathtub. Clearly designed to evacuate stale air into the brick ven-
tilation shaft beyond it, the thing was not only there, but it had already
been pried loose and left opened. I immediately lowered the commode lid,
sat down in the direct view of the long mirror, lit up, coughed wrench-
ingly, teared up dramatically, and generally managed to kill off whatever remaining appetite I had had in the first place, but I was happy, as giddily
happy as I can ever remember having been.

Three and a half hours later, after I had unpacked all the suitcases and
before I began to dress my new bed, I decided to slip downstairs and try
again. This time was a decisively different experience. Though I obviously
still coughed and teared just as much as before, I was also far more relaxed
about the whole thing. To be specific, I was relaxed enough to perceive
that this stark bathroom in this empty and essentially forbidden suite was
very comfortable or maybe somehow just very pleasing to me. There was
to it a kind of familiarity that I was ill-equipped to name, but that I knew
I should be able to articulate. Then it dawned on me, in one of those icy
moments that inform all adult life, that what I recognized was not the
bathroom, but my alert restedness, like a morning's waking, within it.

Arrested completely by this piercing, almost unsettling, new understanding, I stubbed out the half-smoked cigarette in the sink, flipped off
the overhead light, and slid down to a seat on the concrete floor. A bit of
shadowed starglow and a faintly tired breeze came in through the transom
over the tub. Otherwise I was alone as I had been in the playroom at home
and in the forsythia tunnel in the garden. Alone as I had been many times
before, but not the same.

Just here, I think, any responsible storyteller would interrupt the story
long enough to confess the very obvious. That is, how much of what I understood at seventeen about the interior life is impossible to gauge. How
much the nascent actually knew and at what point must stand apart, in all
tales of the heart, from the probability that the teller has often "remembered" more with economy than with accuracy. Compressing long years
of gradual understanding into single epiphanies or even tying revelation to
singular events may allow us to organize our spiritual autobiographies, but
it certainly does not make us fine historians of the actual.

That having been said, let me say (and ask your indulgence in believing me when I do) that long before I left home, I had learned to know my-

self in the playroom, but more by reduction than expansion. And if I were not yet perceptive enough, as I most probably was not, to make such an analysis, I at least knew what I felt in the playroom. That is, I knew I had been able in that happy space of hobbies and delicious distractions to slip without effort into bliss. Both the mini-death of coming back out of that nirvana every time Mother called and the restless yearning I always felt to be done with my chores and homework so I could re-enter it had taught me that much. They both had also taught me—and this I know I knew long before I was seventeen—that I was something I sometimes needed a rest from.

The forsythia tunnel, I had also understood, was similar in result or effect, but directly opposite in its means. The forsythia worked by expansion. Sitting in its golden light and merging through it into the whole unseeing world beyond, I lost all my borders and, for a time or a piece of a time, lost me. But things were not so in the bathroom, nor would they ever be. Once I had tried a cigarette or at the most two in that peculiar and highly unconventional space, there would never be anything else to do, much less anything at all to merge out into the greater world through.

Protected by forbidding signs, by the surrounding suite of rooms, by a closed and bolted door and, if all that should fail to shield me, by the social nicety that stops most of us from opening bathroom doors before we knock—secured by all of these things, I was safe. I was freed by the absence of all things to step out and flow into all things as they can be only when they are no things. I, who was and am God's most gregarious creation, liked sitting on a concrete floor in a half-dark and totally silent cubicle. I liked the fact that I did not have to either do or be to engage aliveness there. And I enjoyed the self in and around me there. I was good company, conscious but easy, in that place. It was a stunning discovery.

Long after I had become a dangerously accomplished smoker, I continued to return to the empty suite. In fact, I returned to it almost daily for the remainder of my freshman year. The following fall brought a larger freshman class; and all the first floor suites, including my plumbed sanctuary, were renovated and returned to full use. I was summarily evicted as a result, but evicted by circumstances and not by people; for to this day I am convinced that no one ever saw me pass in or out of those "No Pass" doors.

By the fall of my sophomore year, of course, I knew the campus intimately enough to also know a good half dozen spaces that were almost, if not quite, as useful and as private. None of them remains with me now as especially memorable, however, and I have gradually subsumed all of them to the overarching memory of the bathroom; for the abandoned bathroom on the lower floor of Cooper Hall at Shorter College in Rome, Georgia, was the place my soul first learned to trust the luminous dark, first learned to dance with it, first learned to follow it as one follows the affianced partner.

The name that one, in full maturity, applies to the waltz of unity— whether contemplation or meditation or inspiration—does not matter. By whatever name, the plains of the fully conscious dance are sacred to all faiths; and by the end of my seventeenth full year, I was already on my way to becoming a devotee to them. What had begun as a semi-rebellious, fully vampish act of self-assertion had become my first mature use of the self. I know now that it had also become my first encounter with the irony of life and the paradox patent in most morality. The poet Cavafy once wrote, "It was in the days of my sensual life that my art was formed," and oh, 'tis true, 'tis true.

6 .

WHEN MOTHER AND I pulled out of the driveway in the freshly waxed Chevrolet that September morning, I may have had the single-minded intention of *savoir vivre* packed snugly into my plans, but my intention had two distinct parts. To become a true sophisticate-at-large, more than smoking was required. I would also have to turn myself into an Episcopalian.

This was the American South of the early 1950s, when everyone was something. Southern culture and Southern business did not tolerate, much less advance, those who were undeclared religiously. There was no question but that like everybody else, I had to be something. Nor was there any question about the fact that in all my life to date, I had never discovered a debonaire Presbyterian. Quite the opposite. They were so Gospel-bound and moral as to be occupying no more than a tenth of life's rich possibilities—or so they seemed to me. Episcopalians, on the other hand . . . ah, they were a different breed of religious cat.

One must understand just here that at seventeen I had not the vaguest concept of what being an Episcopalian meant, nor did I even know many of them. (Truth told, there weren't many of them to be known in upper East Tennessee in the nineteen thirties and forties.) But the ones I did know were very attractive to me. In fact, based on my limited census, all Episcopalians were very wealthy, handsomely turned out, delightfully witty, socially able . . . in short, very sophisticated.

What I was carrying in my head, of course, was a cliché; but the utility of clichés is that they speak the shorthand of the most apparent. By using them, one can perceive a core truth without being burdened by all of its exceptions and peripherals. Nor was my naïve assessment of Episcopalianism totally without merit. It was, in fact, exact enough to have survived to this very day as a fairly universal perception of American Anglicanism; and all my laughing at my seventeen-year-old insouciance will not diminish its half-accuracies.

There was one other subterranean reason driving me toward Episcopalianism. Of all the things I am sure of in this life, few are more firmly fixed than the knowledge that beyond any circumstance or question, I unequivocally both reverenced and adored my father. But I was a teenager at seventeen and at least more or less normal.

My father feared anything papal with a fervor Martin Luther would have admired. His reaction to that branch of the Church was so intense and, for whatever reason, so beyond his control that I would never have even considered becoming a Roman Catholic at that stage of my life. But Anglicans, if one thought about it clearly, did a lot of the things that Roman Catholics did, they just did them as Protestants. Of course, I had never been in an Episcopal church, but I knew from high school literature classes and the occasional British novel that this was true; and that was good enough for me. I had no need to hurt my father, but as with my mother, I did have a considerable need to stand clear of him. Turning Episcopalian, presumably, would accomplish that goal without inflicting any permanent injury. The only real problem was that becoming an Episcopalian was not like becoming a poised smoker. One could not get the hang of it in private.

My first Sunday as a college woman was occupied with required—it was, as I have said, the South—services in the college chapel. On my second Sunday, however, I dressed early to avoid any well-intended but proselytizing invitations elsewhere, called a cab, and paid the man to take me to the nearest Episcopal church. He did, and far too quickly. Standing alone in front of those Chinese red doors, I had not the faintest notion of what to do next. Had there been just a tad less social ambition in my dark soul, I would have bolted on the spot. Blessedly, however, some over-dressed and to me totally daunting old dowager came up the sidewalk behind me. As she navigated her way around me and toward the steps in front of us, she gave me the most singularly arch look of exquisite contempt that I had ever seen. The very perfection of her delivery galvanized me. If something on the other side of those red doors could teach me how to cast that kind of fully nuanced look, then I was going through them, and the devil could take the hindmost.

Reading about liturgical space in half-accomplished novels—or even in fully accomplished ones, I suspect—does little, if anything, to prepare a seventeen-year-old, rather imaginative young woman for the impact of physically entering into it. Or at least reading hadn't prepared me. Once I got myself through the doors and beyond a kind of narthex or entrance area, there was nothing between me and . . . well, between me and "it" is probably the best way of stating the matter.

In retrospect, I have no trouble understanding that before the electrifying moment of my entering St. Paul's, I had never had cause to imagine either my own church or the churches of my schooldays as anything other than some kind of assembly-for-a-purpose places. Churches for me were—had always been—like auditoriums and concert halls. They were municipal spaces built to accommodate a lot of people doing together what they couldn't do in less and/or private space.

My experience of church-as-constructed-space up to that point, in other words, had been of church as human space—human in measure and human in employment. But what I had entered—what, more accurately put, I was standing there gaping at—was the chaotic antithesis of everything I had ever experienced ecclesial space as being. I was daunted for the second time in less than five minutes.

Like Jonah swallowed into the belly of a whale, I had just dumped myself into the most fundamentally, quintessentially sensuous interior I had ever experienced. In its fully vested, bejeweled, and bannered multicolored confusion of line and symbol, this thing—this nave, as I was to discover they called it—bore more resemblance to my dreams than to my sense of architecture. Yet paradoxically, its very bizarreness evoked in me both a painful sense of belittlement and an intense ecstasy. I had stumbled at last into what my father was afraid of.

I melted gratefully into the half-dark of a back pew. From there I watched the drama of my first Eucharist unfold. I managed to stand, a nanosecond late, with everyone else, and to sit and kneel with about the same disjuncture in my timing; but I got there. I even enjoyed the bouncing up and down after a few minutes; it seemed to invite my body into what my head was doing. (The rest of me, presumably, would in time learn to follow suit.) But I didn't attempt to receive communion. Instead, I clung to my pew and shook my head vigorously at the usher who tried to help me out of it. Not only was I paralyzed by my ignorance of what I would be expected to do once I got up to that rail, but I was also overwhelmingly aware that taking that cup and eating that bread would sever me forever from being a Presbyterian. My rebellion literally wilted in the face of such a prospect. I had been ready to deal my father a light blow. I was not ready to deal myself one.

Once the service was ended, I tried to slip out unseen, and I almost made it . . . except that just as I eased my way toward the door he was blocking, the rector turned from talking to some other parishioner and, taking my hand, said, "I trust you will come again." I felt my face flush red with embarrassment at having been noticed at all and with the discomfort of real duplicity. Sophistication had too high a price, and I knew at that moment that I could never pay it. "Yes, thank you," I muttered, and tearing my hand loose, almost ran for the nearest taxi.

Yet the next Sunday, I called another cab and went to the same red doors. For a week, I had been unable to shake off a kind of ill-defined restiveness. I had no idea what to do with my unease, and I certainly was not about to ask anyone for help. (False pride has probably been the most impeding and expensive of the character flaws with which I came equipped into this world, and it was not to fail me now.)

I had grown up Christian and was Protestant; I knew that. What I had never considered about those conditions, however, was that they meant being of a piece with the centuries. Protestant Christianity, up until my seventeenth year, had been a happy and nonabrasive blend of my parents' worldview, my culture's principles, and my friends' social routines. Its very homogeneity had denuded it of any history or context outside its immediate presentations among us.

In all fairness, I have to say here that I had heard a great deal, and that long before I was seventeen, about the "the communion of the saints" concept. As a tenet of the faith, it asserts the unbreakable connection between any confessing Christian and all the other confessing Christians who have preceded him or her as well as amongst all Christians who are presently living out the faith anywhere within current time. The disconnect for me had been that a concept or a tenet is a concept or a tenet. They are both good tools for fleshing out theological conversations or for solving intellectual questions. But for addressing the actuality of the religious life, a concept can never be more than potentially there. It waits always for incorporation, for incarnation, to render it usable.

What happened to me on my first Sunday among the Anglicans, though I didn't understand it at the time, was the substantivization of a tenet. I had slammed head-on into the realization, in physical objects and forms, of what saying, "I am Christian" just might really imply. More than the Eucharist itself, I suspect, this lifting out into the exterior world of the furniture of the interior one had been what so terrified me—that and the fact that giving flesh to human lives that had dared to believe gave flesh to the mass and thereby made it alarmingly more actual.

Whatever the process by which the impact had been created on me, the truth was that on that first Sunday, I had lost something that had been comforting to me. I had been totally unable, during the long and intervening week, to label what it was that had been stripped away. If I were forced today to give it a name, however, I would say that another childhood had been abruptly and cleanly ended, the childhood of my religious self. And while I did not want it back necessarily, I did feel some kind of fitful ache to go back to the place that had severed it from me.

I went to St. Paul's faithfully for most of that autumn, in fact, and fitfully for the rest of the academic year after that. Never quite coming to the point of receiving the Eucharist, I nonetheless came to feel myself enough a part of the place to list it as my church home on college information sheets and to almost believe myself when I did so. But as the first semester of my new life began to unfold, so did my social life. Like many another young American, I didn't hit my stride in high school, but I most surely hit it in college. There were friends everywhere, and especially there were my suitemates.

By late October, the whole freshman class had shaken out all the kinks involved in our living arrangements and had reassigned ourselves, after interminable Saturday morning moves up and down the halls, into clusters of the like-minded. I had never lived among the like-minded before, and I loved it! We five—one of us was wealthy enough to have a private room—had found each other for life.

Most college cliques, I have discovered, remember themselves years later as having been a coterie of the authentic, the daring, and the fractious. Whether we were actually so or not, I can't say; but I do know that we certainly regarded ourselves as such. We went everywhere together, tried our hand at manipulating student politics and student publications together, tested all the rules together, and in general taxed every established academic formality together. For an only child—or a former one—it was heaven. It was also time-consuming and tiring.

To make matters worse, or even better, there were boys. Not on campus, because Shorter was, in the best Southern tradition, a women's college at that time; but there were boys. Everybody but me, it seemed, had a brother or a cousin or a spare boyfriend left over from better times. It really was heaven, and it really was heaven in its most distracting form. The first thing that went was, as always, church. Sunday morning is probably the silliest possible time to schedule anything that one wants young adults to attend anyway, but that is another issue. The issue here is that St. Paul's and any kind of regular attendance at it went for me the way that First Baptist, First Methodist, and even First Pres went for all my classmates, straight down the road of good intentions. Which is to say, of course, that the distancing of intention had slipped into my thinking about St. Paul's. Church once more was becoming not an adventure, but something I expected myself to do.

Over the years, I have forgotten almost everything else about St. Paul's, including the name of its rector whom I remember vaguely as having been very kind to me. Within less than a year and during the first semester of my sophomore year, moreover, I actively rejected both St. Paul's and Anglicanism itself for exercising an antique dogma in a modern world. But before the bitterness of that tragic event could sever me for a while from formal religion, I had managed to file safely under "Interesting—Keep for Later Use" the two things that I can never forget about St. Paul's, *The Book of Common Prayer* and the Psalter it contained. They were the first working tools of my adulthood. The irony was, and is, that as with all superb tools, learning to use them properly requires a lifetime. The art for which they are the means does not take itself lightly.

7.

WALKING FOR THE FIRST TIME as a spiritual innocent into exalted space had been an all-engulfing experience for me, my reactions as much physical as mental. By the time I managed to sink into my half-dark, back pew that first September morning at St. Paul's, I had felt, if not actually ill, then at least a bit wobbly. Entering into what followed next was every bit as all-engulfing, just less dramatic. The bulk of what Christian liturgy creates, it creates by using itself as its own building materials. The resulting structure is far more subtle in its effects, in other words, than is stone and mortared space, and the process itself is much more patient about producing them.

The Book of Common Prayer, or *BCP,* is, as is obvious from its name, a prayer book, though despite its title, not one of either very ordinary or very vernacular prayers. Nor is it a book just of prayers; nothing could be farther from the truth. What the *BCP* . . . (As a sophisticate in training, I had learned early that only rarely does one use the full title. Knowing how and when to abbreviate the title to its initials without hesitation is one of the hallmarks of membership in American Episcopalianism.) What today's *BCP* really is, at least at first blush, is almost a thousand pages of words, some in italics, most in regular type, and far too many of them with maddeningly erratic margins and justifications.

The italicized words are those that one has to look out for. Most of them are there to tell the neophyte, the forgetful, and/or the downright inattentive what to do and say and when to do or say it. The rest of the italicized portions, by and large, are there to tell the priest or officiant pretty much the same things. Irregular margins I still have not managed, in some cases, to figure out the why of to this very day. But the nonitalicized words, I discovered early on, can be divided into two camps—the real stuff and the stuff about the real stuff.

I had never had any experience with a prayer book before. Heavens, I was Presbyterian! The *Westminster Confession of Faith* was the whole library for me in terms of books that could be bandied about like the Bible as some kind of ultimate authority. Thus I lacked at seventeen the reverence that would have lent a more seasoned traveler some greater accuracy of terms. Instead, I can remember quite clearly separating the plain words of the *BCP* into the "stuff" and the "stuff about the stuff."

The latter category is a cook's mix of calendars (I didn't understand them and shall die convinced that mastering them takes either centuries of familiarity or pure ecclesial genius to accomplish); articles of faith (not all that drastically different from the old *Westminster* in its base doctrines, just more elegant and less egalitarian); and passages of bibliographic defense that explain questions no ordinary person would ever have entertained in the first place, at least not in recent memory (which is part of their charm and, as I was to discover, part of the familial record they constitute). The remaining words, my "stuff" itself, are far and away the greatest proportion of the total word count. They are also rife with the analogies, agonies, and awe of the human mind when it seeks to envision and engage the divine.

Rabbis frequently observe that the *Siddur*, the ancient prayer book of Judaism, is in reality a three-thousand-year old history of the Jewish people despite the fact that it was not composed as such until the ninth century. The same may be said for the *BCP*, I think, though the time would have to be changed to the sixteenth century and the frame of reference shifted from Jewish to Christian. Having said that, I must also say that, in 1951, if not now, the human shift would have been narrowed as well from "Christian" to "Protestant Catholic Christian." Such niceties of distinction I more felt than grasped on the day I opened the *BCP* for the first time at St. Paul's, but my original ignorance did not negate their reality. Admittedly, I had been shrewd enough to perceive that receiving the elements of an Episcopal Eucharist would change forever something fundamental to the structuring of my Presbyterianism. What I did not perceive—what I was still far too slow of religious wit to perceive—was that taking in the words of the *BCP* was every bit as dangerous to my general status quo.

Before the sixties with their cultural insurrections opened things up a bit and before Vatican II blasted them around a bit more even for non-Romans, communion was not a weekly occurrence in Episcopal worship. The fact that I had stumbled into a eucharistic Sunday on my first sally forth into the world of Anglo-Catholic worship was another of those events in my life that one can call fortuitous or else parse as something far more directed. Most of the time, in point of fact, however, Episcopal Sabbath services were "Morning Prayer," a fairly euphemistic term for saying little confession, no mass, and nothing personal . . . or that's pretty much how it looked to me on my second Sunday at St. Paul's. I couldn't be sure, of course, because I was very unsure about what it was that was really going on in the first place.

The mass I had at least seen in a movie or two (more or less, that is), but Morning Prayer? Never. From the back of the nave the whole congregation looked a bit like a gathering of possessed dolls, all of them bopping up and down and flipping pages back and forth in keeping with some kind of encrypted sequence only they were wired to respond to. Confused intellectually and thwarted religiously, I left St. Paul's that second Sunday annoyed but determined. I was going to come back for as many Sundays as it might take to get the calendar back to a eucharistic service. I had been possessed of a worldview when I walked into this mess, and I intended to go back to the place where I suspected I had begun to lose it. Fortunately—how that concept does intrude . . . Fortunately, my third Sunday at St. Paul's was not a eucharistic one either. We were back at that Morning Prayer thing again.

The second time around I was less distracted by my own ineptitude. This time I didn't even try to flip around in the *BCP*, having discovered instead that while the whole congregation might wander off to some place known only to themselves and most certainly not to me, they would in time return by some equally obscure way to the page on which we all had started and where I still was. This kind of ecclesial sangfroid served me well in that it allowed me to listen to words that the previous Sunday I had not even been able to hear, and . . . dear God in Heaven!

Whatever other sins I may have, and they are many, speaking the name of God as an expletive is not one of them. Despite my eventual conversion to Anglicanism, I am still far too much of a Presbyterian and far too convinced of what our three-lettered, English rendition of the tetragram invokes to go there. So when I employ it here, I do not do so as an expletive, but as a description that no other word or words can encapsulate. Dear God in Heaven.

The words were everything. They were the whole of my life as I had ever felt it and the whole of beauty as I had ever dared to suspect it. They were, or were so like as to be inseparable from, the song of the playroom and the hum of the forsythia tunnel and the silence of the abandoned bathroom all in one crashing roll of chords; and unlike all those things they subsumed, these words opened up themselves to something that was both of and other than themselves. Dear God in Heaven.

I don't think I had ever known God *was*, until that Sunday. That is, I don't think I had ever envisioned a being that was other than all-present, all-powerful, and handy as a shirt pocket to have around. I mean no irreverence either to God or to my own early self; nor do I mean to imply that all of this epiphany became mine in one brief forty-five minutes of Morning Prayer. I certainly don't mean to suggest that I now know how to catch with words that something that is beyond catching. But I do mean to say that months later, in first-year Greek, I would be assigned *"En arche ein o Logos, kai o Logos ein pros ton Theon, kai o Logos o Theos ein."* "In the beginning was the Word and the Word was with God, and the word was God." And I would physically and rather violently suck in my breath and then tear up because I did understand enough by then to recognize what they were. Dear God in Heaven.

8.

DURING THOSE FIRST MONTHS of my liturgical life, it never once occurred to me to buy a *Book of Common Prayer* for myself. I was at Shorter on a full academic scholarship and, to complement those funds, the college also had arranged a student library clerkship for me. As a result, my supply of discretionary money, though hardly without limits, was still enough to cover both the necessities of college life and most of its reasonable luxuries like cigarettes (rapidly on their way to becoming necessities), the occasional meal out in town with my friends, or the truly coveted book and occasional doodad. Even if all these things had not been true, my father tucked an extra five-dollar bill into his weekly letters about as often as not and without, so far as I can recall now, ever once asking how his largesse was being spent. No, money was not what deterred me.

What deterred me from buying a *BCP* for myself was a lack of imagination. I simply could not conceive of the thing as a book, despite the word *Book* in its title. I could no more have conceptualized the *BCP* as a free-standing entity susceptible to personal ownership than I could have considered setting a chalice as a drinking glass on my nightstand. Both were equally the appointments of a specific and sacred environment; both were equally sacrosanct because of it. The simple truth of the matter is that the option of anyone's privately owning a *BCP* just never crossed my mind.

It wasn't the proper ordering of public worship that I wanted anyway, neither its flow nor its calisthenics. What had me by the hair of my spiritual head was the Psalter in the middle of the *BCP*. The Psalms themselves were hardly new to me, of course. Like most churched people in the early mid-century, I had grown up hearing them read in public worship. I can still remember as well the not-infrequent use of them for responsive reading during Sunday evening services; and though a Psalm was rarely if ever the basis of a Sabbath sermon, then or now, one was frequently the libretto of an anthem or solo.

Admittedly, by the time I was seventeen, some of the Psalms, like the Twenty-third, were more culturally than religiously mine; and I suspect I had been responding to them out of that mind-set for quite some time. Others were relegated to holidays, like the One-hundredth to Thanksgiving, and evoked all the poignancy and distress attendant to those events. Some were even integrated in surprising ways into ordinary life . . . or so I had concluded on that delicious day when I discovered that the 137th is the score of the chorus to "There Is a Tavern in the Town." But all of that was knowledge about the Psalms. What I wanted now was to enter them.

I wanted to learn to sound the Psalms out just like that nave full of Episcopalians at St. Paul's sounded them out. I wanted the familiarity required to make their poetry live first in my chest and then on beyond into the space around me because of my having sent it there. I wanted, for the first time in my life, to possess the skills of sympathetic magic; and even as I was coveting that skill, I also was aware that for the first time in my life I was playing as a grown-up in the gardens of God. All the rules would now apply. It was scary stuff. Or at least it should have been.

The Psalter of the *BCP* is, of course, the Psalter of the *BCP*. It is not, in its cadences and some of its images, the same as the Book of Psalms out of, for example, the King James Bible with which I was familiar. The two are close enough, however, and I decided rather quickly that substituting the one for the other would be sufficient for my initial purposes.

As an incoming freshman, I had been given a sack of printed goodies by one of those zealous organizations that hustle the young toward religion with both earnestness and incredibly bad taste. I was appalled by the tracts, but I had not been unhappy to discover, buried beneath them in the bottom of the sack, a Gideon New Testament in the familiar King James version. Unfortunately and almost immediately afterwards, I also discovered that I didn't like to read out of the Gideon . . . much too small a format to be taken seriously, almost like God on the fly to my young mind. I had noted, however, in the course of rejecting the Gideon, that it contained a complete Book of Psalms on its back pages. Like my parents, never one to throw out a book, I had thrown it instead into the top drawer of my nightstand, along with my cigarettes and my underwear. Thus it was that after one of those Sundays of Morning Prayer at St. Paul's, I went to my room and dug out the Gideon New Testament with the Psalms.

Being skittish about the weirdness of reading Psalms out loud in what, given the constant traffic through our suite, had by then become more or less public space even on Sundays, I waited until after lunch. When everybody around me had settled into the quiet that follows a big meal and the promise of a free afternoon, I did what was by then a natural thing. I took the little testament with its Psalms down to the first floor and locked myself in the bathroom.

Unlike all my previous hours in that place, this time I had to first step into the bathtub and close the transom above it. Otherwise, I told myself, my voice would inevitably filter up the air shaft to the now-occupied floors above me and expose my sanctuary beyond any hope of either explanations or repair. I also had to leave the light on, another less-than-welcome change; but without it I could not see the pages of that down-sized Gideon, much less its words. Despite the slight unease of these necessary adjustments to my routine, I soon settled down into my usual corner where the end of the bathtub met the inside wall of the bathroom and began to read aloud.

Not well at first; not at all well. Probably because of the very informality of my prior exposure to the Psalms, I didn't know most of the verses accurately enough to phrase them initially; and I certainly didn't know their overall content with anything like enough intimacy to anticipate in my delivery of them, but I read.

"Blessed is the man that walketh not in the counsel of the ungodly, nor standeth in the way of sinners, nor sitteth in the seat of the scornful. But his delight is in the law of the Lord; and in his law doth he meditate day and night. And he shall be like a tree planted by the rivers of water, that bringeth forth his fruit in his season . . ." The opening verses of the first Psalm. I read them over and over again. At first I heard my father's voice, or I heard my voice forming itself out of his intonation patterns. Within a few passes, however, I began to find my own voice. I also began to understand, at least at some kind of immature level, the hold that these words had on me.

The difference, as I have already said, between liturgical worship and the nonliturgical worship on which I had grown up is masked, upon one's first few encounters with it, by the sacred space and attitudes within which it occurs. The attention is so riveted to architecture, costume, and usually acoustics that one fails to grasp at first that these things exist in concert with significant other and equally different things. The word *liturgy* itself means work, in this particular case, literally *the work of the people*. What my nave full of marionettes had been doing and what they continued to do at every Morning and Evening Prayer of their lives was work. They did it so well, in fact, that I had completely missed the point until I tried to mimic them while sitting cross-legged on a concrete floor.

I love to read aloud. I always have and, I assume, always will; so the effort and body control involved in the formed delivery of good words were hardly new or distracting sensations for me that Sunday afternoon. Nor, given my seat on the floor, was bobbing up and down any part of my trial run. Yet I felt almost immediately that what I was doing was work, work in some part of me that had been previously unemployed. Yes, there is some muscle involved in sounding words at any time. Yes, there is some discomfort and some rather constant shifting about involved in sitting cross-legged on concrete. Yes, there is some mental labor expended in trying to connect meaning to words, even when the words are already there and require no effort of composition. But there is also another kind of work, as any public speaker can attest and as the good ones are deliberately taught to understand. There is the work of capturing into oneself, at least for a moment or two, the psychology or spirit of the audience to whom one is speaking. Because that's a hard one to either name or define, most accomplished speakers pass the whole process off as being a matter of "intuiting" their audience.

Intuiting, I have discovered, is a code word for internal conversations with what the ancients used to call the genius of a place or a person or an event. In other words, it's an engagement of two or more spirits using a rhetoric and grammar and lexicon that can be translated—artists do it all the time—but cannot be successfully parsed into the pieces of which the translation is the evidence. And that's what I was doing. I knew it, even if not in those clear terms. I knew it and I didn't much like the way it felt or how exhausting it was.

Not only was I annoyed by being forced to admit I had no working idea of who it was I was talking to, but I was also burdened by the weight of the words I was being forced to use. They were indeed not my words, but they introduced into my saying of them centuries of other speakers and whole years of reality that I hadn't lived yet. Watching this process from the back of a nave while someone else did it was one thing. The beauty I had found in it was quite real. It was the beauty of visible and perceived transport. But doing the thing oneself was quite another.

I didn't like not knowing who my audience was, but I most particularly did not like being forced to know that I didn't know. I didn't like having to use other people's words for things I didn't yet want to admit to feeling, much less to have to begin to experience and process. I didn't like the crowd in my bathroom. I didn't like the loss of the restedness I had begun to treasure there. I didn't like any of it, thank you very much. And I left. I was after all a free agent, it was my bathroom, and God and I had got on quite well for seventeen and a half years without any of this silliness. I wasn't about to begin it now.

Of course, nothing is that easy. An adolescent pet is good for about as long as anything else in adolescence is, approximately one afternoon. And then, too, the story of the Garden of Eden and of everything since speaks to the most basic of human foibles: Once some bit of greater or further or deeper understanding is even slightly suggested, we cannot let it be. We must possess it. So I continued to go to Morning Prayer and occasionally Evening Prayer. I continued to be enthralled by the strength of them, but I felt, right through the closing days of second term, little or no willingness to try participating in them publicly.

I didn't take the Gideon and its mini-Psalter back, either, to any of my campus retreats, though I did continue to read the Psalms silently to myself from time to time. My doing so was quite casual at first and randomly executed according to the whim of my spare moments. Gradually, though, the Psalms won.

When at twelve or thirteen I had morosely perceived myself as far too old to be caught taking the *Hurlburt's Story of the Bible* to bed with me, I had begun, more as an acceptable consolation than anything else, taking my Bible instead. It's quite amazing just how much Bible one can absorb in the course of several years of the untutored, semi-conscious reading of its pages. I have been grateful in all the years since, in fact, for the sheer familiarity with text and citation that my sad, young passage from facsimile to original furnished me. I have been grateful as well that what began as an exercise in consolation had, by seventeen, become what it still is, each night's habit, and that eventually, predictably, the Psalms began to insinuate themselves into it. Half-asleep and dreaming, I was drawn like Adam and Eve to the Tree. There was something or other winding and entwining through those words . . . some magic in the patina of their agedness . . . some goodness that might in time give up its beauty.

9.

TO MY WAY OF THINKING, in the years when such things mattered enough to be thought about at all, referring to one's college as "alma mater" was an unfortunate practice that fell somewhere between the pretentious and the downright effete. Now that I am no longer one and twenty, as Housman would say, I find myself to be, if not wiser, then certainly of a more temperate turn of mind. I mention this by way of confessing, of course, that I speak of "alma mater" quite unabashedly myself nowadays. In fact, the only difference between me and those whose conduct I once scorned, so far as I can discover, is that I assign the term to a woman as well as to a place, the former being usually in capitals.

Shorter College was alma mater, the mother of my coming of age, the matrix within which all my pieces of body, soul, heart, spirit, and mind had their first formal and conscious introduction to each other. Dr. Clara Louise Thompson, head of the department of classical and comparative languages, was Alma Mater, the mother of my coming of age, the matrix within which all my pieces of body, soul, heart, spirit, and mind had their first formal and conscious introduction to each other. One contained and protected me during the process, and the other was pleased to effect it.

Shorter, when I matriculated in 1951, had been tucked inconspicuously away in the rolling hill country of north Georgia for most of the ninety years since the War Between the States had decimated the South and most especially those parts of it proximate to Atlanta. The core of the faculty during my years was a body of renegade scholars, many of them women, who had found in a small, isolated Southern college the safety of place in which to do their work and, in each other, the stimulation with which to do it well. Thus I studied anthropology, though under the older names of kinesiology and primitive dance, with Francesca Boas, daughter and intellectual companion of Franz Boas, who had been the father of anthropology as an academic discipline.

I studied ancient and medieval history under Clara Louise Kellogg. According to the received wisdom of the day, she had been born into the social expectations of the cereal family, but had chosen the life of the mind instead. I never discovered anything in her to make me doubt that bit of folklore, though I did find much to admire. And there certainly was no question that she had been one of the few American Egyptologists present at the opening of King Tut's tomb, for she had also been one of the few gassed during that experience. Miss Kellogg—she deplored any other mode of address—could not have weighed, fully dressed, more than eighty pounds; had skin as thin and sere as parchment, so that one could see, in the proper light, the blood pulsating through every artery in her body; ate blackboard chalk, quite literally, by the wooden boxful as she taught, presumably because it was one of the few things that eased her stomach; possessed stamina enough to teach only for three-quarters of an hour or thereabouts at any one time; and spent most of her life resting on a daybed in her high-walled office. I cannot say that she was a brilliant teacher by the time I got to Shorter, but there can be no doubt that she was brilliant. I also remember her with absolute reverence, albeit for a rather aberrant reason.

At the opening of each semester, any humanities major worth her salt who had not yet had Miss Kellogg's courses in ancient and medieval history was at pains to get into them. The presumption, though graciously unstated, was that Professor Kellogg would most assuredly be dead before the end of the present term, much less before another one could begin. The problem of limited classes and patently limited future was compounded as well by the fact that the woman refused to admit freshmen even to her basic lectures.

Being as greedy as the next and about three times as brash, however, I was in line early on the morning of my first college registration in order to sign up for Miss Kellogg's medieval history, and the rules be damned. The registrar looked at me quizzically, trying, I am sure, to gauge my naïveté against my willfulness. "You know you'll have to have her signature on this slip before I can post you to the class on a credit-basis?" she said.

I was prepared for that. I had already found Miss Kellogg's office on the second floor of the administration building. I took my registration slip with all due confidence, therefore, went upstairs to Miss Kellogg's office immediately, made my case earnestly, and was told no summarily. The reason given was that no freshman had or ever could have "the intellectual ma-

turity required for integrating with economy and permanence the principles of ancient social and political organization with those of modern experience." She was probably correct, but it was the wrong reason to offer
me. "Try me," I challenged. "I can do it."

Clara Louise Kellogg looked at me a moment or two, the blood in her
left forearm pulsing erratically in the September light. "Yes," she murmured, "you probably could do it half-well, like a lot of the other young
women in your class. But not as well as if you take a year of basic studies
first." Then, almost seductively, she added, "Beyond that, there is the matter that no beginning freshman can receive an 'A' in these courses, and it
would be a shame for you to damage your grade point in your first semester of college, especially given the quality of your academic record up
to now." That did it. That really was the most wrong of all wrong reasons
to offer me, although I am almost positive in retrospect that it was deliberately fashioned to elicit the result it got. "I can get an 'A,'" I snapped
back. I was furious. "If you'll just give me the chance."

She did and I didn't.

Never before or since have I ever worked so hard on anything as on
that first semester's lectures in history. I read every possible reference and
cross-reference and even chased all the allusions I recognized as such. I also
aced every test, the growing stack of them sitting proudly on the corner
of my desk in the dorm as proof that I was winning. I even succeeded in
getting an "A" on my semester paper, a genuine rarity according to campus scuttlebut.

The final came. I was scared to death I'd fail to cram something and
consequently overlearned it all, proving if nothing else the very lack of intellectual maturity that Miss Kellogg had predicted for me; but I came out
of that final knowing all the way to my toes that I had aced it as well.
When, therefore, the term grades were posted, I was first appalled and
then sick to see not my "A" but a "B+."

I raced up the stairs again and raced as well, with absolutely no grace,
straight into her office. "Miss Kellogg! This can't be! I earned 'A's every
step of the way!"

"Yes," she said without even blinking. "You did."

"Then why the 'B'?"

"First of all, it's a 'B+,'" she said calmly, "and secondly, it is as I told you originally. This lecture room is my domain. I make the rules here. And no beginning freshman makes an 'A' with my material because none is ready to." She was laughing at me, I knew. I could see it in her eyes. But I also knew rather suddenly and instinctively that she was not being cruel or even just plain arbitrary. "It's part of maturity," she said so quietly that I perceived, and not for the first time, just how frail she really was. "It's part of maturity to know what the rules are, but it's especially a part of maturity to learn to distinguish the ones that can be broken from those that can't. And having done that, to choose wisely from those that can't be broken, the one or perhaps two that are really worth risking everything to try to change eventually. Undoubtedly you will remember that a bit better now."

The next semester, in Greco-Roman history, I crammed less, learned far more, and got an "A" for my trouble. I thanked her for the grade just before I left for the summer break. "You're welcome," she said with a tinge of sarcasm, "for both my lectures and your 'A,' but no doubt you'll profit more over the next few years from the 'B+.' " She was absolutely correct; and though hers was hardly a spiritual lesson in its intent, it was to prove so in its application.

In a society built on the moral imperative of individualism and in a mid-century culture of pervasive can-do optimism, nobody before Miss Kellogg had ever shown me in so lucid a way that some of the rules of human circumstance just really and truly are immutable within their own time and place. Certainly no one before her had ever suggested that separating the ones that are from the ones that aren't and picking one's battles accordingly could be an act, not of weak character, but of mature intelligence. And God knows, no one before her had even hinted that the wisdom of such discernments is the wisdom of the spirit living abroad in its secular life.

The 1960s were to stand, of course, as Miss Kellogg's proof text for those of us who tried to enter them vested equally in the Kingdom of God and the Kingdom of Humanity. Just as she had predicted, we came to understand politics, public morality, even contemporary theology and ecclesiology themselves, as being pretty much exercises in distinguishing the currently immutable from the currently mutable and then deciding which of each were worth the price required for their reversal. During all the conversations and upheavals of those disorderly years, Miss Kellogg's "B+" became a kind of sanctuary to my deciding and discerning soul. She had said it would be thus, and it was. *Requiescat in pace.*

But I digress, for it was Clara Louise Thompson and not Clara Louise Kellogg who held center stage in my undergraduate years.

10.

CLARA LOUISE THOMPSON was seventy-plus years old when I came to Shorter College, and even stooped as she was with those years, she stood a good six feet tall. Neither thin nor especially heavy, she had the sharp, straight nose of *Caesar Imperator* and the hair of a lion in prime. Cut straight and short, that thick mane was as white as cotton in the boll and as ill-confined. Directly through the center of it ran a handsome orange streak laid down by the nicotine of innumerable Old Gold cigarettes. The woman held one of them constantly in her left hand, the same hand with which she just as constantly pushed the untamed white hair back out of her eyes. She was to become for me the measure against which every teaching scholar must be gauged.

A graduate of the American School in Rome at a time when nice girls really didn't do that kind of thing, she was also the mother of a daughter whom she had wanted and whose father, purportedly, she had not. Nice girls *really* didn't do that kind of thing. At least they didn't lay public claim to having done it. The only complete text of *Octavia,* once ascribed to Seneca, was, and so far as I know still is, of her critical reconstruction. Her prowess in language, moving easily across the classical languages, the Romance ones that had evolved from them, and the intricacies of both historical Sanskrit and its more modern presentations of Pali and Hindi, was almost beyond my ability to properly appreciate, but not beyond my ability to covet. I wanted what this woman had. In point of fact, I wanted to be what this woman was. Within less than two weeks of her tutelage, sophisticate-at-large had taken on whole new dimensions of meaning.

I first saw Professor Thompson—only her majors were permitted the more familiar "Dr. T." I would eventually come to use—late on the

Thursday afternoon of my first week as a college student. It was the afternoon of language placement tests for all incoming students, and her assistant was overseeing the process. In those days, every collegiate, regardless of future plans or intended major, had to have at least twelve hours in a foreign language to graduate. That was the downside of things. The upside was that anyone coming into Shorter with two or more high school credits in another language could request advanced placement in the same language and cut the language requirement to six hours. Anyone could, that is, if she wanted to and provided she could demonstrate adequate proficiency on both a written and an oral examination. We all wanted to; but by four o'clock and with a lecture room full of nervous girls still waiting for the oral reading segment of the proficiency tests to begin, the process was moving from tedious to painful.

My father had at one time been competent in Spanish; and though he was no longer fluent by the time I began my own formal schooling, he had still loved both the tongue and the culture enough to encourage me in it. As a result, I had not two but three years of Spanish on my high school record, the last one having been a tutorial with a really gifted teacher. As circumstance would have it that day, just as the oral reading segment was to begin, Dr. Thompson walked into the lecture room to observe for a few minutes. She nodded impersonally at the assistant, noticed the room full of us not at all and, stepping up onto the dais, silently took a seat in the chair behind her lecture desk. Again, as circumstance would have it, with a name like Phyllis Alexander, I was both the only "A" in the room and the first to have to read aloud the assigned portion of Spanish text.

As I began to speak, that leonine head shot up; and before I had finished the first two or three sentences, those piercing eyes had pinioned me to the back of the chair in which I was sitting. "Which one are you?" she said, shuffling the papers that were on the desktop before her and were obviously our transcripts and advanced-placement requests.

"Alexander," I answered.

"¿Qué?" she shot back at me.

"¡Dispénseme!" I said, and felt my face flush. "Me llamo Phyllis Alexander."

"¿De donde?"

"East Tennessee." I mumbled the words this time, having become by then totally mindless in the face of her aggression. Everybody else whom I could see around me, including the department assistant, looked about as discomfited as I felt; but while their consternation is amusing to recall now, it was scant protection at the time.

"Ahhh," the woman said, looking first at my paperwork, which she seemed finally to have located in the stack before her, and then at me. The eyebrow went up. "Four years of Latin?" she said.

"Yes, ma'am."

"Don't 'ma'am' me," she snapped.

"No, no, I won't."

She looked at me for a moment or two as if I were some kind of fruit or vegetable that needed washing and trimming to be usable. Then she stepped down off the dais and headed to the oak door that opened into her private office. Just as she passed through the door, she turned and said, more or less in my direction, "¡Venga usted conmigo, por favor!" I came or went or whatever direction one wishes to use, and walked straight into that most elusive of modern American blessings, a fully mentored education. My life as an adult had begun.

Dr. T.'s office was the size of her lecture room. And despite the fact that her intelligence was itself so voracious and palpable a space as to dwarf both of those others, the office also had an appeal of sorts. It was all the things one thinks of as stereotypically academic combined with all the appointments of a female aesthete. Two massive windows, kept shadeless, blindless, and curtainless in defiance of usual office custom, looked down on an unkempt courtyard and, across it, to the brick faced somberness of my dormitory. If there were a single picture or painting on the walls other than one print of the head of Pericles that hung like a talisman just by the lecture room door, I don't recall it. Instead, the three solid walls and what was left of the windowed one were lined with bookshelves and mismatched bookcases, two of them glass-enclosed and all of them stocked in accord with some not immediately decipherable order. Eventually I would conclude that each volume's location was merely a matter of the time of its acquisition. Like Lady Macbeth's guests, Dr. T.'s books seemed to stand upon the order of their coming.

The commanding presence in the room was a desk that was easily seven feet in length and three and a half in width. It was of some kind of imposing, ebonylike wood, and Dr. T. routinely interrupted her office discourses to either brush or blow the ashes and dust particles off its dark surfaces as she talked. She sat behind that desk in an unforgiving straight-back chair which she kept forever poised on only its two back legs. From this position, she rocked back and forth in moments of deep mental activity and hunched forward onto the desk in moments of intense delivery. Rarely, if ever, did she assume any other posture in that chair during the two years I knew her, for rarely, if ever, did she divert herself from the twin exercises of discovery and synthesis or forceful articulation.

There were three other chairs in the room, all wooden and all fairly unforgiving themselves. They were the seats of the elect, for to be invited to occupy one on a routine basis was most surely to be among the chosen. Two of the chairs sat under the curtainless windows and faced the side of the ebony desk. They were the desirable ones. The third chair sat almost directly in front of the desk, but back from it by some three or four feet. It was, or could be, a truly frightening place to be, for Dr. Thompson did not suffer kindly either error or those who engaged in it. Above all of this and tying the whole together, a great, white-lanterned fixture of totally institutionalized design hung by a chain from the center of the room, its inadequacies being the apparent reason for the windows' curtainless state.

I was to spend the most focused and disciplined two years of my life in this idiosyncratic space. Much of it would be in company with another undergraduate or two, the remainder of it alone with Dr. T. All of it, as I recall now and as I perceived it then, was as if the woman were deliberately packing a suitcase each day, every day. I would be the last of her protegées, for she was too old to continue much longer; but by God, I would be as good as she could make me be, and I would leave that room with everything she could possibly conceive of my needing for the journey.

We did not wait for term to start officially, nor did I ever finish my proficiency tests on that Thursday afternoon. Instead, Dr. T. took up her perch behind the dark desk, motioned me to the chair in front of it, took a *De Rerum Natura* from the shelf behind her, and said, "All right, let's see what you can do with this." We stayed there, Lucretius, Clara Louise Thompson, and I, until the light outside was gone and the cafeteria gong was ringing dinner.

11.

CLARA LOUISE THOMPSON was a hard woman. If I had come into her care looking for some kind of approval or emotional connection that Thursday afternoon, I had come to the wrong place, and she let me know that immediately. To rephrase a tiresome cliché, if I now had a nickel for every time Clara Louise Thompson was to hit that ebony desk of hers and half-scream, "No! No! No!" at me, I would be a much wealthier woman.

What redeemed this kind of grinding and omnipresent impatience was its impersonalness. She was never, I think, angry at me, only at the unwieldy and untutored mind out of which I was trying to operate and which, up until that point, I had always really assumed I was . . . or was I, as the case may be. And though I had had a sound education, both formal and otherwise, I certainly had never been given the objectivity needed to "operate" a mind, much less to distinguish my self from it. Clara Louise Thompson had that objectivity, and she intended for me to have it, too.

"Use your head, damn it!" She would more growl than say the words.

"Think of your mind as a machine," on calmer occasions. "Take it out, turn it around, look at it. See what you've got up there and then figure out now what it will and won't do for you."

On better occasions, "Rule your mind, don't let it rule you."

And on the best, "Ah, we are making progress, aren't we! Your instincts were right on that section." But such comments were almost always immediately tempered with, "But remember, instincts can only be as good as what you give them to work with."

There must have been at least a thousand times in my adult life and especially in the fully adult one of my later years when I have wished I could revisit Shorter College as it was in 1951 and not as I remember it. Memory, knowing the end result, recalls only acceptable causes. We construct explanations not on the basis of their actuality so much as on their ability to be the ones we can live with. What is wrong with this process is that it desecrates divine process by rejecting the ordinariness of its means. Nowhere am I more aware of this than just here.

Not all of the rogue scholars at Shorter were female; and not all of the male faculty were of sufficient edge and ambition to be acceptable to the rogues who were the female majority. One who was—one on whom the coterie of the gifted commented as "promising indeed"—was a young man whose first semester at Shorter was also mine. Jack Hornaday was fresh out of Duke University with a Ph.D. that reeked of prestige and almost five years of postgraduate work in something I had never heard of before—parapsychology—and with a scholar/researcher whom I'd never heard of either: J. B. Rhine. And one of those things I would like most to know now, factually and not romantically, is why and/or how he came to be at Shorter.

Looking back from what I am today, I see in 1951 and in that cloistered bit of north Georgia that was Shorter Hill a confluence of circumstances and of intellects so singular as to lie beyond any facile explanation. Looking back, what I see is a small place caught in a small section of time doing things that were so far beyond their time and place as to be almost primitive. While Miss Kellogg, her withered body serving as a constant testament to the arcanum of ancient Egypt, and Francesca Boas, her drums still resonating with aboriginal purposes, may have set the tone of the place, it was the probers, the iconoclasts like Thompson and Hornaday, who gave it substance. They were about more than the business of reporting mystery; they were in the business of disassembling it into its principles and parts. They knew Jung and Teilhard de Chardin, of course, for they spoke of them, of Freud and James, Graves and Frazer. They could not yet, I think, have known of the young Joseph Campbell or the formidable Chomsky or even the other great popularizer Jacob Bronowski, or of dozens more like them still to come, but it didn't matter. They were all plowing in the same forbidden fields. They were compartmentalizing human consciousness and mapping individual life as if it were a universe or a construct, not a sacred creature. They were, in essence, attending the birth pangs of late-twentieth-century spirituality, and, like a kid gawky in my innocence, I was standing there watching.

Hornaday, regardless of how he had gotten to Shorter, set up shop as quickly as any impassioned young man could. Within a few weeks, he had teams of undergraduates sitting, one at a time, alone in empty rooms playing with decks of object cards. Eventually some of us would spend our available Saturday mornings working in two-person teams with Professor Hornaday. As I remember the arrangements on those Saturdays, one of us

would sit alone with the cards in an empty room at the end of a long corridor of equally empty classrooms. The other one of us would be seated in
the last empty room at the far end of the same hall, without cards but with
a pencil and pad. The corridor doors were closed off, and no other human
being was anywhere near either of us. When a timer went off, the one
with the cards would shuffle them. When after that a bell rang, each of us
would take up her assigned role. One of us was to project the image from
the cards as she turned them slowly over; and the other of us was to attempt to receive and then record the images in the order that they were
being sent.

For a little girl from the hills of East Tennessee, it was heady stuff. The
spookiest and most exhilarating experience of my young life, it was also an
attack on all the forbiddens of my childhood, a gift from the gods of gno-
sis that I was smart enough not to write home about. And when Mr.
Hornaday's counting was over and done with, like it or not, the truth was
that some of us clearly and irrefutably were transmitting and receiving information . . . crude information, admittedly, but information. And we
were doing so without any overt connection, one to another. We were, as
Rhine had long since begun to assert, employing an energy, probably an
electrical force, that all primitive peoples and mystics acknowledge, but
that the Enlightenment had not identified, much less dissected.

But that is not the autobiographical point here. The autobiographical
point is that by some process or other I had been drawn at the precisely
correct moment to one of the few places in the South (if indeed, not the
only one) where rogue minds, all well-trained but in disparate disciplines,
had been gathered together in relative safety by an affinity for asking one
central question. While I can never know precisely how or if they worded
that question among themselves, I do know that from where I sat, it was
a very concise one: What is self and how does it communicate with non-
and/or other-self?

None of Shorter's explorers in the world of mystery ever said the word
"god," or "faith," or "religion," or even "prayer" to me, so far as I can remember, except in an academic context like, "Religion among the ancient
Greeks differed from that of the early Indo-Europeans in how it incarnated
its polytheism," etc., etc. They didn't have to. The implications of what
they were doing screamed all these things.

The fact that Dr. T. could so matter-of-factly separate mind out of and away from self and then demand that "I," whoever that was, pick it up and work on it as if it were an object on the edge of her dark desk made perfect sense to me, once I had got used to the notion. It made sense because it was experientially confirmable on a daily basis. But it didn't take me many days of being confirmed to realize as well that redefining "I" had patent in it redefining God and, therefore, everything related to how human beings interact with God.

Jack Hornaday's assumption that the power of the unseen was both absolutely operative among us and ultimately definable had its corollary in his assumption that very physical principles, while still undefined, governed that power and were discoverable. Both made equal sense, for I could grasp Professor Hornaday's proofs as well as I could those of any other science text. Yet it is only a short step from that position to one that begins to scratch its head over miracles and visions and petitions. No, I definitely did not write home about Mr. Hornaday.

I did write home about Dr. T., at least about the accessible, chatty parts of life with Dr. T. As with all her majors, for instance, she had immediately arranged my schedule to suit her purposes. In essence, I was registered for "Thompson." I had to take that Advanced Spanish Conversation in the lecture room along with some dozen or so other undergraduates. I emerged from the experience competent in Spanish, but very aware of the fact that I would never be either a gifted conversationalist in Spanish or even a reasonably fluent one. Other than that, I left Dr. T.'s office only to attend those collateral and required courses that were unavoidable and that, optimally, met when she was herself in lectures. She chose them for me, and only once did I question her choices.

Dr. T.'s best friend on the faculty was Gertrude Von Engles. She was as German as her name suggests and the most bizarre woman I had ever, to that point in my life, known. Equally bizarre, at least to me, was the obvious rapport between her and Dr. T. The only things I could find that they shared were sheer mental agility and a certain kind of European sensibility. But Dr. T.'s regard was enough. I was obliged to take not only freshman English with Dr. Von Engles but, at Dr. T.'s insistence, her advanced lit. course the following autumn. I signed up with less than enthusiasm and, I suspect, with a considerable lack of sangfroid about having to do so.

Von Engles, by her own admission, read thirty-five to forty books a week. To me that translates, now as well as then, to having no life at all outside one's head. It certainly translated then to a sound explanation of why the woman was a nervous wreck. She was in body form a nineteenth-century German dowager, with her pince-nez on her nose, her Gibson girl hairdo constantly in various stages of falling apart, and her corpulence threatening her corset with her every movement, of which there were many. The woman could not stay in one spot for the length of one whole sentence, darting here and there with all the grace of a Sherman tank in motion. I didn't like her, but I grudgingly had to admit I admired her, or if not her, her gifts. Apparently, however, I had been more correct than I would have wished to be about the barrenness of her life, because she took it one weekend of fall term by cyanide inhalation.

I had never known a suicide before, and I was as much grieved by the unwelcome awareness that it could happen to able people as by the loss of Dr. Von Engles. That is, I was thus grieved until we were told that there would be no public funeral services for us to attend. Dr. Von Engles had been, as was Dr. T., an Episcopalian; and Episcopalians did not, in the 1950s, bury suicides on hallowed ground or bring their bodies within hallowed space for the giving of unction or the saying of the mass. I was stopped dead in my tracks.

St. Paul's was closed to one of the most competent and brilliant thinkers in the South! St. Paul's had closed itself, perversely, it seemed to me, to one of its own because it did not approve of an action that neither it nor its rector nor its damned vestry could possibly know any damned thing about!

Ah, the energy of the young when they arrive at the empowerment of righteous anger. How sweet it was to vent my fury at the unfairness of it all, the arrogance, the inhumanity. I who had never had much truck with Gertrude Von Engles suddenly saw her in a much more flattering, even faintly affectionate, light. But when all the telling of the tale is said and done and when all the analysis of it finished, the truth is that I never went back to St. Paul's after that. The passions of the young may be disproportionate, but they are not a whit the less affecting for all their inflation and noise. I simply could not forgive, and I could not embrace that which I could not forgive. I continued to seek my private places of restedness, I read Scripture each night as part of preparing for bed, I continued to ponder on a more or less deliberate basis the content of the Psalms, but I slept in on Sundays for the rest of my college career. My checkered involvement with formal religion had begun.

12.

WHEN I SAY that the rogues—there were more of them than I have named, of course: Griffin in art, Martin in physical science, Grant in religion, a few others—were drawn to the disassembling of mystery into all its component parts, I do not wish to put too fine a point on the matter. What I do wish to describe and what I know to have been absolutely present among them was a seething, pervasive excitement that made each one of them push his or her respective discipline to the limits not only of its content but of its orthodoxies. Perhaps their excitement was itself the heady stuff, their sheer belief in eventual discovery mixed, for most of them, with the urgency of advanced years and diminishing strength. This was probably more true, or perhaps more apparent, with Dr. T. than with any of the others whom I knew and under whom I studied.

Language was the one sure and steady presentation of the sacred in life for Clara Louise Thompson, the one space or exercise in which the human and the divine truly met and in which every act of both was recorded beyond adjustment or deletion. To give oneself to understanding the workings of language was to accept vocation at the high altar. What that elevated process actually translated to on a day-in-day-out basis, however, was quite another matter. What it translated into was all of the dreary mental scut work every undergraduate knows only too well: learning vocabulary, memorizing cases, mastering conjugations, etc. There is nothing romantic or exhilarating or even halfway satisfying about schlocking one's way through either English syntax or Homeric Greek, through either classical or Church Latin, through a reading acquaintance with the major Romance languages or an in-depth intimacy with the history and literature of one of them. Those things are hard-won, and there are no happy little paths winding pleasantly into their domain.

Truth be told, however, none of those things was what my hours of

"Thompson" were really about. Like a well-scrutinized mind, they were simply tools to her. And truth be told again, most of their intricacies are now completely lost to me. I can no more conjugate a Spanish verb now than I can scan a line of Virgil or parse a Portuguese sentence. I keep a parallel Greek/English New Testament on the shelf nearest my desk these days because I long ago ceased to trust my reading of Koine without its help. And while those are regrettable losses, I don't mourn them over much or very frequently; I am sure Dr. T. would not mourn them at all. What she was teaching me employed all of those things, but it was not itself any of them.

Dr. T. understood language as a function of the body. Its messages and even its nuances must be studied, first and foremost, as presenting initially in one's viscera and undifferentiated memory. Only secondarily did language, by way of human neurology and human emotion, become transposed into symbol and order. Both for the individual within his or her own consciousness and for the individual engaging the consciousness of others, language was the rope of connection between the ages gone and the time being lived, between the species and the autobiographical self, between mere existence and life. Language and meta-language were the stuff of God incarnate amongst us, even as Incarnation had said of Itself. Dr. T. knew why I gasped when I first saw *"En arche ein o Logos"* printed out on a page before me. My small cry was her reward, the first proof that she had taught me well; and we both knew it.

Day after long, weary day, she spread the known languages of the world before me as casually and particularly as a skilled astronomer lays open the heavens to a questing child. She cordoned off from them the tongues of the Western world—the so-called Indo-European ones—and by moving backward through them exposed to full view both their history and their evolution from their theoretical original of Proto-Indo-European. She applied Grimm's Law and Verner's Law or the principle of rhotacism with the deftness of a science professor laying out Boyle's law or Planck's constant. But her truest analogues were probably those of archaeologist and psychologist.

No one had ever told me before that language was a thing, a living force, a shifting energy of union possessed of a soul. Certainly nobody had ever laid out its laws or principles. Until Dr. T., I had assumed that the laws of language were the rules of grammar. Not so. What I was to be concerned about, she let me know quite early on, was something quite different. My concern was to be just why and how the concept of a male parent in Proto-Indo-European, for instance, presented millennia later as *pater* in Greek and Latin but as *father* in English (i.e., Grimm's Law, which pertains to shifts in mute consonants and, as a result, manages to explain some several hundred oddities like *frater* and *brother*, or *mater* and *mother*, or *gens* and *kin*). Having conquered that lesson, my next concern was to be learning how to interpret these linguistic phenomena as artifacts, as the extant remains of a culture we could reconstruct by means of them. (In this instance, the artifacts reveal a strong family organization that was first nuclear and then tribal in allegiance and that, as a result, differed markedly from some of the other language cultures of proto-time.

"What," she would say, hunching toward that desk, "is this really telling us? What can you educe from this?" And gradually I learned to see what it was that was there to be seen, even if I never learned to discover it with her clarity and genius.

Nor had anyone ever told me before that language was a thing of the body, though my father had certainly told me often enough that it was a thing made by using the body. The difference between the two was and is, of course, like the difference between the sounding drum and the rawhide of which it is constructed. How far down into the body a sound is made, she argued, determines how deeply the hearer receives its meaning, how totally that hearer will engage its meaning, how completely that hearer will honor the experience of its meaning. The *m*'s of *mother* move us more universally and surely than do the *f*'s of *father* because of where the two sounds are formed or (ah, sweet mystery . . . it was at points like this that she would still the rocking chair) perhaps because mother mattered more than father to the ancients and was therefore assigned quite unself-consciously the tonally deeper, physically richer denominator. (When, years later, pizza came to be associated with the *Mmmmmm*'s, *Ahhhhhh*'s, and *Ohhhhhhhh*'s of Madison Avenue while peanut butter was assigned to the *j*'s of *Jif* and the peppery *p*'s, of *Peter Pan,* I smiled. Of course they were. Those choices elucidate as no words *per se* ever could the difference between the two foods.)

Because it was a thing of the body, the message of language can never be as nuanced in written as in oral delivery, Dr. T. said. The history of grammar and usage is the story of humanity's attempts to grant clarity where civilization has robbed us of audition, she also said. And if I were recalcitrant and disbelieving at first, I soon was forced to accept conversion by means of the simplest of experiments and exercises.

"Assume," she told me one dreary afternoon, "a note stuck on a bulletin board, and the note says . . ." And here she wrote on the back of an old exam paper the words "Ship sails today." "Tell me what it means." The chair rocked forward and the Old Gold was stilled on its way to pushing back the hair.

"I can't," I said.

"Of course not," and the Old Gold continued its journey northward. "Either you are being told to mail some pieces of cloth or you are being told to be patient until something or someone arrives at some dock somewhere."

On another day, when I was slaughtering Virgil, the chair banged down on the floor, the flat of her right hand hit the corner of the ebony desk, and the fierce eyes blazed into my very gut. "No, God damn it, no! It's not the words. Forget the words, get the rhythm!"

She went over to one of the bookcases, searched a second, and pulled down a volume. She opened it and laid in front of me the opening lines of Longfellow's "Evangeline." "Read," she demanded. I read:

This is the forest primeval. The murmuring pines and the hemlocks,
Bearded with moss, and in garments green, indistinct in the twilight . . .

"Feel it?" she half-demanded again. "The rhythm of the sea, the memory of the womb, the sound of ocean's rise and fall like the sound of the mother's heart synchronized with the beat of your own."

Then more quietly, more longingly, "Virgil uses length—*Ārmă vĭrūmquē cānō quī prīmus ŏb ōrīs*—and Longfellow uses beat—'Thĭs ĭs thĕ fór-ĕst prĭmévál. Thĕ múrmŭrĭng pínes ănd thĕ hémlócks'—but they are telling you the same song . . . dead men living on in your body because they speak what your body has brought with it from our beginning."

Then most quietly of all, "How can you dare read Scripture—the Prophets, the Psalms, the Apocalyse—if you don't understand that?" It was a stunning question.

And that was life with Dr. Thompson. She was *magistra ludi, magistra magorum,* and every morning there was some new wonder pulled out of the day's conversation, every afternoon some small mystery set up on the desk to bask in the slanted light from the curtainless window. Day after day after glorious, dreadful day it went until I thought, as I came closer to the end of my second year with her, that Dr. T.'s treasure chest of surprises must surely be near to the point of exhaustion; and that, of course, was when it happened.

It was March. I remember because my birthday is in March; and while I have never been much inclined toward making hoopla over every passing year, I have always had a sense of excitement and anticipation as another birthday approaches. Perhaps it is my greediness for the years or my sense of reward that another, like a notch on one's gunstock, has been bagged and carried home. Who knows? But for whatever reason, the events of each year's early March are etched more finely into my memory as a rule than are those of, for example, a mere April or October. And this one is etched. This one was in March.

Classes, including tutorials, were regulated at Shorter, just as they are everywhere in this country, by the ringing of raucous apparati that sound as if they belong on a shipping dock and not on a campus, and that in some kind of effort to disguise their true character are euphemistically referred to as bells. Shorter's were particularly commercial and imperious in their monotonal splendor; and mercifully, as a result, were not always rung every fifty-five or sixty minutes. Rather, they were used more often to punctuate the larger patterns of each day's course—the opening of classes, the start of chapel, the beginning of afternoon classes, and, of course, our meal breaks.

As a rule, by the time lunch was sounded each day, the one, two, or three of us who were in morning tutorial with Dr. T. felt an enormous hunger, not for food, but for some rest and recreation in less strenuous and demanding company. We were quick to leave, often making it to the office's hall door before the cries of the Rome Hall gong had fully died away. It was an exodus that Dr. T. herself always seemed willing to encourage. In the afternoons and especially at chapel break, she was fierce in her insistence that thoughts be completed, conversational points refined, the ending session summarized before any of us was free to follow the bell. But at lunch things were different. At lunch she was content to see us go, her only words being "Please close that door all the way as you leave."

So it was a normal early March day in north Georgia. The light in the office windows was still gray, and the courtyard world below them was still as quiet as gray. The three of us seated around the ebony desk were in our prelunch mode of "Please, let it ring!" and "I'll personally kill anybody who asks a question before it does." No one asked, and the dong sounded. True to form, we were out the office door and safely into the corridor beyond before its reverberations had stilled. We were, in fact, all the way to the first floor landing before I realized I had left my purse back in Dr. T.'s office.

If I were to make it through the afternoon ahead, I had to stop by the college store and buy cigarettes while we were on lunch break. Annoyed at myself, I turned around and took the steps two at a time to retrieve the purse and rejoin the others as quickly as possible. They, too, were annoyed and not likely to wait long if I appeared to dawdle. Lunch was sacred, and I had already diminished it by three minutes at least.

I more trotted than walked back down the second-floor corridor, had the good manners to at least tap on the door with my left hand even as I was opening it with my right, and burst in, full of eighteen-, almost nineteen-year-old urgency. Dr. T. was still sitting at her desk, still poised precariously on the two back legs of her straight-back chair, still rocking back and forth. But this time there was a rhythm to the tilting up and back that was unlike the more jerky movements of intellectual delivery. Her head was going up and down with the rhythm of her rocking; and her lips were moving in concert with both. In her hands, resting more on her knees than on her lap, was a book. I knew in one fiercely arresting moment what it was. Dr. T. was holding *The Book of Common Prayer*.

She looked up at me, but I am not sure, to this very day, whether or not she perceived me. By the uneasy light of the big windows beyond her, however, I could see her quite clearly. I could see her blank face staring toward the noise that had roused her, could see the muscles in her face move as she struggled to enter again into being where she was . . .

I knew that stare just as I knew where Clara Louise Thompson had been when I interrupted her. My mother went there every afternoon on the long bench in her living room.

I fled back down the hall to the stairwell, took the steps down as rapidly as I had taken them up, borrowed money from a classmate, and was, I am sure, abnormally quiet for all of lunch. Not a word was ever said about that singular interruption of the formal space between Dr. T. and me. Nor, until now, have I ever spoken of it to anyone else; but of all the images burned by a lifetime into the reels of memory none other is more sharply defined or more detailed than is that one instant when the leonine head lifted from its prayers while the aura of them was still visible around it.

If Dr. T. and I never spoke of that moment, we never spoke either of *The Book of Common Prayer.* Within a matter of just a few minutes, of course, it dawned on me that not only was Dr. T. praying during our lunch break, but that she was using the *BCP* in some way as part of the process. This meant both that individuals could own a *BCP* privately and that buried somewhere in its pages there were some usages I had not yet discovered. Both were new considerations for me, but they had come too late to be worthy of pursuit. Dr. Von Engles was already dead, and I had seen beneath the skirts of the virago who masqueraded as Mother Church.

13.

MOST OF THE WORKING TOOLS that my college years provided to my more fully adult ones were shaped and then honed in one office on the second floor of an old brick building in Rome, Georgia. There can be no question about that. The tale of those years and the inventory of what I brought out with me when I left them would be dishonestly truncated, however, if I did not include the discovery, however painful, of one other piece of equipment that, like a good yeoman, has continued to serve me well in all the years since.

By May of my sophomore year it was apparent both to Dr. T. and to those of us who were with her every day that, despite all her wishes and intentions to the contrary, the time had come for her to retire. Even that gargantuan persona could fend off age and situation no longer. Yet I suspect that not one of us in that pale May had even the vaguest of notions just how deeply her retirement would change us as well. Certainly I didn't.

When I was a little girl and long before I had ever even heard of Shorter College, there had been an unstated agreement among us as a family that I would take my undergraduate degree from my father's university. During my senior year in high school, that understanding had shifted from an implied to an overtly stated intention that my father and I had discussed quite fully. He had given his professional life to an institution whose worth and stature he not only believed in, but had helped to create. For his own daughter and only child not to take her degree there would be an intolerable loss of face and public confidence. I would spend one year away from home, not only because everyone needed that pleasure and experience, but also because no one needs to be an incoming freshman at the university where her father is the academic dean. After that first year, however, I was to return without complaint for the bulk of my instruction as well as my degree to the school where he was.

So great and so obvious had been my joy and excitement at Shorter, however, once I got there, that the teacher in my father—never very far below his surfaces at any time—had overridden the politician. He had forgiven rather quickly and without much urging our larger contract and had accepted instead my pledge to spend my senior year with him if only I might have my first three with Dr. T. and the rogues. Now I was to be denied that benediction by her circumstances, not his. At least the irony was not lost on me, even if the consequences were.

As she approached the last few weeks of our time together. Dr. T. became more and more concerned that the tutorial credit hours I had earned toward a Shorter baccalaureate might not fulfill the degree requirements of another school, particularly of a state college like my father's in which neither the classical languages nor courses in comparative linguistics were then taught. As a result, she and I spent a tedious afternoon or two near term's end going over the records of my two years with her. Hunched forward in the tilting chair, she took the catalog of my father's school and painstakingly translated my two years of heaven into the ordinary details of degree requirements for a school I knew intimately but not intellectually. It was like a death for me . . . not even a funeral, but a death. The magic was being folded into the dross the world required, and the rogue was at last conforming for the sake of a beloved.

Despite the poignancy of goodbyes and farewells, I had gone home for the summer of 1953 filled with plans and totally innocent of anything that even approximated anxiety, much less genuine foreboding. I somehow assumed, to the extent that I thought about such matters at all, that I could return as an upperclasswoman in September to a Shorter Hill without Dr. T. and find everything just as it had always been . . . or if not exactly as it had been, then at least familiar and comfortable enough to render her absence a matter more of change than of substance. I was young and very wrong.

The second-floor office, where now some beret-wearing Franco-American sat behind Dr. T.'s desk but not in her hard-bottomed chair, had curtains and two floor lamps. The bookcases were gone, and the few books on the built-in shelves were arranged by content area and then alphabetized within their categories. The print of Pericles had given way to a half dozen of Europe that could as easily have come from any travel agent's posture cache. There was an Oriental rug on the floor, and one upholstered side chair had replaced our austere, wooden perches. In less than one full glance I knew to my toes that the glory that was Greece and the grandeur that was Rome were indeed gone.

I remember that year as a desert of the heart. All the friends whom I had loved, with whom I had shared all my thoughts and most of my emotions, with whom I had in fact passed from girlhood into adulthood were still there. They were still around me every day, still as much a part of my waking hours as ever. They were, as friends should be in such times, comfortable and diverting as well as present and affectionate; but even friendship could not tease away my loss. The intellectual and spiritual excitement—for that is what it had been, of course—of Dr. T.'s tutelage was no longer present in my present.

I went to class, I went to meetings, I ran for and won a campus office or two, I wrote for student publications and even began to seek publication in sources that weren't campus ones. It was not, in other words, that I was unoccupied or even unproductive, but just that I was . . . ?

And that, I discovered, was the problem: I was bored.

Once I had named the beast, I felt a kind of amazement at its presence. I had never been bored before. More to the point and far more frightening to me once I realized what else was wrong, I had never been trapped before either. I had never before been in a situation where passing through a block of time simply to get to the other side of it was the whole point of getting up in the mornings. Yet I was indeed trapped, and trapped in no small part by my own cleverness.

When out of concern for my future, Dr. T. and I had spent those two or three exasperating afternoons tailoring my liberal arts transcript to the expectations of a public university, we also, albeit unwittingly, had boxed me in to a third year at Shorter come hell or high water, though at the time neither of those possibilities had seemed at all likely. Working together, we had first laid out the university's degree requirements. Then we had measured, with total candor between us, exactly where my first two years of undergraduate work could and/or, by any stretch of the creative process, absolutely could not be seen as equivalent to the university's program. Once we had arrived at what amounted to a checklist of the could-nots, Dr. T. had taken Shorter's catalog and preregistered me from its list of always-available courses for those classes that by course description were a legitimate match with the university's required ones.

With my junior year so neatly contrived, it had been a reasonably straightforward, if painful, process to then break our two years together down into satisfactory equivalents to the remaining course requirements. There was no way on God's green earth, however, that I would ever be able to find that same sequence of prescribed classes anywhere else. The whole thing, while more honest and considerably more ethical than I probably have made it sound here, was nonetheless a house of cards destined to tumble down if one card were even breathed upon, much less shuffled about.

When one is nineteen going on twenty, time has a credibility that mercifully it loses to one's advancing years; but more than youthful urgency was involved here. To leave Shorter before I had completed Dr. T.'s junior-year regimen would mean, at the very least, a full semester's delay in receiving my degree anywhere else. Without a college degree, I could not get a teaching certificate, and in those days of the GI Bill and the national teacher glut, no one—but no one—got a teaching position until the fall after he or she had been granted certification. The frustration in all of this was not so much that my young heart was filled with a yearning to teach, although it was, but that my young heart was far more completely filled with yearning toward the other great preoccupation of my Shorter years. Sam Tickle and I were in love; but the cruel realities of our condition were that until I had a job that would support us while he went to medical school, there could be no wedding. It was that simple. I was, in short, threatened as well as trapped and bored.

So it was that for the first of what would be many times in my life, the spooks came out to play; and they did so almost immediately. They were gentle, of course, for they, too, were young. And to their credit, they presented in half-languid ways: "I don't feel very good today." "I'd rather sit here and read as go to the volley ball game." "I don't care enough one way or the other to go all the way to the library to look that one up." And then back again to "I don't feel very good today." What difference did it make how I felt anyway? I wasn't going anywhere and I wasn't going there fast.

What one wants to do with depression, I have decided, is still even today pretty much a matter of what one's own experience with depression has been. I had a much loved uncle once who had outlived his own body by about fifteen years before he finally managed to die; and he referred to the years between his increasing debility and his death as ones of "having the blues." By contrast, I had a first cousin who died of raging, intractable, impenetrable depression in the course of which and despite all medical efforts at intervention she quite literally starved to death out of sheer inability to will herself to eat. On that scale of extremes, I had the blues, though I must say that what I remember feeling at the time was considerably less colorful and benign than Uncle Murph's name for it would imply.

By however charming a label, though, the truth still was that I was blue . . . no, not even blue. I was gray on the inside. All color was so drained from me, in fact, that even the world outside in time went gray as well. Nor did I have even the most primitive notion of how to escape my own grief or of how to gauge the seriousness and longevity of my overwhelming weariness.

No one, not even the most protected of us, arrives at nineteen or twenty years of age without having ridden, at least a few times, atop the emotional yo-yo we refer to as the "ups and downs" of life. Most girls, moreover, rarely escape the pattern of monthly tension and anxiety that gives way in one salvific few days to a cleansing blood tide. Most girls, in fact, by the time they are fifteen, much less twenty, have discovered that in addition to being a monthly phenomenon, this bit of emotional cycling is almost as beneficial as it is predictable. At least the siphoning off of interior angst on a routine basis appears to them to be a potent preventative to the testosterone buildup that vents so unpleasantly and unpredictably in many of their brothers, fathers, and husbands.

That bit of feminist theory aside, however, what was happening to me was none of these ordinary and dynamic things. What was happening to me was neither incapacitating me nor accomplishing anything for me. It was just there, and like me, it appeared not to be going anywhere fast. I and my malaise were trapped together as surely as if we were winged creatures of summer caught in a child's dirty mason jar. Our light and our hope were both in the hands of a naughty and capricious other.

As was true of many another young adult in America's mid-century, I had not yet learned to pray by the time I was nineteen years old and under my first serious attack from the demi-demons of my world. That is, I had passed through the stages of experience that can eventually lead to prayer, but at nineteen and twenty I had neither the maturity nor the native shrewdness to realize that there are stages of religious maturity to be passed through in this life, much less the discernment to know where I was in that process or how best to attend to it.

I had, of course, perfected the rote "God blesses" of infancy long before I was six and "big enough to no longer need to be listened to," as my mother had put it. Undeterred when she and my father quit "hearing" my small prayers, I had persisted alone, posting them off each bedtime like little Valentines through a kind of inner-office mail that we all three had once agreed was real, even if a bit concocted.

In early adolescence, as I had begun to keep daily rhythms that were separate from those of my parents and as my maturing body had begun to write its own needs into my scheme of things, I had just as innocently picked up the proportionally larger petitions of my larger life. I added to my "God bless"s the untutored "I want"s and "Please give me"s that are the natural conversation of older childhood and that pretty much sustain most of us on into early adulthood. Or at least, they had sustained me quite nicely for the eight to ten years that preceded my first crisis of the spirit. What I had not perceived, of course, for I had had no need to do so, was that as my prayers had changed with my changing years, so too had their intended recipient. God had morphed subtly but surely from some benign power who wore my father's face to an un-imaged concept; and while concepts can be helpful, they have never been known to be warm or consoling in times of deep distress.

Equally true and ultimately to my benefit was the fact that when, at seventeen, I had taken up smoking and fallen into grace, I had fallen as well into a practice that, if not itself prayer, would certainly come in time to serve me well as adjunctive to prayer. I already knew, for instance, and directly because of it, that I had an interior world larger than the playroom or the forsythia tunnel. I knew also that that world had another being who was in it, as well as of which it was. None of these things, however, meant that I had yet learned to know this presence as a persona, a living construct. It was, after all, the very maturity of the Psalms on this one point that had made their rending so arduous for me; but I had no way of knowing that as I lay joyless beneath the weight of my own immobility.

Thus it is that I cannot honestly say I prayed in my distress. Rather, as the weeks dragged on and as even food grew increasingly tasteless and unappealing, I began a kind of internal conversation with something far less elevated than the term "God" usually indicates. I said, "Oh, God, help me," and meant it; but I didn't for one minute think I was asking for effectual relief so much as I was just giving vent to the sickness I felt.

There is, however, one thing that writers and apparently all artists eventually learn about depression; something I most surely did not know as an ailing junior at Shorter College; something that I was to have to learn and relearn and then learn again for years before I could finally come to trust its infallibility as a principle: There is—there can be—no creativity without depression. Just as surely as fever and the sniffles precede and signal a baby's teething or a chronic bellyache precedes and forecasts an older child's sudden jumps in height, just so surely does depression of the spirit always precede a spurt of internal growth and perception . . . which, of course, takes us to what psychologists refer to as the three-hundred-pound gorilla in the living room.

Depression as a term bandied about in slick media and everyday conversation is not the name of a disease so much as it is, like "the flu" or "a virus," the descriptive title of a set of symptoms. Those symptoms can arise from any number of pathologies that do indeed range in etiology and destructiveness anywhere from my blues to Cousin Norton's hideous death. To speak of all of these presentations as "depression" is dangerous in no small part because it obscures the lines between disease and natural process. I was in the grip of natural process; and while it felt convincingly pathological, it was not. Rather it was a harbinger that, as Shakespeare would have it, was cruel only that it might be kind. It was, in short, a snake.

One Saturday afternoon, then, in late March and deep into my depression, while I was physically at my desk in the dorm and actually wading around like Bunyan's Pilgrim in the slough of my own despond, I began to make a list of all the things that, despite my misery, I had to do if I were ever to escape it. By what grace I came to this idea I do not know. I only know that I did.

That list was, as I had known all along it would be (it was, after all, the basic fact from which I was running so hard) singularly without substance. Presumably, of course, my showing up for work did matter if I wanted to keep on smoking, and I checked it off as necessary, if not morally significant. And like it or not, I had to show up for lectures because colleges in those days, even ones as bound as Shorter was by honor codes, really did demand attendance as well as performance.

I took out another piece of typing paper and idly blocked it off into the seven columns of my week, dropping those class times in under the five weekdays and then adding my work schedule. Halfheartedly, I penciled in the two or three routine meetings I still cared about or was pledged to each week and then, for a lark, shaded the times I liked to slip away to be alone as well as the half hour or so before retiring. I looked at the result and, again for a lark, penciled in meals. I even allowed for the fact that some of us liked to eat off campus on Friday nights with our dates or, sometimes, just with each other before our dates.

What was interesting, as I looked at the emerging schemata of my life, was just how regular it was. Where, minutes before, I had perceived a kind of lumpy pointlessness, now there was at least a pattern. I could sit at my desk and accurately plot out my days on a piece of paper because—and only because—they had a form of order or internal integrity I had never before perceived in them. From that discovery, however inane it may now sound, it was a very short leap—less than half a breath, in fact—to realizing that I was a life. That is, with all due respect to Descartes' earlier solution, the truth for me at that moment was that if what I was had pattern, then I was.

I'm never quite sure what the word *epiphany* means when I use it these days. Like *depression*, we have tossed it about so casually of late that we seem to have spent its discrete meaning in order to buy an easier, vaguer one. In 1954, however, *epiphany* was spoken rarely and always judiciously; and we all knew what it meant. *Epiphany* was—and still is for me—the name of that moment, that instant, in which a clarity so brilliant as to be only divinely possible drops into human life and takes up permanent residence there. Epiphany is the ripping apart of the obscuring veil, the cautery of healing fire, the bursting open of the chrysalis . . . and as was true with my Saturday list, it always comes wearing the humblest of clothes.

The problem with epiphanies, of course, is their very clarity and ordinariness of circumstance; for both of those qualities defy easy, or even credible, description. Nonetheless, everyone who has an epiphany seems to feel a compulsive need to try; and I am no exception.

What happened for me in my Saturday instant was a shift of consciousness from inside my self to a point of perspective outside my self. I had lurched out into an awareness that, whatever else I might be and have thought up to that point I was, I was also and just as actually a freestanding piece in life. I was, because I had pattern; and I had agency because I was . . . which is not to suggest that I was thinking any of these things at that moment or even during that entire afternoon. I was far too stunned to think about anything—too stunned and too busy feeling, for suddenly and for the first time in months, I was alive again. The world was full of color and I was starving to death for a good steak dinner and a Saturday night on the town with whoever was financially able and willing to join me.

Within a day or two, of course, my euphoria settled down into the realm of thought, and I had to consider what had happened to me. I knew quite clearly that where once I had had only one perspective from which to look at my self, I now had two, one of them from inside and one of them from something much nearer to an outside. I knew that I had escaped something so dreadful as to be demonic as well as deadly and that I had done so through no skill of my own. I knew as well that the lifting of this particular siege was a permanent one. But it followed that if the demons had come once, they could come again; and one had best keep a keen watch out for them. As part of that watch, I completed with reverential care the listing of my hours that the Saturday epiphany had interrupted. I lived it for a week, checking and adjusting it for accuracy and then, taping my corrected copy up on the wall beside my bed, I followed my pattern as if it were a schedule, as if I and it were one and the same.

The freedom of arbitrarily setting aside one class's set of assigned texts for the books of another simply because the wall schedule said that American History got forty-five minutes from four fifteen to five and Latin American Poetry got the hour from five until six was enormous. The list made my decisions; and what the list didn't govern was mine to do with as I pleased, to squander or to invest in any way I pleased, so long as I did neither in any of the areas already covered by the list. American History was over and done with, finished or not, at five o'clock. That was all of me American History required and all it could have. The resulting economy of my focus and effort was likewise enormous. So too, interestingly enough, with my times of retreat, my bedtime Scriptures, my sleepy repeating of the Psalms.

Ah, that innocence of mine in the closing minutes of each day. How indirectly the Psalms had come upon me. How rudely I had been thrust into them. And oh, how very poorly I understood in my own youth the age and power of their vocation.

PART THREE

*The House at the
Top of the Hill*

14.

MY MOTHER'S GREAT WHITE KITCHEN was pierced by two oversized windows through which daily streamed the mountain light beyond us, and by three very ordinary-sized doors through which daily streamed the rest of life. Because that pristine kitchen was, by position anyway, the operative corner of an architectural rectangle, two of its three doors served as little more than facilitators of family traffic from bed and bath and hall through to breakfast room, dining room, living room, and back to hall, bed, and bath. The third door was what mattered.

The third door opened out onto what my father referred to as "the back porch" and what anybody of a less euphemistic bent would have referred to as a "stoop." By any honest measure, the thing could not have been more than eight feet long and four feet wide. It was, at best, utilitarian. At worst it was inelegant, a contrivance clearly born in the lean days after the house's original owner had suffered his reverses and before he had given up entirely on the dream of finishing his home.

As was typical of his own husbandry and natural pride, my father spent hours every spring of his life painting that stoop a high-gloss, battleship gray that glistened in the sunlight and was slick as the proverbial sheet of glass during the six to eight months of our winter. He designed and built elegant—they really were quite elegant, actually—trellises as side walls for the porch and then spent more hours every spring and summer training roses and clematis to grow the height of them. Two or three years after we moved into the house, he replaced the original plank steps with sturdier new ones and then proceeded to paint them the same slick, glistening, battleship gray. In time, he laid the brick mini-terrace at the foot of the steps and hedged it with the high boxwoods that for the rest of his life would form both an opening to our driveway and a serene, cordial entrance into his garden.

In those long-ago days when groceries were delivered and when careful housewives knew from experience that fresh-today meat was the safest, when shirts had to be sent out to the laundry to be properly starched and sweaters to the dry cleaners to be properly blocked, when in-season produce came from hucksters bargaining at the kitchen door, when Coca-Cola and 7–Up were delivered by the case to that same door, when do–it–yourself would have been a scandal and artisans still worked for themselves out of small trucks, when neighbors were supposed to share coffee each morning and a cup of soup and a sandwich each lunchtime—in those days of my growing up, in other words, it was the back door that accessed the texture and magic of life. I loved it.

I would perch for hours on the wooden step stool Mother kept beside the back door, waiting for the next excitement to enter our lives and giving up my vantage point only when some bit of juicy gossip or some adversarial encounter with a tradesman required my leaving the room. To this day, I think that the bulk of what I learned about being female I learned sitting on the step stool just inside the back door of my mother's kitchen. That, however, is not why I have mentioned all of this just here; for as I came into late adolescence, my father's fancied-up stoop took on a much more mature place in my life.

When one went out the kitchen door onto the stoop, one could look left, through the oval window of the rose trellis into the beauty of the flower beds beyond. If, on the other hand, one looked right, through the opposite trellis, one saw part of our driveway, a portion of the avenue in front of our house, and a fairly confined slice of the terrain on the other side of it. The view was confined not only by the oval of the trellis itself, but by the fact that the terrain just beyond our street went almost straight up, as is the way of mountain neighborhoods. And in the house at the top of the hill there lived a boy; his name was Sam Tickle.

We first met, that boy and I, when he was exactly thirteen months old and I exactly six weeks. We accomplished this in the newborn nursery at First Presbyterian Church in Johnson City, Tennessee. And, according to both our mothers, from that day forward they only trusted each other with the care of either of us. As a result, the two of them spent the next year and a half alternating Sundays of nursery duty while Sam and I presumably learned to teethe, toddle, and shove each other.

But as is the way of the world, Sam grew too old for Nursery a year before I did and was summarily hustled away to the more decorous environment of Pre-School. After that, we rarely if ever saw one another. Going to different schools as well as different Sunday school classes—after Pre-School, children were separated in those days by gender as well as age—meant that we had no easy contact in the daily course of things. And our mothers, while obviously respectful of each other, were no more than acquaintances for whom church duties were the only real connection.

That separation of lives all changed when I was sixteen (nice girls, one must understand, couldn't date in the 1940s until they had turned sixteen). When I was at last sixteen and Sam was seventeen, we found each other as naturally as if we had suffered no interruption at all in our conversation. It was not that we dated constantly—my father would have perished or seen to it that Sam did—or even that we went steady; it was just that our awareness of each other was steady and solid and even had a few of its own bells and whistles.

When eighteen months later at seventeen and a half I went off to Rome, Georgia, Sam saw to it that he made the same journey at least once a month for the three years I was in college there. He dated other girls from time to time, of course; and I certainly took full advantage of the three remaining weekends in every month of my Georgia life, at least for the first two years of them. I don't mean to suggest otherwise. But what I do mean is that there was, I think, never any real question for either of us about who the life partner was to be. That sounds a bit unromantic, perhaps, or even worse, a bit too much like the idealized foolishness of "the boy next door," but it's our truth.

There is, of course, another truth here that must be acknowledged also, and that is that I have forgotten the boy who courted me, have lost him seamlessly in the man who still does. Whatever clear otherness there was to him in those long-ago days, whatever otherness there still is in either of us, exists now more as a particularity of the what-we-are than as the border marker of a neighboring territory. To try to claim here that things are otherwise would be a travesty against, almost a defilement of, our half century of life together. That caveat having been offered, I do remember the things that in our youth excited me, for they are the things that still do—and shamelessly so.

In our youth, Sam had that baby face that looks too cherubic to be the comfortable possession of any young American male. He used to complain of it intermittently, claiming that he would have to be forty before he looked old enough to be a physician, much less to be taken seriously as one. The first part of his prediction proved true, but not the second; for what has most riveted me to him over the years is what made him a physician in the first place: Sam possesses in his hands a kind of charisma or white magic or genius for which I have never managed to find a safer or less freighted name.

The boy with the angel's face and the man he has become have always carried in their touch a life force that is shamanistic. All things in distress— plants, creatures, human beings, even stretches of barren earth—react to Sam as heliotropes react to light or as withering plants do to water. The *ruach* flows from him as history says it flowed from St. Francis of Assisi, though I am willing to wager in greater quantities from the former than from the latter.

There is no point in making a virtue of this peculiar gift, and Sam himself is the first to say so. Rather, it is simply so much a part of his being as to be his chief characteristic, the virtue, as he would say, being in how one uses such rare gifts. And not only is the virtue in the using, but so also are the daily excitements and amazements of his gift. Nothing is ever disposable with Sam Tickle. Nothing is so broken as to not be fixable or, if by rare chance really so fractured, then still not so broken as to not have pieces and parts of itself that could prove useful. Nor is anything allowed to die around him until such time as compassion perceives that life itself wants to pass to its next permutation. As a result, we have always lived—often to my consternation—in the near-junglelike excesses of stray things in waiting: stray animals on the mend, temporarily stray children in need, weakened plants or threatened trees, bowls of life forms that are aberrant and want watching to be defined, and saucers of accidentally discovered seeds that having been found must be sprouted to be realized . . . the list goes on, and so do the infinite variety and acts of constant discovery that are to this day no small part of the man's abiding power upon me.

When I think of Sam as a man having a physical appearance, however—that is, when I am asked by strangers to describe him—I have to conjure the image of a recent photograph and describe the features caught there, for I have no adequate semblance of him in my head to describe. In me there are only the stories, the word pictures. . . . The way he once puzzled over why the tap water was colder in his mother's kitchen than in mine until he concluded the difference had to be a matter of flow, researched the city's water lines, and established that the main coming into town out of the mountains was not separated into feeder lines until it had passed his house and before it reached ours. The way he carved from a burl of wood a carburetor valve for an old car whose parts could no longer be replaced and how that car ran on that burl for a good seven years and even passed to two other owners after undergoing such peculiar surgery. The time I discovered he was really identifying all the species of trees on the Shorter campus while I had naïvely assumed that all he was doing was strolling with me. The time in 1952 when I had the most stunning corsage at Shorter's Spring Formal, not because I thought so, but because everybody else from the dean of women to my roommates said so. Working at a florist's in Johnson City to make his spending (he says "traveling") money, he had found eighteen or twenty white rosebuds that, having fallen or been broken off of other arrangements, had been swept into the garbage bin. Retrieving them, he had painstakingly driven a wire through the base of each bud, wrapped the wires in white florist's tape, and then woven the whole lot of them into a tapestry of buds that followed the contour of my shoulder. It was, as the dean kept insisting, a work of art . . . which word is probably still the most applicable one. Sam Tickle is an artist with a practical turn and a genius with a healer's agenda. He was so in the beginning and, God willing, he will be so to the end.

But when all of that is said and done, the real truth—the one that time and familiarity have not sculpted to their own purposes—is that things were for us as they were, and our simple commitment to each other every bit as simple and unpretentious as I have made it sound. And so it was that on the late summer evenings of my Shorter years I would step, after supper clean-up, through the back door of the kitchen, turn right onto the stoop, and stare straight up the hill beyond, waiting for Sam to come out of his own back door and start down the hill to pick me up.

In late May of 1954, after my junior year at Shorter was at last over and done with, I fell back quite naturally into old habits, taking up my customary post on the stoop each evening. The difference in May of 1954 as opposed, for example, to May of 1953 was that I was wearing a diamond. Sam and I were to be married in thirteen months.

15.

IN MID-TWENTIETH-CENTURY AMERICA or at least in my part of mid-twentieth-century Appalachian America, the conventions of marriage were quite fixed. Vestigial remains of the farmer-planters who had settled the area two hundred years earlier, the rules were inviolate reminders of the fears and accommodations of a structured, almost feudal society. Landowning farmers had, from the first, protected their fiefdoms against fragmentation and parceling by primogeniture and the careful breeding of their sons and daughters. In time, the primogeniture had had to go, forced out by ungrateful younger sons who took strong exception to the process. The part about careful breeding, however, had withstood the onslaughts of both sons and daughters. Thus, aberrant and offensive as it may sound today, I had been given a list, just before the week of my sixteenth birthday, of the nine young men whom I might "go out with."

The nine boys on that list—seven of whom could not have been less interested, I am sure, and who today might still get a chuckle out of knowing that they had even appeared on the list—had been chosen very carefully and with considerable discussion back and forth not only between my parents, but also amongst a few of my mother's most trusted friends. The first rule governing good breeding was that one never, never went out alone with a young man whom one could not marry. That interdiction presumed a prior principle, which was that parents were the ones who made all determinations of acceptability. (At least those were the principles and rules until one could escape the parental eye by going off to Rome, Georgia, but that's irrelevant here.) Thus the assembling of the list.

To the partial redemption of this process for our own later and more democratic times, it must be said here that the criteria for establishing the list were far more physical than social or frivolous. My mother's greatest concern—she had been very vocal about this—was the health history of both sides of a boy's family. Any debilitating disease that was known to run in the family? Any history of mental illness or even peculiar behavior? Any alcoholics in either bloodline? After that, the next tier of questions was about ambition, future intentions toward a working life, the probable ability to support a wife and children. Closely aligned to that was the sober question of general intelligence, and especially of whether the boy were as bright as, or even better, brighter than, the daughter for whom one was preparing the list of suitors. Once a boy's conduct to date had been checked thoroughly, interestingly enough the listing next considered his physical appearance; handsome was considered to be a good sign and not a merely transient vanity. Good looks prove good stock, as my mother so candidly put it. Sam Tickle made the list.

Because Sam had made the cut and because there had even been a list in the first place, I was stunned at my father's reaction four years later when I had just turned twenty and Sam, at twenty-one, was ready to begin the next step in the process. No girl could accept a boy's offer of marriage until her father had given his consent and expressed a willingness to announce publicly his blessing upon the union. The request to marry was made always in a late afternoon or evening call upon the girl's father. There was no contact between the two lovers on that visit. Rather, the girl's mother admitted the young man, took him to her husband, and left the room. No young man in his right mind, of course, ever went through this troublesome and potentially dangerous procedure without the girl's having first tested the waters with her father and, often, even having arranged the details of the prenuptial call itself—which was all I had been doing on the first evening of Easter break in April of my junior and final year at Shorter.

We were standing in the kitchen, my father and I, just talking in the easy way we had between us. The supper dishes were done, and I was about to go stand on the back stoop and watch for Sam. Without giving the matter any preliminary thought at all, I simply said in an "Oh, by the way" kind of fashion that Sam would like to come calling the next evening to ask formal permission for our marriage.

If I had struck my mother in front of him, I would not have shocked my father any more completely than I did with that simple sentence. And if he had struck me back, he would not have stunned me any more by that action than he did by his reaction to my statement. He quite literally blanched gray, fell back two full steps against the kitchen wall, and said, as if it should be as obvious to me as it was to him, "But I don't want you to marry! I don't want you to marry now or ever! Whatever gave you such an idea?"

Well, what had given me the idea was the damned list for one thing, not to mention almost four years of rather heavy and very obvious courtship, not to mention elaborate educational gerry-rigging and maneuvering to which he had been privy, not to mention all the kitchen conversations that had been going on for months between Mother and me and that he most surely had to have overheard! I was livid for the first time in my life, and most certainly for the first time in my life at my father. Mother, who was still at the sink wiping the counters dry, stopped dead in midwipe. The room was as silent as arcing electricity can make a room, and not one of us made a move to help either of the rest of us. How long we stood there in locked positions I don't know, but it felt like the slow-frame time of impending death.

"I mean," he finally stammered, "I mean marriage will distract you. You're born to be an academic, to run a college curriculum like me." And then the one I shall never forget, said heart-wrenchingly and from the very core of his whole life as a parent: "I didn't rear you to be a girl."

In that blazing minute of confessing, I knew he had spoken truth. Things I had never understood before, things I had remarked upon to myself but had more taken for granted than pondered, fell into place. All the professional meetings I had been taken to when no other children were there, and especially no other girl children of any age. All the hours of teaching me first the power of words and then the principles of their effective delivery. All the forcing of what I had thought of as "boy skills" like the hammering and sawing of my playroom. I had accepted them all as proof that an only child is always indulged or else is, as I had sometimes said smartly to my friends, "the only basket available to carry the parental eggs." But he was telling me it had been more than that, much more deliberate than that.

"But I *am* a girl," I said softly.

"Yes, yes, I know that. I wanted you to be a girl. I prayed you would be when you were on the way, but I didn't want you to be a girl when you grew up!"

Whether it was the sincerity or the illogic of the whole thing I don't know, but suddenly my mother laughed one of those hearty belly laughs that good women can sometimes produce with great political skill and no evidence of premeditation or unkindness. He fled the kitchen and we heard the door to his den bang shut, something it never did. I felt ill. I had surmounted the problem of transcripts and endured hell for months as a result, only to find that there was to be another obstacle in the most ridiculous and essential of places.

He came back to the kitchen almost as abruptly as he had left it. His face was still ashen, but his lips were set now, not quivering. "I do not want you to do this thing," he said quite calmly.

"But I will do it," I answered just as softly, "with or without your permission." Then I played my trump card. "And you will be a lot less embarrassed if I do it with than without." He looked at me hard, gauging what I had just said and, I think now, probably admiring for just an instant how well he had taught me to fight. Suddenly, his body relaxed and the funny little smile that often teased his lower lip came back. "Good," he said. "If you must do it, then I'd rather it was Sam than any other young man I know. Tell him to come Saturday afternoon at three, though. I have a meeting tomorrow night," and he was gone again, back to his den.

For the almost fifty-five weeks between the time I came home at the end of my junior year and the time I left home as a bride on my way to becoming a wife, that kitchen confrontation remains my dominant memory, just as it is even today one of my few surviving ones of that time in my life. In fact, my prenuptial months really began, not with my final return from Shorter in June of 1954, but with that Easter exchange two months earlier. Like one of two bookends on a shelf, my father's grief—for that is what it was—opened those months. The other bookend, the one that would close them, was the similar and equal grief of Sam's mother.

Mrs. Tickle—I could not call her by her familiar name of Mamaw until after the wedding—Mrs. Tickle and my father were as similar in substance as they were different in élan. Both born in 1890, they had come of county gentry in a time when that social distinction carried more pride than hard cash and when appearances were an expression of sound self-discipline rather than a pretension. His father—my grandfather—had been an elected magistrate and landed farmer of cotton and timber in the upper reaches of West Tennessee just below where the Ohio crooks around to its confluence with the Mississippi and just above where the last of the extended Delta ends. Her father—Sam's grandfather—had been a landed farmer on terrain that had been ceded his family six generations before by George III of England for services rendered, the signed, royal grant for which was still on file in the county courthouse when Grandpa Witcher died. In those only slightly dissimilar origins lay the explanation for most of the differences as well as the parallels between Mrs. John Crockett Tickle and Dr. Philip Wade Alexander.

For county gentry of the old school, survival was the first and greatest imperative. Education, closely aligned as both tool for and proof of the first, was the second; and God was the whole point. But while education and God might have enjoyed more or less the same definition in the rocky hill country of East Tennessee as in the warm alluvial flatlands of West Tennessee, survival did not. East Tennessee required that everybody—sons and daughters alike—work to make the crop; that everybody learn how to manipulate every detail of a place from its cash flow to the breeding schedules of its animals, and this with constant self-critiquing for efficiency; that everybody be skilled in bartering for and then preserving the massive amounts of provender required to see a large farm and its dependents through the long winters—in other words, that everybody, male and female alike, keep a shoulder to the wheel, as Mamaw used to say. Survival in Appalachia was rooted in daily conversation as surely and constantly as entropy is in reality.

In the kinder climate of West Tennessee, survival in the late 1800s meant controlling the Mississippi. It was the river that would wash away everybody and everything if the levees didn't hold, if the autumn rains went too long, if the snows didn't melt and run off before the spring thaws began upstream, if any one of a dozen other such caprices of nature should occur. In West Tennessee's cotton and timber lands, little could be backlogged or assumed, and real security was the means with which to get out quickly. In such a system, sociability mattered. The land was one's work and income, but it was not a dependable, often not even a permanent, possession. Social contacts and alliances, on the other hand, were the coin of the realm. They were routes of escape and safe havens in distress.

Both Dad and Mamaw had assimilated flawlessly the ways of their rural, nineteenth-century backgrounds. By the time Sam and I had come along four decades later, they had also superimposed those ways with total self-assurance upon their own twentieth-century, urban lives and, with equal self-assurance, upon those of us with whom they shared those lives. Each ruled his or her respective household imperiously, to say the least, yet without being either conscious of that fact or offensive in effecting it on a daily basis. Their moral certitude was far too commanding to admit of either of those possibilities.

That having been said in their defense, however, I have to emphasize as gently as possible that the only accurate word here really is "ruled." There could be no question that the tenor of both households was set by the intensity and surety of my father and Sam's mother. The amusing thing for me, as I became more and more intimately aware of the senior Tickles' *modus operandi*, was that Sam's father—Papaw—had developed the same compensatory mechanisms for dealing with his situation as my mother had developed for dealing with hers. Both Mother and Papaw lived their domestic lives as jesters to the king—or in his case, to the queen. Both of them enjoyed all the impunity from royal disfavor of the medieval jester as well as all of the jester's traditional position as counselor of record and trimmer of the imperial ego; and they both did it by drollness and wit, a running acerbic commentary on everything, and a kind of self-contained existence that remained just slightly aloof and above the fray at all times.

There was, in time, even a kind of beneficial, or at least useful, side to all of this alikeness of attitude for Sam and me and our children. If one knew Mamaw Tickle or Granddaddy Alexander at all well, then one could predict the other with alarming accuracy. One could, that is, if one allowed for their being mirror images of one another, rather than exact copies. Where one was spare and orderly to excess (one cannot carry excess when a river is constantly rising all around one), the other was excessive, comfortable only when in the midst of stacks of supplies and food and tools. (There might be a fierce blizzard at any time or a late spring that would delay the first crop or, worst of all, a bank failure. Who knew?) Where one was diplomatic and sometimes given to circumlocution, the other was candid and direct to a fault, but to nobody's confusion. Where one was vague about money as well as about the need for improving personal efficiency, the other was precise to the penny, intentionally generous, and compulsive about the betterment of all personal effort. And so it went.

Suffice it to say, then, that by the time June of 1955 had finally arrived and the long months of prenuptial waiting had wound themselves down to a matter of only a few days, I had become sensitive enough to the dynamics of my new life to perceive quite clearly that the politics in the house at the top of the hill were comfortably familiar, as were the dispositions of its principals. That may have been the only thing that saved me from destructing on June 13, 1955.

Sam and I were to be married on Friday, the seventeenth. On that

Monday afternoon, he was still in first-year finals at the University of Tennessee College of Medicine in Memphis, but his last examination was to be on Wednesday. He planned to drive home afterward. It was a ten-hour trip in those days from the lower corner of West Tennessee to the upper corner of East Tennessee, so he would drive all night, sleep Thursday until noon, and then go downtown with me in the afternoon to get our marriage license. We would end the day at our rehearsal and, later, at our rehearsal dinner. But even given all the tedious details required to make that final week work, I cannot for the life of me remember now which one in particular would have taken me up the hill to Mamaw's on Monday afternoon. Apparently, what she did once I arrived has completely obliterated the preliminaries from my mind.

For whatever forgotten reason then, I drove up the hill that Monday afternoon, parked in front (once an engagement had been announced, backyards like back doors were *verboten* again until after the service itself; another inconvenience of mountain propriety), and rang the bell.

Mamaw—still Mrs. Tickle at that point—took my hand and led me directly to the sofa in the parlor. What my mother as an outlander called a living room, Mamaw referred to by the Appalachian name of "parlor," but either way it was serious to be taken in and set down there, that much I understood. Still holding my hand, she began without any fanfare or social preliminaries. "Phyllis, I want you to do something for me," she said. "It is something you *must* do, in fact."

"Certainly," I said, still innocent of where this could all be going, even if I were already uncomfortably aware of the probable weightiness of it.

"I want you to call off the wedding now before Samuel comes home, and I want you to promise me that you will never tell him that I have asked you to do this."

There could have been no possible doubt at that moment that Mamaw was as sincere in what she was saying as she was earnest in how she was saying it. Too stunned to respond in any way, I simply sat there looking at her—rather stupidly, I am sure. Misunderstanding my silence for the beginning of my compliance, she lowered her voice and went on as if we were simply chatting now, although perhaps about some faintly unpleasant subject like a troublesome neighbor or a bastard cousin.

"I've given this a great deal of thought," she said, "and it's the only way. I just wish I had realized it sooner and spared us all a great deal of time and distress."

At this point, I managed to squeak out a "Why?" of sorts.

"Why?" she said. "Why, because Samuel must not marry, now or ever. Marriage is not right for him. You would only divert his attention from his studies now and then later from his career. He's going to be a truly gifted doctor, and you and I have to do everything we can to help him do that."

"But . . ." I started to say.

"There are no 'buts' to it! If you love him, you'll help him, and you'll never tell him why. It's that simple"

By this point I had got my land legs back beneath me and had even begun to realize that I had been here once before fourteen months earlier. "No," I said.

To her credit, Mamaw looked as honestly shocked as my father had. It was her turn to say, "But . . ."

"No," I repeated. "Even if I thought for one minute it was better for Sam to come home to my saying 'Go away, I've changed my mind'— which I don't and haven't—this is my life, too. So the answer is no."

At that point she did what my father had not. Instead of storming out of the room, she crumpled and cried. I had never seen her cry before (and rarely would I see her do so ever again), so I was more nonplussed than I had been in our kitchen.

"You don't really think that this is what Sam would want, do you?" I asked her as tenderly as I could manage at that point.

She shook her head. "No," she said, "but it's such a waste, and you're both too young to know what marriage will take out of you, how it will take from your careers, your work." She was crying more quietly now, and an old, wadded-up Kleenex had appeared from somewhere or other. We sat a minute or two longer before she finally began to dab at her cheeks. "I was afraid you might not do it," she said. "But I had to ask for his sake, for Samuel's, you know. He could be such a fine doctor."

"He still will be," I said, but she shook her head. "Not the same," she said, "Not the same as if he weren't thinking about you and babies for the rest of his life."

"No," I said softly, because I understood at last what she was saying.

"No, not the same." I kissed her still-wet cheek and left. We never spoke of that conversation again.

We never spoke of it, but I have never forgotten it. It was the beginning of my deep, abiding affection for my mother-in-law. Whether part of my emotional reaction was what psychologists would simply call transference of love from my father to her similar personality or whether, as I would prefer to think, I was really old enough at twenty-one to reverence the purity and depth of her love for her son, I can't say. What I can say is that she and I, from that day forth, became a team. Like two workhorses harnessed in the same yoke, we lived out the rest of our time together united by our shared absorption with one man.

Mamaw had come late in life to marriage, had borne six children, buried three of them at birth and a fourth at age five. She was no fool about the ways of the world, and she was tough as the mountains that had bred her. By the time of her death some twenty-odd years later, I loved her without reservation and for herself alone. Near that death, she took my hand one more time, pulled me down to her, and said, "I have loved you best of all." It was pure Mamaw. I was the youngest of her children, the last to come within her sphere; and all that she had learned of love she had improved and applied to me. It was the final piece of self-monitoring; she was satisfied at last with her own performance.

"Yes," I said, knowing there was no way to go where she was just then and no need to try. She had earned her moment of quietness at the border.

"You'll have to take care of Samuel alone now."

"Yes," I said again; and she squeezed my hand.

May her God be my God as surely as her people have become my people, and may I go whither she has gone.

16.

WHEN, LATE IN MAY 1954, I had packed up my things to leave Shorter for good, I had taken the by-then fading schedule down from its place on the wall beside my bed, had folded it carefully into a brown envelope, and then had slipped that envelope securely into the front pocket of my zippered notebook. I did not for one minute think that the particulars on that schedule would ever be the particulars of any other part of my life; but I could no more have left it behind than I could have dropped the attenuated Gideon into the dormitory's hall trash bin, and for dangerously similar reasons. To me, on that overheated May afternoon when I was packing the last of Shorter into suitcases and memories, a schedule was the fetish that kept my own pointlessness at bay. Like insulin to a diabetic, the regimenting of time would, I assumed, be a part of the rest of my life because it appeared to be a requisite to the sunniness of my life. I was, of course, wrong, as I discovered on the Sunday evening of my second week back at home.

I was alone in the house that night and doing the most conventional of things. Summer classes were to begin the next day, and I was about the business of reassembling all the paraphernalia it takes to be a student at any time anywhere. I went looking through my closet for the zippered notebook when, with a sense almost of dislocation, I realized that not only had I not once thought about the Shorter schedule inside it, but also that I had not once felt any need to map out a new schedule for living at home. I sat down on the edge of my bed, completely stilled by the fact that for two unregimented weeks I had felt . . . ?

Well, to be honest, I had felt not much of anything at all for the previous two weeks.

Sitting there on my own bed in the room where I had sorted my way through the adolescent confusions of life, I now began to sort my way through some much more mature ones. What I discovered in doing so was a life that had absolutely no need for wall charts to govern its affairs. What I discovered was that I was already living inside the ultimate schedule, that I was, in fact, living inside a script.

The problem with life in a script, at least for the formation of a young adult, is that the processes of living are external to it, or at best they are relevant only upon its outer surfaces. Even consummate actors who spend months learning the interiors of their assigned characters must come to familiarity with them by moving from the outside in; besides which, learning to successfully re-create the emotions of completed personalities is vastly different, as a piece of work, from experiencing all the distresses and joys that forge the emotional cores of living ones.

Even if that were not true, life inside a script can never evade flawless regimenting anyway, for a script knows its own ways before the fact, knows what the course of those ways is going to be, knows the final resolution to which they shall come. It lacks all the uncertainties of change or responsibility, of ambition or love; and there is a kind of freedom in that. There is also a loss of all the painful scabs and scars on which memory hangs—which is why I have almost no memory of my final months in my mother's house and why the one memory remaining to me is of my spiritual, rather than of my physical or emotional life. It is also, at best, far more diffuse than specific.

Lest I overstate things, let me say immediately that of course I remember many of the appointments and activities that organized and distracted me during those months. It's just that there's little magic and little memory in such a feat, for most of them are recorded in my bride's diary. I can remember other events and deadlines as well, not because they are recorded anywhere, but because they must have happened. Those fourteen months could not have come to an end with all their purposes and intentions at last accomplished had things been otherwise. That, too, involves neither magic nor memory, only surmise and logic. What I have little recall of from those months, though, is of myself as a participant in the overt activities that constituted them; what I have little or no recall of, in other words, is how most of them "felt" to me, or even if they did, which is what I now suspect was the truth of the matter. Physically and emotionally, as I have said and as most brides know, I was the lead actress in a very old and highly stylized production that would be done with me when it was done with me, and there was no good to be gained by chafing at the conventions that held me in so golden and velvet a cage.

With my life thus comfortably anesthetized, it was easy during my first weeks back home for my prayers to slip into rote editions of what had been the vital conversations of my earlier years. It was easy, with my mind happily engaged outside itself, for my Scripture reading to devolve once more into being a sedative at bedtime. It was easy and probably unavoidable for one as young and inexperienced as I; but the soul will not have her internal balances so cavalierly set askew even in the young and inexperienced. As a result, my one integrating, surviving memory of the months from the evening confrontation with my father to my painful afternoon with Mamaw is of a kind of gnawing, unstated, low-keyed spiritual lonesomeness. Like a child bereft of playmates or a traveler bereft of home, my spirit mourned softly for its former pleasures.

No longer were there any stealable quarter hours for hiding in empty bathrooms to read the Psalms; no longer were there whole private hours for watching the light show of connections with which introspection can instruct us. No longer, either, were there the rich study hours spent with the questions of the ancients and the polished clarity of their answers. No more of Homer's grand loyalties, no more of the scrutinizing Plato in paean to a Socrates who may or may not have so spoken himself, no more of the sad ordinariness of the extraordinary Cicero, the florid paganism of the dissolute Lucretius, the deep and accepting wisdom of my beloved Aurelius . . .

. . . I had not known how much they fed me, had never suspected how much they tutored my soul while showing me how to follow the intricacies of their native grammars. I had never guessed in my days with them how effortlessly they had carried me, like a small companion, into the realms of the spirit; nor had I perceived, until suddenly they were gone, how completely they had addicted me to such travel. I was bereft.

There was grace, however; or there was a book, and its coming to me was a matter of grace. Which is to say that I, who am pathologically resistant to pasting labels like grace on things that seem to me just as easily and accurately labeled as subconscious intention fulfilled or fortunate happenstance experienced, can apply only grace here. The book was *The Soul's Sincere Desire,* by Glenn Clark; and the truth of the thing is that I have absolutely no idea where I got that book, how I acquired it, whence it came. For that matter, I have no idea who Glenn Clark was, though I assume I could discover the answer to that question even now, were it pertinent, which it is not and never has been.

What is pertinent is the fact that *The Soul's Sincere Desire* was published in 1954, meaning that it was to all intents and purposes a new release at the time of its coming to me. As such, it certainly was not a book I would have found lying idly about the house somewhere, nor one I could have borrowed from a neighbor who would never again have inquired about it, nor even one that could have come home by mistake from Shorter with me. None of us, be it at home or at school, had enough money in those days to suffer that kind of misplacement quietly and, more to the point, none of us in those days would have suffered the loss of a book in silence. No, the miraculous appearance of *Sincere Desire* remains for me to this day as an evidence of grace primarily because it lacks any other explanation and because of the perfection of its timing and the utility of its impact.

Timing may be the only unmitigated perfection in *The Soul's Sincere Desire*, and I need to say so before I go much farther in the tale of my time spent poring over its pages. For the forty-two years that stretched from 1954 to 1996, I thought I owned the only extant copy of *Sincere Desire* in America and was quite possibly the only American who had ever read it— which statement is a bit of a reach, of course, but one with some truth to it. I can remember for years looking almost surreptitiously in bookstores, both new and used, to see if I could discover another copy of Clark's work, but to no avail. And I can also remember being faintly relieved each time I failed. It was not, after all, as if my own bruised copy were not still safely hidden away among all my old college texts in our basement.

Out of some kind of perverse loyalty either to Clark or to the pre-sumed benefits of spiritual candor, I would occasionally over those same years mention the book as having been significant to me, only to have those around me look blank and shrug, or else give me the even more dis-tancing response of "Hmmm, I never heard of that one before." And I was always relieved again. The last thing I wanted at such times was a conver-sation about a book that I remembered fondly, but whose actual content and details I had long since managed to forget. In 1996, however, a small publisher of religion books, Macalester Park, reissued *The Soul's Sincere Desire*, and the gig was up.

I was, by 1996, religion editor for *Publishers Weekly*, the international journal for the book publishing industry, which is to say that *PW* occupies in the business of books a position exactly analogous to that occupied by the magazine *VARIETY* in the entertainment and media business. As *PW*'s religion editor I traveled the country attending book shows, talking to publishers, constantly observing and analyzing religion in all its forms and varieties. It is and was an endlessly absorbing work, but one rarely filled with shock in the usual sense of that word. In fact, one of the very few "shocks" I can remember in my years as a student of religion publishing is the moment when I rounded a corner at a national book show and ran straight into Macalester Park's stall and Macalester Park's banners declaring as their lead title for the season the reissue of *The Soul's Sincere Desire*. I stopped dead in the aisle, the breath quite literally taken from me by the words on the banner.

Publishers are born knowing the power of the media to make or break a book; and as luck would have it, the publisher of Macalester Park was in his booth, as I so abruptly stopped dead in front of it. "You know the book!" He was on me like a hawk on a field mouse, in the aisle and in my face before I could put up even a modicum of professional defense.

"Yes," I said, "once was the time it meant a great deal to me."

"You're not alone," he said; and to his credit, he backed away a step or two and let me have my moment of reconnection. But he was a publisher, as I, too, have been; and he did what I also would have done in his position. "Would you consider giving us a blurb for the dust jacket . . . just a few words or so about what the book has meant to you?"

I shook my head out of trained response this time, rather than thought process. So long as I am on the staff of *PW*, I may not furnish any book with a jacket blurb; that part was easy. What was not easy was the next part. "Then won't you just take a galley for your own use. We'd just love for you to have an opportunity to see what we've done with the volume."

A galley in the book business is a kind of dummy or first printing of a book that is done as both a final proofing and also as a relatively cheap way of getting a forthcoming title out to reviewers well before the book's actual release to bookstores. Being offered galleys is standard operating procedure, and taking them graciously is also standard operating procedure. I should have by all rights, in other words, reached out my hand, accepted the galley, and moved along. I couldn't.

I couldn't take that galley and, as I realized immediately, I couldn't because I didn't want it. I positively and actively did not want either the means for rereading *The Soul's Sincere Desire* nor the professional obligation to do so. It was at that moment that I had to admit to myself that I was afraid of what I would find there . . . afraid to my toes of what rereading those pages would force me to remember and acknowledge about the long months of my prenuptial life and about me during them. But such avoidance is an unaffordable luxury of pride and self-protection if one is looking back over one's shoulder at the long way of one's becoming. So it was that not too long ago I finally went into the recesses our basement and retrieved from its nearly inaccessible cubbyhole my original copy of *The Soul's Sincere Desire*. As a body of writing, it both was and was not exactly as I had feared it would be.

I remember keenly that in 1954 it was the title of Clark's book, taken from that of an old hymn, that first compelled me to it. That is, I remember seeing that title among my books one early autumn day and thinking that whoever he was, Glenn Clark was right about one thing: The soul can feel desire in ways as engulfing and disassociating as can either the body or the mind. That much I had by then discovered for myself. I likewise remember thinking that the words "soul's sincere desire" were themselves so insightful—and so beyond anything anyone else had ever suggested to me before—that Glenn Clark must be a man, if not of great wisdom, then most certainly of desirable knowledge. How otherwise could he have chosen so piercing a title for what he had to say. My soul was filled with an uneasy and roaming desire, and this man had to have known the same hunger; otherwise he could not have so precisely named our shared condition.

If I were indeed obliged by fate and circumstance to fall defenseless into the mentoring of an unknown teacher, I probably could not have chosen a better one than Clark; of that much my recent rereading of him has reassured me. He was, and still is, as quintessentially American 1950s as those twin phenomena of Norman Vincent Peale and Norman Rockwell were, and just about as weighty. Like them, Clark spoke to an era of optimism just beginning to miss its traces a bit, to calculate the estrangements as well as the means of success, and to experience the self as cut a mite too free of tedium and necessity for its own comfort. Clark was also my first Christian teacher in book form unless one wishes to count Professor Hurlburt of *Hurlburt's Story of the Bible,* but that hardly seems a fair analogy, for Clark was interpreting what Hurlburt was merely retelling. The fact that Hurlburt's was the infinitely better theology is a moot point now just as it was then.

The Soul's Sincere Desire is a small monument to the 1950s view that reality is in the eye of the beholder rather than in the actuality of events. The miracles of Jesus, according to Clark, were the result of Jesus' ability to see correctly and with divine accuracy what He was really looking at rather than what the rest of us mortals only thought we were looking at. It was, in effect, as if the dead daughter of Jairus were not so much dead as that her parents were confused. As if the hungry multitudes were not a day's journey from food so much as that they were simply unaware of the plentitude of loaves and fishes which not only were in their own pockets, but which had been in those pockets all along. As if a storm were not swamping the Disciples' fishing boat so much as that there was a lake's worth of troubled winds yearning to be calmed. Pushed to any kind of logical extension, such a position not only breaks down under common sense, but it also robs the New Testament narratives at an almost heretical level of their potency. One should note as well that it also relieves Christianity of most of the burdens of faith, not an insignificant problem in and of itself.

Part of what frightened me in the aisle of that book show, I now know, was the awareness of how cheaply bought and pedestrian such thinking is and the memory, which I had tried to deny, of how faulty an interpreter of Scripture it had made Glenn Clark. The larger part of my discomfort, I also now know, was something nearer to pure dread . . . the dread of having to face once again my twenty-year-old self and the spiritual bereavement that had made me the willing recipient of such utopian and almost gnostic instruction in the first place.

Facing specters, especially fifty years later, can almost always be an exercise with substantial benefits, however; certainly facing this one was. For example, while there may have been most of the great weaknesses of his era and place in the work of Glenn Clark, there are also great strengths in it, ones that were, so far as I know, almost singularly his in that time and place. In my need to push away the uncomfortable memories of my spiritual life at twenty and twenty-one I had pushed away as well my memory of what *The Soul's Sincere Desire* is really about. *The Soul's Sincere Desire* is about prayer. Specifically, it is about prayer as the soul's desire.

Part manual of how-to and part explanation of why, this one slender book is from introduction to closing examples firmly based on the tacit assumption that prayer is the natural habitat and function of the soul as well as its natural desire. Even more specifically, Clark holds the basically un-American and certainly non-1950s idea that prayer doesn't have to ask for anything. Prayer wants, first and foremost, just the freedom of being prayer, of being the words and expressions of the spirit at large in the estates of the spirit. And for the exercise of such freedom and for its perfecting, Clark recommends . . . But of course, what else could he have recommended? The use of the Psalms in close conjunction with the use of the set prayers of Christianity, especially the "Our Father," and especially in the early morning when body and mind are likewise refreshed and at peace.

The girl sitting in the upstairs bedroom of an otherwise empty house on that early summer evening so many years ago and remarking upon the stillness in her life would give way, within only a matter of weeks, to a girl/woman who still felt herself mightily attended in body and mind, but abandoned in soul. Abandoned, that is, until a strangely present book by a strangely uneven Christian would, more by assumption than assertion, expose the spirit as the third provenance of living and then send her forth into a lifetime of mapping its domains. My embarrassment over having been homesick of spirit in the midst of such physical and emotional largesse as I was enjoying and my later sense of having compromised myself by clinging to a piece of writing that is intellectually flawed were in the end unfortunate only in so far as they prevented me for years from embracing the loneliness of the girl with the zippered notebook and from naming accurately the gift of a poor thinker with, as I had suspected from the beginning, a great deal of highly useful information.

17.

DESPITE THE NOURISHMENT for my spirit from Glenn Clark's words and his prayer exercises, I lived the closing months of 1954 and the opening ones of 1955 primarily at the front door of my life, rarely traveling farther into it than where its parlor would have been, if lives had parlors. There was little need most days to go farther back, and certainly there was little impetus. The parade was all outside on the street. It was a time that I would never, never wish to live through again, not because it was dreadful, but because it was so dreadfully, damningly, anesthetizingly pleasant. No soul, at least not mine, could afford two such ruptures in its education.

I don't mean that I sat, like Miss Muffet upon her tuffet, and managed not to lift a hand for thirteen months. Obviously I didn't. But there was in those months a pervasive sense of festive interruption that distanced me even from the things that were most familiar and routine in my life, not to mention from the ones that I was most earnest and intentional about accomplishing. I resumed all the household assignments of supper dishes and errands that had been mine before I left for college and that had reverted to being mine every time I had returned for holidays or summer break. But beyond that kind of natural, undiscussed settling back into the familiar, I was an adult whom once the house had known as a child and whom now it served as would an innkeeper.

I registered, as planned, for summer school classes and then for the fall and winter quarters, thereby managing to fulfill my degree requirements as well as those for my teacher certification in March rather than June, also as planned. If I slugged my way ungraciously through some dreadful classes in how to complete a Tennessee Daily Register and build bulletin boards that state supervisors would approve, I also rejoiced through some sinewy courses in economics (which I had never had before and which I have thought ever since should be required as a liberal art) and some eternally useful ones in geography, which I had also never had previously. I got a student job in the university's athletics department as a file clerk and then added another as ticket agent, loving both of them for their very lack of connection to much of anything besides themselves.

In March, as soon as I had completed my degree requirements, our engagement was announced in the local paper. That evening Papaw and Mamaw came calling, just as the rules of etiquette said they must do and just as if they and my parents hadn't already spoken a half dozen times by phone that very day. Papaw brought me a bouquet of bachelor's buttons from his winter garden, winked when he handed them to me, mumbled "Brought you these, Baby. You're probably going to need them" in my ear, and promptly settled into his customary disengagement for the rest of the whole artificial hour. He also winked at me as he left. I remember these details because at that point in time Papaw was the only real person in my immediate surroundings. We were both equally useless and powerless in the midst of a lovely carnival.

Middle-class weddings in the bewilderingly affluent 1950s were overwrought affairs that verged on, sometimes merged quite naturally with, vulgarity. Given that fact, my father's position in the community, and Mamaw's deep, broad roots in the whole region, there was indeed no hope that ours could be anything other than a carnival.

Sam and I married outdoors on the college campus in an amphitheater on whose steps and stage I had played as a child and whose shaded grounds, fortuitously enough, were designed for large lawn parties. While I have no idea how many people actually came to witness our vows, I do know that twelve hundred people came through the receiving line afterward. I know, because that was when the caterers ran out of white sheet cake and good humor simultaneously.

I am almost sure, also, that at least half of those twelve hundred guests had sent or brought wedding gifts. That was certainly the way it looked in Mother's living and dining rooms, anyway. Throughout April, May, and even into early June, she and I had spent hours managing the flow of gifts. I had done the unwrapping, recording, and thanking. She had done the arranging and most of the entertaining of the neighbors and friends who came every afternoon for a cup of coffee and an intimate view of everything that had arrived since the previous day's inspection. The two of us had shared equally in the ooohhhing and aaahhhhing, first with the arrival of each new gift and then later with my father with whom we had to repeat the whole process. Dad's pleasure in the gifts was palpable. For a man who had not wanted an adult daughter, he certainly was enjoying the final procedures involved in producing one, and that with an unabashed candor and openness.

For me as for most young brides, the gifts at first had been an extended stay in fairyland. I had greedily unboxed and unwrapped them each day as they came in the front door by post or by hand; and I had rejoiced my way through many an early evening in April and May, imagining my use of them—which was pretty much how the 1950s saw prenuptial gifts. Although given to a couple, most wedding gifts, then as now, were domestic goods and as such fell, almost by default, into the bride's governance. Then slowly and so quietly that I had not even perceived my own evolving, an understanding of what the governance of goods really meant began to intrude into my day's thoughts along with my fantasies. By mid-May ownership had become a very conscious part of my self-image, and its arrival a change of circumstance more pleasant to ponder than even the gifts themselves.

I had never had property before (not that I had ever realized that fact before, either, because I hadn't). I had had all the usual transient goods like clothes that I outgrew and passed on to younger cousins or the consumables of notebooks and makeup and phonograph records. I had called them all "mine," and so they had been for the brief time they were able to serve me and/or for as long as Mother agreed their presence was still justified in her house. But the wedding gifts, as I watched them grow in number and utility, were different. The wedding gifts were goods under my control and, beyond that, the bulk of them were china, crystal, silver, statuary— permanent objects, substantial, bequeathable. Subtly but irrevocably, I had been changed by their coming into my domain. I had been made into an owner of things. No longer a dependent, I was an enfranchised citizen, and I loved it.

There were some practical problems involved in all of this heady bliss and changing identity. The truth was that Sam and I could no more afford to use most of what kindness had provided us than we could have afforded to buy the Taj Mahal. Like it, all that china and crystal was an affluence we were leaving. Except for the most basic things like sheets and cooking utensils, our gifts were the tools and appointments of a lifestyle that we would not be able to sustain for at least the remaining three years of med- ical school and internship and perhaps longer. The rules saw to this as well; for the rules said quite clearly that if one were old enough to marry, one was old enough to support oneself. Properly reared young people did not ask for or expect financial help once they had married, because properly reared young people did not give in to the desire for marriage until they could support its obligations as well as its pleasures . . . or such was the thinking of the times. The only exception was that parents could supply tuition money, and Mamaw, I always hoped with Papaw's compliance, had agreed to that. Otherwise, Sam and I were to be on our own as of 6:00 P.M. on Friday, June 17, 1955.

Sam and I had both worked through high school and college, and each of us had saved some money. Even put together, however, our checkbooks would barely be enough to get us through moving, getting settled in, and the coming summer. I had applied for and, blessedly, had received an ap- pointment in the Memphis City School System as a Latin and English teacher, but my salary of two hundred and twenty-five dollars a month for ten months a year was not about to support the use of formal china and crystal. It would not, in fact, even support the kind of apartment that was large enough to store formal china and crystal . . . or Chinese vases, or thirty-six pairs of pillow cases, or brass umbrella stands or . . .

By 6:00 P.M. on June 17, however, the conundrum of too many goods and too little money had slipped benignly into abeyance. Sam and I really were on our own at last, and we took off like fleeing deer to a perfectly normal mountain resort that we spent six days not seeing. And where there had been an engulfing silence in my life for fourteen months, now there were whole afternoons of the "Anvil Chorus." It was, I thought, a fair swap-off.

Honeymoons, at least good ones, have to nestle down into intimate memory, however, if they are to complete the domestic work they are designed to accomplish. I could feel ours already beginning to do just that as Sam drove us back toward Johnson City late on Thursday afternoon. We had had no choice in the matter, actually. His classes were to resume in less than two weeks . . . not much time by any tally to deal with those gifts that were still spread out all over Mother's house or to pack up the Bel Air Chevrolet Papaw and Mamaw had given us as a wedding present. Certainly not enough time to make anything other than a forced march back across Tennessee to Memphis and a quick business out of settling us in before Sam had to turn back into a student again. Nobody—not Sam nor I nor his parents nor mine—thought any of this was going to be easy. It just simply was necessary and, therefore, had to be possible as well. Such was and is the code of the mountains.

After supper with my parents that night and after everything had been put away, the four of us stood in the kitchen a minute or two longer, making idle conversation. Finally, Sam began the process of trying to excuse us up to my bedroom. He mentioned in particular the herculean tasks facing us the next few days as a plausible, if partial, explanation for our early retirement. When that did not seem to bring about any graceful closure, he took my hand and began physically edging his way out the door toward the hallway. Dad followed right along behind us. Even when we were halfway up the stairs to my room, he was still in the hall, still projecting bits of commentary up to us. As I glanced down to respond to something or other that he had just said and to offer a final good-night, I saw my father—really saw my father—for the first time that night.

He was standing in the doorway to the downstairs bedroom. The wash of light from the hall's ceiling lamp, falling in a yellow slant onto his face, had caught his features as completely as if they had been cast in sculptor's clay. Such a mixture of anguish and helplessness was visible across that dear face that the very look of him moved me to a quickening of tears. Instead of crying, though, and much to my own surprise, I laughed. Holding the bannister in one hand and Sam by the other, I laughed.

"It's okay, Dad," I said. "We're legal now."

"I know," he said, nodding his head just once before he went into the bedroom and closed the door behind him. Sam and I went quietly up the rest of the steps and to a good night's slumber.

There was no cruelty in that Thursday night laugh, no cruelty either in its retelling here or in the moment when it first flew out of me. There was no more cruelty, that is, than had been resident in my mother's evening laugh fourteen months earlier. But I did know, and knew instantly, that it was a new laugh for me, one that I had neither owned nor could have released less than a week earlier. That Thursday night, as if by the waters of an irrevocable baptism, I grasped the difference between a girl and a woman. I also understood for the first time why men desire the former and often fear the latter. I had laughed.

18.

EVIL, that unholy force of intricate construction and exquisite entrapments, had not played a big part in my spiritual considerations until Sam and I married. I don't mean that I had not been merrily sinning away for a decade or so. I most assuredly had been, I just didn't know it. That is to say that any sophisticated knowledge of the true skills and fatal enticements of Evil requires some conscious awareness that It is there; and that awareness had for years been occluded for me by something that I can now describe only as a variant of moral smugness.

By any criteria, moral smugness is a frightening condition, threatening to the health of the soul, and never subject to total cure. Untreated, it is a silent killer. Treated, it may go into remission from time to time and occasionally even for extended periods of time; but it never entirely leaves a soul it has successfully invaded. As is true with most diseases, it is also not a condition one just goes out and catches out of some act of willfulness or some misguided sense of adventure. Instead, it is a bequest from one's heritage mixed with associations from one's environs.

I don't offer this as an excuse for my having fallen victim to it, but as a reminder that the ill are rarely the sources of their own illness. The ill are responsible only for their conduct during the course of their sickness and for their responses to it. In my case, I didn't even perceive that anything was amiss until the second week of my marriage, a fact that had nothing to do with either Sam or marriage itself except in the most tangential of ways. Part of the irony in all of this, at least for me as an adult, is also its poignancy. Once and only once in my growing-up years did I ever engage Evil with any kind of conscious awareness of what it was. And because I had more or less resolved that struggle to my own satisfaction, it never once occurred to me thereafter to remember—poor foolish child—that few things breed infection more effectively than does the closeness of hand-to-hand combat.

From the time I entered first grade until the time that I graduated from high school, I attended classes in only one institution. Called in those days the Training School and later the University School, it was a strong and effective combination of a tuition-free private school and a laboratory in which master teachers, hired by the university, taught aspiring teachers who were students at the university how to exercise their profession well. Quite logically, the Training School was located on the college campus, approximately a mile and a quarter from our house.

Because the 1940s were at first the pinched days of wartime gas rationing and later the rugged days of pervasive national self-assurance, my father walked the mile and a quarter between our house and the Training School twice a day every single day of them. It will come as no surprise, of course, when I say that on school days I trudged the mile and a quarter with him, though I was considerably less gratified than he about our contribution first to the war and later to America's image of itself.

As the forties went along and I arrived at prepubescent maturity, I was granted the great freedom of being able to walk home alone in the afternoons instead of having to wait in Dad's office for the end of his day as well as mine. This was, initially anyway, a delicious improvement in life, for it not only put me home earlier, but it also let me dawdle along with three or four friends who lived almost as far away as I did. Somewhere around the fifth or sixth grade, however, and as my books began to increase in weight and number, it began to dawn on me that the whole business of lugging four or five extra pounds two and a half miles every day was a high price to pay for the pleasure of my schoolmates' extended company. This growing irritation on my part was exacerbated by the fact that more and more of them were being allowed to ride the city bus most of the way home, their books having also become more weighty and more numerous.

The problem with the city bus was that it cost money, a nickel a trip for students, if I remember correctly. While that seems like a modest sum, and was even then, it was far beyond the reach of my fifty-cents-a-week allowance if I wanted chewing gum after school or a Coke with lunch. My father, who was of a generous turn always, was also God-and-Country to an excess. He was duly appalled, consequently, on the few times I petitioned for bus money. The answer was most emphatically no. Walking was good for youngsters, very good. It built character (I think now that he was probably right, though I remain unclear about exactly how) and strong bones (that part was both correct and is ever increasingly clear to contemporary medicine). As a result, if I wished to ride on those desperate days when the load of books was just too overwhelming or the group of other kids on the bus just too appealing, I would have to do so out of my allowance. Like a normal child faced with such a parental position, I grew more and more sulky about my lack of privilege and more and more resentful.

Then there came the afternoon of truth. It was a clear day in an early April spring, not even as cold as such days usually were in our part of the world. There was a stiff breeze outside; and of all God's extraordinary gifts of nature, none delights me more than wind. Wind makes my spirits soar and causes my laughter to rise in their company. I had very few books that day as well, so few in fact that I could even do a kind of jig across the kickball field, toeing up tufts of new grass as I went. There was money in my pocket, for I had been careful of my funds the week before; and I was thinking seriously of spending some of it to reward myself and the wind with an ice cream on a stick.

Just beyond the campus gates and the Training School wall, there was a fairly sizable neighborhood grocery called Scott's. The Scott brothers were my mother's grocers of choice, and their delivery boy went in and out of her kitchen door far more often than did anyone else's. As a result of this mutually satisfactory commercial arrangement, the Scotts and all their entourage of staff knew me by name, and their store was a permitted stop on the way home. Ice cream on a stick, however, and not conversation with the Messrs. Scott, was my usual motivation for stopping in.

Scott's was located on a corner, almost directly across the street from the city bus stop. To get to it from the kickball field, one had to walk as if to the bus stop and then cross just beyond it over to the store itself. As I got almost even with the stop that afternoon and was working my way along through the friends and acquaintances waiting there, the bus pulled up, opened its doors, and began loading up. The minute I saw that flow of college and Training School students begin to mount the steps, I knew I was going to join them.

. . . And "know" is exactly what I mean. I did not *intend* to join them, I did not *will* to join them, I just perceived that I was about to. I perceived as well that I was not going to pay for my ride. Spending my money to treat myself to a lift home on a lovely, windy day made no sense, my newly found knowing told me. The wind was more exciting than that and so was ice cream. But what was more exciting than either wind or ice cream, I knew with amazing clarity, was what I was going to do.

I took out of my purse what we used to call a slug and what is now more commonly referred to as a knockout. They are the round bits of metal that are incised in fuse boxes and electrical housings and that work-men "knock out" as they wire a building. I suspect that children have been picking them up around construction sites for as long as there has been electricity. I certainly had been for as long as I could remember. What I had not done before that moment, however, was appreciate the fact that a slug was just about the size and weight of a bus token. All I would have to do was slide one of mine quickly into the token rather than the coin slot of the till box, and I would be on that bus with no one the wiser.

I crowded as closely as possible into the woman ahead of me, thrust my hand at the token slot at the exact same moment she thrust hers at the coin slot, and then tried to ease along with her into the aisle beyond. I didn't make it. The driver half-rose from his seat and, to the irritation of the woman, grabbed behind her coat to gain a firm grip on mine. He knew, probably from experience, exactly what I had done.

He was kind. I will say that for him. "You'll have to get off now," was all he said, and I didn't argue. I wormed my way back out the open door of the bus and through the queue of still boarding passengers. Once clear of them, I ran, humiliated and more frightened than I had ever been in my life before, up the street away from Scott's and as fast as I could toward home.

So kind had the driver been, in fact, that none of my friends had even noticed what he had done, nor were they ever aware apparently that I had tried to get on the bus in the first place; but I didn't know that as I went racing for home. All I knew was that I had to get there before one of them and/or the bus company could call and report me to my mother. I had to circumvent those calls by some means or another. They never came, of course, but I suffered the terrors of Dante's damned waiting for them.

I spent most of that evening trying to convince my mother that I was sick with something too awful to go to school with but not awful enough to see a doctor about. Since I loved school and was never sick, I almost persuaded her. All I lacked was a perceivable fever, and God knows I can't fancy to this day why my level of agitation didn't in and of itself produce one. The point is, though, that it didn't, and I dragged my unwilling self behind my father the next morning, sure that I was walking into the worst day of my life. Again nothing happened. The week dragged on, and nairy a word from anybody, friend or authority. I had not gotten away with my petty thievery exactly, but at least I had escaped it unscathed . . . well, initially I had anyway.

My first few days as a thief were energized entirely by concerns for saving first my life and then, as the week wore on, my face. Within less than another week, however, I had begun to spend more time and energy in replaying the whole sad event in my head than in trying to escape from the horrors of its possible consequences. The strange thing to me—the gripping thing that I could not let go of—was my absolute belief that I had not done what Phyllis Alexander had done. The result of that conviction was that I was not sorry for what I had done, I was terrified by it.

Not guilt but an escalating sense of vulnerability to invasion became the order of my days. Something had taken me over, something that had been beyond my will, something that had been external to me. Like a top spinning on an open-ended shaft, I had been a closed little world of me until something had swooped up through that opened point, spun around inside me ripping every thing out of place and then, having wreaked its havoc, had whirred out the top again, leaving me empty and destroyed.

It is a crude image, as well as a rather archaic one. Nowadays a child in my state would probably image her self as more like the good ship *Enterprise* boarded and usurped by aliens. Whichever metaphor one chooses, however, the end result is the same. I knew I had been invaded by something as separate from me as the Devil was separate from . . . Ah, within a matter of a few days I had named my beast as well as his mode of operation. To my young mind, I had met the enemy of church and story, and I had lost the battle. My terror grew with each passing day of internal conversation.

One of the great advantages of Roman Catholicism is its rite of confession, even if that confession is only one of being host to an escalating anguish. For a Protestant child there is no such surcease and, therefore, no access to either spiritual comfort or spiritual counseling. Thus I soldiered on unaided. So far as I can remember now, because I had no guilt about the actual act of thieving, I never thought to confess to God, who obviously was available, my failure to resist the Devil's power in driving me to it. Instead, I began to see with the earnestness born of genuine fear that my duty to my self, my parents and, by a somewhat vague extension, to God was to man the turrets of my conduct, patrolling its parapets like a stalwart trooper determined never to suffer invasion or even a small breach in its walls again.

This may all sound terribly silly and terribly inflated, I don't know. I have no way to gauge it, for never before this have I ever spoken to anyone about my April in Gehenna. As a child I could not because of fear and shame. As an adult, I have not because of some feeling that the whole tawdry event may appear distorted beyond credibility by its own lack of proportion. The only bit of reassurance I have ever received on this score, in fact, comes from St. Augustine's *Confessions*. In telling the story of stealing his mother's pears he seems to me to record the kind of exquisite agony I endured. Unfortunately, the incidents have no other similarities, having borne substantially more and better fruit in him as well as a humility of character and spirit with which I shall never be blessed, at least in this lifetime. No, what I got out of my experience was a frantic concern with my own good behavior—that, and all the arrogance that usually accompanies the successful hefting of such a burden.

The rules were so clear in mid-twentieth-century America, and so generally agreed upon, that almost no one bothered in those days to separate divine laws out either from social rules or from the working tenets of a public good. The result was a self-perpetuating confusion that relegated all of them as equals to the category of moral principles. Too much unanimity of moral opinion can be as dangerous to souls—maybe even more so, I think now—than no moral unanimity at all, though neither extreme is to be desired. What too much did for me at least, in my post–bus-stop rigor, was to obscure any clear view of sin that I might otherwise have formed and allowed me instead to define evil as being synonymous with infraction of the rules. Because my opportunities to err were far more confined than would be those of a youngster today, my uprightness was also less expensive, which is to say, of far less worth than would be true today or than would have been true in a less homogeneous society.

In any case, rectitude without godliness is a sad, weakened way to enter adulthood. It was our wedding gifts which were to expose that truth to me by fully exposing my self to me for the first time in my life.

19.

DURING THE SIX DAYS that Sam and I had been away honeymooning, my father had been busy in his own, kind way, though without our knowing it. Houses like ours, built in the 1920s before parts standardization and modular construction, were as often the product of some builder's on-the-job decisions as of preplanning and architectural foresight. They were also and almost without exception the products of a compulsive frugality that is alien to our aesthetic today. Every square inch of space that could be enclosed and finished out in them usually was, generally as irregularly shaped cupboards or garbled closets. Of the latter, the most garbled on record, I am sure, was an under-the-eaves, walk-in space that for all the years of our tenure in the house had masqueraded as an unused closet just across the hall from my upstairs bedroom. The thing had two narrow, side wings that almost resembled normal closet space. It was the walk-in center part between them that was the problem; it was walk-in for only about three feet before it became a crouch-in and, eventually, a wiggle-in with erratic contours and inopportune recesses. Here, in this center portion of salvaged space, my father, during our absence, had hired one of the university carpenters to build shelves on which to store our gifts.

As shelves go, these were truly impressive, solid enough to hold cider kegs without bowing and deep enough to hold a double row of them without any fear of the frontmost's tumbling out. I never quite knew whether Dad had, in his usual way, just said "shelves" and left the man to his own imagination or whether he had, also in his usual way, simply been a bit fey about the mechanics of storage; but it didn't matter much because even Gabriel and his angels could not have blasted those shelves back out of there by the time we got back home and ready to use them.

Sam had stood in front of them our first morning back and, literally, massaged his forehead as if something buried behind it were troubling him considerably. "My word," was all he said, but only because we hadn't been married long enough for him to be more candid. "Not very practical," I submitted. "Not very," he responded, and we left it there for the time being.

The chores ahead of us, ones that we really had envisioned for weeks as herculean, turned out, in point of fact, to be the amiable occupations of a very pleasant few days. They also have turned out to be the only days of sorting and packing, out of a long life of sorting and packing, that I have ever managed to recall in quite those terms. I hate moving. Let the record show: I hate moving. But this one time it was an adventure of the imagination more than a trial of the back and psyche, at least at first. For one thing, in June 1955 Sam and I were still trying as hard to please each other as we were to get our possessions someplace other than where they were. Such grace does not live long in this world, primarily because it's not very efficient, but it does make for amiable and pleasant memories.

So bathed in what I recall as a mild and courtesy-laced euphoria, we left off staring at the too-deep-to-be-believed shelves on Friday morning and set about the business of getting ourselves divided into two piles: what went to Memphis and what stayed in Johnson City, the latter being a euphemism for what had to be wedged safely into the too-deep-to-be-useful-as-well-as-to-be-believed shelves. Friday was almost fun, and that's not romanticized memory; that's hard fact.

As I have said, the Tickles had given us, for a wedding gift, one of those bulbous, limitlessly capacious 1950s tanks that General Motors insisted on calling Bel Air sedans, and we began to use it as a holding station. The first things into it were all the clothes, books, and memorabilia that I would need in Memphis but not for the rest of the immediate week. Easy. I had already stacked most of them up in the guest room before the wedding. Sam drove them up to Mamaw, who had dedicated her parlor to serving as our loading dock. By the time he had got back from the top of the hill, I had made my first pass through the living and dining rooms, lifting out onto the floor all the things that we would need to conduct even the most elemental of housekeeping arrangements.

Our gifts had fallen, more by chance than plan, into three broad divisions—the formal and elegant, the quirky, and the utilitarian. To be honest, it was the utilitarian gifts that had given me the most contentment and satisfaction over the months of their being on display. The formal things—the china and crystal and silver—were by definition the tools of formal life, and I already knew I despised most formal life and all formal dining experiences. More accurately, I already knew I deplored them, especially the dining parts.

My mother was a consummate hostess, as skilled as ever any human being could be in the arts of graciousness and hospitable elegance. As a child, I admired her inordinately for those gifts, but as a child I also took serious note of the hours and the labor required by her kind of formal domestic entertaining. I had, in other words, decided quite early in my life that when my time came, I wanted people in my house for supper not dinner, and I most certainly wanted them there for evenings when conversation, not convention, would be my hospitality to them. Thus it was that the twig was already bent where the tree would grow.

Like a dutiful middle-class daughter, however, I had picked out, with Sam's help, the "good" china that was still sitting on Mother's dining room table, the crystal and sterling that complemented it spread tastefully in an arch around it. I had selected, also with Sam, the "Sunday" or family china with its crystal and silverplate, also tastefully and almost as grandly spread over the other end of the same dining room table. But without Sam, for he was already gone to Memphis by then, I had selected a set of everyday pottery dishes that clearly belonged in the utilitarian division.

They were heavy, thick things with no design, each piece being just one solid, unmitigated color—either solid black or solid red. As a set of dishes, they were so completely California fifties that words could never honor them enough, much less do justice to their appeal for me. They were as self-satisfied as the Bel Air and every bit as voguish. Sam, whose tastes have always run to the classic, at least in contrast to mine, had been appalled the first time he saw the dishes. He was even more appalled that Friday morning when he came back from delivering my clothes to Mamaw's and discovered I had packed the red and black California ware as his next load for her parlor. He balked, but I assured him that two eggs sunny-side-up would look smashing on one of the black plates. He allowed that they would look quite otherwise were they to show up one morning by mistake on a red plate instead, but we both let it pass. The pottery dishes went up the hill.

Then there were all the other things, too, from among the utilitarian gifts, things that I had rejoiced in and that went up the hill that day. A Betty Crocker iron was tall cotton for me. All the irons I had ever used at Mother's or at school had had a heat selection system that involved pulling their cords in and out of a wall outlet. Whoever heard of actually owning an automatic one! Affordable electric home mixers were a post–World War II indulgence that had certainly not made it to my mother's kitchen by 1955; but, wonder of wonders, Sam and I had received one of them as well. And so it went for hours. My sorting, Mother's helping me in boxing, and Sam loading and unloading the Bel Air. The only thing I couldn't determine was how Mamaw was doing at her end of things, but Sam reported she was being quite sanguine about the whole thing. He even reported, by midafternoon, that she had sorted all our boxes into various parts of her parlor and begun inventorying what was in each sort so we would know how to pack the trailer most securely. She was, as I have said, Mamaw and a piece of work.

By Saturday evening the three of us with Mamaw's unseen assistance and Dad's late-afternoon help had managed to get the obvious and easy decisions either out of Mother's and up to Mamaw's or else returned as duplicate goods to the stores from which they had come. That got me to the unique and the quirky, and they were much harder because with few exceptions each of them was the work of a wry disposition or a tender generosity: A perfect pair of Venetian crystal bud vases that, along with my adapted transcript, were the last tangible gifts I would ever receive from Clara Louise Thompson. A set of tin measuring spoons on a cobalt blue ring from a neighbor child. A yardstick embedded with a metal strip to keep its edges true. A tiny ceramic butter warmer with its own iron stand and—for heaven's sakes—a votive candle, something I had never seen before in a domestic context. The list went on and on, but the truth was then, and still is today half a century later, that they were the things whose givers I remembered by name. An aqua ceramic butter warmer pitched precariously over a votive candle does not get lost in the hullabaloo nearly as easily as one more Floral Chintz dinner plate by Picard, nor does its giver. I wanted them all . . . wanted them all around me . . . wanted the humor or the sense of affection they elicited every time I picked one of them up. That wasn't going to happen, of course, but making the cut was exhausting for me and, I suspect though he didn't say so, exasperating for Sam to watch. When on Monday night, as he was making his final run of the day to Mamaw, I grabbed up the butter warmer at the last minute and shoved it into a box, he just shook his head and said, "Honestly!"

All of which got us, weary but basically unbowed, to Tuesday, the formal ware, and the shelves. One did not have to be an engineer to perceive that whatever went to the back of those shelves would never again be seen in our lifetime . . . or at least not unless we could invent a retrieval system that worked. The only solution, crude as it was, that we could contrive was to wrap and box up all the odd-shaped things like cups and bowls and platters—things that would not stack but would break—number each box, and then tack to each shelf the inventory of the boxes on it along with a catalogue of what was stored in each. Warehousing 101, by whatever name one might wish to call it. Mamaw would have loved it, had she been able to watch us.

Having determined the system, implementing it was more or less a one-person-at-a-time process. One person had to move back and forth from goods to boxes, packing each breakable both where it mechanically would fit and where it logically could be expected to be located. One memory and one set of criteria were all that kind of sort and pack could tolerate. Until one of us had completed it, moreover, there was no way either of us could begin to stack the shelves. Until every box was inventoried and sealed, no one knew which of them should go all the way to the back and into never-never land, which should be put nearer to the front in the vicinity of the possible, and which should go in last as citizens of the probable.

Mother was at an all-day church meeting that Tuesday, one I thought she had been singularly eager to be off to, as a matter of fact; and Dad was at work. It seemed logical, therefore, for me to be the one to begin separating the formal ware into boxes while Sam, who had not yet really seen either his mother or his two best friends, should go visit with them. He left, telling me his plans and where he could be reached if I got through early or just changed my mind about needing help. I was unlikely to change my mind, I thought, but I didn't say so.

Sam had scarcely done more than turn the Bel Air right at the bottom of the driveway and point it toward town before the house began to nod off around me, obviously intending to nap its way through the few hours of inactivity being granted it. Almost as content myself, I sat down to the task of the dining room. It was the first time I had been alone in almost two weeks . . . the first time, I realized, that I had been both alert and alone at the same time in almost a year. The sensation of solitude with no fear of interruption was as dear to me just then as the odors and sunny half-shadows of the dozing house itself.

My hands began to work the dishes and the tissue. Select, wrap, position, cushion, record. Select, wrap, position, cushion, record. The very rhythm itself lightened the work, making a kind of dance out of its tedium. Then, within no more than five or ten minutes of my beginning, there was the tiniest, most imperceptible of movements . . . a shift in presence as unhurried as a mist when it rises from off a summer pond and hangs there a while, being neither air nor water, neither tangible nor yet refutable, neither substance nor the lack of substance.

I was quieted by the paradox. My hands stopped their packing; and I was filled with that kind of half-sweet, almost welcome, resignation which comes when news one has dreaded receiving is at last delivered and demands to be heard or when something one has spent inordinate amounts of time and energy trying to outrun finally overtakes one and must at last be engaged.

Please understand, this thing that had come to join me was no creature of substance at which, for lack of an inkpot, I could have thrown a tea cup or goblet; but it was not an interior act of imagination, either. It most certainly was not some agitated shard of morality spawned at a bus stop and bouncing all over the place. More nearly than anything else I could think of at the time, it was simply a gnawing, almost familiar presence that I would have preferred to avoid a bit longer but toward which I was inexorably attracted—an instructing awareness, or perhaps an accusing grace, that was using the quiet of my mind to force a conversation about the nature and condition of my soul. I can say that now, but I could not have said it then, because that Tuesday morning was the first time Spirit and I had ever met, at least to the best of my knowledge and face-to-face, so to speak.

The dining room grayed and then receded, my attention having shifted to follow neither my hands nor my own thoughts but those of my inquisitor.

To say we "spoke" that morning is foolishness, of course, but it is a foolishness born of inadequacy. There are no words to name conversations that do not emanate from geographically fixed sources, no words to name encounters that embrace and surround at all places evenly and outside of time. The words—or better, the three words—that we do have simply acknowledge the mystery; they do not attempt to name the process or the sensation. Moreover, we tend to use them almost exclusively in non-spiritual contexts. *Intuition*, like *intuiting* itself, we apply to some kind of subjective knowing that comes from no obvious or identifiable source and that has practical, almost always successful, consequences. *Inspiration* we apply most frequently to externally presented stimulus that, like a moon to an ocean, pulls us into tides of greater purpose and well-being. Either that, or we apply it more academically to the arts and then cavalierly define it as "flashes of genius" without troubling ourselves overmuch about the meaning of "genius." The third word, *epiphany*, should be the one nearest to the crux of the matter; but as I have already lamented, it tends in our usage to exist either as a specifically liturgical word or as one that nicely covers discoveries and breakthroughs in practical knowledge. Perhaps the very smallness of our vocabulary is advantageous, however, for it spares us the desecration of facile use from which these others have suffered.

By whatever inadequate name is most comfortable, then, I was brought, on that sunny and unportentous morning, into my first understanding of "Phyllis" as the equally inadequate name for a congress of parts, each one of which had a vested interest in what this life was and each one of which had a different agency and role in how it played itself out. Certainly there is nothing startling in such a discovery, or there shouldn't have been for one who had enjoyed Jack Hornaday's lectures and company as much as I had. The surprise was not in the knowing, therefore, but in the actual experiencing of what up to that morning had been only intellectual data. The surprise also, I know now, lay as well in discovering that this congress of all my parts had a member that felt or presented as considerably different from what Mr. Hornaday had passed off as id, ego, and/or super ego, a piece that seemed, if not divine, then at least luminous from contact with the divine.

Because, as all who have also walked this path already know, my dining room experience was hardly to be some rare, isolated, or singular one, I do not wish to exaggerate it here, nor do I wish to fall into the autobiographer's eternal trap of imposing today's understanding on yesterday's confusions. Suffice it to say here that had the Paraclete and I engaged ourselves in words that morning, which we did not, the conversation could be reported now as having gone more or less like this:

"What in the world are you doing all this for?" asked of me as if in some kind of half-amused scorn.

"Because I have to," I would have answered.

"Why?"

"Because the shelves are too deep for us to retrieve any of this stuff later if we don't store it now in boxes we can grab."

"Stuff?" There would have been just a tinge of sarcasm.

"Stuff," I repeat. "I hate formal dinner parties and all the paraphernalia that it takes to make them work, all the hours it takes to wash this mess by hand and store it afterwards, all of that."

"You know, of course, that you'll be wrapping and unwrapping your so-called 'stuff' for the rest of your life, don't you? The hours and hours of packing and unpacking it every time you move or buy new furniture or paint your dining room will waste more of you and your time than washing up after a party ever will."

"Yes, but that's partly because I don't intend to ever actually 'use' them all that much anyway."

"So why did you ask for them all?"

"Because I was supposed to," I said. "I didn't have any choice. It's what brides do. You know, it's how the system works."

I knew, of course—had known, as I have said, for weeks—that my sense of being propertied and therefore enfranchised had come from receiving the things before me. I knew as well—dammit, both of us sitting there knew—that, despite my protestations of powerless conformity, I had eagerly participated in the process. I had participated so eagerly, in fact, that the change in my status had become far more important to me than any particular gift or giver. I wasn't about to let go of that little bit of shameful self-perception just then, however.

I also knew, though I had not taken time to think about it before that very moment, that there had been a growing fatness in my heart as the quantity of gifts had mounted over the weeks, a sense of validation and approval and reward for a life lived in accord with expectation, at least up to that point. I could even recall without any effort, though with some embarrassment, a few times when in unwrapping and recording a day's presents I had had a nasty but delicious moment of thinking, "I bet we've got more stuff than any other couple this year." But what was all of that? some part of my self thought. A little ambition here, a tad of jealousy there, a good deal of pure greed with some lust of the eye—at worst no more than what could be expected, given the circumstances . . . and even at their very worst, all quite natural.

"Perfectly natural," said the other as easily as if all thoughts were spoken ones. "It's naturally, precisely who you are . . . a smidgen of ambition, a snippet of jealousy, a bit of greed, a lusting eye . . . in sum, the sins of the parents visited upon the children. But tell me one more thing. Now that the system as you call it has been satisfied, why not simply take the whole lot of these things back to the stores they came from?"

"I couldn't do that!" The thought or question was genuinely shocking to me.

"Why not? Why would you want to carry this kind of time-consuming baggage into life when you can just set it down right now before it's too late?"

"Because . . ." I was by this point in a pain of soul and self that rested just on the brink of agony.

"Because what?"

"Because I need them, I want them."

"Why?"

"So people will know who I am . . . you know, what kind of people we have come from."

"Ahhh, so now we have a modicum of false pride in us as well."

And then it was over. I was back within time and back to being only one awareness. The chirp of some fledglings out in the side yard, the faint crackly pop of the upstairs floor as the house began to heat up in the noon-day sun, the slap of the mailbox lid as the postman dropped the day's de-livery through it . . . they all began again; and life picked up where it had left off less than a hour earlier.

". . . a smidgen of ambition, a snippet of jealousy, a bit of greed, a lust-ing eye, a modicum of false pride . . ." The words—for they were words now—wound their way through my head, and I repeated their litany like a penitent telling her beads, though I was not praying. Rather, I was feel-ing the first swells of something very close to joy.

". . . a smidgen of ambition, a snippet of jealousy, a bit of greed, a lust-ing eye, a modicum of false pride . . ." I didn't have to worry any longer about being taken over by evil; I already had been. I had been fair game for it all along, had domesticated and housed it, in fact, from the begin-ning and never recognized it, never suspected that it had a being existence much more powerful than its doing one.

". . . a smidgen of ambition, a snippet of jealousy, a bit of greed, a lust-ing eye, a modicum of false pride . . ." Just the acknowledgment itself was as sweet as any absolution from a priest ever could be, or so I thought in those first giddy minutes of acceptance.

Whether that release of heart and soul was spiritually healthy or not doesn't matter much now. The fact still remains that no Christian in his-tory—Orthodox, Roman, or Protestant—ever embraced Original Sin with any more relief and any less contrition than I did on that Tuesday morning. The fact that I would spend the rest of my days trying to extract my life from out of sin, both original and acquired, didn't matter much just then either, because I had just engaged the mystery of the bronze snake in a new way: It is wrestling alone with sin that leads to sure and painful death just as it is looking up for help while wrestling that leads so abundantly into life.

When Sam came home four hours later, he said he figured I must be through with the bulk of the packing because he could hear me humming from the kitchen. He was right about the dishes and wrong about the rea-son for my humming. But for whatever reason, after that our work pro-gressed as easily as it had originally. By suppertime on Friday, the impossible shelves were full and Mamaw's parlor-load of goods packed into a trailer in just the way she thought it should be.

Early Saturday morning, Sam pulled the Bel Air up in front of the house so he and Mother could wedge our picnic lunch and my overnight case into two spaces that plainly weren't there. I left them struggling and went back inside to make one final check for anything we might have left behind and to lower the upstairs windows.

The night before had been stuffy as late June sometimes can be. Sam had opened the playroom door before we went to bed, propping the dormer windows as wide as they would go in hopes that some small breeze might circulate our way. As I went into the playroom now to close and latch the dormers back, a breeze come too late to relieve us began perversely to tease the maple trees in the front yard. Through their leaves I could catch little flashes of the Bel Air parked on the street beyond, the orangey-yellow trailer hasped securely to its back bumper.

The morning sun was already making the dust motes dance, and I smiled briefly over all the hours I had sat on that floor, content just to watch the unceasing ballet of motes when they are in love with light. The playroom was about such hours, of course: time translating space into the force of memory.

In the corner just to the right of the dormers was a tumbled stack of cushions. I had sat there for whole other mornings, not watching but working, making clothes for the dolls that lay, undisturbed but fully clothed, in beds and cribs and carriages about the room. The table where for five glorious years I had made model airplanes, painstakingly carving their fuselages from balsa wood and papering their wingspans with tissue and shellac, still sat exactly where I had always had it near the hall door, my tools neatly in their accustomed places on its scarred top. On the east wall, holding pride of place as he had for years, was a collage of Little Jack Horner, his thumb red with a just-extracted ripe plum. A co-ed babysitter had cut him out for me, building him up piece by bright piece out of construction paper, and I, who had never seen such a thing before, had always treasured him. The stack of castoff alarm clocks, most of them heavily cannibalized, sat where I had abandoned it under the left dormer on the winter afternoon when I had finally had to admit I would never understand how a clock really worked, much less how to repair one. And there was Papaw's bouquet as well.

I had brought his bachelor's buttons up and dried them here weeks before. They hung now on a nail just to the left of Little Jack Horner's head, suspended by the same blue ribbon with which he had originally bound them. "Here, baby," Papaw had said. "You'll probably need them before this is over." And he was right; I had.

I had needed all these things at one time or another . . . I had needed them and they had been provided. For most of my remembered years, I had been so much a part of the playroom and it of me that I could no more have parsed it objectively than I could have parsed my father's love or my mother's care. Now we were no longer of a piece, the room and I. We had ceased to be so, I think, on the afternoon when I had hung Papaw's flowers beside Jack Horner's picture and experienced for the first time in my life the amazement of gratitude, though not yet its humility. That would take far more years of living than the twenty-one I had acquired. For the time being, however, amazement was more than sufficient.

The horn of the Bel Air tooted twice. I finished locking the playroom door and went down to my waiting husband. We were going to Memphis.

PART FOUR

*Upstairs and
to Your Left*

20.

ACCORDING TO our most revered storytellers, or at least according to our most romantically inclined ones, every young life has one golden summer somewhere in it. Somewhere there are supposed to be those few fecund days or weeks when the business of growing up catches each of us in a final embrace, dances awhile to a haunting but still unfamiliar tune, pivots ever so wistfully, and then, like a good sorting machine, drops us summarily into our appointed places in the greater scheme of things. Whether that plot line is true to life or simply to the requirements of the storytelling craft, I have never quite known. I do know, however, that I had such a summer, or a piece thereof. It began when Sam parked the Bel Air and its trailer in the back drive of 1094 Poplar Avenue in Memphis, Tennessee, and it ended the last Thursday morning in August when I headed out that same drive to begin my brief career as a public school teacher.

It was 95 degrees' worth of hot as Sam and I drove in that first time—95 only because it was also well after 9:00 P.M. when we arrived and only because Memphis had had a small shower the day before. If it had been hot in the Bel Air with the windows rolled down and the car moving at highway speeds, it was purgatory to be stopped dead on a concrete parking apron in the country's most airless town.

Sam cut the lights and then the motor on the Bel Air and leaned back against the seat, too exhausted from thirteen hours of towing a trailer to even get out of the car. As the low drone of the motor ceased, the braided noises and syncopation that have become "the Memphis Sound" began to encircle us as if we were alien visitors whom they had come first to inspect and perhaps, if all else appeared in order, eventually to greet.

In the half-day of Poplar Avenue's streetlights, 1094 was a mountain of darkness hunkered down for the night, but it was also the only thing within the range of sight or sound that was hunkered. Everything else was honking or singing or throbbing or flashing or shouting. There once had been the time, back when Memphis was just a river town, that the hoi polloi had been confined by its own circumstances to hovels along the Mississippi and to shanties cobbled together around Beale Street. In that turn-of-the-century era of order and good sense when a man could tell the way of things by another man's clothes or another man's color, Poplar had been the avenue of kings . . . or more correctly, the avenue of barons and princes, for cotton was Memphis's always and only king in those days.

Long before Prohibition had become an expensive memory, however, the rich cultural soup of stevedores and steamboat crews, roustabouts and displaced ne'er-do-wells had begun to escape their appointed places along the river. Bringing their bars and tenements and gaming houses with them as they came, they had begun more to trickle than to flow east away from the river and the Front Street cotton markets toward the public parks and shady belvederes of the wealthy. Over the decades of such slow human erosion, the old Victorian mansions of an earlier Memphis had fallen, one by one, from their former glory. A few had survived the Depression as tenements, but most had been razed to make way for housing projects, ghetto stores, and, most significantly, the world's largest medical school. With its acres and acres of campus, public clinics and inner-city teaching hospitals, the University of Tennessee College of Medicine had originally been welcomed more as an early form of state-funded urban renewal than as a boon to human well-being. By 1955, however, it had become Memphis's proudest landmark and the city's most touted proof of benevolent municipal government. In all of this, 1094 Poplar was a bit of a well-kept anomaly. (It was also the property of an anomaly, but that's another, if related, story.)

The upper or eastern end of the ten-hundred block of Poplar ended at Waldran Boulevard. The lone survivor of old Memphis's original boulevards, Waldran was hardly more than a ghost of its earlier self, more a boulevard in name than in effect or presence. The only vestige of graciousness left to it in 1955 was the remnant of a belvedere, still trimmed and sometimes tended, that ran north from Poplar for almost four blocks before it gave up and became just a dusty median in another low-rent neighborhood. It was this intersection of diminishing boulevard and dwindling prestige that 1094 commanded, unlit and haughty as if it were still the chosen retreat of a dowager, and just as self-referencing.

Built of cut stone and standing three storeys high above its fully habitable basement, 1094 still looked as solid and square as a mansion, but it certainly could no longer claim the elitism of being a one-family dwelling nor the hauteur of having servants rather than renters in its habitable basement.

The place was, in point of fact, home to three families (of whom we were about to be the third) and three single med students (of whom Sam had been one up until he had gone home to marry me).

But that kind of concentration of people was as nothing compared to the house next door. Even in the artificial twilight of the street lamps, 1090 did not appear ever to have been much of a house, architecturally speaking, though it was difficult to be absolutely sure from where I sat. Hard on the western property line of 1094 and as jammed up against the intervening fence as any city's ordinances would allow, 1090 had belonged to a dental fraternity for so long that it had lost all the contours and amenities of its original self to decades of unrestrained bonhomie. One thing 1090 most certainly did have, however, was the neighborhood's prize for overpopulation. This was especially relevant because the one thing the place plainly did not have was any cooling system other than open windows and loud fans, all of which were buzzing and commenting as Sam and I drove in. That is, the fans were whirring and the males in front of them were shouting to one another above the general fray.

Almost as diverting as a fraternity house next door—I was, after all, a married woman now—was the two-story wooden building that sat behind 1094 and was the northern boundary of the parking lot. Originally the carriage house for a fleet of horse-drawn vehicles, the place was, by 1955, a multiplex of doors and families. I was destined never to have a firm grasp on the carriage house during the months that we lived across the backyard parking lot from its residents. Just as I would think I had figured out who belonged with whom, the thing would do a kind of mighty burp, spew all its pieces and parts out into the street somewhere, and begin to collect a new set of inhabitants. The regularity of this process would eventually persuade me that either the spaces were let by the week or chronic nonpayment of rent might be a problem in the back house. None of that mattered at the time, however, because on that first night in our first few minutes of arriving, the carriage house and the fraternity house together were the biggest party in town.

"Is it like that all the time?" I asked Sam.

"Yep, all night every night, but you'll get used to it."

He had said the words as if I should study to become resigned, but I didn't want to be resigned. Even tired and hot as I was, I hoped to my soul that I would never, ever become resigned to the sounds of beer and camaraderie and radios and one truly awe-inspiring bass who appeared to be in one of the upstairs rooms of the fraternity house. Becoming resigned to that would be worse than old age, I thought. I'd just moved into the French Quarter, for goodness' sake, and nobody and no thing was going to separate me from all that raucous energy, that beautiful flood of boozy anger and rich sadness. I was, thank you very much, home at last, right where I had been meant all of my life to be, right in the heart of reality, at least reality as I had always imagined it. Sam, on the other hand, was re-signed both by his hours of towing and his months of prior exposure. He crawled out of the car, plowed around behind his seat, and extracted my overnight case and our picnic basket as well as the paper sack in which he had dropped the last of his shaving gear so many hours earlier. "Come on," he mumbled as he started across the lighted lot toward the darkness be-yond. I followed him around the corner of the house and up a set of heavy stone steps to a side entrance. A single lamp burned in the porte-cochere ceiling above us, and through the beveled glass mullions on either side of the locked door I could see the low, yellow glow of at least two more fix-tures inside. Otherwise, the place was as silent and unlit as the mausoleum it resembled.

Behind us the dental students were still making beginning-of-term mayhem, the cars on Poplar were still whipping down the avenue honk-ing, the carriage house was engaging in some kind of intra-familial argu-ment, but 1094 was above it all, removed from it all. Sam sat down my suitcase, his sack, and the basket to fish the side-door key out of his pocket. "I'll get one made for you on Monday," he said, as he shoved the door open and stood back to let me pass. Then he added, as if in afterthought, "It's upstairs and to your left."

21.

THE BUSINESS of understanding the new lives of old houses is expe-dited greatly, or so the theory goes, by understanding first the original pur-poses of each part of a structure. Nowhere was this principle ever more applicable than it was with the apartment upstairs and to the left at 1094 Poplar.

In fact, to call the thing an apartment was a bit of an indulgence. What it was was one huge, perfectly square box, half of which was inside another box. On its southern and only truly interior wall, the box opened out into a richly paneled, pretentiously Edwardian space that we referred to as the upstairs hall, but that came nearer in size and grandeur to being a lobby of sorts. The west wall of our room, by contrast, was its only truly exterior one, though with no windows—at least no windows for all practical purposes. Technically speaking, there really were two of them, eight feet tall and heavily draped, on that wall. My first domestic act, on the morning after our late arrival, had been to pop out of bed and throw open the drapes to the morning sun. Just as I pulled the cord, Sam said, "Don't!" but it was too late. A naked or half-naked, I couldn't be sure, dentist-to-be was doing his morning exercises not thirty feet away. He waved, I waved, Sam rolled across the bed, crazed with laughter . . . all of which is to say "no windows," for I never opened the drapes again.

The apartment, which was how we continued to refer to it simply because we had no better or abler term, had been the mansion's nursery, a role that accounted for the peculiarities of the box's other two sides. It accounted as well for both the space's greatest virtues and its most singular inconveniences. On the plus side, the nursery cum apartment had a door on its north wall that opened out onto the most remarkably cheerful enclosed porch I have ever been pleasured by. Running along some ten or twelve feet of the back wall of the house, the porch had done dual duty, I surmised, as a sun porch and as a summer sleeping porch for little fellows. Certainly, it was tailored to the size of babies and cribs; but even the porch's minuscule size couldn't diminish the ocean of sunshine and health that washed through its windows on all but the most daunting of winter days.

As something of an extra bonus, the windows of the porch looked straight down on the parking lot as well as straight across and down to the menage of the carriage house. Neither of them could have been of any use to infants and toddlers, I'm sure, but both were endlessly absorbing to me, better than a balcony at Mardi Gras on some days, in fact. Since the porch itself was only about five feet wide from windows to wall, there was just enough room under the windows for one of those small chrome dinette sets that were the hallmark of the 1950s, domestically speaking. Number 1094's was of egg-yolk yellow and possessed of two chairs, one of them of questionable stability. I was to spend hours and hours of my life in one or the other of them over the next few months.

While the dining-room porch appeared at first glance to be just a sunny space built between the nursery itself and the mansion's exterior walls, it actually was not so much a discrete space as the shorter side of an "L"—an "L" whose long side burrowed its way for some fifteen or more feet behind the apartment's east wall and toward the rest of the mansion's interior. This was our kitchen, and such a kitchen as I have never seen before or since. Like the rest of the mansion, its ceiling was twelve feet high. Like the sun porch, its width could not have been much more than five feet. But its walls! Oh, my! Had there been any light at all, even the smallest of transom windows, in that corridor, the marble of those walls would have made one weep. Even in the incandescent dusk of the distant ceiling fixture, that marble could make me catch my breath on most days. The place had been the nursery's wash and laundry room, its original elegance no more, probably, than the waterproofing solution of its era; but what largesse to the eye and heart in 1955.

As a kitchen, of course, the space was a disaster, as anyone who has ever cooked in a corridor can attest. Everything was in a straight line, with the sink's being plumbed in at the upper end and the stove being wired in at the turn of the "L." There was a very practical reason for this latter positioning, of course. The place was so narrow that to open the oven door completely, one had to step back into the porch and then pull the handle of the oven door. But amusing accommodations were not inconveniences as such, just quirky bits of structural character. The inconvenience was that infants and even toddlers use diapers, thus necessitating the presence of a sizable laundry near their quarters, but obviating any need for more adult facilities. The bathroom was down the hall and to your left, as they say.

Actually there were two bathrooms; they just didn't contain the same things. If one went out our door into the foyer or lobby and made a sharp left, one passed into a narrow hall that apparently paralleled the south end of our thin kitchen and then terminated in a truly remarkable marble-walled room the size of my mother's breakfast room. One stepped up six inches onto a marble floor, looked up to twelve-foot walls marbled halfway up their full height on all four sides, and stood in homage before what I was sure was the only working water closet left in America. It was the only thing in the entire room, but its grandeur gave a whole new level of appreciation to the term "throne room." This, Sam had explained within minutes of our Saturday night arrival, we were to share with the three single medical students who lived across the hall lobby from us.

While I could readily understand that no house could afford two of the things I was looking at, I did balk briefly at the notion of passing back and forth among med students in all states of disarray and at all hours of the night. Since Sam for the life of him could not comprehend why this would be a problem for me, it wasn't. That resolution, more tacit than arbitrated, was the first time I, road-weary or not, began to perceive that like our parents we would develop—were already developing—a politics of marriage, but I let it slide.

I had let it slide in part because we were both too tired that first night to care about much of anything except sleep and because there was one interesting compensation in all of this, namely the other bathroom. It too was accessed by means of the narrow hall, but through a door that was always kept closed. Once that door was opened, however! Once that door was opened, one stepped into plumbing heaven, and it was ours, all ours, just ours. A wondrously sunny room some ten by fifteen feet, it, too, was solid marble, but with a glorious, watery-paned window and the space to complement it. There were only a wash basin and a tub in the entire room, but they were enough.

The basin, of heavy china or porcelain and poised on an equally brilliant pedestal, was like a great flat disk with a scoop in its middle. The tub, not quite so pristine but regal upon its clawed feet, had to have been somewhere between six and seven feet long, for I could lie flat in it without touching either end. For that tub, that wash basin, and that sun porch, I would have endured anything, including a shared w.c. Maybe, I thought, in one of those charitable minutes that are so easy in the first few months of marriage, maybe Sam knew I'd feel this way, and that's why he brushed away my anxiety over the bathroom itself. Maybe, but as an older and wiser woman would have said, not very likely.

22.

OUR FIRST TWO DAYS in our new quarters are lost to me in the minutiae that composed them. We have to have unloaded the car, returned the trailer, got me a door key, hauled boxes up two flights of stairs, and even, at some point, eaten and slept. I know that, I just don't remember doing any of it. What I do remember was our first visitor and our first trip to the grocery store.

Number 1094 was owned by the Jimersons, and Mrs. Jim—I never heard her called by any other name—was our first visitor, arriving just shortly after the episode of the drapes and just before I had had time to get fully dressed. Sam answered the knock on the door, and there she stood— no surprise to him, a total astonishment to me.

As human exteriors go, Mrs. Jim's will always stand in my mind as being among the more memorable. The woman was all edges and lines. Part of that effect, admittedly, was a result of her size and thinness; fully turned out, she could not have weighed ninety pounds or stood much more than two or three inches over five feet. It was the bones beneath the thinness, however, that were so arresting, so elegant in their straightness and visible sharpness. Her face, too, was sharp and narrow (it was, in fact, about as narrow as a face could be and still provide for all the usual appointments of eyes and nose and mouth) and had the most clearly demarcated midline I have ever known a face to have. It looked as if someone or something had gently compressed it cheek-toward-cheek just enough to express and exaggerate the center seam of her entire facial structure. Even her teeth gave the impression of confined space, the left inside corner of her right front tooth lapping just by a fraction of a hair over the inside right corner of her left front tooth, the result being that the two appeared to be holding hands in the middle of Mrs. Jim's mouth. I was drawn to her immediately.

I've never had trouble liking people or even engaging strangers with true pleasure, but my attraction to Mrs. Jim was cut from a different cloth. She was, for one thing, as completely resident in her body as a coquette is and as clearly in control of its distortions as a fine actress has to be. More to the point, though, with her perpetual profile and her henna-dyed hair she was as near as our times are likely ever to come to the Nefertiti of history. Wherever she had come from, and she never told me of her origins, Mrs. Jim was a genetic throwback to something very ancient and very well-bred. The only dissonance was that even though her stock might still run close to its original pride and visage, it had wandered far away from any of its original privilege.

The mansion at 1094 Poplar was patently more than Mrs. Jim had ever had in her youth and far more than she had originally had any reason to anticipate. She was, as a result, ferociously protective of the place. She fit that house like a key fits a lock and, God willing, the two of them were never going to be separated from one another again. Holding on to 1094 was also, I always suspected, the whole *raison d'être* for her life with Mr. Jim. She needed his policeman's salary to help with the bills, his policeman's connections to negotiate code and ordinance details, and his policeman's strength to stave off the deterioration incipient in old mansions. Beyond that, so far as I could ever tell, Mr. Jim was of no apparent value or interest to her.

I can't remember ever seeing Mrs. Jim without a cigarette in one hand and an ashtray in the other. She certainly had one on that first Sunday morning when she stood in our doorway, the cigarette in her right hand and her petite, china ashtray in the left. "I came to welcome you home," she said, as Sam opened the door. Then she reached up and touched his face lightly with her right hand, haloing him with a trail of smoke and affection while he smiled and bent to her in return.

Even had I been fully clothed and in command of my senses, I could not have been more shocked than I was by that five seconds of familiar greeting. This curiously appealing woman knew, liked, and greeted my husband in the way that grown women know, like, and greet grown men—and Sam had responded in kind! I was stunned into silence, my whole being transfixed by what I had just seen.

Up until that moment, it had never occurred to me to think of Sam as a man. Artless as it may sound, up until the exact moment of Mrs. Jim's welcome, Sam Tickle had been the boy I grew up with and then, more recently, the boy I had married, primarily so we could play together for the rest of our lives. Mrs. Jim, on the other hand, looked at Sam Tickle and saw a trusted and proven tenant, a professional with one degree in hand and another in the offing, a competent manager of relationships as well as arrangements.

Standing there barefoot and with my dress not yet entirely buttoned, I could feel the boy slipping away from me, drifting into photo albums and memory as he went. I had never been caught by the hinges of time before, had never had to accept the inevitability of their closing, had never entered a new place while still filled with a sweet, sad longing for the old. I more sank than sat down on the edge of the unmade bed.

"Come in, come in." Sam stepped back from the door to make room for her.

"No," she said, keeping her place in the hall, "I just came to say I'm glad you made it back home safely and to see Phyllis." She turned her head slightly, cocking it in my direction as if she were a bird rather than a woman, and I again had the sensation that, like an Egyptian silhouette, she used only one side of her face at a time.

"You're tired," she observed, and there was a kindness in her words that exceeded mere courtesy by years of living. "We'll talk later when he's gone off to school." She gestured toward Sam with the left, ashtray hand. "I'm downstairs if you get lonesome." And she left; but she proved as good as her words about providing companionship.

If anybody had been counting, I suspect the tally would have shown that I spent more waking hours in Mrs. Jim's company that summer than in Sam's. By the clock, most of those hours would have been evening ones spent watching television together in the cavernous entrance hall/parlor that she referred to as the front living room; but interspersed throughout the television hours and through some just-visiting ones as well was my first substantial instruction in Roman Catholicism.

Mrs. Jim lived in that strip of grace that is called being sensibly devout and that seems to be the purview of Roman, but almost never of Protestant, Christians. She never confused her religion, which was belief in God's willingness to do business with humanity, with her Church, which was there to expedite the arrangements and give some order to their effecting. She was neither afraid of her own sin—she could go to confession and get herself back out of it—nor pleased about it. Penance, after all, was real and frequently inconvenient. She absolutely believed the priest and the Church about the rules and then prayed to Mary for help with everything else. She was as easy in all of this as she was content in her mansion and sure in her body. She was, in fact, an attractive proof text for the truth that had sat in my mother's dining room and chided me about the dangers to grace of unholy rectitude.

But if Mrs. Jim's morning visit had been a dramatic beginning to a happy relationship as well as to my new domesticity, our afternoon trip to the grocery store was neither. Shopping for food, in my opinion, is and always was in the same category as doing the laundry, washing dishes, or paying the bills. At their best, such chores are rendered almost invisible by their repetitiveness. At their worst, they are mildly annoying because they are never done with for very long, and mildly stressful because they require the expenditure of time and money. Grocery shopping should not, however, be the cause of emotional meltdown, or that was my unexamined opinion as I went cheerfully out the door with my husband just after two o'clock that Sunday afternoon.

In 1955, Memphis still had rather rigid blue laws. While I have no idea how Sabbath ordinances came to be called by their incongruous name, I do have a keen memory of the inconveniences they imposed on most Southern towns, large or small, at mid-century. In Memphis, the blue laws shut down everything except churches and public parks from Saturday evening until Monday morning with few exceptions. Obvious necessities like hospitals and police and fire departments were permitted skeleton crews as were public works and the telephone companies. There just were no stores, no gas stations, and, oddly enough, no pharmacies. Grocery stores sat somewhere in the middle of this great divide between the essential yesses and the nonessential nos.

To solve that conundrum, Memphis's blue laws allowed grocery stores to be open until six o'clock on the Sabbath, but prohibited them from selling nonessential and/or work-provoking goods until after one o'clock, that is, until after morning services were over and before evening ones could begin. Thus, one could buy milk all day, but one could not buy the coffee to put the milk into until after one o'clock and before six. The reason was regarded as blatantly obvious: coffee has to be perked, boiled, or dripped; milk requires none of the above. To further assure the absolute integrity of the system, each grocery also had to drape all the shelf and bin areas where the prohibited goods were stocked. The draping was undoubtedly an irritant for the grocer, but the undraping was pure vexation for customers. It meant, effectively speaking, that most stores were not really operational until close to two o'clock.

In the winter this added delay was not so dreadful, but in the summer things were different. In the summer nobody in his or her right mind would go grocery shopping at two in the afternoon in Memphis, Tennessee, especially not in un-air-conditioned cars. There was not a vegetable short of a turnip that could survive a trip in that heat without wilting beyond repair. There certainly was not a cut of meat that would survive for more than a few hours after it, even if refrigerated. Things like butter and cheese lost their contours permanently, and milk followed the path of meat toward early demise. So when I say I was cheerful at two o'clock on that first Sunday, I mean cheerful within reason. We were off to accomplish a necessary chore under awkward circumstances and only because we really could not wait until Monday morning. We had skipped breakfast and eaten the last of Mother's picnic for lunch because we were down to $32.67 between us, and according to our budget, that was supposed to last until the fifteenth. It certainly had to last in those ATM-less days until the university opened for classes and Sam could cash a check at the bursar's office. If we were going to eat supper, we were definitely going to have to cook it at home. In an unstocked apartment, that meant the grocery store.

We had no grocery list as we left. I had begun one, but Sam had almost immediately stopped me because, according to him, we could not possibly make a list since we had no idea what the market's specials and promotional items would be that afternoon. To the extent that I had ever thought about the matter—which was little, if any—I had always seen grocery shopping as divided into two separate types of activity. There was the routine, day-by-day business of fresh meat, bread, and produce, and there was the once-a-month business of staples, household supplies, and those commodities either not available or not affordable in neighborhood groceries. Though different in substance, both required a list. For the routine foodstuffs, the list was called in and the goods delivered. For the major purchases, the list got taken to a store where everything on it was collected into a buggy, paid for, and hauled home with a certain dispatch. Given this clear-cut and long-standing scenario, Sam's position seemed to me to be rather inefficient and time-consuming, but other than that, it was irrefutably logical. We set out list-less.

I had never watched Sam shop for groceries before. To be honest, I had never watched myself doing it either—had never thought of grocery shopping as a watchable exercise, in fact, until that Sunday afternoon. Once we arrived at the store, however, the man—his newly acquired denominator in my mind—was positively tedious he was so deliberate. Not only did every special have to be checked out, but almost every one of them had to be bought (in as much as each was a bargain). I, who had always bought what the weather felt like or the menu called for, was a bit unsettled to discover that what we ate was going to be determined by what was cheap without any regard to whether or not we liked that particular food, much less to whether or not it made a balanced meal with anything else we had. I protested a time or two, specifically that I detest rabbit in any form known to mankind for cooking it, but we ended up with two (it took us a week to eat them fried, baked, and finally barbecued). We spent a good twenty or twenty-five minutes just figuring unit costs per pound on all our staples, and thus ended up buying five pounds of corn meal instead of two, ten pounds of dried beans instead of one sackful, and four sticks of butter instead of one. I did protest these things as excessive beyond any stretch of good sense much less of our limited space, but to no avail.

At the checkout our bill was just over twenty-five of our thirty-two-plus dollars, and the hunter/gatherer in my husband was as happy as I ever hope to see him be. The only spot of discontent in his euphoria, as he explained to me on the way home, was that I appeared to be a profligate shopper whom he would have to oversee and instruct from now on. In short, Mrs. John C. Tickle had just crashed head on into Dr. Philip Wade Alexander, except that now the two were not only mirror images of each other but they had also crossed gender lines and gotten married. It was not a good afternoon, and no amount of tongue-in-cheek levity can change that fact. That having been said, however, the truth also is that any marriage of passion needs an edge on which to hone its affection, and the tensions and incompatibilities we discovered on that first Sunday afternoon have remained for five decades as the uncomfortable but effective edge in ours.

23.

MY FAVORITE ONE-LINER out of America's vast repertoire of one-liners has always been "Other than that, Mrs. Lincoln, how was the play?" It seems especially appropriate here, and the answer about the rest of that long-ago summer is that by grace and mercy it was, and remains, singular among all the summers of my life.

Sam's classes had begun on Wednesday. He was out the door by seven or seven-thirty each morning and sometimes not back in it until well after dark. I was alone at last and alive with the joy of a house, albeit a humble one, to keep and a home to make. Those first days are still a bright, shimmering memory in my head. If I lived them at a most unoriginal level of elation—and I very much doubt that my edenic content was very different from that of most other brides . . . If I lived them in an unremarkable delight, I also lived them consumed in unremarkable occupations. I unpacked and arranged, dusted and repositioned, unpacked some more, dusted again and then rearranged the whole configuration all over again. Every piece of everything we owned—bric-a-brac, underwear, cutlery, notepaper, it didn't matter—everything must have occupied at least three separate locations in that boxy apartment before my first days of wifedom were over.

Those days themselves were few in number, however. Like the five-year-old I had been when life gave me a doll house and started to train me for this new job of mine, I reveled only briefly in the warmth of my own domestic imagination. After that, the laundry kicked in, thank God . . . and this time the capitalized "G" lies at the heart of the matter.

In the old days when medical education was a trial by fire as much as a course of study, and psychic and/or physical stamina almost as important to one's success as one's grade point, the laundry mattered. Once a young man arrived, as Sam had, at second-year status (there were only three women in Sam's class and therefore not yet enough to affect the university's nouns and pronouns of reference), he was expected to appear each morning in a stiffly starched, impeccably ironed, blindingly white lab coat, one that had to be pristine each day. Even worse was the expectation that a second-year man would unhesitatingly change his coat for a fresh one during the course of the day should the Memphis heat and the university's lack of air-conditioning prove stronger than the inordinate amounts of starch in his jacket.

Sam had bought his coats before he had left for Johnson City. He had even unwrapped and hung them in one of Mrs. Jim's spare closets so they would be ready. That wasn't the problem. The problem was that because they cost a fortune, there were only six of the things. The even greater problem was that the laundry charged a dollar a pop to bleach, starch (vulcanize, actually), and press a coat, a routine and ongoing expense so far beyond the pale of our budget as to not be even visible. Closely related to both those problems was the fact that starching and ironing one of those lab coats by hand at home played out at about an hour a jacket, even with the help of Betty Crocker. What Betty and I could not do, and never could, was the blindingly white part of the equation. Civilization simply never made a domestic bleach strong enough to chase out all the blood, tissue, chemicals, and general detritus of a medical student's clothing. Thus the compromise.

I never knew whether or not Peery's Laundromat (which in those days was not a self-help operation as its name would now signify, but a bank of commercial washing machines run by Mrs. Peery on clothes that had been presorted and pretreated by their owners) or Hurlburt's Laundry (which had a disconcertingly familiar name for me, the compiler of my Bible storybook and the owner of that laundry being the only two Hurlburts I had ever heard of). I never knew whether or not those two family-owned businesses were just Good Samaritans in a medical neighborhood or whether they actually made some small profit off the arrangement; but both of them would professionally bleach those coats, giving them back to us unstarched and unironed for a dime a coat. And both of them were located just across Poplar and south a matter or no more than five or six blocks. Thus it was that on my second Monday morning as a housewife, I betook myself and my sack of four lab coats—we had got down to the wire while I tried to prove I could bleach them at home—and headed out on foot for Hurlburt's, the closer of the two laundries.

It had not dawned on me up until that July morning that I had never lived in a city before, much less that I had never walked around alone in one before. I stood on the curb in front of 1094, looked across four lanes of traffic with no signal lights in sight anywhere and perceived immediately that I had a problem for which I had been singularly unprepared by any previous experience or education. Laundry sack and all, I had to get across that street if I were to be a serious and dutiful wife, though I honestly suspect now that I was driven to courage less by love and duty than by my fear of shame in front of Sam should I decide to tuck tail and run.

I watched the west-bounds for a break—it took me an embarrassingly protracted period of time to locate a break I trusted myself in—made it to the center, stood exultant while a new wave of west-bounds fanned my back and an onslaught of east-bounds polished my front. One foot back or one foot forward, I realized, and I was dead. One foot back or one foot forward . . .

Like every child reared in mountain terrain, I had grown up aware of the call of the precipice. Like every child proximate enough to roam in mountain terrain with familiarity and frequency, I had stood more than a few times as an adolescent on that crumbling margin where the edge of an asphalt road gives way to a verge of gravel and beyond that to the loamy, untrustworthy rim of a deep and rocky valley. I had stood in such places, allowing my feet to lose their hold as bits of rock and earth slipped out from beneath them and tumbled downward. Always I had jumped back, but only at the last minute and always with an almost sweet regret. It was not that I wished to throw myself into those green and fecund abysses, but that the tease of the possibility and the enticement of a knowledge beyond the ken of all knowing were always there, always splendidly present just on the other side of the waiting valley . . .

One foot back or one foot forward . . . The traffic zipped along all around me while I stood in the midst of it tasting for the first time in several years that remembered sweetness, that faint rush of longing and amazement that are the beauty of the sirens' song in any place or time.

I made it the rest of the way across Poplar, of course, and with considerably less deliberation and hesitation than originally, my head now being more occupied with memories than with immediacies. I was walking south on Waldran toward Hurlburt's, still lugging the lab coats and still absorbed in my own thoughts, when I glanced down and discovered that there was an impoverished patch of grass growing like a border along the sidewalk beside me. What church or apartment building could have afforded or maintained even so modest a pretense of a lawn in that section of town is beyond me now, but there it was anyway, just to my left. I

stopped and looked down at it, startled at first by its presence and then curious within myself that I had been startled. Grass, like the mountains of a
few moments earlier, had obviously dropped away from my circumstances
as easily as baby fat drifts off a toddler. They were caught, like photographs,
in the album of my used-to-be's, and instead of them I now had . . . ? I
turned toward the honking, raucous traffic weaving impatiently in and out
of itself before me. Instead of grass and mountains, I realized, I now had
the city or perhaps, said more accurately, I now had "city" as a frame of
reference as well as a place.

Let me say just here and before I go any farther that I have never lost
my sense of the romance of a city. It makes no difference how many times
I fly into New York or Boston, San Francisco or Chicago, my reaction is
the same. Just as the pilot begins to circle and the wings start their final
dance of lift-and-dip, I still have that same rush of need to embrace it all
that I first had when Sam cut the Bel Air's engine behind 1094 and told
me we were home. That, however, is a quirk of personality born of who
knows what. Being apprehended by the concept of "city" is quite something else; and while it may not be universal to all human beings, it certainly is not the quirk of only a few. That is to say that at that particular
moment on the July morning of my discovery, when I turned my back on
the grass beside me and turned my face to the fractured boulevard in front
of me, I also walked, however unintentionally, straight into Western religion's most ubiquitous pair of twinned metaphors.

The Psalmist had written—and had I not read and loved his words for
years?—"I will lift up mine eyes unto the hills, from whence cometh my
help. My help cometh from the Lord, which made heaven and earth. He
will not suffer thy foot to be moved; he that keepeth thee will not slumber. Behold, he that keepeth Israel shall neither slumber nor sleep." But I
had loved the singer's words for the sound of them, the rhythm of their cohesion, the flow of their mist-shrouded images. I had never, ever been able
to possess them for themselves. The grandeur to which they played seemed
always to me a bit overwrought, a bit out of proportion to the naturalness
of a mountain or even a whole range of mountains. As well for me to say,
"I will drag mine eyes down onto the meadow or walk them over toward
the stream," as to find commerce with divinity in hills.

Part of my childhood's puzzlement with the 121st Psalm was undoubtedly a result of the fact that my sheer familiarity with mountains made an

association between them and God seem slightly irreverent. As I had grown older, I had also perceived, and quite consciously so, that religious statements like the 121st that relate trees and rocks and hills to spiritual contact make me intellectually uncomfortable in direct proportion to how suggestive they are of human neuroses and/or pagan explanations. A city, on the other hand, I understood as I watched this one exercising its enormous vitality against the backdrop of the July heat—a city is a different thing. Clearly, a city—any city—is like a mountain range in the sense that both are made of intransigent principles and circumstances as well as of fluid, living things. Like a mountain range, too, a city is an impenetrable (not to mention highly addictive) mix of anonymity and intimacy and of the liberty and vulnerability each of those ways of being brings to us. But unlike the eternal hills of poetry, city is us. We are the stuff of it. Its grandeur and accomplishments are the first fruits of our longings; its very existence, the dynamic and roiling expression of our imperfect yearnings. And therein lay a difference I had never engaged before that very moment, a distinction I had never even been equipped to perceive before that moment.

"If I forget thee, O Jerusalem, let my right hand forget her cunning." The Psalmist had written those words, too.

And "Jerusalem is builded as a city that is compact together: Whither the tribes go up, the tribes of the Lord, unto the testimony of Israel, to give thanks unto the name of the Lord. Pray for the peace of Jerusalem: they shall prosper that love thee. Peace be within thy walls, and prosperity within thy palaces. For my brethren and companions' sakes, I will now say, Peace be within thee."

And "Lift up your heads, O ye gates; and be ye lifted up, ye everlasting doors; and the King of glory shall come in. Who is this King of glory? The Lord strong and mighty, the Lord mighty in battle."

Had I not loved all these words of his also? Had I not spent hours of my near-sleep in reading them to myself until they flowed like the breath of me, in and out unthinkingly? Even though I could not in those college days plumb the nature of their hold on me, had I not claimed them anyway?

And what of all the other, half-remembered passages that now stirred me? What, for instance, of the Apocalypse? "I saw a new heaven and a new earth: for the first heaven and the first earth were passed away; and there was no more sea. And I John saw the holy city, new Jerusalem, coming down from God out of heaven, prepared as a bride adorned for her husband."

And what of Isaiah who had put mountain and city together, though always before to my faint displeasure at what I saw as a confusion of metaphors? What of "And it shall come to pass in the last days that the mountain of the Lord's house shall be established in the top of the mountains, and shall be exalted above the hills; and all nations shall flow unto it. And many people shall go and say, Come ye, and let us go up to the mountain of the Lord, to the house of the God of Jacob; and he will teach us of his ways, and we will walk in his paths; for out of Zion shall go forth the law and the word of the Lord from Jerusalem. And he shall judge among the nations, and shall rebuke many people: and they shall beat their swords into plowshares, and their spears into pruning hooks: nation shall not lift up sword against nation, neither shall they learn war anymore."

And what, I thought suddenly and just as clearly as if the poets themselves were watching the traffic with me, what to make of a wistful T. S. Eliot as he watched a crowd flowing over London Bridge and, yearning toward them, heard again Dante's lament of "I had not known death had undone so many." What of that?

I half-ran the rest of the way to Hurlburt's, threw Sam's coats at a heavily perspiring clerk, grabbed my claim check, and half-ran the whole way back home, totally oblivious now to traffic and its hazards. Once there, it took me a few minutes to locate the right volumes in the still-unfamiliar bookcase, but once I had, I took Mr. Thomas Stearns Eliot out onto my sun-drenched porch and set us both down at the egg-yolk yellow dinette with the wobbly chair. Thus and in that place began my life as an intentional Christian.

24.

For the forty-five years that stretched from the summer of 1955 to the changing of the millennium in 2000, I rather tacitly assumed that I was one of only a few Christians who had ever been rescued from spiritual stasis by T. S. Eliot—that is, who had ever been lifted out of the cultural mind-set of Christianized theism and set back down again in the highly personal role of confessing Christian. This presumption of differentness, for once in my life, was not born of arrogance, but of a kind of embarrassment that made me shy of sharing with others just how irregular, nonclerical, and non-pentecostal had been my own passage from hereditary to convicted Christian. In the closing days of the twentieth century, however, when the whole of Western society fell into the silly distraction of making lists of every imaginable thing that had been halfway noteworthy in the passing millennium, there near the top of list after list of the best Christian writers sat T. S. Eliot.

My suspicion is that Mr. Eliot, while he might be pleased by this positioning, would also be somewhat befuddled by it. That is, I don't think he saw himself as an evangelizer so much as an Anglican who heard pieces and parts of a mystery and recorded them. The fact that it is the poetry of religion and not its doctrine that persuades the soul was for him, I suspect, a corollary to his occupations, but not their source or reason. Certainly on that first day of my long trek toward confessional living, I sat on the sunporch from late morning until late afternoon at last hearing *The Waste Land* for what it is, a magnificent intimation of a music too contoured and full for mere theology.

Seers, of whom artists and poets are the most accessible order, are always pieces of a chain, grip knots along a cord of rope that comes from what cannot be fathomed and moves on toward what cannot be envisioned. In some dumb, half-thought-out way, I had probably understood that for two or three years at least, maybe more. Eliot sees through the lens of Dante as Dante had seen through the lens of Virgil who had seen through the lens of Homer who had seen through the lens of the mythmakers. Or if the ordering were reversed, then the recorders of myth and sacred symbol had passed to Homer devices and conventions that he had passed as tools to Virgil who had passed them and some of his own contriving as tools to Dante who had passed them and more as ways of seeing and saying to Eliot who earlier that morning had used them all to expose the essentialness of noisy traffic in a raucous American river town. It was the relevance of the thing, its immediacy, that had shaken me.

Back home, once I had checked Eliot's lines to confirm that they were as I had remembered them, the inevitable second question was how. Not how in general, but how in particular and with what effect. The most basic class in art history or literary criticism will answer the "how in general" one quite effortlessly. Art in any form works and lasts in proportion to its creator's ability to represent and interpret our constancy as an order of creatures, the solid sameness of our reach and our origin, the inescapable "am-ness" that is each of us. The "how in particular" is a bit trickier.

In my own case that July day it presented as a question about what after all really had been folded into the stoicism of the privileged Aurelius or the dualism of the cerebral Plato. What within them had imbued me with a sense of spiritual, rather than academic, impoverishment when I had had to set them aside for a while? What had it been within Virgil that actually protected him, but not many of his peers, from obsolescence throughout the passing of two millennia and evolving circumstances? All well and good to say, as was true, that Virgil's canon, but not those of his contemporaries, had been spared from the bonfires of later Christian ages because he alone seemed to write within the prophetic tradition; but what did that mean? What was the prophetic tradition and how had it equipped the poet for survival long after the centuries of political danger and censorship had passed? For that matter, what exactly was it within Dante—and where exactly within the vaulted beauty of his *Divine Comedy*—that made him the guide of choice nearly seven hundred years later in a seamy London he had never known? What and where, as well, was the strength that carried his words securely enough so I had heard the echo of them above rude traffic that very morning?

Those are questions of the particular that, because of their greater specificity, can entertain scholars and theorists for whole lifetimes. I knew that. By age twenty-one I had certainly studied under and read my fair share of some solid critical thinkers; but critics tend to particularize by focusing on a single artist and to explicate by discussing objective things like craft and available mediums or vaguer ones like voice and eye or affections and physical health. What if particularity were both simpler and more complex than that? What if particularity lay not in cells of time and situation but rather, like the rings of Dante's Paradise, in levels or tiers of intimacy with What Wants to Be Known?

Such a question—such a set of possibilities—marks the beginning not of a fact-finding exploration with a terminus but of a process; or at least it did so for me. Where the process led me first and almost immediately was to two things. It led me first to the realization that while I had up until that very day believed in God as a distant, if irrefutable, given and in Jesus as a semifictionalized example of that given in real-time application, Eliot worked from a base of personal familiarity with both of them. In fact, what just a few minutes of rereading led me to was the sure knowledge that whatever it was that Eliot was about, it most certainly was not in response to theories, givens, examples, or applications. Rather, it was in response to something as visible, central, and experienced for him as a cup of tea or an afternoon stroll—Something that was as much borne in his rhythms as his words, and as much captured and exposed in his choosing to see a thing as in his choice of words to depict what he saw.

The same process led me to a second discovery as well. It led me to understand that for Eliot—for this poet above all poets, this thinker of a depth unsounded by any other of our contemporaries—for this man all history is of but one telling. All history, for Eliot, leads inexorably and irrefutably to only one purpose: God's, for the glory of His Name. Nothing—not confluence or paradox, not able story or falsified accounts, not beauty of word or grotesqueries of image—nothing could escape from the all-incorporating reach of that purpose. Which is why I can only say that my conversion was effected in a most irregular, nonclerical, and totally nonpentecostal manner. In the beginning, that is, all I wanted was to test Eliot's reality and that of his mentors. The fact that I was permanently convicted and consumed by their reality in the process was as much a surprise to me as birth itself must always be, if only we could remember it.

Almost as if by chance thereafter, my days fell into a kind of loose schedule that paced the rhythms of my physical life with those of my newly discovered religio-intellectual and aesthetic one. In the mornings before the breakfast dishes were cleared away and washed up, I would sit at the dinette table with the Psalms before me. Following Glenn Clark's instructions, I asked nothing of those prayer-poems; I just read one, two, sometimes three of them. As Clark had also urged, I offered from time to time the set prayers to which the Psalms so cordially incline us—the Our Father, the Gloria, the Doxology.

Whatever the faults of Glenn Clark's theology may have been, here in this one place his teaching was superb and served me well. I had not, before he taught me, known how to meditate upon the set prayers of the faith, or even that such an exercise was there to be done. But now, with his guidance and the surrounding benediction of the Psalms' phrases and refrains, I began to pull apart the ancient prayers, peering into them like a child into a box . . . like a delighted child into a just-discovered box, in fact.

". . . As it was in the beginning and is now and evermore shall be. . . ." Eliot's unity. And let all creatures cry "Glory!," each in its own tongue, each in its own way.

"Our Father," replete in its "ourness" with the messiness of confrater-nity and the expectations of a mutual grace.

". . . Who art in Heaven. . . ." Where? . . . Where? A place far away? Every part of my experience and Mr. Hornaday's lectures told me no. Heaven? Somewhere, I thought, just on the other side of seeing, but very now and very here.

And what to make of this "Who" as opposed to all the "whos" of Greco-Roman myth? Why always "Who" anyway? Why not the "Its" of golden calves and sacred poles?

And so the questions went. Some of them really were meditative. The bulk of them, at least in the beginning, were academic. A few were theo-logical, but in the main only primitively so. All of them, though, were of a piece, held together by the context in which I was pursuing them and, more especially, by the company in which they had come to me. It would be almost ten years before I would discover, actually with some amuse-ment, that what I was doing in those first few minutes of each new day was reinventing the wheel; what I was doing, in point of fact, was some-thing remarkably close to the office of Terce in the Liturgy of the Hours. But what twenty-one-year-old lapsed Presbyterian living in Memphis, Tennessee, in 1955 knew that? Certainly not me.

Because I was compulsive, however, even at twenty-one, I had to ac-tually wash those dishes and make our bed before I could consider a day as having officially started. Once I had done these things, once every dish was in the drainer and all the pillows in place, it was Eliot's time, or perhaps better said, it was time for trying to backtrack along the trail Eliot had come from. I went to the porch again, this time with my Bible, my refer-ence copy of Gayley's *Classic Myths*, and my notebook.

I had brought the zippered notebook with me to Memphis almost as a caprice, a bit of sentimental fondness thrown into the mix at the last minute of our sorting. Now it served me well. Worn, familiar, self-contained, its flaps already sprung and receptive, the notebook became my first studio, a kind of portable variation on the playroom I had left behind me. This time, however, it was words and not clocks or dolls that were my subject as well as my object. If I began on my first morning or two simply by making notes and recording ideas, I had begun within two or three more to write. I had begun to write, that is, as a writer writes, although I am almost positive that I did not make that distinction until a year or two later.

I had always written as a child reared in a word-laden environment could normally be expected to write. I had employed words with acumen and sensitivity and with delight as well, this last being always a good sign. I had "written" my first formal piece—a backyard melodrama produced by my older playmates in a neighbor's garage to resounding neighborhood applause—at seven. I had learned, irrevocably, from that experience the uncanny power well-tempered words can wield over one's betters, as well as the rather ironic gratification of being praised by them for having done so. No, it was not that I had not written before or never published before or never made some small sums of money before. I had. I just had no more been a writer before that summer than I had been a Christian. An adequate wordsmith and an eccentric cultural conformist, I would believe, but not a writer or a Christian.

In hindsight I know now that any psychologist (or even half-astute student of human behavior, for that matter) could look at my 1955 July and August and see that what appeared to me at the time to be dramatic amazements and tectonic shifts without prior history was really quite the opposite. Looking back now, I, too, see the same thing; I, too, see only an emerging adult who had just been given one of a young life's greatest gifts, a holiday.

Life was going to sustain me for those two months whether I did anything or not, but life was not going to interrupt me either. In all truth, there was neither an event nor a person, all things being equal, *to* interrupt me. I knew no one except my husband and my landlady, and neither of them was around me all day, much less desirous of being interrupted by me even when they were. I had no obligations aside from a few household ones, and even they were fluid still, our domestic patterns and mutual expectations having not yet been closely defined. I wanted nothing, and no one and no thing wanted anything of me, yet every one and every thing seemed perfectly content to have me around as companion and/or observer. It was, in summary, a holiday, a time of physical and emotional well-being when the self's normal defenses of tension, focus, image, and desire were in abeyance, a time when everything that had been planted could safely creep up through the soil and begin to live in consciousness.

When I say, therefore, that I was transmuted from an adequate craftswoman to a writer on that porch in that green time of summer, I mean simply that unself-consciously and as naturally as if I had known all my life how to do so, I discovered then and there to appreciate the clarity of early morning for seeing the true edges and definition of things; the imperative of sustained writing even if the phrases and sentences are as uninspired as finger exercises; and the skill, like a beagle in the autumn hunt, of following without question the scent, the perfume, the irresistible musk of Keats's truth that is beauty.

I wrote poetry in those first hours of the morning. Most of it was images awkwardly connected to one another. Most of it, even when rhythmic, was still badly disciplined. Most of it was slender in its soul and young in its grasp . . . most, but not all. Even I knew that some of it had the cachet of the glen, that some of it carried the suggestion and first melodies of a music yet to be scored.

I will never be a poet, of course; I was never intended to be, but I didn't know that in 1955. In fact, I remember that by the end of those summer weeks I rather assumed I was a poet, or at the very least, so intended. Eventually, years of trying would show me otherwise, but they would show me as well that my weeks and later my months and years of apprenticeship to poetry were the optimal education for anyone who wished to ply the writer's craft. If I am not a poet, as I am not, then I am nonetheless a most grateful graduate of poetry's tutelage, and nowhere am I more indebted than for my freshman weeks as a holidaying bride under her instruction.

25.

MY MORNING HOURS of writing were also hours of reading, though not of poetry; that came later in my day. Rather, the mornings on the porch belonged to the Bible and Gayley's as much as to the notebook; I was busy chasing Eliot's patterns, happily busy chasing both him and his mentors to their sources. I who no more than a year previous, would have been scandalized to find myself reading Gayley's *Classic Myths* for its stories rather than for its charts and explanations of literary allusions, now fell to devouring them like a ravening beast, and most assuredly not for their referencing value. This time I was reading for the threads of connection that wove them together into a cohesive, utile aesthetic. I had had no idea! Equally as aberrant, I who had so passionately adored *Hurlburt's* as story was now scouring the Hebrew Old Testament for the progressive revelation and centrality of which each of his tales was but a motley part. I had had no idea!

Dotted all through both the Greco-Roman and the Hebrew stories, of course, are the similarities and the familiar (though some were not so familiar at that stage of my life) parallels that comparative mythologists have become so fond of noting. Between the two of them, for instance, Venus and Eve certainly can make one wonder what ever was wrong with apples in prehistory. The Titans bear a wondrous resemblance to the Nephilim, and Ajax to Og of Bashan. Tamar and Dinah routinely seem to have embarrassed Dr. Hurlburt into silence, but goodness knows both Professor Gayley and Homer seemed comfortable enough with Hera as well as Helen.

The similarities and the parallels, however, whether familiar or newly unearthed, were not what I was digging my way toward on those mornings, because academic curiosity was not the tool I was digging with. I was digging toward my own need with Dante's assumption that Virgil's command of classical mythology could illuminate Hebrew/Christian history and with Eliot's blatant assumption that Dante was correct. I was digging toward God with Dante's assumption that every human story and every twist of human circumstance was part of, or attracted to, or decipherable in terms of, Hebrew and Christian sacred narrative and with Eliot's blatant assumption that Dante was correct on that score as well. I was, in effect, teaching myself to till by watching two master groundskeepers, both of whom knew for a personal, experienced fact that God was the material as well as the point of their efforts.

Day after day, my mornings wandered down dozens of such sometimes open and sometimes opaque paths, and each noontime I came back smaller and often sorer than when I had left. I would eat my lunch occupied as much by my thoughts as by my food.

On most summer days the porch was too warm by midday for comfortable reading, so after lunch I would do one of two things according to the day of the week. On midweek days, after I had put away my notebook, the Bible, and my *Classic Myths*, I simply moved back inside to the apartment. Lacking as it did any useful windows, the old nursery was always dark as well as moderately cool. It was so dark in fact that from the beginning, I had had to leave at least one light on all day just so I could find my way around the furniture and through our constantly shifting piles of personal possessions. The pooling of lamplight, however, mixed with the shadows just beyond its reach and the stillness of an empty house, creates an ambience even at midday and even for the young. So it was after lunch and in the apartment itself that on most Tuesdays, Wednesdays, and Thursdays I would at last take down my volumes of Eliot or Dante (and sometimes of Longfellow or Whitman or Auden, all of whom, by extension, I had also begun to recognize) and settle down on the sofa to read. On most Mondays and Fridays, by contrast, I had to attend to Sam's socks after lunch.

Socks were our other laundry problem. There were no vented Nikes in 1955, and they would not have been permitted second-year men, even if there had been. Instead, second-year men wore wing-tips. Laced-up wing-tips undoubtedly were a sight more agreeable to wear than were the low-heeled pumps second-year women wore, but that was small advantage. The truth about wing-tips in summer is that they are a perpetual steam bath for the feet laced into them. Sam had sampled every foot potion and salve known to science during the previous summer, trying to keep his feet from falling victim to something that looked, for all the world, very much like jungle rot. Unfortunately, none of his tinctures and creams had worked very well, and even the few that did had not done so for very long.

He had complained bitterly about his problem during his time at home and, after our honeymoon especially, about how much he dreaded another four months of walking around in the sauna that is a Memphis summer. Mamaw had, however, made a suggestion that, like most of her suggestions, turned out to be right on the money. Wear two or three pairs of cotton socks at a time, and the cotton will wick the moisture out of your shoes and back into the air. The idea was indeed on the money, but regrettably, neither Hurlburt's nor Peery's was in the business of washing sweaty socks on the cheap.

Mamaw had anticipated this problem as well and, to solve it, had given me one of the two old washboards with which she herself had begun keeping house. I had seen washboards many a time before, of course, but only hanging somewhere in abandonment, never in use. Mamaw had assured me, however, that I would be grateful in the long run, and she was right about that, too. After lunch, therefore, on Mondays and Fridays, and sometimes in between, I took not poetry, but a mountain of soured and/or drenched socks into our marble bathroom, drew that massive tub a quarter full of hot water, put two pillows on the floor to protect my knees, set the washboard into the curve of the tub's back, and commenced the business of scrubbing my husband's socks.

It doesn't take many minutes of working a washboard while kneeling upon a marble floor before something begins to protest. Usually it was my knuckles that gave out first, and I would roll off the pillows, change the water, and decide to let the whole mess soak for a while. When exactly it was, in this long, damp process, that my after-lunch preoccupations slipped away from the business of doing laundry and into the business of studying the bathtub room itself, I am honestly not sure. My progress into the heart of its subtleties was too gradual for that. The truth remains, nonetheless, that although the space certainly had drawn me from the moment Sam had first shown it to me, its hold on me had become, by the end of July, much nearer to the grip of an astonishment than to the pull of a small delight.

At first it had seemed no more than sensible that, lying flat on the cool floor and waiting for Sam's socks and my water and soap to do their thing together, I should use the time to think my way back through the pages of poetry, history, and myth that I had worked with earlier in the day. Around me as I would drop into this deliberate act of recall, the wavy sunlight from the massive window would suffuse across marble walls that glowed but, mysteriously, like the forsythia of my tunnel, did not heat. Above my head and to the side of the window, the elegantly cupped washbasin with its perfect porcelain pedestal ran a constant trickle of cold water, the faucet's antique washer being no longer able to restrain it; but even that small annoyance would soon become indistinguishable from the musical play of a fountain.

In my mother's living room, as in the living rooms and parlors of many a post–World War I home, there was a print of Maxfield Parrish's *Daybreak*. Large and framed in a substantially gilded molding, the Parrish was almost an icon for my mother, who refused to have it hung anywhere else than in this honored spot and who refused to part with it long after its inks had faded into a near unanimity of hue. When I was a child and the print was still in its glory, it had fascinated me, too.

Against a distant background of pink-tinged and just-suggested blue mountains, two female figures occupy the print's foreground. One of them, a young woman dressed in a short, gossamer toga and with her cropped, curly hair confined by a delicate fillet, is lying on the marble porch of what appears to have once been a Greek temple. At least a column or two that are reminiscent of one still stand just beyond her head. She rests with one leg bent up and one arm raised across her forehead as if to shield her still-sleep-darkened soul from rousing out of its dreams. Bending over her is the other female form, this one scarcely clothed at all but with the same classically styled hair. Her hands upon her knees, the apparition leans almost playfully over the sleeper, trying to entice her into the soft glow that limns valleys as the sun breaks across mountain peaks and before the dawn light can wash down into the meadows below.

In 1955, *Daybreak* was as close as I had ever been to a Greek or Roman temple. Even given my erstwhile major in classical languages, *Daybreak* was as close to one as I had ever really wanted to be, in fact. Or it was until I took up washing socks in one.

I can remember that one afternoon fairly early in my laundress days (though, strangely, I cannot remember precisely which afternoon it was in that summer of discoveries), lifting my left leg to ease my back as I lay waiting on the marble floor, I was amused by the thought that with my short, curly hair and my loose housedress, I could be taken for a poor woman's edition of *Daybreak*. Diverted by this conceit from my thoughts of Gayley and God and Eliot, I raised my left arm and deliberately set it across my forehead. Softly, smoothly, I was in . . . not inside the print, of course, but inside what made it an icon for my mother, inside the experience that was its seduction as well as its content.

I am not an Orthodox Christian of any flavor—Greek, Russian, Eastern, Armenian, Whatever—nor have I ever been a visitor at Orthodox worship more than two or three times in my life; but central to Orthodoxy, as I understand it, is the iconostasis and the veneration of icons within sacred space. For twenty-one years my Presbyterian self and later my young Anglican self had cringed before such notions as icons and venerations, cringed almost to the extreme of wanting to lift two crossed forefingers before me and run as fast as possible in the other direction. The afternoon in the bathtub room made a humbler woman of me.

On the other side of the Parrish print there was an idea of which the print was the expression. More to the point, that idea was so much more actual than the print as to make the latter seem to the reality as an outside window is to a lovely and inviting room.

When in the 1960s and '70s talk of altered states of consciousness became as common as houseflies and just about as astute, I was to spend a good deal of time listening to what those conversations were actually about and then trying to lay their descriptions upon my own experience. Rightly or wrongly, it seems to me that the experiences of my college bathroom retreat and even of the forsythia tunnel were ones of joy, in part at least, because they enabled an expansion of my self out into its surroundings. Those experiences and times enabled a traveling abroad of my awareness. There was to those hours even a kind of playful daring that invites an alteration of consciousness by allowing the self to dissolve its borders and to lay down its role as gatekeeper between two worlds.

What happened in my Maxfield Parrish moments was very different. I simply as myself stepped over or through. That may be altered consciousness; but if so, there's a large part of me that would ask for a more specific definition of altered consciousness before we go applying it here. I would argue that where I was, the consciousness is absolutely intact; it is simply intact in a different place.

Suffice it to say here, however, that by whatever name one uses, that sock-washing afternoon was the first time (though hardly the last) that I had ever traveled anywhere even close to the land of my mother's afternoon journeys or of Dr. T.'s midday ones. Of course there was the problem that while they both got where they went by prayer, I seemed to have arrived by sheer blind luck. But even on that first afternoon I was experienced enough to know that though I might be in a territory somewhat similar to, and probably even in the same general landmass as, theirs, I most certainly was not in the same place as they. For one thing, I had no desire to pray where I was. Where I was, it was enough just to be and, far more significantly, there was in that place none of the otherness that undergirds prayer.

Where I was, I concluded, must be close as well to the "inexplicable splendor" Mr. Eliot found in "the Ionian white and gold" of the walls at the Church of Magnus Martyr; and if Eliot himself declined to dissect that splendor, then better and far wiser simply to experience this peculiar tesseract of mine than to chafe at any obscurities in its mapping.

26.

READING POETRY and scrubbing socks may sit at opposite ends of the aesthetic spectrum, but they had one thing in common in 1955. They both had to come to an end in time for me either to iron Sam's coats or, on the good afternoons, walk to Hurlburt's to exchange dirty coats for clean ones. This part of my life varied according to where in the unremitting coat cycle Sam's laboratory classes and Memphis's weather had put us in any given week.

Although I have always rather enjoyed ironing for its mindlessness and its reassuring sense that one really is accomplishing something, I hated those coats. Ironing them was like ironing a pastiche of circus canvas and just about as likely to eventuate in anything crisp and professional. My frustration with ironing the coats, and within just a few days my outright exasperation, were not the reason, however, for my joy in the afternoons of walking to Hurlburt's. My joy in those afternoons emanated, instead, from my hours of reading about Eliot's sawdust-floored restaurants and public bars.

I had never been in a bar in my life before 1955, primarily because there were no "bar" bars to go to in the places where I had lived before. That is to say that I had been to an isolated dive or two and found them unsociably loud and entirely threatening; they hardly seemed the stuff of good sense much less of poetry. A true bar, on the other hand, is the functionary of its neighborhood. A true bar is a pub, not a bar. As a pub it presupposes not just any neighborhood, but a particular one of some density which it serves not as a private home or a public husting would, but as "that third good place" of satisfactory human intimacy.

A bar is a continuous conversation, albeit sometimes a laconic or even silent one, that is as fluid as the needs of its foot traffic and as constant as the idiosyncrasies of its regulars. A good one is a predictable coterie of familiars with whom one may or may not have much truck in the larger world, but with whom one can enjoy a state of near empathy inside the smaller one of the bar's walls. Not that I knew any of this in 1955. What I did know, however (and without even realizing at first that I knew it), was that there was a bar on my way to Hurlburt's, or if not on it, then at least close enough for me to see the sign up a side street. I was curious; that was all, just curious.

My decision, one afternoon early in the coat parade, to turn up that street on my way home and check out the Pigskin Bar and Grill seemed a matter of no great moment to me at the time. It never once occurred to me as I was turning that my presence in the Pigskin would be anything other than ordinary, either for me or the Pigskin; and to the barkeeper's credit, it never was. I walked in, my clean coats rolled up in a sack in my arms, and immediately was as blind as the proverbial bat . . . but then I thought I had gone deaf as well. The place was abruptly as quiet as death is supposed to be, again proverbially speaking. By the time my eyes had adjusted enough for me to see through the darkness (which turned out not to be dark after all, just restfully dim), the barkeep had picked up a towel and was wiping his hands. "Hey, Bud, let the young lady by," was all he said to the Quasimodo lookalike sitting in the bend of the bar just where the stool and the front door made a tight passage. Bud grumbled something I couldn't hear, somebody farther up the bar gave him an "Ah, Bud!," and the hum was back in the place.

I went, not to the bar itself, but to the center table in a row of five tables that paralleled the bar and ran along the other side wall. I threw my sack on the table, sat down, and perceived without too much effort that I was the only woman in the place. That didn't disturb me as much, however, as the barkeeper's saying, "You want a beer, Miss?" Heavens, no, I didn't want a beer! I didn't drink alcohol often enough for the thought to even have occurred to me, and I certainly didn't have any money. If I had any, I thought, I'd be paying Hurlburt's to do the blasted coats and not drinking beer with it. Instead, I said out loud, "No, thanks, just to sit awhile."

"Go ahead," he said. "Be our guest," and went back to arguing what I took to be local politics with some man at the far end of the bar. After a minute or two, as if he'd just suddenly thought of it, the barkeeper—his name, I discovered later, was Mike—poured a cup of coffee from somewhere and came around the bar, setting it in front of me. "Thought you might like a cuppa," he said.

"Thanks," I said.

"You live around here?"

"Yes, over on Poplar."

"Just move?"

"Yes."

"Husband at the university?"

"Yes."

"Good. You come back anytime you want to. Not many of the ladies come in here. Too bad, too. It'd pick the place up a bit." He turned his head and looked back toward the customer just three stools beyond Bud and right against the wall. "Hey, Gunner," he said, "her husband's at the university. You outta give her a few pointers."

"Maybe some other day," Gunner called back and finished his beer, banging the mug lightly on the bar to indicate his displeasure at its empty state.

I sat there as long as I dared dally, eavesdropping on the conversations and studying the grouping and regrouping of customers as they came and went; the neighborhood's three-to-eleven shift was apparently fortifying itself for a day's labor and the seven-to-three shift was definitely recovering from one. As Gunner, who was fifty if he were a day, rather stocky, and a seven-to-three'er, got up to leave, he paid his tab, and then came over to me. "I wasn't being rude," he said. "I'll talk tomorrow."

"Okay," I said, and he left; but I had heard enough to recognize the accent as well as seen enough to identify the body stock. Gunner was German and, unless I was crazy, not long away from home.

"He's a good man, Gunner is," Mike offered as the door closed. And that was the sum of my first day in the Pigskin. I thanked Mike for the coffee, picked up my coats, and went out into the life-defying heat.

I never went back to the Pigskin after the summer of 1955, and I couldn't have gone to it more than eight or ten times during it. There simply weren't that many weeks or walks to Hurlburt's. But I began my lifelong love affair with pubs and bars in the weeks and walks there were, as well as my lifelong respect for their role as way stations and sanctuaries.

I had figured out by my second visit to the Pigskin that I could afford a Coke, if not a beer, though about as often as not I was given coffee before I had a chance to ask for anything. Sometimes I gave up the center table for the companionship of a stool at the bar itself. Sometimes I went back to the table and sank, as one can so easily do in a good bar, into anonymity, occupying myself with just listening and enjoying. There were afternoons when I wanted my notebook and pen so desperately my fingers hurt for them, but I never brought either with me. I was afraid of offending my fellow customers or, worse, of transforming them into self-conscious performers. I listened and tried to remember.

Gunner was indeed German. A scientist and now in this country a medical assistant of sorts, he had lost his family in the war and come to Memphis because of the university. He was as alone as any man I have ever known, and the bar was, so far as I could ascertain, his only safe place. On the days when he was morose, no one fretted him; on the days when he was more cheerful, no one probed. They all just let it be, leaving it to Gunner to call his own shots in a way that seemed to me at the time to be the most guileless expression of charity I had ever watched.

I never learned the names of most of the other men, and they neither asked nor knew mine. I was "Hey there" when I went in and "See ya" or "Be good" when I left. But the Pigskin didn't need to know me in order to give me what I wanted. All the Pigskin had to do was to let me be a part of its daily human mix, let me be the observing and unobserved; and this it did.

The habitués of the Pigskin had a flow of conversation that had nothing to do with the economic, social, and intellectual circumstances from which I had come and in which I still belonged, at least more or less; but they did have some intriguing economic, social, and intellectual variations upon the themes we held in common: the shape of the world we were leaving to our kids (McCarthyism had long since peaked and hit the credibility skids in my world, but not in the Pigskin's); the proper role of the sexes (by which the men on their stools meant gender and occasionally turned to say, "No offense, young lady"); the fear of accident or breakup or layoff ("Jesus Christ, I don't know what me and the old lady will do if they get me").

There were, of course, more themes that we did not hold in common than that we did, but the discrepancy was due more to their age and level of adulthood than to anything else. "Can you lend me a sawbuck 'til tomorrow?" "Damned kid's driving her crazy and she's driving me right behind 'em both. Can't beat any sense into him, and I've sure as hell tried six ways from Sunday!" "Hey, Mike, you know anybody as has got a beat-up old truck he'd sell me for a couple of hundred? Mine's dead in the street in front of my place, and she ain't gonna fix this time." But always there were courtesies like those extended to Gunner, always generosities like my coffees; and sometimes there were even conventions and mores that brought me up short with their authenticity.

The requested sawbuck was almost always handed over to the asker by someone or other of the men at the bar. The only consistent exception, so far as I could ever see, was one man whose name I never caught—the regulars addressed him only as "Fella"—and whose requests for a loan were always refused as dispassionately as had been those of the hoboes in my father's alleyway; Fella apparently never got home with what he borrowed. It was a kind of group-administered code that I had never been privy to before. The question was not, as it would have been in my experience, whether or not one went gambling, whoring, and/or liquoring. The scandalous question apparently was whether or not one saw to his family before doing so.

The whole world, and most certainly the whole of Memphis, was Elvis-mad in 1955. Two of the afternoon regulars claimed to have worked for him at one time, and I was fascinated by the stature that that past contact had gained them among their present company at the Pigskin. Who even knew, I asked myself, whether the two of them were telling the truth or simply engaging in the name-dropping process we all try at one time or another . . . or I wondered that until I realized I believed the men, too. I believed them because they always said "Mr. Presley" when they told their anecdotes, even though everybody else said "Elvis" in telling theirs. The two of them had obviously gotten just close enough to the King to respect him. I had grown up on the old saw that familiarity breeds contempt, and I had observed for myself that great distance, by contrast, breeds a flip ir-reverence. Never before, however, had I considered the uses or the power of that station in-between where the vision is in focus. After the Pigskin, the stories and opinions of those who are midway of an issue took on an authority I had not known to assign them before.

When all of that is said and done, though, romanticizing a bar is much like romanticizing a city. The theory of each may be an easy subject for eulogy, but the underside of each is dark and messy. Eulogy is for what has been and now is static enough to be described; dark and messy are for what is and does not yet know what it shall be.

I never saw a fight in the Pigskin or knew Mike to tolerate any abuse of his clientele on the premises, but I saw a lot of posturing that was its own escape from private truth and I saw a lot of affection given that was too cheap to survive in the sun outside the place. I saw men who felt constantly and knew it, yet had nowhere else to go with what they felt. Whether ill-equipped by natural bent or past example for the work of introspection, whether tethered to a wracked acceptance by personal history and station, or whether just simply exhausted and externalized by their own constant necessities, they in the end all seemed to share one thing: The specter of serfdom was waiting for each of them just on the other side of the Pigskin's front door, waiting patiently until it was time to walk them home again.

The Pigskin, like the pubs of Eliot's London, was a temporary way sta-tion, an entry into a briefly manageable reality. It was a place of human in-tercourse for those who lived by necessity on the outside of their lives and whose measure of good and bad was taken on the yardstick of pain and pleasure. But Eliot was also right. In that place and in its transient relief the men of the Pigskin bar talked their souls to each other the way I talked mine only in secret to my self and God. I could no more have spoken the candor of their pain and the passion of their physical joys than I could have explained at that point what it was that prevented my doing so. But I knew one thing and knew it well. If these were the hollow men, then their hol-lowness was like that of the well-crafted violin, a cache of air resonant with our music.

27.

MY SUMMER DAYS may have been filled with adventures of the spirit, but my summer evenings were just as filled with adventures of the mind—though my husband thought, and said at the time, that those hours would have been more aptly described either as misadventures of the mind or else as adventures of no-mindedness. By whichever term, my summer evenings of 1955 were to uncover in me tastes and pleasures that I had never even suspected I had before, and that's adventure enough in anybody's dictionary.

When Sam came home at each day's end, we did the things that most married couples do. We talked and munched and flirted from the minute he came in until dinner was over, regrettably, and study time could be put off no longer. Once he had settled into his work, I began to clean up supper. Actually I was as intent usually on catching his signals about what type of evening this one was to be as on washing dishes and putting away food. Some evenings he wanted to talk, not about life but about the day's lectures and the next day's quizzes.

It didn't take me long to realize, of course, that a parrot or a mannequin could have served him quite as well as I on such evenings. Sam is what we now call an external thinker, which is to say that he has to vocalize what he's learning in order to fix it firmly in place. The result of those externalizing evenings, which extended for years beyond medical school into his internship, residency, and later fellowships, was two-pronged: I learned an alarming amount of half-understood physiology, pharmacology, pathology, and clinical medicine. It is an accomplishment that still annoys both of us to this day, for it makes me a difficult patient and sometimes a combative wife. That I can't help. The other result of Sam's need to talk everything out was my discovery of pop literature. That discovery has been far more productive than has my M.D.-by-proxy, although it originally was the reason for Sam's charges of misspent time and misguided mentation.

When two people are in a box for three and four hours at a time at the end of a full working day and when one of them is talking an on-again-off-again flow of half neo-Latin and half totally esoteric gibberish, it is very hard for the other to concentrate at any consequential or productive level. This is a provable fact and not my imagination. As a fact, it becomes particularly relevant when the first person expects of the second an occasional response of some cogency or, at worst, of feigned comprehension. On the other hand and equally important, when two people are engaged in this way, both must be occupied lest the idle one distract the occupied one. Enter Erle Stanley Gardner, stage left.

In many ways—I can hear the cries of "Heresy!" even as I say the words—Erle Stanley Gardner was the Arthur Conan Doyle of mid-twentieth-century America, and Perry Mason was Sherlock Holmes. All America was reading Perry Mason novels. How, despite that fact, I came to have a generous supply of them in 1955 is still something of a mystery to me. I simply can't remember when or where I got the things. They most certainly did not come to Memphis with us; I had never seen a Perry Mason novel in my life before we arrived at 1094. The Memphis Public Library was half a day's journey from us, figuratively if not literally, so I am quite sure my supply did not come from there. There was no money for a bookstore, even if there had been one near us. The only feasible explanation now seems to be that the books were stashed on Mrs. Jim's shelves in the Edwardian hall or else in one of the closets off of it. The only thing I'm sure of is that there were dozens of them, or so it seemed.

It doesn't take much focus to follow the plot of a Perry Mason mystery. Though I rarely figured out the murderer's true identity any sooner than Paul Drake/Dr. Watson did, I had to admit that sometimes my obtuseness was born, more than anything else, out of the desire to be tantalized for as long as possible. In the beginning, of course, when my Perry Mason evenings first started, I knew quite clearly what I was doing; I was occupying the corners of my mind so the center of it could say, "Goodness, I never knew that before!" (How could I? I'd never been to medical school before.) Or "Wait, say that again." (Always a good idea when he hesitated and had to look back at his notes in saying it the first time.)

Within a week or so and after no more than three or four novels, however, something else had begun to check in. I was enjoying these things! They were so unlike anything I had ever read before that originally I had not even thought of them as reading, simply as a pretense of occupation; but I had been wrong. These were books. They had the internally consistent characters and the internally consistent voice that are prerequisites of good writing. They had well constructed and credible plots and employed, if not a broad vocabulary, then certainly one varied enough to not be tedious. They had, in other words, the characteristics of solid craft; they just weren't literature as Sam and I had been taught to define it.

Erle Stanley Gardner referenced contemporary places and people, and used ordinary language to do it. So also, according to Dr. T., had Homer. The incisive difference between the two seemed to be that where Homer had cited and interwoven the men, women, gods, wars, and wonders of his Hellenic past, Gardner rarely referenced and cited anything farther back than 1929 or more lasting than a politician. The attraction in this was its ease. I was never distracted from Gardner's story, because I could connect immediately to his allusions and citations. Homer's and Virgil's I had spent hours of interruption looking up in *Classic Myths*. No, Gardner was definitely not concerned with assuming and passing on a people's long heritage, nor was he involved with any reality other than the immediately apparent one, the life of the surface. In sum, Gardner was in the entertainment, not the culture business. The irony was that the two couldn't be separated anymore. I just didn't know that yet.

One of the deficits of having been reared always in the presence of ideas is that I had never learned either to imagine or respect a world that did not give pride of place to ideas in their purest form. Yet here in front of me were lives, albeit fictional ones, who lived with sufficient intricacy and emotion to hold my interest while never once looking beyond themselves. In addition, I was learning something from reading their stories. Admittedly, my command of bad law is almost as impressive as my command of bad medicine from those years, but facts and profession-specific details are not what I mean when I say I was learning something. Rather, I mean I was being forced, novel by novel, to admit that there was a kind of spirit or set of shared sensibilities shaping Gardner's characters and informing the whole surface upon which they played out their lives, and that that context was mine. It was American, or perhaps 1950s America. And whether he intended to or not, Erle Stanley Gardner was modifying and refining the ongoing evolution of that set of sensibilities just by talking so entertainingly and unpretentiously about them, especially since he was saying the exact same things simultaneously to so many of us while he was being entertaining and unpretentious! Popular culture.

There was, in 1955, little talk of popular culture, little bandying about of the term in either polite conversation or academic lectures; but it was to become a major influence in my life just as my ever-increasing respect for the power of it was to become a formidable determinant in my creative and professional interests. The old "high culture" of Western art and literature in which I had been shaped as a child will never leave me, and I would not want it to. I treasure and daily employ its appreciations and the rich intricacies of its interdependencies as well as the shorthand of its associations; I hope I always will. What 1955 opened to me, however, was something as potent and necessary as the second half of a two-part equation. What 1955 began leading me to see was the emergence-in-process of another construct of appreciations and cross-references, one that had been created almost entirely by universal literacy, by the mass production of books and magazines, by a shortened work day and its resulting free time, by the increased human contact of urbanization, by the more fluid values of a mobile society, and by a dozen other such social changes that had changed the intellectual, spiritual, and psychological shape of Euro-America.

Eventually, pop culture was to win out over high culture in its influence on all of us, because eventually it would command a far larger citizenry and a far fatter purse and also because its inherent humility would admit of far more participants. In time, pop culture would grow so strong that it could look not only with scorn but also with pity and a hint of curiosity upon the heirs of high culture. Nobody knew that in 1955, of course, least of all me. I only knew I was fascinated by the tease of a different and fully formed perspective that winked at me every time I picked up a Perry Mason or—and Perry led me here as well before the summer was over—every time I began to read one of the abridged novels in the *Reader's Digest Condensed Books* that I truly do remember finding in Mrs. Jim's shelves.

I should not lay my discoveries and their pleasures all at the door of books, however. There were evenings when Sam needed our box all to himself, or to a friend or two and himself. Usually the friend or two showed up only when there was a major exam the next day. The other evenings alone usually happened when he was organizing material or writing up lab experiments and records. On those evenings when my absence was more desired than my presence, I betook myself quite happily down to Mrs. Jim and her front living room.

I saw my first television show in high school when my homeroom was invited to a classmate's house to watch General MacArthur fade away, something he managed quite literally to do two or three times while we sat there listening to him talk about it. Shortly after that my father's Sunday school class, a group of men whom he taught for almost four decades, gave him for Christmas a massive Zenith television that he set in the living room across from Mother's Maxfield Parrish print and with more or less her same attitudes of reverence and pride. We watched it there from time to time, but primarily we honored it as a good and proper thing to own, if not actually employ. At Shorter and later back at home there had been little time to watch television and, in all honesty, not a lot of television to watch in the early days. By the summer of 1955, all those things were changing.

Mrs. Jim's front living room was a kind of cliché, given the house it fronted. Dark even in the broad light of day and paneled as heavily as our upstairs hall, the front living room was itself a bit of a box, though slightly thinner on its east-west axis. It was an ideal configuration for watching television. Mrs. Jim's four foot by two-and-a-half foot by three foot set with its fifteen-inch fish bowl screen could not have been seen in anything wider. As it was, I pulled my chair closer many a night before our evening together was finally done. Of course, the truth was that a lot of those times I adjusted my chair so I could better see, not the television, but Mrs. Jim.

Mrs. Jim sat every night on an overstuffed and tapestry-upholstered chair while she kept her feet and legs ever so slightly crooked in front of her on a hassock of similar proportions and texture. Logically, she should have been lost within the tufts and recesses of both, but she wasn't. Instead, she rode upon their brocade surfaces as elegantly as a queen upon her barge, scarcely depressing any part of either the chair or its footrest. The porcelain ashtray was beside her, but the crassness of matches and cigarette packs was fastidiously secreted out of sight in a pocket somewhere. I loved this woman, loved her tough refinement, her strange and almost aberrant delicacy, and her kindness, for she was as kind a human being as God ever fashioned. But before that summer was over, I valued her conversation as well.

Mrs. Jim was not a chatterer. That doesn't mean that she was laconic exactly, only that she was not given to roving commentary on everything that happened by. She picked what we were to watch each evening and then sat in silence while we did so; talking and watching were complementary, not contemporaneous activities in the front living room of 1094. As soon as Mrs. Jim was satisfied that a segment had arrived at resolution, however, she would turn her sharp head, fix me with her left eye, and begin to speak. Sometimes she would ask me something like, "So, what did you think of that?" Other times she would tell me what she was thinking, and hers were the more interesting observations. "My mother would have thought that was funny," after a Groucho Marx show she had enjoyed. "Things as painful as that are not pleasant to watch if you can see their faces," after a rather imperfect gymnastics performance on, I think, "The Ed Sullivan Show." "I despise clowns. They always seem so mean-spirited and too contrary to admit it," after a Red Skelton show.

I don't know how much the feminist movement in this country was influenced and abetted by the spoofing of traditional marriage that Jackie Gleason and Art Carney achieved on "The Honeymooners." I do know Mrs. Jim never missed a show. "He's a wise man, that Gleason fellow. Not pretty, but he has a good soul."

I don't know how much America's acceptance of Latinos as cultural as well as geographic near kin was due in the beginning to "I Love Lucy," but I do know Mrs. Jim would just shake her head after one and say, "That Ricky! He's no better or worse than any other man I ever knew."

For that matter, I don't know how much American foreign policy came to be shaped by Edward R. Murrow, but I do know Mrs. Jim would shake her head after he was done, too, this time saying, "What bothers me is all the folks who'll never take the time to watch him and will still go vote."

I may not know the how-much of such changes, yet I do know the by-whom of most of them, thanks to Mrs. Jim and Erle Stanley Gardner. Between them, they gave me that summer the gentlest but most forceful introduction imaginable to the coming world of democratized experience and information. What none of us, especially the devout Mrs. Jim, could have imagined in 1955 was that religion, theology, spirituality, even faith and praxis themselves would also be democratized by the same processes. By the time that had happened, she would be dead but I would still be watching as she had first shown me how to. I would be monitoring Western religion publishing for *Publishers Weekly* and writing books with insubordinate titles like *God-Talk in America*, but I would also be remembering with gratitude, as I am now when I say in public what I have so often whispered to myself in private: "God bless you, Mrs. Jim."

28.

THE DAYS and early evenings that were the shimmering summer of 1955 were no different from any other days and evenings in that each of them had to wind down eventually into bedtime and sleep. Sam was not only a beleaguered student in those days, but he also was, and is, a happy insomniac of sorts. I have never been sure whether his body just doesn't need as much sleep as most bodies do, or whether his mind is simply unwilling to quit thinking for more than four or five hours out of any given twenty-four. Whatever the cause, the end result was the same. By ten-thirty I wanted to be in bed, and by ten-thirty he was just beginning to enjoy himself.

The study mates would be gone by then or, if it had been a learning evening for him, the new material would all be comfortably in place. Ten-thirty meant he could concentrate on postmortem reports and lab protocols as well as diagnostic procedures. None of them required any conversation, and quiet would at last blanket us both. In that quiet, in that generous bed, by the wash of yellowed light from Sam's student lamp across the room, I read again, this time from the writings of the Apostles.

I had read the Gospels in Greek with Dr. T., but not these other books of the New Testament. I had never paid much attention to the Book of Acts over the years except when Sunday school classes on the journeys of St. Paul or college lectures on the same subject had forced the issue. I had not paid serious attention at all to the content of the Apocalypse of St. John, only to the roll of its magnificent words. I had, of course, read the letters of the Apostles many times over; but even in doing so, I had given them a kind of personal short shrift. That is, I had always read them for their moral and religious content—their applicable sound bites, as we would say nowadays—and not for where the arguments of each fit into Christianity's evolving history. Now I needed something else. Now I needed to see for myself how—and even if, for I still was keeping an open mind on the matter—the works of the Apostles interlocked to form a cohesive whole.

For a young woman reading in bed and on her way to sleep, my choice of material was singularly counterproductive on many nights. On many nights, I was still reading at midnight, still flipping back and forth from letter to letter or, and this was far more frequently the case, from New to Old Testament. I had been reared on the so-called Scofield Bible, which for half the twentieth century was the be-all and end-all of biblical authority for Protestants. In Scofield, the text was the King James translation, as befitted any Bible that wished to be considered biblical in those years. Thus the remarkable hallmark of the Scofield was hardly its text but rather its elaborate set of cross-references and notes. The notes were all at the bottom of a page, as is standard procedure, but the references were split between a column running down the center of each page and the notation section at the bottom. The columnar references were the big, obvious connections. The references at the bottom were the doozies. Dr. Hugh Scofield was a genius, not to mention tireless, at chasing biblical allusions and citations from one snippet of Holy Writ back and forth to other, equally minute snippets. Over the years since 1955 many of Scofield's notes and much of his commentary have wilted into disrepute and/or been seared by outright, better informed scorn. They have, but not his notated references.

Growing up, I had used Scofield because almost every Bible we owned was a Scofield; and I had read it just as I would have read any other Bible. As I had matured a bit in my curiosities, I had begun to read Scofield's notes from time to time when doing so pleased my fancy. I had even chased back through some of his columnar references, but almost never had I bothered with the cross-references at the bottom of his pages and/or with those buried in the notations there. It was not that I chose to ignore these things; I just had never known I needed them until the day that T. S. Eliot began his work on my soul.

There, in bed with Dr. Scofield's endless references, was where I discovered for the first time the full story of my bronze serpent, discovered how from my childish recognition of the importance and utility of him he trailed like a cable backward through history from the Apostles' use of him to Jesus of Nazareth's claim on him to King Hezekiah's righteous fury over him to Moses' lifting up of him in Sinai's desert.

It was in Scofield's citations that I stumbled across the fullness of Melchizedec, that noble king of Salem, who threads back through the Judeo-Christian story from the epistoler's assertion of the Christ's priestly heritage in him to the Psalmist's adoration of him to Abraham's homage and obeisance before him.

It was in Scofield's citations that I found exposed before me that strain of mystical and radiant allusions that courses from the four-square city of St. John's New Jerusalem back to the Prophets' visions and through David's lineage on back to the trees and rivers of Eden's gardens. It was in Scofield's citations that Mr. Eliot's thesis was nightly affirmed and reaffirmed.

As if Scofield were not enough, my perverse and charmingly iconoclastic mother had given me for graduation a copy of Goodspeed's *New Testament: An American Translation*. Now this gift was hardly elegant, being instead a most utilitarian kind of hardback volume printed on the most ordinary of paper in the most mundane of typefaces, nor was Goodspeed's translation, having been in print for some thirty years at that point, all that new. I had, therefore, received the gift as yet another example of Mother's quixoticism. Being attracted neither by the volume's physical appearance nor its content, I had laid the Goodspeed aside without opening it and had brought it with me only to avoid any possible hurt should Mother ever chance upon it still at home in my old bedroom's bookshelves. When, however, I ran amok one night of a bit of St. Paul's chronically convoluted syntax, I got out of bed and fetched the Goodspeed just to see what he could add to the discussion . . . oh, boy!

Edgar Goodspeed had not been jesting when he had argued the need for a translation of the Scriptures into American vernacular, and Mother hadn't been fey or innocent when she thrust him upon me in a way I could not easily abandon. Here lay unlocked before me half of the obtuse puzzles of King James's translation of Paul, and here too lay all the appeal of prose made easy and accessible. It was Erle Stanley Gardner's rendition of Holy Writ mixed with the dramatic intimacy and relevance of Eliot's lines on the July morning that had begun this whole consuming pilgrimage of mine.

What Goodspeed lacked in euphony and elevated style he more than compensated for with clarity and concision. The result, inevitably, was that I understood a great deal of what I was reading and/or of what always before I had half-understood but passed over as not being worth the bother. There was Paul, that Jew in transition, who suddenly began to exercise a human appeal I had never seen before. There was an early or emerging Church made out of people with emotions and concerns other than religion. There was Virgil's world recorded in first-person, unornamented, epistolary prose. These people and issues had been real, had lived in real time, had in their reality directly shaped my own. It sounds obvious, maybe even simpleminded now, but in 1955 for me it was an extravaganza of the spirit.

The luxury of memory—the privilege of being able to look back now on those long-ago days and evenings that were my July and August of 1955—still revives in me some of that sense of carnival and adventure. I know now, of course, where the girl was going because I have become the woman she made, but I still shake my head sometimes at the strange way of our arriving. If ever any human being came to religious enthusiasm in a more cerebral way than I, I hope to meet him or her before I die. We would have much of the peculiar to share. And if ever any human being since St. Paul himself came to Jesus of Nazareth through Old Testament Yahweh and New Testament *Christos* by a more deliberated and obdurate way than I, I hope never to meet him or her before I die. We would burden one another into early death with our intricacies. But if the soul of Eliot lives on as Eliot, I hope to meet him shortly after I die, for it will have been his insistent loyalty to the eventual triumph of the Story that set me on the road to that place of conversation.

29.

THE CELTS, I am told by a friend who knows such things, valued greatly the skill of extra-physical vision. According to my friend, who claims an Irish heritage and cultivates an Irish persona, his people to this day speak of this feat as "seeing with the third eye." By this, the best I can determine, they really mean the ability to perceive agencies in the natural world that the rest of us read over, so to speak. In the play of light on a lake ripple, most of us see the play of light on a lake ripple. Not so those who see with the third eye. The cavorting light is not light at all for them, but the presence of the water sprite who lives in the lake and stirs its waters with her beauty when she is pleased, disturbing them with her anger when she is provoked. Those of us who see only light refracted in water call the peckish sprite a fairy or a piece of folklore or a residual from less civilized days—this despite the fact that many of us seem nonetheless to enjoy beguiling ourselves from time to time with the fancy of a world inhabited by more animas than our own.

I, unfortunately, have never seen a water sprite, nor have I ever been able to delude myself into thinking otherwise. This does not mean that wee people and nymphs don't exist; it just means that I am not so turned as to see them. Because more of our predecessors have believed in such agencies than have not, however, I am inclined not to scoff at the Irish for holding on so fondly to their ancestral beliefs. Beyond that, I have come over the years to an increasing regard for the benefits that can sometimes accrue from being reared to believe on a daily basis in the presence of things not seen. Water sprites as such probably have not taken the Irish anywhere remarkable or productive; the Irish openness to the possibility of sprites and creatures like them, on the other hand, seems to me to have taken them quite a long way, especially as Christians.

We talk a great deal in the Church today about Celtic spirituality, as well we should. What we mean by the term, however, is sometimes very dependent for its definition on the person or group doing the talking. There is a constant that informs our multiple conversations, though. The strength of the Celtic Christian experience is still in place today for one reason: It rose up out of a people who, long before they were Christianized, valued seeing what was not. They valued it so wholeheartedly, in fact, that they retained their cultural penchant for seeing with the third eye even through conversion, incorporating it seamlessly and unselfconsciously into their practice of the New Testament experience.

I say all of this just here not because I am interested in Celts, although I am, but because I have come to the time in this story when I must speak again of things unseen. This time I must speak of an unseen more specific than my dining room inquisitor; and for many of us today a respect, however tenuous, for the Irish sensibility is the most familiar and palatable way into such conversations.

It began in the mornings. To be exact, it began in those after-breakfast, precleanup few minutes when I sat at the dinette table on the sunporch, reading the Psalms and repeating the prayers of our heritage pretty much as Clark had suggested. I do not know, and will not pretend here to know, when it was in the course of that long-ago summer that one morning I ceased to read and repeat and began instead to know the words as being nearer to the sprite than to refracted light in their substance, but I did. That is, at some small, innocent moment in time, I knew that beyond the meaning of the words I was dealing with and beyond even their emotional and religious impact and beyond my conditioned response to them was an alive presence.

I said earlier that when strangers or acquaintances ask me to describe Sam, I cannot do so—that instead I have to summon the image in a recent photograph and, as best I can, describe it. The same is true just here. I have lived so long with that which I am trying to describe that I neither remember how it was with us in those early days nor when it was that I learned which particulars of our being together. As with Sam's hand-carved carburetor piece or my rosebud corsage, however, I can tell our stories.

In the beginning, somewhere on the other side of something, there was another whom/which that I perceived as there when I was with the Psalms and the set prayers. I did conclude fairly early on that the "something" which it was on the other side of was the margin or perimeter or property line of my mind. What was, was; but it was so different from mind as to not be reachable by mind, much less susceptible to a languaged knowing. What was—and I use this word only for the want of a better one—was also comfortable. Not comforting, but comfortable, or the creator of a comfortableness.

If one can imagine the domain of thought or mentation as a thick but semitransparent and very pliant and encapsulating bubble, then one can imagine as well an area on the side of the bubble where something on the other side stands so close against the bubble's wall as to warm that space. Standing on my side of the bubble and up against that inaccessible warmth is what I mean by comfortable. Like most pleasures, this one, too, began gradually to lose its strangeness and to become instead a perceived need as well as an amazing gift.

At some point before September came and my holiday was over and gone, I began to think of the warm spot and of the aliveness that was its source during times other than those spent in morning prayer. I say "think," but that may be too harsh and aggressive a word for what I mean to convey. More than deliberately pondering or purposefully recalling the essence and the sensations of my prayer time, I simply began to carry with me an awareness of an other's always being there in a somewhere I couldn't go, but which I could approach. I began as well to address, albeit wordlessly, that good spot in the bubble, or not the spot so much as the presence on the other side of it; and talking to another invites it into—in a manner of speaking, animates it in—one's own mind, as we all know . . . which is how it was in the beginning.

30.

SAM AND I may have been young in 1955, but neither of us was entirely dewy-eyed or foolish. We had both foreseen, and talked many times before our wedding about, the restrictions of a med student's studies on his time and the demands on him not only of his present schedule but also of his future profession. I went into marriage, in other words, expecting that as Sam and I began to build a life together, I would also have to begin building a separate and complementary one. Part of that bifurcation is the normal work of early marriage anyway, anytime; but there was an arguably greater urgency to it for those of us married to a physician in the days when medicine was a priestly art more than a technical skill.

All of which means that while I was, in my waking hours, at play that first summer, I was also building a life that would create and be me. It means as well that play is important not only to our lives as children while we learn through absorption how to build and be in the mature world, but equally so to our lives as young adults while we learn through pleasure and diversion how to build and be in an even more mature world. Sam and I both knew that as premises go, this one is as operative in joined lives as in single ones. Whether we articulated all of that or not, I very much doubt. We just understood that given a schedule like Sam's and a future like ours, playing was essential.

On Saturdays, Sam was usually home by lunch, and the next thirty-six hours were ours, with only minor adjustments for academic emergencies like major exams on Monday. We relished those weekends as much as any honeymooners ever did. Often we went to the zoo in the afternoon on Saturday. Memphis has a superb one, and in 1955 it was free for the coming. We held hands and sweated, retreated frequently into the cool thickness of the carnivore house to recover, and then went right back out again to the aviary that Sam loved and to the hippos I found so amusing. On Saturday night without fail—and variations of this have remained a habit throughout our years together, though no longer affixed so rigidly to Saturday evenings—we bathed and, as Sam said, "gussied up." In our best clothes, we got in the Bel Air and drove ourselves downtown to see the sights. When we had money, we treated ourselves to a movie. When the groceries or laundry had overshot the week's allotted funds, we simply walked back and forth along the length of Main Street, window-shopping and telling each other what we would do with all the items we saw, were we actually to someday be able to acquire them.

On Sundays, we were a mixed bag of religious decorum. Sam was still dedicated to his Presbyterianism and a Calvinist way of seeing things. Since I was by now firmly Anglican in my sympathies, but still disenchanted, where we worshiped mattered little to me. The problem was not, therefore, where we worshiped; the problem was getting ourselves in gear for doing it somewhere. There were four sizable Presbyterian churches within reasonable driving distance of 1094, and we really did visit each of them once during our first summer. We also agreed that the old church downtown just above the river was the congregation we should join. In itself, that decision seems to have constituted in our minds a fair summer's work, for most Sundays we were stay-at-homes, still in our pj's long after brunch should have been and sometimes right into when lunch was.

Some Sundays would be so simple a thing as walking out to get a paper and then occupying ourselves with reading it for the rest of the afternoon. Sometimes it involved getting in the Bel Air again and just riding. Such a thing sounds quaint now, but we had grown up with parents for whom the ability to move around over large areas easily and see varieties and wonders in a short time was the great, core gift and accomplishment of the twentieth century. Some of that sense of a drive as a mini-holiday or small adventure had stuck to us, and we would start up that car with all the anticipations of travelers to distant lands. In the course of things, we learned a lot about Memphis and its environs, but we also learned a great deal about each other as forming adults as well as beloveds.

Sam knew, at least to some degree, what was occupying my time and thoughts while he was in classes or studying. There was little way, actually, that he could have avoided knowing, for I talked to him incessantly then as now. My occupations that summer were, in the main, ones I would label now as spirituality, but in 1955 Sam or I would have called them—in fact, we did call them—theology and religion. If there were anything Sam Tickle loved almost as much as talking medicine in those days, it was talking religion. So it was no surprise that regardless of whatever else we did or did not do with our weekend hours, we always spent an animated segment of them arguing and discussing the operations and principles of Christianity. This usually meant over our lazy midday meal Sunday and, after our newspaper or our drives, over our equally lazy Sunday night suppers. We were playing, but at a deadly serious game called life.

As those weekend hours of happiness grew and extended further over toward the end of August, they increased in me as well a kind of poignancy. The more we were together, the more I realized that we were two people, that we would always be two people, that there is no other option given in creation. The realization filled me with a soft, pervasive mourning—mourning that it must be so with us and mourning for the loss of a sweetness I had dreamed and would never have. Once or twice when we were lying abed that summer, I took my forefinger and ran it up Sam's abdomen to his breast bone and said, "I wish I could unzip you right here and just crawl in forever." I stopped my half-serious foolishness when I realized my words were upsetting to him. Whether they seemed animalistic or too dependent or embarrassingly puerile, he never said, and I never asked. I just simply stopped expressing, but not feeling, that feminine pull toward a more perfect union, toward the return of two into the primordial whole. I wanted with all my soul to be a rib again inside the man I loved, yet . . .

. . . Yet—it is a hard-nosed word, that one—Yet increasingly, while our lives continued to re-form as two individuals within a mated pair and while my sorrow over the inevitability of that subtle change settled into grief, so increasingly did my sense of the presence on the other side of the soft, supple, semitransparent wall of the bubble intensify. Near summer's end, I had to admit to myself that I could almost sense the suggestion of a shape through the bubble—not a shape as of a creature, but as of a steady intention.

Plato would have called it the Idea or the Ideal, and he might have been right in his day. St. Paul had already described my perception much more simply as seeing through a glass darkly, but it would be years before I would make that connection. Thus, mistrusting Plato's dualism and not yet laying claim to St. Paul's, I accepted this nuance of shape on the other side of somewhere as just there. At some point, the intimation or presence began to seem almost familiar as well as expected. Over the months that followed, it would also come to seem less impersonal, more sympathetic. Eventually, of course, it would become my schoolmaster, and not the smallest of its lessons would be about the redemptive, if painful, necessity of separateness in life.

But before August was to have done with us, there was one other weekend that needs mentioning, one that would indeed mold us not as individuals but as a marriage. On the second Saturday morning in August I woke up not feeling well. At first I couldn't figure out exactly what part of me was out of kilter, but by lunch when Sam came back from the school, I knew. I was bent double with pain and had begun to stain a bit with pinkish blood. I also knew that I had not had a period since Johnson City, a fact the two of us had noted but brushed off as a normal response to so much change and physical activity. For heaven's sake, we both certainly knew where babies came from, and even in our youthful enthusiasms we knew how intelligent, responsible people prevented their coming. By three or four o'clock, when I was bleeding and cramping and gagging, we finally said the word to each other: miscarriage.

We had no doctor in Memphis and we had no medicines of any sort. Actually, it hadn't occurred to us that we might possibly need either of them that summer. Moreover, Sam didn't know the Ob–Gyn teaching faculty well enough yet to call for help unless help were really needed. (A student's calling teaching staff at home was strongly discouraged at all times and required a blatantly obvious crisis to be regarded as acceptable conduct at any time.) Even if we had had the money to do so, we would not have gone to an emergency room. In those more matter-of-fact days, most ER's would have looked askance at anything short of hemorrhage itself. Given the circumstances, then, Sam did what many a good husband has done. He went to the liquor store before it closed, got a pint of Old Crow, and nursed me through it.

Every time I would come up out of my fog, he would have another small cup of warm whiskey cut heavily with water and fortified with sugar waiting for me—a toddy in anybody's book. During the twenty-four hours it took—the body parts with new life so unwillingly—during those twenty-four hours, I'm sure he must have done with love as well as skill all the things he would have done had I been in his clinic and not his bed. I don't remember, however, any of what he did or whether he ever evidenced what he himself had to have been feeling. I do remember that by Sunday afternoon, although I was shaky, the ordeal itself was over.

I lay in bed while he sat beside me and we discussed how the whole episode could not possibly have happened—not to us, not in the face of all our preventive measures. As marital conversations go, this particular one is among the oldest in modern times, I suspect, but we were sincere participants in it, nonetheless . . . sincere enough so that by Sunday night we had almost persuaded ourselves that we had been mistaken. Such a thing could not have happened. What we should have been worrying about, of course, was not the impossibility of the thing, but the possibility of its happening again. We gave that not a thought, though, and by Wednesday or Thursday, we were our usual young selves again.

The only apparent consequence of our weekend, so far as we could tell, was that I seemed to have developed an aversion to cheap whiskey— or better put, a gag reflex that kicked in every time I even smelled the stuff. It would take me, quite literally, almost twenty years to overcome that piece of weird conditioning. Otherwise, things seemed as ordinary as if nothing untoward had happened; and almost three weeks later, on a hot Thursday morning, I straightened the seams in my stockings one last time and went jauntily out the door toward Messick High School. I might never be a Dr. T., but by the grace of God, I could be a Latin teacher. And I intended to do it with all the passion she had had and all the reverence for my subject that she had taught me.

PART FIVE

Messick High School,
Building D

31.

WE AMERICANS have never been entirely clear about the ownership of our public school systems. As a result, we have never been entirely clear about what we want them to accomplish, much less how we want them to do it. In most human enterprises it is a given that ownership is control and that policy rests in control. Almost without reservation over its democratic lifetime, we have sought to apply that same principle to our national ideal of compulsory, universal education. The compulsory and the universal parts of the equation are, however, pure paradox in a democracy. They are also the headwaters for much of the fractiousness and waffling intentions that have characterized our educational efforts from the outset.

Public schools, inasmuch as they are paid for by tax dollars and administered by professionals who are under contract to the state, would seem logically to be extensions of the state. They would, that is, just about anywhere else except here. We Americans come from a different bent of character, a slightly more anarchistic and suspicious bent than that of our fellow Westerners. Our forefathers crossed oceans to escape from the hierarchical systems of traditional European governance, and they neither forgot that heritage of individualism nor left us a system capable of abandoning it. Historically for us, the central *raison d'être* for compulsory, universal education was, and still is, the creation of an informed citizenry capable of controlling the state and even, should such be necessary, overthrowing the state and reconfiguring it with political intelligence afterward.

Ironically, of course, even the most patriotic, tax-paying parents among us, when pushed, will deny vehemently that there is a state; we are, we will be pleased to tell you, the state. Inherent in that position is the strong sentiment that public schools are the property of parents who, beleaguered already, certainly do not wish it to teach any further means of eroding their authority, much less of furthering their own overthrow. Public schooling, under this way of seeing things, is really only home schooling that happens in a place other than home and is conducted by hired professionals whose purposes must be those of the parents for whom they serve as proxies. And the truth is that in most homes, American or otherwise, the chief and informing concern of parents is not the transmittal of academic knowledge *per se,* but of morally, culturally, and familially acceptable and operative ways of being in the world.

Such a complex of opposing tensions is inherently chaotic. As a *modus operandi* it can survive and be academically effective only where almost all the parents involved are of similar backgrounds and aims; where most of them also know without hesitation that they are the state or controlling political power, at least in the small area which their school services; and where they are not besieged by contrary, external, and/or more empowered aims, values, and necessities. The minute any one piece of that triad gets knocked askew, the whole thing begins to career like a gyroscope out of control.

In 1955 Messick High School was beginning that career. Within a quarter century, it would succumb to our American contradictions. Closed as a school, its generous spaces and well-tended halls would be turned into a distribution center for community services, its laboratories and manual arts shops into facilities for adult job-training, and Building D would be boarded up for good. But I didn't know any of this on that August morning when I parked the Bel Air—proudly, may I say, and with flair—in the parking area marked "Faculty," and went inside.

In 1955 Messick was not so much a school as a sprawl, a prodigious maze of classroom buildings and playing fields and parking spaces that were all attached by walkways to each other and to the original Messick from which they had grown, but apparently never separated. That building sat, self-assured as a dowager, on the campus's northeast corner where its wine-red brick walls, gray stone caps, and broad front doors marked it forever as quintessentially early-twentieth-century American. It was a love of a building, as solid and unimaginative as one would wish a good institution to be and as commodious and adaptable as one would wish home to be. When I opened the double doors that first morning, it smelled of years of books and oiled floors and hot, cafeteria-baked pan rolls. It smelled of years, and I knew a rush of excitement unlike any I can ever remember having had before or since. I was going to teach. I was going to teach here. We had made a pact, this place and I, and we were about to have a love affair.

I never saw the label "Building D" on any chart or memos after that

Thursday morning when we were handed maps of the campus in our first faculty meeting and given our room assignments. Always thereafter my building was simply "the far building," "the new building," or "the other building," none of which, as it turned out, was a bad thing at all. I liked the notion of being far away from administrative eyes. I had no idea what I was going to do that would be administratively unacceptable conduct, but I was pretty sure I would manage at some point or other to misspeak (after all, I always had, so why would I stop now?) or bend professional decorum a bit (I did . . . to its limits, actually, but only once or twice).

I liked being in "the new building" as well. Despite its lack of élan and cachet, it had the distinctly desirable advantage of an uninterrupted wall of windows, all of which actually worked and all of which opened in so that even on rainy days the room could stay dry and still be ventilated. The result—i.e., a dependable breeze that was ever on the ready—made my second-floor space into heaven itself, especially in a climate like that of Memphis and in those years when un-air-conditioned schools were not yet regarded as municipal child abuse (which they are, believe me). The new building, by virtue of its newness, also had blackboards so copious and ample that even my penchant for long, tedious arguments and elaborate schemata never managed to fill them completely. And last as well as best, the newness of Building D meant light—great, modern, tube-laden fixtures that hung over our heads and pressed their soft fluorescence into every crack and crevice of that angular space. There was not a cloudy day or even a thunderstorm daunting enough to discourage the light from those fixtures; and the kids and I reveled in the openness and constancy of them.

But it was Building D's status as "other" that was to give texture to my new career. I am reasonably sure that nowadays faculty room assignments in public schools are set on some principle of logic like grade levels or content areas or traffic-flow patterns, and not on the more freighted ones of slightly aberrant personalities or subtle degrees of *outré*ness among a building's faculty. I am sure of that in terms of present policy, but I shall never be sure about it as an operative precept in 1955. Certainly no one could have proved it by looking at the motley crew of us who taught in the "other building." By and large, we were about as other and as disparate as we could be and still keep our positions.

One of us was divorced, a scandal in 1955, a sign of personal failure and the sure mark of a bad moral example for young adolescents. Even worse, one of us was in the process of getting a divorce! Unheard of! One of us had a tongue in her head that was as incisive (and insightful) as a surgeon's knife, especially when discussing educational theory and the illogics of its applications in the Memphis City System. She was also as funny a curmudgeon as I have ever known, not to mention one of the brightest. One of us, unfortunately, was a martinet with an absolutistic world view that not only made her a poor confidante, but also a constant visitor to the principal's office. Her removal to our building was apparently a last-ditch effort to make her reports of infractions and misdemeanors as difficult as possible to deliver and, hopefully, as infrequent as possible. One of us was a widow with children and a contagious despair that only her classroom seemed to relieve. Watching her teach was like watching the gods at play; eating lunch with her was hell on earth, an exercise in depression that could last the rest of the afternoon if one weren't careful to tune her out early enough in the process.

My qualifying characteristic in all of this seemed, on the surface anyway, to have been that I was the youngest and least experienced of Messick's faculty and that I was going to teach Latin to working-class kids, most of whom had no intention of going on to college and none of whom wanted to learn the stuff in the first place. Beyond this native reluctance on their part lay an also native resentment: The college-prep freshmen, almost all of whom were from the neighborhood's older, middle-class homes, were taking their Latin in the main building from the senior faculty who had taught their parents before them. In other words, while the whirring of the careen may have been little more than a low hum in 1955, it was nonetheless audible.

My other qualification for assignment to Building D, I thought and still think, was the fact that I had presented as that unknown factor a professional legacy. There was no question in my mind or anybody else's that I had received my appointment not so much because of my own merits as because of my father's. He might be five hundred and fifty miles away in East Tennessee, but P. W. Alexander was still a well-known and much respected Southern educator. Until I could prove my own mettle, however (or the lack thereof), better to keep me as far as possible from public view and patron scrutiny.

Ultimately, of course, the vulnerabilities that got me relegated to Building D in the first place also served me well once I had arrived. Everybody wanted to help me out, show me the ropes, teach me which rules would bend and which would break. Everyone also, even our moralist, seemed pleased to give me the benefit of the doubt, as well as of each day's gossip. Within a week I knew I was a piece of a whole, a spoke in a wheel that while wobbly was still efficient and, as I told Sam, was "giving me one heck of a wild ride."

3 2 .

EVERY SCHOOLTEACHER I ever knew has his or her own survival stories, every one of them more or less self-congratulatory and every one of them faintly impossible. My own are only two in number, totally self-congratulatory, and much too bizarre to be either contrived or impossible.

Early on Friday morning when classes were to assemble on short schedule for half a day and immediately after our homeroom rolls had been handed out, my friendly moralist called me out into the hallway. I had inherited, she said, the terror of Messick High, and she thought it her duty to warn me. She thought it as well, she added, a singular piece of meanness and mischief that such a thing should have happened to me, but it was nonetheless true. I had been given a boy who had already been "held back" twice, but—oh, too horrible to say except in a whisper!—one who purportedly had been convicted three times of statutory rape.

I hadn't the faintest inkling, on that previously pleasant morning, of what the statutory part of her *sotto voce* phrase had to do with anything, but I most surely grasped the rape part of it. My throat tightened and my heart picked up an extra beat or two. After I went back into my classroom and looked at the boy she had pointed out from the hallway, it picked up several more beats. If that kid were a boy, then I had never seen a man. Muscular and taut, he was also drop-dead handsome. As I moved back to my desk, he turned his head, sized me up as dispassionately as a lion sizes up dinner before he lunges for it, and in general let me know with an insolent nod that he understood exactly what had just happened in the hall.

We made it through homeroom—it was, after all, only a ten-minute, roll-calling, seat-assigning event that day—and we made it by some act of mercy through Monday's opening and closing homerooms. By Tuesday, I was beginning to like these kids a lot. By week's end, I was beginning to feel almost proprietary about them as "mine," and just a little bit enchanted by the integer they were making of themselves as "Tickle's homeroom." In all of this, however, I was avoiding the alleged rapist as assiduously as I was building connections with his classmates.

I had never been afraid of another human being before in my life, never been in a place or position before where fear of a fellow creature would have been a reasonable response. Now I was. Even Sam was concerned, something that more excited than allayed my own anxieties. He was primarily concerned about my passing from the building to the car in the afternoons and insisted that I do so only in the company of some other faculty member. Within a week or so of such, however, most twenty-one-year-olds give up on fear. It's just too demeaning to carry around for longer than that, especially when it's unsubstantiated, as mine increasingly seemed to be.

I had looked up "statutory" as it relates to rape the minute I had gotten home on the Friday of my first meeting it in that context, and I had been relieved to discover that it meant any intercourse, consensual or otherwise, with a girl under sixteen. The longer I looked at the accused and the longer he sat in my classroom, the surer I was that consent had most probably been involved. I could not, in fact, imagine otherwise. Even more reassuring was the fact that while my young man might indeed be fully and magnificently a man, he was also what educational psychologists call an early maturer. According to my register, he had just turned seventeen himself, a circumstance that seemed to me to somewhat diminish, if not legally obliterate, his guilt.

The more I watched my supposed culprit, the less intimidating he seemed. True, his physical maturity and presumed prowess made him a kind of titulary don among the other boys and true, he and his reactions seemed to be arbitrators of the behavior and attitudes of the group as a whole, but he appeared to be neutrally inclined toward me. Almost as if he were measuring me as I measured him, we began to do a kind of dance around each other, neither of us crossing that line at which the other's domain and autonomy would be on the block. Then it happened, and it had nothing to do with either of us or our intentions toward each other.

It was Friday of the second full week of classes, and everyone including me was tired, cranky, ready to go home, ready to escape the heat. We were in closing homeroom, waiting for the dismissal bell and not doing anything significant. I was leaning against my desk, half propped on its edge, and the students were all in their appointed seats in various stages of disarray and impatience. One of the girls was talking to me about something or other, probably an assignment, and I was watching her as I answered when suddenly a tennis shoe came flying from the far back right-hand corner of the room, sailed by my hand, and landed on the desk behind me.

I was so instantly and totally angry that without missing a beat, I picked the shoe up and flung it back as hard as I could at the boy who had just sent it whirling by me. It hit him dead-on, right in the bend where his head and neck met his shoulder, and he hollered in pain.

"Don't you ever, ever, ever do such a thing again in my classroom!" I said with a deadly calm that I can still taste in my mouth to this day.

There was a fury in me I had never before thought possible, but this kid had just violated the one secular thing I held sacred. He had just violated Dr. Thompson's premise of the classroom as holy ground.

For just an instant the room was a still frame of life interrupted. I glared, immobile in the grip of my own emotions. The kid, who had obviously been hurt, whimpered and then hushed, the imprint of the shoe sole now flaming on the side of his face and down the side of his neck. Then softly, from the chair just in front of me, came the laughter. Fully bass and laconic but filled with approval, it came and grew and set the pace until the entire room was filled with laughter and then, unhappily, with scorn for the boy who had started the whole incident by throwing the shoe in the first place.

"I didn't mean to," he kept protesting. "I was trying to throw it up there to Buck. For gosh sakes, it's his shoe. Come on, guys, I didn't throw it at her, honest!"

But nobody cared, or else nobody chose to care. The laugh of my supposed rapist had been the laugh of approval. I was in.

We never had any trouble after that for as long as I was at Messick High

School. Of course the truth was that I had no more acted maturely or professionally than I had acted consciously. I had simply acted; and lest there be any mistake, I had also meant to hurt every bit as badly as I did. The same response today would have lost me my license and probably triggered a lawsuit or two to boot. Things in 1955 were simpler, and all I got out of it was respect—an almost frightening, but highly useful and most accommodating denouement.

As things turned out, of course, while I never managed to become at ease in dealing with my don, I did come to understand and appreciate him. He could not have afforded any cordiality between us anyway. Familiarity with faculty would have compromised completely his standing as class authority on macho and mean and, as I have said, those gifts were real enough and always present enough in him so that I could never quite persuade myself to lower my own guard either. We settled for a workable accommodation of mutual regard. In due time I even told my moralist she was probably full of malarkey as well as of potentially actionable slander. That kid was an empowered braggart too politically savvy to squelch licentious rumors about himself, be they true or false; but his parents, I suggested to her, might be of a different mind. For once in her life, she seemed to grasp the wisdom of silence, and none of us heard any more about statutory rape.

Discipline is undoubtedly the prime bugaboo of new, young teachers and the hurdle which by some means or other must be jumped before anything constructive can take place. Latin teachers, alas, have another, almost equally pivotal problem. They must also establish that they are hip enough to be worth following through all the winding paths and obscure valleys of a patently dead language. This second test was a bit more tenuous for me and my freshmen. The fact that I was young helped. The fact that I was young and still a bride helped a lot, especially with the girls who wanted more details than grammar after class, but who were willing to settle for proximity. The boys were less easily seduced into *Italia peninsula est.*

We were struggling in those first few days, me with trying to make the wonders of life's most fascinating study seem even faintly deserving of their interest and the boys with trying to figure out whether or not I really knew the good from the bad in life's giant bowlful of jollies. One morning—I think it was in the third week of class—one of the ringleaders among my hold-outs was right on the cusp of late when he came into class with a "Sorry" and a scurry past my desk to his.

"Been into the Chesterfields again, I note." I said it sarcastically and without thinking.

His hand flew to his shirt pocket, which was empty, and he turned to look me dead in the face.

"What did you just say?" he asked, not as a challenge, but as an honest question.

Taking him at face value, I repeated what I had said. "Unless my nose fools me, you've been out there smoking a Chesterfield instead of paying attention to the time." Of course, smoking on campus was the offense in those days, but it was being almost late to Latin that was at the root of my rancor.

His hand went up to the pocket again, as if perhaps he had misinterpreted its emptiness before.

"How'd you know that?" This time I heard that funny edge of respect that I had been looking for. I drove it home.

"I can tell Chesterfields from anything else—Lucky Strikes, Pall Malls, Carltons—by their smell." Then cruelly, but edges are hard to come by, "Can't you?"

"Prove it," he said, and motioned to one of the other boys who had reeked earlier with what I now prayed was the odor of a Carlton. "Go up there and let her smell you," he said.

The boy came to the front beside my desk, I made a show of taking one whiff and then gambled. "Carlton," I said.

"Gaaawlly," or something like that was the response. Then he motioned another boy to the front. This time it was easy. I knew that smell better than I knew my own Pall Malls.

"Old Gold," I said.

"Well, I'll be damned," he said, and I was so grateful I never even thought to correct him.

Latin class was singularly successful that day and, by and large, every day thereafter. And that, as they say, is my set of stories, and I'm sticking to them.

33.

AS CATEGORIES of human beings go, Mary Ada Singleton will always stand in my experience as a species, if not a genus, unto herself. Thin, but more trim than bony; curly haired with a salt-and-pepper coif that was neither dyed nor permed nor particularly well tended; cynical in discipline and worldview yet like all classical cynics, convinced first that there was hope for humankind and second that that hope was already and everywhere resident within humanity itself if only it could be elicited and properly tutored; a giantess in presence who in actual stature could not have exceeded five and a half feet; possessed of an acerbic wit that expected the worst and, to her delight, almost never found it—all these things and more may be said of her. As a result of them, Mary Ada was a kind of roving circus of a woman whose contrary and opposing sureties were held together only by the tensions inherent in their being juxtaposed within her particular scheme of things. She presented, as Mimi Minsky told her one morning, like a sharp-tongued and utterly charming crank who was in a perpetual state of wonderment that things were not as bad as she was eternally sure they, by rights, should be.

Minsky, who was Mary Ada's best friend, was also a perfect counterpoint to her. Mary Ada taught algebra by the slash-burn-and-terrorize method. Students didn't cross her, but they didn't waste any emotional effort pursuing her affections either. The ones who were good and/or academically ambitious sought her classes as earnestly as I had pursued Miss Kellogg's and with about the same personal and intellectual result. The woman was good. Minsky, on the other hand, taught American history with a passion that approached Dr. T.'s sacramentalizing treatment of language. Minsky soared, and even the dullest kid would occasionally be heard to come out of her classroom, stop dead in the hall, and say, "Wow!" with genuine homage, if not admirable retention.

Minsky was thin too. Her hair was browned with help and set every few days by an accomplished beautician. Her clothes, carefully selected, were hardly ostentatious, but they were expensive. Even more to the point, she had the full, beautifully rounded bosom that defines feminine elegance for most of the Western world and the statuesque height that good clothes love to complement. And while she herself was hardly the soul of optimism or jolly good humor every day, she was the soul of a tart optimism and brusque affection that drew students like sugar draws flies. I cannot even begin to count the number of times I watched a cache of students pursue her all the way to the door of the faculty lounge and only cease talking after she had slipped through that door and shut it firmly in their faces.

The commonality between Mary Ada and Minsky, other than a certain natural *sangfroid* and depth of spirit, was that they both smoked with a truly remarkable dedication. My own habit, which by 1955 was approaching the pack-a-day status, paled before the earnestness of theirs; yet it was our mutual bad habit that also drew me in to them, or that was the explanation the two of them always offered for, as Minsky often said, "having taken the kid on."

One of the more appealing parts of my new schedule as a professional was that I had to have the Bel Air to go ten miles diagonally across a big city in order to get to work. I loved driving, and while walking can produce good cardiovascular systems and interesting side trips, it by and large does not offer quite the freedom and broad vistas of driving a car, especially not to a twenty-one-year-old. The disadvantage to my having the car, of course, was that Sam still had to get to the university. Hooking a ride home at the end of a day was rarely a problem for him, but arranging a ride in the mornings proved almost impossible. The senior who had been his ride the year before had graduated, and the new students at 1094 were not on his schedule. The obvious solution was for me to take Sam two miles south and west to school each morning before I turned back east and farther south to Messick. Such an arrangement would be a chore to me now, but I remember it as a morning pleasantry with only one disadvantage.

I think I had known almost from their beginning that my cloistered summer mornings with the great voices of Hebrew scripture and English poetry were a gift that would not come to me again, except perhaps in old age. When they ended with the beginning of the fall term at Messick, I did not so much miss or mourn them as I reverenced and incorporated the gift of them. It was my morning prayers that I could not be so sanguine about; and it was my morning prayers that first introduced me to Mary Ada and, through her, to Minsky.

I have never been able to rush my prayers in the morning. I would that I could say the same of those occurring later in the day, but my track record there is a bit shakier. Morning prayer, however, once I had got the habit of it, had to be thoughtful, intentional, receptive. Yet there was no way that I, who love to sleep more than to eat, could rouse myself early enough, much less to levels of alertness sufficient enough, to enter my prayers before Sam and I had to leave our apartment at seven or a bit before. Wrong woman, wrong set of biological skills. It wasn't going to happen.

More to the point, though I've never been sure whether this is a theologically acceptable position or not, the truth was, and very much still is, that I "enjoy" my morning prayers; and I do mean enjoy—not "value" or "need" or "am addicted to" or "am afraid to omit" or any other of a dozen more credible reasons for prayer, but just plain old, simple "enjoy." Losing them to an early-morning departure time was just not acceptable. There had to be a solution and there was: the faculty lounge.

By skillful (read here "aggressive" with a smattering of "foolhardy") driving, I learned within a week of my time at Messick to get from the University of Tennessee's College of Medicine to the faculty lounge at Messick High School in thirty minutes or less. Since that can't be done on a weekday, not even at seven o'clock in the morning, I have to assume the angels offered help, because I, or we, did it. By and frequently before seven-thirty each morning, I would be sitting in a wooden chair in front of a big window in a totally empty faculty lounge in a still, almost totally empty building. The Psalter in my hand, I would begin my day:

Lord God of hosts, hear my prayer; harken, O God of Jacob . . .

Let us come before his presence with thanksgiving and raise a loud shout to him with psalms . . .

On this day the Lord has acted; I will rejoice and be glad within it . . .

Whom have I in heaven but you? And having you I desire nothing upon earth . . .

Our God will come and will not keep silence; before him there is a consuming flame, and around him a raging storm . . .

The contradictions, the "otherness," the majesty of Israel's God flowed through me as I sat beneath that window morning after morning, self-taught and spirit-taught to claim them as my own by birthright and by crucifixion's bounty. Adding my words, my small petitions and mighty concerns, to the anguish and the glory of my kind, I passed those few stolen minutes each morning oblivious to all save the conversation I was in . . . or I did until the third week of term and the Tuesday morning that Mary Ada Singleton opened the faculty lounge door at 7:25 A.M., took a look at me, said "I'm an old high-church Methodist," and then sat down to light up as nonchalantly as if nothing untoward or noteworthy had just transpired.

I closed the Psalter, embarrassed at having been caught and annoyed at having been interrupted . . . interrupted, I now know, by one of the more consequential interruptions in a life that has been blessed with them. "I'm Mary Ada Singleton, algebra," she said after I'd closed the book. "You're the one who's Wade Alexander's daughter, aren't you? . . . the new one in freshman Latin and English?"

"Yes," was all I managed before she sailed on. "I grew up in the crook of the river, too, up in Tiptonville with your daddy's people. My father owned the dry goods store on Church Street. You tell Wade that Mary Ada Caldwell—don't use Singleton, he won't remember that—said 'hello' and he'll remember." She snuffed out the cigarette and headed to the door. "And don't worry, I really am high-church Methodist." And that was the end of that.

Mary Ada was right about one thing. I called home that night, and my father did remember. "Oh, dear!" was his initial response, followed by, "You watch that woman and don't let her get you into trouble. She has a good mind and a reputation for saying things better left unsaid."

"You mean principals and superintendents don't much like her?"

"I'm saying they don't appreciate what she says or where and to whom she says it. I'm also saying that associating too frequently with her might get you seen in an unfavorable light, especially as a new teacher just beginning your career."

That was all it took to rouse the insurrectionist in me; I was hooked. Whoever she was, Mary Ada Singleton was perverse enough and skilled enough to have evoked the parental censure. It followed that she must also be interesting. I dedicated myself to finding out how and why.

The next morning Mary Ada did not show up until seven forty-five, by which time I had finished my prayers and was waiting for her. By seven forty-five I had also rediscovered bathrooms. There were two capacious faculty ones that opened off the lounge. Since the possibility of interruption is all it takes to distract my attention beyond any hope of repair, I had locked myself early that morning into one of the stalls as unthinkingly and naturally as if I had been praying in bathrooms all my life—which, as I realized later, was exactly what I had been doing for a sizable portion of it.

By the time Mary Ada came, I was safely back in my chair under the window and smoking away. "Morning." The way she said it, it was as much an observation as a greeting. "Did you call home last night?"

I was a bit nonplussed at having been caught out again. "Yes," I admitted.

"What did your father say?"

I was into it by now, determined to match directness with directness. "He said to watch out for you and not associate too closely this early in my career."

"Good," she responded and struck her match. "It's reassuring to know that some things don't change in this world of change."

"Meaning my father?"

"Meaning your father. Has he ever seen you smoke?"

I really was aghast. "Good Lord, no!"

"Too bad. I'd love to see his face the first time he does," and she chuckled.

Not knowing what else to say, I said, "You weren't in here last week, were you? I mean, I didn't see you."

"No," she said. "Usually I don't come in here until my first break, but yesterday I had to take my car to the shop and the mechanic dropped me off early."

"So is it still in the shop today?" I asked.

"No, it's fixed. I came this morning to see you."

I really was stunned. "You did?"

"Yes. Any daughter of Wade Alexander's is bound to have some kind of potential, especially one gutsy enough to smoke behind his back."

Before she could say anything else, the door opened and in came Minsky. "This is Mimi Minsky," Mary Ada said, "but we call her Minsky. She's Jewish, so she'll understand, too."

Minsky's sole comment was, "Oh, for mercy's sake, Mary Ada!" and then the warning bell rang, calling us to our homerooms.

Despite all my father's fair warning, we three became within a matter of just a few days the fastest of friends. Or I know that was how I saw things. Looking back, I suspect that the two of them probably saw themselves, just as Minsky said, as having taken on a youngster who desperately needed friends, not to mention some serious exposure to common sense and instructional reality. In addition, it didn't take me long to perceive that Mary Ada, for all her words to the contrary, held my father in the highest esteem and, though she was some several years younger than he, still saw her tutelage of me as a means of repaying his past courtesies to her and her family. All that having been said, however, the effect of their interest evolved into something that functioned and felt for all the world like friendship and that became my greatest single delight during my time at Messick.

The two of them began coming into the lounge for a few minutes each morning, thereby allowing us to commence our day together with gossip and complaints and general running commentary on the state of the world. In order to accommodate this new and unexpected happiness, I continued to lock myself into one of the lounge's faculty bathrooms early each morning and, on most mornings, to be back in my window chair and already smoking by the time they arrived.

Mary Ada never said anything else about what I had been doing on the day of our first meeting, nor did she ever offer any clarification of her "She's Jewish, she'll understand" introduction of Minsky; but they stuck in my head like hooks in a fish's throat . . . stuck until finally, like all good hooks, they reeled me in.

34.

TIMING, as they say, is everything; and while I have been slow to accept that truism over the years—primarily, I suspect, because I am constitutionally suspicious of truisms—I am beginning of late to experience a certain surprised respect for the underlying accuracy of this one. The change in my own attitude is a product not so much of advancing years and the wisdom they are supposed to bring—mine seem, alas, to have failed me on that front—but of the process of reducing the course of those years to paper.

Few of us are ever granted an opportunity near the end of life to look back and, through the prism of what is, formally interpret what has been. I appreciate that rareness of occasion far more keenly now than when I first began this project, just as I sense within myself each morning an ever growing gratitude for it as I sit down to address the day's business of re-membering, sorting, pondering, recording. The places that have contained and secured me, the events and circumstances that have determined the courses of my life, the people who have been and still are the extensions and extenders of my being—they came and went, almost all of them, in the company of myriad other places, events, and people; and though I still remember many, if scarcely all, of that host, I have up until now remem-bered them as covalent neighbors in a small geography.

There is a kind of spiritual laziness—perhaps even an ingratitude—in living, as I have, too actively to scrutinize and sort the stages of life as one passes through them. There is also, as the ancients themselves have said, a diminishment of vista . . . or I now know in retrospect that there has been for me. Had I been a more reverent watcher of my own life, I might have exposed its patterns far earlier. I most assuredly would have accepted and used its gifts more humbly and less conventionally. All of which is not so much a *mea culpa* (though it is) as an observation of some personal be-musement and regret. It is also an explanation in part for my failure to ap-preciate timing appropriately.

Timing, if not everything, certainly seems to me now to be the most mysterious of the exigencies that sculpt and burnish life. Timing, ordering, sequencing—call it what one may—appears to me now as the enabler and potentiator of all the rest. Thus it would be unreasonable to say that Mary Ada Singleton set the course of my life. She would be as appalled at that statement as I would be. It is, however, more than accurate to say that her cryptic comments about her Methodism and Minsky's Jewishness came to me at precisely the right time; they were the first clearly identifiable ar-rows pointing toward what was to be. They were also, I think now, the first significant words of my life as a grown-up, for adulthood, of course, was exactly what had happened to me.

If I knew clearly—and I did—that my childhood ended at the exact moment when my mother drove out of sight through Shorter's gates, then I knew even more clearly that my girlhood had ended at the exact moment when I first walked through Messick's double front doors as a member of its faculty. As surely as if someone or something had dropped a mantle around my shoulders, I had felt, as I passed through that doorway, a settling down upon me of a *persona* I had not been before. I knew to the bottom of my soul that I had become an adult.

I had planned and daydreamed for months my passage out of childhood. I was totally unprepared for my passage out of girlhood. Such a dramatic, complete, and exquisitely defined translation in so specific and discretely defined a place as the front door of a public school had simply not been part of my prior or anticipatory thoughts. Nor, I discovered very quickly, was it reversible. I could no longer be girlish, even with Sam . . . seductive yes, girlish no. The tenor of our life changed as a result.

We began for the first time to engage each other as working partners as well as lovers and best friends. That, too, was an astonishment, since I had not perceived before then that we were still living as overage playmates. The richness of giving to a partner exceeds that of lending and sharing with a playmate by as many degrees of clarity as the light of diamonds exceeds the dark of coal, and I had been quick first to marvel at, and then rejoice in, this unforeseen enlargement in our lives. I should, therefore, have also been self-aware enough to know that the impact and clarity of most other relationships would shift as well.

The most visible shift, at least at the time and to me, was an abrupt about-face in our relationship as a married couple to institutional religion. In 1955 I would have stated the matter more simply, of course. I would have described what was happening to us as a shift in our relationship with church. I'm a bit more chary now than once I was of using that catchall label without qualification, however; and what Sam and I engaged in our time of my shifting was far more naïve than what I would hope the two of us engage now. That is, in 1955 there was in our heads—or at least in mine—no concept of church as a timeless organism. Never once in my life to that point had I (nor could I have) conceptualized "church" as a corpus, a composition of human lives, a holy entity made up in the same way that every living thing is, of differentiated cells, but sustained by divine intention.

Rather, in those long-ago days of our beginning, church was a location to be gone to, a means for effecting and deploying social mercy, a body of chronically outdated but defensible and evolving dogma, a grouping of constitutionally similar folk, a sustaining community offering identity and context as well as acceptable human contact, an arena for the exercise and experience of ecstacy . . . The list goes on, all of the items on it (and more to boot) being true. All of them, in other words, would be perfectly applicable to every Christian congregation I have ever known. As defining characteristics, they are, nonetheless, more descriptive of institutional or organized religion in general and anywhere than they are in the particular of Christian "church" as a body preparing itself for translation.

Sam and I did not concern ourselves with any of these niceties of ecclesial theory, however, when we went trucking back to Mother Church. Instead, we were following—and I mean no unfairness to our youthful selves here, just a useful candor—a kind of lemminglike, mindless, unthought-out instinct. The shift in me had at last made adults of us both; and where the two of us had come from, sleeping in was what college kids did. Getting up and going to church was what adults did. Our new selves got up and went.

I can't say that I found membership in First Presbyterian Church in downtown Memphis to be any more or less inspiring and exhilarating than had been membership in First Presbyterian Church in Johnson City. They were, in point of fact, remarkably alike, such predictability and constancy being two of the virtues as well as curses of organized religion. I can say, however, that Sam and I found there exactly what we needed at the time. We found a small group of four or five young couples who, having been reared in the faith, were now trying to discover how to put it on and wear it every day as an informing garment.

Our Sunday mornings together as a group of young marrieds, though they were destined to be interrupted from time to time for Sam and me, would gradually evolve into extremely literate as well as confessional discussions of theology and faith. Part of this freedom to roam and still arrive was due to Bill Johnson. What my father would have called "one fine figure of a man," Bill worked for a local educational broadcasting station. He had a speaking voice the four archangels probably coveted and a remarkably low threshold of tolerance for intellectual pretension regardless of who was employing it. He let us know early in our life as a group that if media work had taught him anything at all, it most certainly had taught him that when there are too many words in play at one time, there is almost always a vast and compromising ignorance buried beneath them. "Thus," he declared on our third Sunday morning together, "I honestly believe that when I die, I'm going to look up and see the clouds part and there, shining out at me, will be the words 'Two plus two equals four.' It will be just that simple, once we understand it."

Sam, who finds great beauty in intricacy and chaotic excess, took serious exception to Bill's reductionism; and between the two of them, they kept the rest of us honest, if not relaxed. When Cootsie Schippers would go too far over into determinism (which she tended to do on a regular basis), Bill would say in his maple syrup bass, "And two plus two always . . . always . . . equals four. For this you're blaming God?" If, on the other hand, Jim McKnight tried to take conciseness of interpretation very far into our discussion of a troublesome parable or an annoying epistle, Sam would mutter under his breath something like "Two plus two's boring without 'x' and 'y,' " and we would welcome the unknowns of theology back into the conversation for the rest of that Sunday.

Understandably, although unintentionally, our Sunday school discussions began, within a matter of weeks, to run over into the time allotted for formal worship—which is a politically correct way of saying that we began more and more to shamelessly skip services in order to continue our talking and arguing, sometimes until long after lunch itself had also come and gone. Even that bit of truancy seemed to bond us, making us miscreants together in a delicious naughtiness.

Out of that strange group of earnest seekers, both Bill Johnson and Cootsie's husband, Smitty, are dead now. Every time I think of that, I wonder about two-plus-two and whether or not Bill finally saw the clouds roll back away from that emblazoned statement; but then, I never, ever hear anybody say "Two plus two equal four" without thinking of Bill and Doris Johnson. Jim McKnight, who in those years was head of pedodontics at the university, went on to become a nonstipendary Episcopal priest as well. He and Sussie, his wife, became our first and most enduring barter friends. Sam has been their physician for decades. Jim, having shepherded us through numerous pediatric dental crises, ended up officiating at the marriage of one of our daughters, and as I said not long ago, please God, he shows every sign of intending to stay around long enough to bury at least one or two of us as well.

Like Jim and Sussie, Sam and I have both moved on, me once again and he at last to Episcopalianism. One or two of the other couples we've lost contact with entirely now. But I still remember our time as Presbyterians together as having been, for the Tickles anyway, our first participation in mature community as well as our first introduction to what it means to be incorporated into Church with a capital "C."

Even if our reincorporation into institutional Christianity were the most immediate and visible result of my shift into adulthood, however, it was nonetheless Mary Ada Singleton's words that were to be the more formative for me personally; but I didn't know that at the time. All I knew was that a stranger who had become my warm friend had begun our time together by catching me at prayer and that she had somehow recognized not only what I was doing, but how I was doing it. I knew, in other words, that Mary Ada's recognition, or her response to her recognition, had had to do not with my praying *per se*, but with the presence of that slender Psalter while I was doing so. I understood as well that Mary Ada had meant to convey safety and acceptance when she tossed out her, "She's Jewish. She'll understand, too," at me by way of introducing Minsky.

My mother might have inadvertently taught me the habit of prayer and Dr. T. might have, with equal lack of intent, suggested to me the uses and validity of a prayer book in one's doing so, but Mary Ada gave me something far more consequential. Mary Ada lifted individual prayer out of the realm of the idiosyncratic and plopped it down squarely in the midst of a broad and ample tradition. The informing difference in all of this was not, of course, that tradition is any more compelling or effective than prayer itself or even than the use of manuals in the course of prayer, but that Mary Ada acted, first, nondogmatically and, second, toward an adult. The difference also was that Mary Ada Singleton was the first person in my life to offhandedly and almost artlessly lay Jewish and Christian praxis side by side in the same sentence as part and parcel of one another.

There would, of course, be little or no mystery nowadays about what Mary Ada was referring to in her gestures of kindness. Phrases like "fixed-hour prayer," "the keeping of the hours," "the liturgy of the hours," "the daily offices," "the chanting of the offices," "the *opus dei*" are all terms in more or less general usage today; but they certainly weren't in 1955, at least not in the part of East Tennessee I had come from. To put the matter even more emphatically, it was not that I was an anomaly in my religious naïveté but rather that I was a positively exemplary reflection of the religious naïveté of the times and places that were my part of creation. In my natal frames of reference, the possibility, had Mary Ada pushed it, that any human being might routinely pray at several fixed and sustained times of the day and night, much less that he or she might do so by using a fixed arrangement of set prayers, would have been alien, if not just a little bit reprehensible, to me. In East Tennessee the common wisdom was that "too much praying don't get the wood chopped," a colloquialism frequently expressed a bit more grammatically in other parts of the country as "God helps those who help themselves." Little did I know then—little could I even have guessed—that Mary Ada's almost flip reassurances were actually the first hints, the first suggestions in my mature life, of the discipline that would become my spirit's vocation; and little did I know that the next eight and a half years were to be directed almost entirely toward preparing me to assume it.

35.

THERE IS GREAT DANGER, if not outright presumption, in declaring a single event to have been the most pivotal in one's life. I do not wish to fall into that trap. On the other hand, I am equally reluctant to treat what must follow here as anything less than what it was—a determinant of my years and my self that began quite innocuously and, as has been the pattern of my life, in the most unexciting and unimaginative of places.

We were in that warm, sunny space of Memphis seasons in which October has cooled to morning sweaters and November has not yet turned to raincoats and nasty chills. The day could not have been more tourist-bureau perfect than that Thursday afternoon was. It was late, the sun low in the sky, when Sam picked me up at Messick. We had reversed our pattern that day, and for good reason. I had an after-school faculty meeting, and Sam had driven me to Messick instead of the other way around. The idea was that if he had the car, he could pick me up after my meeting and his classes but still in time for us to go to the grocery store that afternoon. By now I knew all too well that grocery shopping was not my favorite shared activity, and by unspoken consent we had moved it to weekdays in order to avoid tarnishing our weekends with its stresses. In addition, Memphis's grocers all announced the week's specials on Thursdays and, as every dullard knows, the early bird gets the worm. One really had to care about groceries . . . !

Anyway, the *sine qua non* of the specials-of-the-week that week was unfortunately at a singularly dirty and unpleasant supermarket located not more than three miles from Messick and on the fringe of what was close to a ghetto of deteriorating businesses and a devolving neighborhood. I despised the place, but as I have already noted, I despised even more the particular special it was about to will upon me . . . rabbit. Rabbit in those days was sold not by the pound but by the head, and the rabbits that week were going at the unheard of price of forty-nine cents a pop. Even I was smart enough to know that we couldn't afford to not buy the miserable things.

The minute we pushed open the door to the grocery store, I was assaulted—which is how it felt—by the offense of its odors. I swore to Sam that I could smell the rabbits from the distance of the first aisle and that every one of them was cheap because every one of them was either rotten or well on its way there. The closer we got to the meats, the more light-headed and gagged I felt. And sure enough, once we arrived, there in the middle of the floor were two or three tubs of dead rabbits lying whole though headless and skinned in piles of ice that seemed to be chilling only parts of any of them. Sam dug around in the ice to extract the coldest three, our permitted limit, and we finished our shopping.

We were at the checkout counter, Sam in front of our buggy and me behind it, when the black-and-white tiles of the floor began floating up toward me. I remember thinking how odd that anything so nasty could feel so cool and . . .

. . . I had never fainted in my life before and I have never fainted since; but one time was enough to verify the truth of what folk say about floors rising up to meet one. They do, or at least this one did.

Sam, since, has confessed that at first he really thought I was doing some kind of manipulative trick or perhaps engaging in a hysterical over-reaction to the rabbits. While I find that assessment to be singularly un-complimentary, I also believe it was honestly his at the time and not entirely unreasonable, given our brief history as grocery shoppers together. He got me to the car, therefore, less with sympathy than with expedi-tiousness, and we went home. I remember the silence of that drive—it was total—and I remember that before we got all the way to 1094 I felt a small, cramplike pain, a kind of grinding discomfort I remembered having had once before and all too recently. Without saying anything, I let Sam walk me upstairs to bed and then unload the groceries and our things by him-self; but by the time he had them all put away, I had to tell him I thought we were in trouble. This time, though, there was to be no cheap whiskey.

We had assumed that the events of our Old Crow weekend in August were simply too recent to have allowed my body to right itself. We had, more to the point, been almost pathologically intentional about all the sub-tleties of birth control. I had even stained for a day or two in September, and we had been mildly relieved, but neither surprised nor concerned about the scarcity and brevity of that flow. After our August experience, however, Sam, ever the wise companion, had sought out a member of the university's Ob-Gyn faculty for counsel. Now, shortly before supper on that fateful Thursday evening, Sam called him for the second time. We had no phone, of course, so I did not hear the conversation, but my husband's face said a great deal when he came back from using Mrs. Jim's. "I'm go-ing to go pick up some medicine for you," he said.

"I don't need anything yet," I answered. "I'm not hurting, just kind of aching. Why don't you wait until we see if we need it?"

"Because we have to try to prevent a miscarriage if that's what's hap-pening. This is a new drug, he says, and it won't hurt anything if you're not pregnant and it should stop the aching and cramping if you are."

"You think I am?"

"He thinks so, especially given the fainting."

"Oh."

Sam left and came back shortly with a vial of pills, the first of which he gave me before he brought me some supper. I slept as if Thursday had been the most ordinary of days. The next morning Sam stopped on his way to classes and called Messick with the word that I was suffering from some kind of stomachache and would return on Monday. I dutifully took a pill every four hours as prescribed and alternated between dozing and fretting about how much damage such early absenteeism might do to my teaching record. Sam came home, once again cooked supper, and once again gave me a pill before turning out the lights. We were encouraged.

I woke up to the funniest thing . . . the most bizarre thing . . . the most confusing thing . . .

. . . somewhere . . . somewhere over there Sam was screaming . . . but somewhere else over here he was on top of me, still screaming . . .

. . . I was on my stomach . . . our door was open . . . Sam was just yelling and yelling . . . yelling for Mrs. Jim in the middle of the night with our door open . . . I drifted off . . .

. . . I heard them . . . I mean, they made so much noise that the dead would have heard them! . . . Sam looked funny with his pants on over his pajamas and no shirt except his pajama tops . . .

. . . as they carried me around the bend of the stairs, I saw Mrs. Jim crowded back into the corner saying her rosary and crying. She even touched me as I went by, but I couldn't feel her . . . couldn't feel Mrs. Jim's dear hand . . .

The roof above me was metal and all exposed, with no upholstery or paint . . . the siren at least was familiar . . . if I were going to be in an ambulance, I would really like to be able to enjoy it . . . so sleepy . . . and old Sam just slapping me and sticking a mask in my face . . . so funny really, all of it so funnnnnn . . .

36.

THERE ARE amongst us human beings and especially amongst our theologians and philosophers a veritable bevy of low-key but ubiquitous arguments about the standards and definitions of truth once it has entered into time and turned into event. Which is more accurate, they argue, the truth of an action as it is remembered or the truth of something as it actually happened? Is there—can there ever be—any accuracy about such matters anyway, any pure record of what happens in our temporal existence? That is, can there ever be a record so all-encompassing as to be complete or, more to the point, can there ever be a recorded event that is not itself polluted or colored simply by the very process of having been recorded? Is the notion of absolute accuracy of record within the course of human activities and happenings even appropriate in the first place? Is such not rather a kind of platonic ideal that pales in relevance before the consequences and sequelae of experienced reality, an ideal which, by its very stipulated presence, more frustrates than advances human society with its pronouncements about what must or should have been?

The questions are as tedious as they are elderly, and it seems safe to assume that most of us will never resolve our own answers to them with any kind of abiding consistency. Perhaps we are not even supposed to. Perhaps the arguments alone and their attendant incongruities are, as some say, present among us not as constants in search of reconciliation, but as discomforts sent to remind us we are individual components of a much larger whole. We would be but poor, encapsulated microcosms forever bouncing off of and bumping into one another, so the apologia goes, were we not goaded beyond our own experiences and perceptions and memories by the tease of other and differing actualities possible within time. We would, each of us, be little more than childish and destructive victims of our own individual rightness were there no contrary precepts to challenge that rightness's integrity or its natural dearth of compassion. That's the theory of some theologians and thinkers anyway. I have to confess that it is also my theory, more or less and at least for the time being, though it may not be my position six months from now and it most certainly was not my position forty-five years ago. Forty-five years ago, I could not even have conceived of the possibility, much less the utility, of there being various degrees of accuracy operative within human events. I could not have, that is, prior to the chain of them that began with my Friday night ride to the hospital.

My total recall of that dramatic evening is no more and no less than what I have already recorded here. I know now, but only because I have been told so, that I stopped breathing just after midnight and that Sam, who had had his arm around me as we slept, had been wakened almost immediately by my stillness. Even if I had understood all of this at the time, however, I doubt that I would have been disturbed by it. I was much too comfortable to be disturbed. My only memory of any distress at all, in fact, is of those few seconds when I realized Mrs. Jim was touching me and that I couldn't feel the warmth or pressure of her hand. Even that fleeting moment of sadness was washed away almost immediately, however, by a kind of detached and pleasant euphoria. Undoubtedly I would have enjoyed such a state of well-being enormously if only I had been able to stay awake. For some reason I just couldn't. I drifted off instead . . .

There is in me absolutely no memory, corrupted or otherwise, of what happened after I slipped back into unconsciousness in the ambulance, just as there basically is little or no memory of the four months that were to follow. Despite the assurances of doctor after doctor that the memories of those lost weeks would eventually surface again, they have not. More telling, probably, is the fact that after so many years without them I would be loath to receive those memories back again, even if some shaman or magus of such matters could offer them to me. I have built a life instead on the memories I do have and/or on my selective recall of them. It is, as the philosophers and theologians have said, what I do remember and how I have remembered it that have shaped my life. My house is built, in other words, and whether it be founded on rock or sand only God in the end will say; but it is built, and there will not be another now.

Suffice it here to say that the next time I woke up, I was in a hospital bed and it was broad daylight. I woke up amused . . . amused that my body was so still it was making almost no rumples in the sheets that were covering me. I wondered where it had gone off to, that body of mine, and how it had left me behind, so neat and straight, without it. Then I saw Sam sitting beside my bed looking as if he'd never shaved or washed or slept in all of time. I think he said something . . . I know he smiled . . . but I couldn't hear him very well, or else couldn't follow the sense of what he was saying, which was the same thing, I decided. Some nurse was standing there, too, and gave me another one of my pills. "Good," I thought, "I'm still pregnant," and went back to sleep.

The next time I woke up was apparently only an hour or so later. I was up in the corner of the room just above my bed. That is, I was in the space where the outside wall and one of the inside walls of the room converged with one another and the ceiling. To say I was sitting there would not be quite accurate, inasmuch as the upper corners of rooms do not admit of sitting *per se,* so much as of crouching or wedging. By whatever method one calls it though, my back was curved into the juncture of the two walls and the ceiling while my legs were drawn up in front of me and my chin was resting on my fists which were resting quite comfortably on my knees, thank you very much. I was pleased to discover as well that in this perch, I felt exactly like a gargoyle snugly fashioned up under the overhang of a cathedral roof. I was even more delighted to discover that I could move back away from me and see that I also looked like a gargoyle up there against the unforgiving plaster of the corner. It was all quite charming really until Sam began to make another ruckus.

This time he made so much noise that I had to look down, and when I did I lost my gargoyle existence. In fact, just by looking down at Sam and his annoying racket, I lost all my body, either recent or past. I was nothing but an awareness devoid of any agency beyond itself because, as I discovered, I really was down there in that hospital bed, and Sam really was beating on me again and he really was yelling again and buzzers really were going off and nurses really were scurrying. But I couldn't be bothered by any of that, for I was no longer looking down. Instead, something or someone had caused me to look to my right; and there in that spot where there should have been only more ceiling, there was only light.

Without a care for anything that had ever been or ever was or ever might be, I lifted toward the light as lithely as if I had been a sparrow upon the courses of the early morning wind. The light toward which I floated had the soft brilliance of a luminous lily, and it radiated out in sweetness from a marvelous tunnel that was green like summer grass and perfectly round. I moved into the tunnel and thought to myself that it was like a glowing culvert between two meadows; and the light at the other end was sending out the blessing of that place, and it said, "Come."

And I wanted to. All of me wanted to . . . all except the part that for just an instant looked back through the tunnel to Sam, still bent over my bed. That part said to me and to the light, "I can't come now. I have to go back to him and the children we are going to have." And the light said, "Yes, go." And I did, except that I don't remember any of my return.

37.

WHAT I HAVE DESCRIBED is, of course, a textbook-perfect case of what we now call a near-death experience, or in popular parlance, an NDE. The only slightly unusual variation in what happened to me is the fact that it was immediately preceded by a vivid and equally classic out-of-body experience, or OBE, again in popular parlance. The distresses—at times the near-agonies, in fact—Sam and I were to endure as a result of my experiences arose not from any question about the orthodoxy of the episodes themselves but from the time of their happening. In 1955 there were no vernacular names, no popular parlance, for either near-death or out-of-body experiences. For all practical purposes, there was no professional literature about them either; there certainly was no lay literature and almost no body of experiential records. What happened to me happened, in other words, in a medical and theological vacuum that carried with it the stigma of ignorance, the suggestion of a kind of derangement or instability that was best not talked about, even within one's family. It would take me several weeks to find the energy and strength requisite to making that sad discovery, but I had to get well first.

The next time I roused, it was late at night, dark everywhere except for the lamp by my bed. I could see Sam dozing in the hospital chair. Somewhere along the way he had changed clothes and shaved, but he still looked puffy and blanched. "What's wrong?" I said, and he was instantly on his feet and over me again.

"It's the drug," he said. "I've stopped it. Can you hear me? It's the drug. Don't let them give you any more of anything unless I'm here. Do you understand?"

I nodded. Thus reassured, he pulled the chair closer to the bed and taking my hand in his, sank down into it and was asleep almost instantly. I watched him for a while, dozing off now and then myself. He roused several times to say, "You all right?" or "You still awake? Good," and then was gone again. Finally I woke up enough to say, "Go home now. You look awful."

Nurses came in and out, and even when I had drifted back into sleep, they woke me by shaking my bed vigorously. They also woke Sam, primarily to also tell him to go home. Everything was going to be all right. Everything was under control. Eventually either he believed them or his own exhaustion defeated him. I remember only that he took a piece of paper off the nightstand, showed it to me, and said, "Give it to Dr. Calliston when he comes. Do you understand what I'm saying?" I must have nodded again, because the next thing I remember is waking up to Marcus

Calliston standing by my bed and reading the paper on which Sam had worked out the cause-and-effect relationship between my clinical symptoms and the pharmacology of the drug I had been taking.

I'd never met Dr. Calliston before that midnight meeting, but I knew who he was. He was one of the most revered, if not outright feared, internal medicine men in the South at that time, and he would shortly thereafter go on to become dean of the Medical College as a result of his superb abilities as both a physician and a teacher. He was also indefatigable, famous for making his final hospital rounds after midnight just to be sure all was well with his patients through the night watches. He must have introduced himself, but I have no memory of anything save seeing him read by the glow of the lamp and hearing him say to me, "You tell that young husband of yours that he's a Damned Good Diagnostician."

Compliments from Calliston may have been hard to come by in those days, but once given, they were generously continued; and the tale of Sam's medical prowess began that evening with Dean Calliston and spread from there. So, too, did the jesting that Sam's first advanced degree was a D.G.D., granted that night by Marcus Calliston and perpetuated by him ever afterwards. The D.G.D. appellation we have treasured, though, not so much because it was flattering and accurate, but because it was to be the only moment of emotional relief or beneficence in our lives for quite a while.

My antimiscarriage drug had been an anticholinergic-blocking agent, something that, in medical terms, can block the autonomic nervous system and obscure the proprioception if used in the wrong dosages or chemical combinations. In lay terms, it can in the wrong situation or mixture shut down one part of one's nerve pathways so completely that no incoming signals are received, much less interpreted. The patient is, in effect, bodiless because, as I was to discover, there is no sensation coming in from anywhere, not from the soles of one's feet to the diaphragm beneath one's lungs to the pain in one's cramped or unchanged positioning.

My particular nemesis had been a very new drug and on the market just less than a year when it almost killed me. Before I left the hospital, most of the neurologists at the university and/or their students trooped through my room, or so it seemed. I don't remember any of their names or much of what they said except their assurance that the drug was suspected of having been involved in the deaths of five other women and that their reports of my experience should be enough to remove it forever from the market. That having been said, they stuck me with straight pins I couldn't feel and tested me with charts of red and green dots whose variations in hue I couldn't perceive much less name. They asked me stupid questions about the day of the week and the name of the president which so annoyed me that they finally concluded it was my body and not my mentation that was in trouble and began instead to spend their visits trying to persuade me that all the other parts of me would also return to their proper functioning within a matter of just a few weeks. After that, my brief life in the hospital, as I remember it, was not unpleasant. Nurses came in and moved my legs for me or washed me and in general took care of all the tiresome things one has to do to maintain a body. Since I could not feel mine, I was grateful.

At some point we lost the baby and at some other point we went back to number 1094, but I have no idea when or how either happened. I only know that I remember being in our bed again, and that Aunt Maggie was talking to me. Aunt Maggie had always seemed to Sam and me to be a spinster removed from reality and bent by her years, though she could not have been quite seventy when we married. Mamaw's oldest sister, Maggie had spent her youth and fertile adulthood, as did so many firstborn women in the nineteenth-century, in caring for the babies, the ill, and then the aging of her birth family. All those obligations had eventually been met and, in her full maturity, Aunt Maggie had gone on to become the only thing she knew how to be, a home-care nurse. She had always been rather cheerful about this career shift, claiming that her life really had changed only in that she had moved from a barter to a cash economy. While she was in later life paid for her services, she was also expected for the first time in her life to buy her own food and pay her own rent. Where was the gain or the loss in that? In retirement, however, she had at last struck a balance by taking up permanent residence as a nonpaying but companionable guest with Mamaw and Papaw.

How and when Aunt Maggie got to Memphis is beyond me now, as are the questions of exactly how long she stayed with us or where in that house Mrs. Jim and Sam found space to sleep her. Almost every memory I have from the weeks of November and early December, though, is of Aunt Maggie's sitting beside my bed tatting, watching me, and talking.

Eventually it began to dawn on me that Miss Maggie was not making idle chatter, either, but rather that she was quite deliberately filling in the gaps in my missing weeks . . . what Sam had done and was doing, what my parents had done while they were there (I have no memory to this day of their having come), what Mamaw had written in her almost daily letters, what Mrs. Jim had done for Sam while I was in hospital and what she had done since, what the larger world was up to and had managed to accomplish while I was *non compos mentis*. I recall none of it now, of course, only my sense of amusement at, and gratitude for, her skillful concern.

I can remember quite clearly the day in early December when Sam stuck a pin in my leg and I felt it. We were all drunk with relief, and a few days thereafter he got me up on my feet for a moment or two, and shortly after that he began walking me in the evenings when he came home. With my elbows pressed into the palms of his hands, he walked behind me bending his knees just slightly into the backs of mine, shoving the toe of each shoe under the corresponding heel of mine, and then nudging my feet forward, one after the other. Once I could keep my balance enough to walk, albeit with help, we knew we were on our way.

Aunt Maggie went home for Christmas, and Sam cooked the biggest pot of the best spaghetti I have ever tasted. We ate on it for a week, and he laughed like a boy again when he came home with a stub of a Christmas tree, flocked it with the foam off of whipped detergent, and lit it from below by clipping our bed light to the edge of the card table on which he had set it. There were even presents sent from Johnson City and some from my students, one each from Minsky and Mary Ada, and one or two from med student and church friends who had endured with Sam and sustained him through it all.

To this day I think that neither of us knows quite how Sam managed to stay in school that dreadful term; but when his grades came just after Christmas, we knew he had not only stayed, he had survived. The Damned Good Diagnostician had proved his stamina as well as his skill. That left only the near-death experience to be dealt with as 1956 slipped, cold and rainy, into its appointed place on the new kitchen calendar that one of my students had included in our Christmas gifts.

38.

AS MY STRENGTH RETURNED with the advancing days of the new year, so did my desire to talk and talk and talk, and then talk some more. Unfortunately, since I was still confined more or less to the small path between bed and chair and sofa, since I was now alone all day, and since my control of my eyes still did not allow much if any reading, Sam was the sole recipient of all I wanted to say and ask. My returning health, in other words, was almost a greater burden than had been my illness . . . or if not burden, then certainly as great a threat to his own survival. I knew that, of course—knew that he had to study and knew as well that he was now also bearing all the demands of our domestic life alone—but knowing and respecting those facts were not enough always to rein in my own need to talk through what had happened to me and what it meant.

I was like a person who had come up out of days and days lost in a deep fog and who, emerging, found herself somehow possessed of a great gift that she had stumbled across in the mist. Or, no, stumbled across is wrong, though not entirely; rather and more accurately said, a great gift she had been allowed to stumble upon and then given to take back with her beyond the fog. I needed, with all the passion of the recent traveler as well as all the loneliness of a long confinement, to show off my treasure. I needed for Sam to let me show it to him, and I needed for him to puzzle out its intricacies with me, not for me. He could do neither.

I know now—we both know now—that what prevented him was not the tensions and burdens of school or the time drains of domestic obligations or even his own emotional exhaustion from so harrowing a few weeks as he himself had endured. What prevented him was a kind of low-grade fear, a repugnance toward what I was trying to express, and—this is inevitable in such gripping experiences—an inability to comprehend in any useful way what I was, as he said, "babbling about."

The first thing, then, that must be said about my near-death experience is that it was also the first thing in our lives that we could not talk about, and it was to remain so until quite recently. Every marriage of any length develops those emotional no-go areas which the partners simply seal off and refuse to enter, not out of courtesy or affection, but out of a commonsense recognition that irreparable destruction lies there. The pain of that discovery—first of making it and then, second, of having to live with it—was for me the keenest agony of my extended illness, just as learning to forgive Sam for his part in it has constituted much of the major work laid upon my soul by the whole affair. How badly my NDE threatened Sam's soul—threatened everything he believed in, in fact—was obscured for me by the driving hunger of my own need to show and tell and be told.

Over the years, of course, much of my forgiveness of Sam has come from the same anguished discoveries we all have to make as we mature. Much of our singularity—and ultimately of our utility to the larger machinations of life—is fashioned out of the emotions we can't share, the agonies of our truncations and the wounds of our isolations. We forgive each other, in such cases, not for our sins, but for our innocent guilt in being co-existents in a system that makes our offenses against one another inevitable, co-existents in a system that indeed militates for and is dependent upon those offenses. Forgiveness for how things are is forgiveness of God. It is, finally, self-subjugation into a searing praise of such a majesty as only the soul can know, and then can address only as mystery.

That understanding, torturous as has been its coming, stands as the great gift of my NDE. The other consequences and sequelae of that event I am less sure of. That is, I still do not know whether they were circumstances I have squandered or ones I have used correctly. In many ways, like the state of my house's foundation, the question itself is moot now.

Having never before heard of or known about a near-death event and being confined to my own resources for considering it, I interpreted what I had experienced, understandably enough, at its most primitive and obvious level. I thought I had seen heaven itself and heard the voice of, if not God or Jesus, then certainly one of the archangels. I not only thought that at the time, but I continued to be sure of it right up until I was well over fifty years of age. And while I am no longer so sure as once I was about NDEs, I still cringe when someone who, like Sam, has never had one cavalierly pooh-poohs the possibilities of God and heaven and archangels as participants in them. That is to say that although I am increasingly convinced I experienced a physiological event that I interpreted simplistically for years, I am not to this day sure enough of that conclusion to go on record as saying so without some caveats. Nor am I at all sure that divine and physiological agency are either mutually exclusive or necessarily distinct from one another. I can, nonetheless, say quite unconditionally that I find the interpretation of NDEs as physiological (or partially physiological) phenomena to be much more exciting theologically and intellectually than are the more standard interpretations of them as solely and only meetings in time between God and humankind.

Regardless of how one evaluates or explains NDEs, however, there are still certain things one must acknowledge about them—or that I have had to acknowledge about my own. Not the least of these is the fact—the hard, constantly reported fact—that with very few exceptions NDEs are inexpressibly beautiful, suffused with a joy far beyond the paltry reaches of that word. There is, in those brief encounters, all the sureness of acceptance and sustaining, unending being that the soul has ever longed toward or any life has ever labored to achieve. It is all there, and all given without restraint or cost. One emerges from such an interruption of ordinary life . . . No, that is perhaps presumptuous. I must say instead that I emerged from the interruption in my ordinary life, persuaded that death was a good and welcoming thing, a state to be anticipated, hoped for, relished as my inherited portion within eternity's peace and security.

Let me hasten to say that there is not, and never was, anything suicidal associated with such convictions. I simply understood from the very beginning that in having asked to return, I had also assumed unto myself the responsibilities as well as the joys of continuing to live. There would be no physical ending for me until the pledges implicit in my having asked for husband and children had been either fulfilled or else fulfilled as completely as circumstances external to my will would permit. From the very first days of my returning normalcy, there was no question for me but that the remainder of my secular life would forever after be first and foremost about the one man and the one group of children for whom I had asked. Whatever might come after that or as attendant to that, the vows I had taken on earth in marriage had been repeated as vows made, if not in heaven, then in some place of unutterable glory. It was so for me then, and it has remained so through all the years since.

What the beauty and exquisite goodness of near-death caused me to do, then, was not to pursue death, but rather to domesticate it. To this day, I still do not know whether that has been a good or a bad thing, a productive or debilitating factor in how my life has lived out its time and informed my soul. That, too, is a moot question, for the truth is that for years—decades—after 1955 I simply could not fear death. I could, and did, fear the horrors of pain and sorrow and/or of the half-deaths that leave our poor bodies broken and prisoners of themselves; but I could not fear death itself. What the loss of that particular fear does to one's spiritual life is to instantly remove from it much of what institutional religion and formal dogma use as glue for holding the faith and the faithful together. The effect of having the fear of death be obviated is, as a result, a little like the flabbiness and disorganization that obtain in a marriage which has suddenly lost every trace of its former eroticism. The rules not only change, but their very absence dramatically exposes the absolute lack of any secondary or substitutable ones.

Like a good knife, the loss of all fear of death cuts two ways, of course, or it did for me. That is, it allowed me to obey and to worship, however inadequately, out of overwhelming love and conviction and, to the extent there was any fear at all, out of a fear of displeasing or damaging or violating a beloved communion, not out of some dark dread or sureness of unending punishment, though in this, too, I am no longer so completely persuaded.

What the removal of any fear of death also did was stifle any real desire in me to live for the sake of life. I passed through years after my NDE rejoicing in what was waiting for me when I was done here, but more or less oblivious to what was being given now. I could pray for the goodness of God in this world, in other words, but not for life itself as a divine desire extending always from before into beyond. That is such a limitation as one never recovers from probably . . . unless perchance my NDE were accurate and "all things are well, and all things shall be well."

Another sad limitation accruing from my more or less Sunday school interpretation of my own near-death experience was that I was so persuaded by the comforting perfection of it that I refused to consider any less mystical and more physiological explanations. This was, in part, the fault of my pushing Sam, against his wishes, to talk to me about what had happened. The more I pushed, the more he protected himself in scientific jargon and physiological explanations. The more I insisted, the more he resisted with polysyllabic words and tedious disquisitions about what happens to the body when there is oxygen deprivation and about levels of consciousness and about the intricacies of cortical stimulation, any one of which, he assured me, could account for what I was describing. Having no science, or at least none at his level of sophistication, I retreated stubbornly into what I had ascertained experientially. Eventually, as I have said, we simply quit talking at all; and when that happened, I entered a mental and spiritual landscape known for its great and considerable hazards.

Historically, there are and have been few dangers to the soul more seductive or more insidious than having the human mind accept into itself as divine that which is really only mechanically or physically explicable. Perhaps nothing, in fact, threatens the health and well-being of our contemporary religious and spiritual practice, either individually or as a people, than does this very thing. Our human inability or our proud unwillingness to separate the mechanism from the designer far too often creates an idolatry replete with whole panoplies of false but attractive prophets. Not for nothing, I have learned the hard way, did the ancients hold discernment of the spirits to be among the noblest and more difficultly acquired gifts of the Spirit.

Beyond danger, however, there was also a certain loss of richness that came when Sam and I quit talking. That is, we lost for years any opportunity to apply his very real and verifiable observations to my personally sustained ones, and thereby we both lost an opportunity to enhance ourselves as well as each other. In all fairness one must also note here and now, of course, that in this instance at least most of our present knowledge was not even dreamed of in 1955. Sam's observations, in other words, about the brain and how it operates were as crude in relation to what he knows and would say to me today as a caveman's sharpened flint is to a Henckels knife.

One of the things, obviously, that has led me out of my entrenched insistence about having seen heaven in a hospital room in 1955 is the fact that much of the research that has been done since seems to establish irrefutably that we are indeed most marvelously made, far more marvelously than anyone could have guessed in the middle decades of the twentieth century—and that we are far beyond our consciousnesses; that the sum of each of us exceeds the tabulation of our parts; and that those parts in their union do indeed seem to be indwelt by life, by the *rauch*, as I now embrace, celebrate, and adore it. But, as Henry Van Dyke once said in his story of the other wise man, that is the product for me of my long way of coming and my strange way of arriving.

But enough. It is sufficient here to say that my final secular vows had been taken and then sanctified by 1955 and that the courses of much of my Christian life, as well as the vocation and vows that would define it, had likewise been set by that strange and powerful year. The new one into which Sam and I were just entering would both continue that work and, incredibly enough, discipline, but not diminish, its pace.

PART SIX

East Norhall Circle

39.

MY FATHER, who by any set of standards was a man of considerable accomplishment, was also a man not much given to talking about either himself or his attainments. This was not a result of any natural or even any studied modesty on his part so much as of a kind of quiet ease he had with himself and with what he had done with his years. In truth, I can remember his bragging with earnestness and consistency about only two things during the time I was growing up.

One of these sources of pride was that he and Mother had survived the Great Depression, admittedly by means of grace and good fortune, but also by means of a certain degree of sheer cleverness on his part. He had gotten the two of them through those years with a roof still over their heads, food in their bellies, and clothes of a sort on their backs. They had neither frozen in winter nor begged and pilfered in summer. It was he who, when Mother's overshoes—a necessity in our mountain winters—finally frayed beyond use, contrived a pair of new ones for her out of old, abandoned inner tubes. It was he who collected all the little chips and slathers of used-up soap bars and, soaking them in glasses of water, melted them into a second life as the viscous liquid with which they bathed. It was he who had struck the grocery agreement with the Scott brothers that was to last a lifetime. It was he who had found and then cultivated the wild mint that made unsweetened hot water into an acceptable tealess tea and even, in some more romantic moments, into a coffeeless after-dinner treat. It was he . . .

The stories were as long and graphic as the years that had evoked them. Like all stories, they grew in their elaborations and heroic proportions with each retelling; but by and large, I never sensed that the retelling had as much to do with me or the refining of his stories as it had to do with him. There was no question that he was telling me tales about the most difficult period in his life and Mother's, but mainly, I thought, he was telling the tales to himself even while he was directing them at me. He seemed to need those stories the way a soldier needs his trophies. He certainly opened them up to me with the satisfaction of a veteran unlocking a display case of battle treasures. Though he might have become an intellectual and a member of the academy, he seemed to be telling us both, he still was a man for all that, a man who under impossible circumstances had provided for his family as adequately and successfully as his times and heritage said a true man must provide. Of this he was proud, and by this he was affirmed.

The other of his accomplishments that drifted from time to time into my father's conversations with me was the fact that he had been the first Southerner to be sent by Columbia University to do graduate work abroad. This he always mentioned with a kind of wonderment tinged with poignancy—wonderment that Wade Alexander from tiny Tiptonville, Tennessee, should somehow have become the acceptable recipient of such an honor, and poignancy that he had left one Wade Alexander somewhere in Scotland or on the Continent and had not entirely succeeded in coming home with another.

"Foreign travel," he would say with a slight shake of his head, "foreign travel changes one forever," and then he would grow quiet, as if he were testing the implications of that observation for the first time. "Domestic travel—going down the road or going a continent away, that part doesn't matter—opens your eyes to new possibilities and new ways of seeing things, but they're still your eyes when you get back home with them. But going abroad, that's different. That makes you different."

In our own era of a rampant globalization that drives ever-increasing numbers of us to trot all over the world as easily and with as little fuss as our great-grandparents used in going to the grocery store, my father's observations seem now to lie somewhere between quaint and antique. If, however, one remembers that he was making them within the context of events, and the effect of events, that took place in the 1920s, they take on a different cast and go looking for a different analogy. I think, in other words, that my father's early-twentieth-century experience of foreign travel was far more analogous to the outer-space travel of the later twentieth century than to my deciding, for example, that I should go to Japan for a series of meetings a month hence or to Chile for a week's holiday with friends.

What my father was trying to articulate to me was his discovery that travel into an other and alien world makes one a citizen of neither the country of one's origin nor the country of one's transient habitation, but rather a dweller in some place between the two of them. It makes one a dweller in a kind of corridor that tunnels along between the two, in fact. And while that corridor's doors and windows may open broadly onto the two worlds that run beside it, it is still the corridor, not either of the two discrete worlds forming it, that becomes one's context and frame of reference thereafter. If I did not understand this as a child under my father's tutelage or even as a young woman in his beloved presence, I certainly had begun to understand it by the end of January 1956. I, too, had been a traveler in an alien world. I, too, would spend the rest of my life in a corridor that ran between what I had seen and been in one place and what I had seen and been in another. All the distancing and shotgun focus which that image implies would accrue to me as well. So too would all its advantages, though in my initial isolation I would never have believed that.

Instead, in those days of returning sensations, I struggled with confusion like Jacob with his angel, knowing only that I felt disjointed. Feeling blessed would take considerably longer for me than a single night of wrestling, but it would come. It would come with the years, just as, at last, a pure gratitude has come . . .

And that's my one and only tribute, at least on these pages, to Pollyanna, the saint of the annoyingly compliant. While I could never bring myself to join her chorus of devotees, I do have to acknowledge that she sometimes sees clearly and speaks true.

40.

"THE TIGER SPRINGS in the new year. Us he devours." Eliot had written those words and then gone on to assert in poetry, as only he could, that we human beings "have not reached conclusion" when we "stiffen in a rented house," nor have we "made this show purposelessly." Himself a permanent immigrant, Eliot had had the immigrant's way of knowing, my father's way of knowing, my new way of knowing . . .

The minute I thought of T. S. Eliot, the minute he jumped into my thoughts for the first time in weeks, I knew that, in whatever shape or condition, I, too, was on my way home. A pinprick perceived may signal health to the body, but poetry in one's head sings of the reestablishment of reason and vitality in its interior. I reached for my Norton's and found, with tearful delight, that at last I could hold the lines separate and apart enough to read a little. Had Eliot known more of alien worlds than his self-imposed transplantation to England? It didn't matter. It was January, and I was reading again.

Most of January and February are lost to me except as detached memories of the bits and pieces of improvement, the little instances of minor triumphs and small joys, that mark any patient's march back toward full activity. Spring came, as it tends to do in Tennessee, twice that year, once in late January and once in April. When it came in January, I was balancing well enough to make my way unaided and at my own volition to the dining room/sleeping porch with its cheery yellow chairs and its relentlessly absorbing view of the carriage house. I read as much as I could each day before my eye muscles rebelled, and then I stared shamelessly and for hours at the life going on below me both in the back house and along the small stretches of Waldran that I could see from my windows. It was television without commercials and without censors. I loved it.

The Memphis City School system, however, to their eternal credit and our still-loyal gratitude, had not only continued to pay my whole salary during November and December, but they were still continuing to do so in January and then February. My sense of obligation for this constancy grew with every passing week, and by Valentine's Day all I wanted from Sam or the doctors was their certification to Messick that I was fit to return. I didn't get it, of course, until March, but I did get it. The real obstacle was unfortunately not the certification of my restored health, however, but the complexities of effecting its freedoms. I still could not tell red from green or from most other shades and hues in between and surrounding them.

In point of fact, it would be almost a year before I could look at a stoplight in broad daylight and say with confidence, "That thing's red." The people who issued the state of Tennessee's drivers' licenses in 1956, however, seemed to think that such an ordinary thing as distinguishing red from green was essential to the well-being of the general populace, if not to Sam's and mine; thus and also in point of fact, we had a real problem.

Folk wisdom has always held that it's the little things in life that destroy us; and those ten miles of Memphis that ran diagonally south and east from 1094 Poplar to Messick High School almost destroyed us, primarily because being diagonal, they also ran contrary to every route in the entire public bus system. We simply could not figure out a way to negotiate those miles without my being able to drive, although goodness only knows we tried everything, including ourselves and our friends.

At first, Sam got up even earlier to drive me to Messick in time to get back to the university for his own classes, and then repeated the whole process in reverse in the afternoons. The flaw in that was apparent almost immediately; I was still too compromised to sustain such long hours. Minsky, who lived only two miles due east of us, tried driving me in for a few mornings. Mary Ada, who lived literally in the shadow of Messick but was not going to be outdone because of it, dutifully drove me back home in the afternoons; but neither of them could be expected to support that kind of drain on their own time and energy for long. Yet I had to work. While the city might have generously continued my check, that check was nowhere near enough to cover our bills, not even in those days of professional-courtesy billing. Long before the end of March, we both knew we were going to have to move close enough to Messick for me to walk to work, and that if we wished to have any friends and/or any sanity left, we were going to have to do so quickly.

The years caught between the end of World War II and the resolution of the war in Korea were a near-decade of great disjuncture in this country. The older I grow and the further I live on out beyond them, the more I appreciate the social, cultural, and political magnitude of those eight or nine years in which capitalism and Yankee ingenuity began to translate the technology of war into a whole new set of definitions for the good life and the American way. The areas of the country that had from their beginnings been primarily agrarian in life-style were especially susceptible to postwar visions of a better, or at least physically easier, life.

Oriented by heritage toward acquiring goods and services through the expenditure of time and sweat more than through the outlay of cash, organized by homogeneous moral and social codes, and anchored by family, the rural citizens of our dying order all too rapidly became uneasy constituents in our new and still undefined technological one. Cities that before the world war had had ample housing suddenly had none, especially for the less affluent. Towns that before Pearl Harbor had provided adequate social services suddenly found themselves possessed not only of systems burdened to the breaking point but also of tax bases incapable of assuming debt for the repair and expansion of those systems. Municipalities that had come out of the Great Depression blessed with abundant public grounds now found civic parks to be totally incapable of diverting rural physicality into anything even approaching orderly urban living.

The restiveness and social unease of that decade, which would finally find full expression in the sixties and seventies, were especially obvious during the mid-1950s in the South, particularly in Memphis. With its proximity to Mississippi's rural poor, its direct corridor upriver to Chicago, and its heritage of Beale Street and easy living, Memphis was the nearest and most conceivable portal to the promised land of better times. As a result, there was little or nothing to rent in Memphis during those years of influx. Especially was this true in neighborhoods that lay, like Messick's, along the southernmost borders of the city. By 1950, everything habitable and not already inhabited was let and/or sublet, and even sometimes sublet again. But Yankee ingenuity is Yankee ingenuity even in the South.

As the glut of the unhoused grew, so, too, did the glut of inexpensive little cookie-cutter houses. Built of clapboard and with modest to moderate square footage, they had been thrown up by the handfuls in the areas surrounding Messick. Where there had been a cotton patch one month, there could by the end of the next month be sewers and driveways filled with tricycles. "Fields of instant slums," one city councilman was to tell the Memphis paper time and again during those years; but Sam and I were oblivious. Like all the rest of the unhoused, we were far more desperate than aesthetic.

By April we had found a house in one of those converted cotton fields, a playdough house that, being almost nine years old, was a senior citizen among its kind and already showing signs either of its age or its less than exemplary construction. It was, however, close enough for me to walk to school and cheap enough for us to afford. The monthly house note, including taxes and insurance, was fifty-five dollars. We were paying Mrs. Jim fifty-eight, a three-dollar difference that might help defray part of the increase we would have as a result of increased utility usage. Aunt Maggie, who had almost adopted us after the weeks of her time with us, volunteered the fifteen-hundred-dollar down payment and, once the purchase papers were actually signed, gave all fifteen hundred to us as a gift.

Almost before we ourselves knew it, we were homeowners and we were moving. When spring came the second time that year, we were in our own home.

41.

APRIL IS THE CRUELEST MONTH, according to Eliot's now overly famous line; and cliché or no, his observation is accurate, at least in the countries of the Northern Hemisphere. Being the most life-bearing, life-infused month of our year, April is the one of all the twelve that exercises among us the least compassion for past pain and the least respect for earlier loss. According to many romanticists and even more preachers, April should be celebrated—congratulated, even—for this. They would have us honor elaborately April's annual reenactment of the miracle involved in taking the weary bulbs of the previous summer and the dead leaves of the previous fall and then forcing them to abandon the last vestiges of their past glory in order to become what they do not yet know how to be: bulbs and seeds to perfumes and pollens, humus and a dank crumble to color and dancing shade. As the things of earth go, this may all be well and good. That is, as the nonsentient things of earth go. But people are sentient. I am sentient; and I was not ready for April. Alas, however, April brooks no holdouts, and in 1956 it was feeling especially cruel.

The truth is that I remember almost nothing about that April. To complain of it, then, may seem to be a work of self-indulgence and little more than the petulance of a whiner; but I would prefer to think of what I am about to say as a record of lamentation, a description of a grief that, whether I wished it or not, had its ultimate uses. What I remember of actual events and people and places is minimal, in other words; nonetheless,

I still hold my own sorrow over what I do remember in too much reverence and respect to try ever to expurgate it.

How much of my vagueness about the physical details of April was still drug-induced and how much was due to my attention's having been so dramatically internalized, I don't know. It certainly is not relevant to the end result. Also pertinent to understanding my dearth of specifics about April is the fact that I remember even less about March and little more about May. They all three, in effect, are gone for me. The sum total of what I do remember about March is exactly what I have already recorded, though I can recall almost none of the context within which most of even those few tidbits took place. I know we moved, for instance, because obviously we must have; but I have little memory of how we found the house at 1075 East Norhall Circle and none about how we got ourselves moved into it; no memory of who, except Aunt Maggie, helped us with what; no memory of leaving Mrs. Jim. Even more wrenching, I have no memory of having gone back to my students and my classroom. There is forever in that particular place a blankness that breaks my heart. The only thing more painful now is that I can remember how the blankness began to recede in April and how for weeks I wished only to be blank again.

I had left Messick on an October afternoon so many experiences and so few weeks earlier as a young woman sure of where she was in life and of who she was. By April I was beginning to understand that I had returned to it possessed of an entirely different set of definitions for each of my former sureties. By April I was being overtaken by moments when, standing in front of my Latin class, I wanted more to weep than to teach, for I had lost the beauty of it. Somewhere in the bright recesses of a tunnel, the near-divine precision of grammar and the brilliant joy of lifting one tongue out into the patterns of another had been blanched into dullness and then, ultimately, had leached away. I would never know them or feel them again; and I could not teach what I no longer had. Instead, I taught the utility of grammar and the intellectual rewards of accomplished translation. The kids believed me and, I am very sure, perceived no difference. That, in and of itself, was a great part of my grief. I could mourn for what might have been. They had no experience from which to do so, and now never would.

By April I also knew that I no longer thought of my classroom as being in and of itself holy ground, for I now had a much broader set of standards against which to gauge the uses of that term. A classroom—my classroom, any classroom—was now by definition a place of preparation, not of being. If it were hallowed at all—and I still knew that the good ones always are—then it was hallowed by human affection and by human discipline, albeit both often exercised with holy intent.

In October I had embraced my students psychologically, using a banter that played constantly to the sparkling miracles of their energy and of their youthful ability to still be surprised. In April, I wanted to embrace each and every one of them physically as they walked back and forth in front of my desk on their way to and from their own. I could not do that, of course, and so my classroom became a place enlivened first by my obligation to them and, only second, by my wonder before the intricacies of them.

How much of all of this was apparent to either my supervisors or my fellow teachers I shall never know, for nothing beyond "How are you feeling these days?" was ever said one way or another, just as "Good to have you back" and later "You're looking well these days" were as close to intimacy as most of their conversations ever got. Not so Mary Ada and Minsky. They, too, were oblique and therefore not intrusive, but they were there.

Within a month of my return, Minsky had taken to walking over to my classroom at lunch from time to time, something she had never done before. There was always an excuse: Mary Ada was too crabby that day for anyone to have to endure her alone, there was a special notice about an in-service meeting she wanted to be sure I'd gotten, Mary Ada was saving us seats at the corner faculty table if we'd just hurry up and get to the lunchroom early. The inventiveness of it all was impressive, but neither of us believed the content. Or at least I didn't, not after the day I looked up near the end of class and saw Minsky already outside. She was not only waiting, she was also obviously listening.

"You're a good teacher, kid," she said to me later as we were walking toward the cafeteria.

"Still?" I said, and saw the tears start in her eyes.

"Still," she said. "I wouldn't lie to you for all the money in the world, not about that."

"It's different now," I said.

"Of course," she said. And then she added, "You wanted maybe to be Peter Pan all of your life?" Which was as close as she ever cut to the bone of my pain, but it was enough.

Mary Ada was never able to say big things flippy. That was Minsky's gift. Instead, Mary Ada would bide her time until she knew precisely what wanted saying and then deliver it. As a result, for several weeks she became more and more silent during our early-morning conversations. I'd catch her almost every morning, at one time or another, cocking her head and studying me when she thought I wasn't watching. I would be talking to Minsky and there would be Mary Ada scrutinizing me from behind the smoke of her cigarette. One April morning after I had caught her puzzling more intently than usual over my face, she put her hand on my shoulder as she got up to go to class. "So," she said as brusquely as ever, "I'm praying for you."

"Thanks," I said, being very sure she meant it and very unsure, at that point in my life, about which of us would benefit more from her doing so. But apparently it satisfied Mary Ada, for after that she went back to being her normal, curmudgeon self, and no more was ever said about my state of disorientation.

None of this means that teaching died for me that April. It did not. I was to teach professionally for another decade and a half before the classroom and lecture hall had taught me all I could accept from them and before they had honed for me, insofar as I could receive them, all the skills I would need for life outside the academy. For most of those years, Sam would still be a student himself, and teaching would support and feed us. But by April of 1956 I had ordered and synthesized enough of my short life as a traveler to know that I was no longer a teacher by eventual purpose; and I found that conviction a heavy load to carry as well as a threat to my understanding of how the devices of life are shaped.

Everything that had been needed to make a teacher out of me had been given, I kept saying to myself, everything. Why? To the extent that I had ever questioned my career choice, had I misread the signs, had I misunderstood the gifts? Or had I—a far more threatening possibility—simply not really stopped to look at all? Had I, instead, gone pell-mell along the easy route of adored role models and well-memorized patterns?

I prayed during those weeks in the greatest disorder. "Why?" as a silent cry, is rarely quiet enough to hear anything but itself. In general, it rarely wants an answer anyway. Certainly my "Why?" as I remember it now wanted none. It wanted only to celebrate its own presence in my remembering life. So, too, did my "If not this, then what?" If being wife and mother were henceforth to be the vowed discipline of my hands and if teaching were now to be no longer its own end but a servant to theirs, what then was the use of all my acquired passion, my now-chronic sense of something "other," or for that matter, of my travels themselves. My blankness became my first trip out into the desert.

Lest all of this become maudlin, however, or just plain unrelieved rather than revelatory, let me say that I do remember discovering quite by accident in that fecund April a most curious and far knottier addendum to my tunnel experience, one that has stayed with me through all the years since.

Christian mythology is no better than, or very different from, the mythology that inevitably grows up around any organized religion. They all indulge in delightful flights of human fancy and charming anecdotes more insightful about the ways of their authors than of their deities. Christianity's canon of myths, however, contains one or two tales that are especial favorites of mine; and given my own experiences, none more than the tale of Lazarus's later years. Lazarus was the beloved friend of Our Lord, and the story of his succumbing to a fatal illness is quite canonical, being as it is, fully recorded in the eleventh chapter of St. John's Gospel. Equally canonical is the story of his being raised from the dead by Our Lord. What I hope is pure myth is the tradition which holds that after being returned to life, Lazarus never laughed again.

Most of my fascination with this particular tale has to do with the fact that in the almost fifty years since 1956, I have never quite decided how to arbitrate the conundrum it presents. There seem to me, in other words, to be only two possible explanations for Lazarus's abrupt loss of laughter, yet neither of them can be established and only one of them is easy to accept: Either the chatterers who created and then perpetuated the tradition of Lazarus's strange loss had never had near-death experiences themselves and therefore had no grasp of what its logical consequences would be; or else one of us—the mythmakers or I—had had an aberrant, even possibly an apostate, episode whilst traveling abroad. Over the years, I have been inclined toward, though not entirely persuaded by, the former because, unlike Lazarus, I came back laughing.

My laughing was no contradiction of my sorrow, but almost an en-richment from or extension of it, one that has been an inextricable part of me ever since. Life for us while we are here is absolutely, irrefutably, and irreparably contained by time and, of course, by length, breadth, and height, although we tend to confuse the role and nature of the latter three dimensions, more than we do those of time, with the role and nature of our own bodies. When one steps, even briefly and through whatever means, outside of the box of our four dimensions, however, one never quite sees life again as being so clearly and formally contained within that box. More to the point here, most of us who by means of an NDE step out of the box come back seeing it as a four-sided playpen that has been placed as a loving but necessary restriction around the glorious and infi-nitely more dangerous world that is embodied but dimensionless life. The result of this shift in awareness is a kind of wry recognition that playpens and being stuck in one are comic in direct proportion to just how deadly serious a playpen's purposes and activities are. Thus my enduring hope that the mythographers were merely innocents in pursuit of a story and that Lazarus also laughed. I pray so anyway, for otherwise the alternative would seem to be that death and NDEs may in fact pass us through to two very distinct and disparate places.

Kyrie eleison. Christe eleison. Kyrie eleison. Lord, have mercy. Christ, have mercy. Lord, have mercy. Amen.

42.

IF THERE IS ANYTHING in this life more annoying and tedious than sitting in a doctor's waiting room while ill, it is sitting in a doctor's wait-ing room among the ill while no longer ailing. Thus, though my few memories of April may be gray and sad, my more numerous memories of May are not only much sunnier but also of a much more irascible turn. If those events of waiting did anything at all to my spiritual life, it was of a repentable and not a recordable nature. The most that can be said for them is that I endured and, for the first time in months, tried earnestly to forget many a day's experiences. Other than that, the rest of May, with its returning vitality, is captured now in images that still make me smile. It was in early May, for instance, that I discovered the rich goodness and energy of strong emotion again.

Number 1075 East Norhall Circle had come with an ancient, almost primitive, barrel-shaped washing machine in its kitchen and a slightly listing clothesline already strung in its backyard, both of them left by former owners on their way to better things. Obviously I had known this intellectually from the beginning—I had been using them both, for goodness' sake—but as functioning facts and pieces of heaven-sent relief, the washing machine and the clothesline didn't penetrate my fog until early May. To be exact, they penetrated on the first Saturday morning in May when I walked into the kitchen and saw my new old washing machine in pieces and parts over the floor and on the counter tops. I thought I was going to die for sure and certain right on the spot, thus the flash of intense emotion that translated into memory. Then I thought I might kill Sam Tickle instead, another intense and equally memorable emotion.

The said Sam Tickle was lying on the floor, which I might add was already smeared with black grease and general muck from the dining room door to the outside back one, with his hand up in the guts of my machine and the silliest damned grin of little-boy pleasure I had seen on his face in months. It was the grin that saved me from instant widowhood. His excuse for his condition was that the machine had had a trickle of water around it the night before, and he didn't want the floor to rot out from a slow leak. The truth was—and I suddenly remembered this in a blinding flash of returning memory—the truth was that the man had been eying that antiquated machine since the day we first walked into the place. He had an itch in his psyche like the itch of a kid closed up in a playroom with a pile of dysfunctional clocks. All I could do for the rest of that weekend was pray the end result of the former would not be the same as the end result of the latter.

By Sunday afternoon, I was scrubbing up mess from my kitchen counters and mopping up even more from around the washing machine; but true to his record, Sam had fixed the leak. We spent a marvelous and slow evening thereafter eating homemade pizza while he explained to me in exquisite detail just exactly how our archaic machine worked. By bedtime we both were happy. Life, at last, was beginning to bear some resemblance to what we once had known. Life, at last, was becoming familiar again, and something we could both recognize.

As May marched toward its midpoint, however, and as we came nearer and nearer to the realities of three summer months without my paycheck, a less ebullient but equally familiar part of life checked in as well. We had to have money. We had managed to acquire furniture by hook and crook, not to mention the kindness of family and friends as well as the luck of the draw at a few sales. Ours might be a discordant, sparse, and well-worn decor, but it was an adequate one. It had, however, cost us the last vestiges of what we had managed to hold on to from our combined premarriage funds. We were, in short, broke and with bills to pay.

Sam's solution to part of our dilemma was fairly straightforward. There was an opening in the medical laboratory at Methodist Hospital. The position required that one work the all-night shift every third night, running the tests that make any major hospital function even during its night hours. It involved as well actually drawing and/or collecting many of the blood, urine, fecal, and tissue samples on which the tests were to be run. The position was, in short, tailor-made for a medical student in mid-training and, as a result, was usually held by one. Sam applied and immediately received the job.

Working all night every third night—and there was no dozing, much less sleeping on this watch—is a drain on anybody, especially on one who is also in medical classes all of the days in between. Sam, however, even on those evenings when he would drag home haggard and totally depleted from his thirty-six sleepless hours of classes and work, seemed nonetheless to be pleased with his situation as well as motivated by more than our need for money. He was learning, he kept telling me, things he could never have learned in the classroom or clinic. He was also gaining valuable contact with the senior physicians in town. This job, though utterly exhausting, was a blessing beyond anything we had any right to expect, he said, and eventually I began to believe him. As it turned out, I should have believed him from the very first, because he was right. My own solution to our financial crisis, on the other hand, while equally beneficent, was far less predictably or obviously so.

PART SEVEN

*The Jewish
Community Center*

43.

FINDING A SUMMER-ONLY JOB, even in good times, is well nigh to impossible, as any teenager or schoolteacher can attest. It was beyond impossible in 1956. The nearer we got to the end of the term, the more frantic I became. Within days I was doing that silly thing of calling about every position listed in the want ads regardless of how unlikely, but all to no avail. There were no jobs for married women without prior experience in bookkeeping, lingerie sales, or cosmetology; and there were no summer-only jobs for anybody, not even in those elect areas. Then on Monday of the last full week of classes, I was in the hall outside my door during a class break and singing the got-no-money-got-no-job blues to our moralist when she said, as indifferently as if my whole life were not about to be changed by her words, "I heard there's an opening for a crafts teacher in the summer camp program at the Jewish Community Center, but I don't know a thing about crafts, do you?"

Of course I didn't know anything about crafts. Nothing, in fact, could be farther from knowing about crafts than an education in classical languages, but I wasn't about to say so, not at that point and most certainly not to her. Instead I said something noncommittal like, "Well, it might at least be worth checking out," and then went for the clincher. "How did you hear about it?"

She thought a minute and said, "You know, I honestly can't remember who told me. I just know you call a man named Paul Schwartz at the JCC, if you're interested."

"Interested," as a word was so far removed from the depth of my need that I didn't even bother to respond beyond thanking her for the information. That afternoon, fortifying myself with that same depth of need, I went home and called Paul Schwartz. Yes, he said, there was an opening, and it was one he was eager to fill as soon as possible, since the summer was essentially upon us all. Did I have any qualifications?

I did not lie. Let the record show, I did not lie. I did, however, exercise a good deal of what can only be called *chutzpah,* a nice Yiddish term that describes in quintessential completeness what other lexicons must cobble together as sheer gutsiness mixed with bald-faced brashness and a monumental disregard for horse sense. I did an end run, in other words. I told him I could teach like there was no tomorrow and suggested he call my principal or any of my colleagues, the names and phone numbers of whom I would be more than happy to mail to him that afternoon or give directly to his secretary as soon as I could look them all up or which I could look up right now while he waited, if he preferred, and . . .

When Mr. Schwartz seemed sufficiently diverted by this energetic and related, but less than coherent, outpouring, I jumped immediately to some of the projects I felt would be age-appropriate for his campers as well as effective precursors for later skills they might need to acquire, because, as we both knew, sequential building was pivotal to sound content determination which . . .

What I was doing, of course, and with absolutely no caution, was mixing all the things I could remember from those miserable educational theories classes with all the things I could remember from very happy years of Girl Scout camp and Daily Vacation Bible School and then throwing in a little bit of the playroom for spice and originality.

He said, "Hmmm," and I was encouraged. He said call back with those numbers before five o'clock, if I could, along with the one at which I could be reached. I thanked him. I also thought, as I hung up, that I had hoodwinked him. I thought so only because I was young, fairly unsophisticated, and totally ignorant about Paul Schwartz. He, before summer's end, would turn out to be one of the shrewdest, gruffest, and most enabling human beings I would ever work for. Part of that shrewdness, moreover, evidenced itself in an almost eerie ability to let other people talk themselves into whatever hole, corner, or commitment they might choose before he attempted to determine his own position. I have envied him that skill for years now; but that comes later in the story, not here.

On Wednesday his secretary called to arrange a time the next afternoon when I could come for an interview; and on Thursday at the appointed hour I went trooping into the JCC. I still was more emboldened by desperation than inspired by any sense of a natural fit between my skills and this job, but I went. Thinking about whether or not I could really do the thing was a luxury I just couldn't afford at that moment. Paul took one long look at me from my hair down to my shoes, turned to his desk and held up three or four sheets full of notes just so I would understand that he had indeed checked all my references right down to Mary Ada and Minsky, and said, without ever inviting me to sit down, "What do you know about our program?"

I was caught out, as they say, caught out and then nailed to the wall. "Not much," I said, realizing far too late to do any good that I should have asked Minsky about the camp program itself as well as for a reference. The truth was that it had no more occurred to me to ask her about the JCC than it had occurred to me earlier to ask Mary Ada about the Methodist Hospital system when Sam was applying there. I couldn't believe my own lapse in common sense, and my will began to melt before the total illogic and impossibility of what I had tried to pull off. Suddenly I was embarrassed as I had been embarrassed only once before in my life. I was embarrassed as I had been on a long-ago afternoon when, standing in front of a bus driver whose token box I had just jammed with a knockout, I was told to get off his bus.

At that moment I wanted to flee Paul Schwartz's office and the whole Jewish Community Center as desperately as once I had wanted to flee my bus driver and the whole Johnson City transit system. I could actually feel my face flushing. He looked at me again with one of those impervious head-to-toe inspections of his and, apparently satisfied that I had been humbled into honesty, said, not unkindly, "Knowing the details of a program beforehand doesn't always determine whether or not you can do it well. I'll give you the details and you tell me whether or not you can do it." We sat down at long last.

For fifteen minutes or so, he showed me both the craft and the general camp schedules, the age groupings, and the preregistration records. Then we got up, and he showed me the JCC in general and the Crafts Room in particular. "Can you do it?" he asked when our tour was done. I looked at Paul Schwartz that time as directly as he had looked at me earlier and said "Yes," because I knew to my very toes that I could indeed do this job.

"Good," was all he said, and shook my hand. Back in his office, I filled out an application form somewhat belatedly, got the requisition forms for all the materials and supplies I would need, was given a key to the Crafts Room so I could inventory what was there and begin to sort and shelve what would be coming in, and was handed the employee pamphlet that explained everything else. I went home elated out of my mind. It was the first job I had ever landed on my own and without any reference to what or whom I had come from. It was not until Sam and I were talking over our great good fortune that evening that I realized I had never once asked Paul Schwartz how much his job paid; but then, as I also realized, Paul Schwartz had never once asked me if I were Jewish. We had, in effect, taken each other on faith, no pun intended.

44.

THE MEMPHIS JEWISH COMMUNITY CENTER, in 1956, was a wonderfully inadequate building pinned together with good humor, hope, and Paul Schwartz's bullheadedness. A new—most would even say splendid—JCC has been built long since; and though I have been in that spectacular facility many times, I still regard it as something of a charlatan, a pretender to former riches of light and texture it can never hope actually to attain.

The old Center—my Center—is boarded up now. When from time to time I am in Memphis and chance to pass it, I have a lurch of the heart that is almost inevitably followed by a sense of peace. The old building is aging, not like urban buildings usually do, but with the dignity and deliberateness of an elderly tree. It is not so much tumbling down in disrepair as simply melting a little deeper each year into the grounds that surround it. Even now, all of its natural diminishments seem still to be protected from overmuch haste by fondness as well as a comfortable removal from the changing patterns of urban life. If anyone had chanced to ask me in 1956, I think I probably would have predicted that kind of demise for the Center. I am enough of a romanticist to think that those who live generously are often granted the final grace of a quiet dying. Not concerns about mortality, however, but decrepitude and certain idiosyncratic twists to its mechanical disposition were the place's informing characteristics when it took me into its embrace in 1956.

My most enduring impressions of the Center as a physical plant, that is, as a campus of sorts, are all ones full of fresh air and light. Sunniness as a summer memory is hardly remarkable, of course, especially not in the American South. By their very definition, summer camps in our climes are sun-drenched experiences that are infamous for being sweat-drenched and mosquito-, wasp-, and bee-laden as well. If there's anything curious about my memories of the JCC as a place, then, it is not so much that they are painted in broad strokes of warm, airy brightness, but that they are so totally devoid of summer's attendant unpleasantnesses. The very absence of these discomforts from my recall speaks, more than anything else, I think, to the depth of the darkness out of which I was myself emerging and to the intensity of my need to walk again in the light and the sun and the free air of God's outdoors.

Each day, the outside facilities of the Center were given over entirely to camp activities until 2:00 P.M. No adults except Center and camp staff allowed. The kids loved the freedom of that, and they would shriek with *joie de vivre* as they raced about doing all the shoving and jumping and raucous horseplay that annoys parents and that counselors are paid to be amused by. And everything that a child could need for running off energy was amply provided. There was an old but sizable swimming pool with old but plentiful and very comfortable deck chairs around it. There was the usual smaller pool for the younger children; and while there was no golf course at that time, there were volleyball courts and tennis courts and hopscotch walks. The parklike areas surrounding the building were limited, admittedly, but they had paths enough for short nature walks, and there was archery for everyone, staff as well as campers.

Although archery is one of the few sports I have ever truly enjoyed to the point of mindless addiction, it is also not a sport that most city-dwellers can just go out and practice in the nearest backyard. As a result, in my off-duty hour each weekday, I joined the kids in taking full advantage of that archery range. I spent half the summer, of course, with some telltale bow-string bruises on my arms and a few honestly painful burns on the inside of my left wrist. Those discomforts I do remember. I also remember that I could not have cared less. The shooting and the sunshine and the cavorting swimmers were a carnival of therapeutic distractions to which my spirit went each morning like a hungry child to its breakfast, except that hungry at the JCC really meant lunch, not breakfast, for me.

It took me one day and one day only to ascertain that, despite all prior assumptions, I actually had never experienced food before that summer, not in my entire life. My day of lost opportunity was due only to my ignorance. There was, poolside at the Center, a capacious, but again hardly elegant or impressive, snack bar that was the whole sum of the place's food facilities during camp hours. I stood in line the first day and ordered up a kosher hot dog with relish. I was enjoying it, too, until one of the other counselors at our table looked at my hot dog and then at me as if I were lacking in every shred of good sense God had promised an adult. "You're not eating the pastrami on rye?" she asked, though there was more pity than question in her comment.

"No," I said. "Should I be?"

"Try it," she said; and the next day I did.

I'd never had kosher pastrami on rye in my life before, primarily because I'd never heard of kosher beef pastrami on rye before. We didn't grow the stuff in either East Tennessee or northern Georgia. I had heard of kosher pickles, however; and even though I'd never eaten one of them either, when the teenager filling my lunch order asked, "Want a pickle with that?," I thought why not go all the way, and said yes.

Oh, my! Oh, my, my! I am a vegetarian now, for no good reason other than the fact that I just don't like the taste and texture of meat in my mouth anymore; but if there's anything on this earth that may someday tempt me back to the meat side of a menu, it will be a really superb sandwich of kosher beef pastrami on rye with sauerkraut, mustard, and a pickle to the side. I thought I was going to die!

I spent every lunch for the rest of that summer and all the lunch allowance I could squeeze out of our budget on those poolside, snack-bar sandwiches. I also spent every lunchtime being amazed all over again at how I could have lived for twenty-two years ignorant of life's greatest culinary blessing. My amazement was not entirely uncalled for, as a matter of fact, because the reason that neither East Tennessee nor northern Georgia offered their citizens kosher cuisine was a result of assimilation, not of any lack of once-upon-a-time exposure.

The South's story is one that I have disciplined myself over the years to tell as infrequently and as neutrally as possible. There comes a time at which the recitation of pain becomes instead a celebration of it, one that destroys the celebrants more than it relieves their anguish. I am old now, the child of a father who was a bit older than the norm when I was born and who himself was born late in his own father's life. That unusual chain of delayed births means that I grew up around dinner tables and family reunions that were rife with tales of "the War," meaning the War Between the States.

Right and wrong are never as clear during or immediately following a war as they are after history has had time to write large its own definitions of them; and those family stories of my girlhood were always tinged with bitterness. Even the rich, colorful ones—even sometimes the arrestingly poignant ones—still had folded into them dark strands of resentment, if no longer of hatred. There were accounts about how Grandpa had been shot at Shiloh and how for three days he had hovered between life and death there; about how, afterward, he could never walk again without a limp; about how fellow Americans had swept through and decimated what they could not pillage, rape, or carry off with them; about how there had been nothing for the family for decades afterwards but the suppressed and humiliating life of a people conquered and then demeaned by their own, English-speaking kin.

Such tales are not told so much these days because mine—pray God—will be the last generation ever to be fed upon them in infancy. That wise and healing change in the content of Southern suppertime stories does not mean that the tales I grew up on were not true, because they were. Nor does it mean that the mind-set of the exile, the vanquished, and the oppressed did not shade and inform every part of Southern life when I was a child there, because it did. I and the friends of my girlhood came up Southern and second-rate just because every part of the larger culture let us know that if the former were true, the latter most assuredly was.

The sensibility of the exile—the pariah syndrome, so to speak—sometimes lends a kind of compassion to those whom it afflicts. It has for the South, anyway, where the experience of disenfranchisement has mellowed out into the mannered friendliness and easiness of disposition for which we now are regionally and personally famous. That is good. That is as it should be. But pariah status, or perhaps life as a pariah for several generations, also recognizes itself in others who are equally the victims of man's inhumanity to man. That particular turn of mind-set explains, at least in part, why during the twentieth century there was by and large little anti-Semitism in the American South. The major reason for the South's cordiality toward Jewry, however, is much more intimate than mere empathy and is called marriage.

When my grandfather came limping home from Shiloh, he shortly thereafter married my grandmother. I never knew her, because she and Grandpa were both dead long before my father was grown and, therefore, obviously long before I was even thought of, much less running about underfoot. Grandma's maiden name, however, had been Wahl, which by anybody's understanding of derivations is not your usual Scots-Irish surname. The family wisdom had always been that Grandma was of Jewish descent, her forebears having been merchants originally. If this were true—and it apparently was—then the Wahls and the Alexanders were only following a regional norm when they intermarried. That is, during the nineteenth century and especially in the years after the war, mercantile-based Jewry married and intermarried more and more frequently with landowning goyim as the economic circumstances of each had need for the protective buffer of the other.

Until the summer of 1956, I had accepted this quasi-fact, to the extent I had even thought about it at all, as neither remarkable nor personal. It was simply the ordinary way of things in my part of the world. Because I had never known my grandmother, I had never had any opportunity to ask her about her origins, assuming I might ever have wished to do so; nor had there been any opportunity to observe in her the vestigial remains of possible Jewish ancestry, assuming that there ever were any to observe. Nonetheless, it is still something of a personal as well as a regional *non sequitur* to me that during every lunch break for almost three weeks I could have sat at that sunny, poolside table rejoicing in sandwiches while never one time suspecting something more than the gratification of a robust predilection for kosher pastrami was also waiting for me at the Memphis Jewish Community Center.

45.

THE CRAFTS ROOM at the JCC was unlike every other part of the Center in that it was the only part of the whole complex that admitted any variations to speak of in its climate. That is, only Crafts had weather changes every day that were predictable and all its own. Cheerfully sunny in the morning, bright but never, never hot at noon, softly limned and cool by early afternoon, the room was a great long rectangle of a space with banks of windows and well-paned doors on its outside wall and storage closets and display boards and student cubbies on all three of its interior ones. Its cordial predisposition toward changing measures and depths of light and warmth was due primarily to the fact that the place was more recessed than built into the Center's concrete-floored, lower storey. The theory, according to Paul Schwartz, was that Crafts were the messiest part of the Center's program, and being able to hose the room down from time to time was a virtue. I soon discovered, although he would never admit it to me, that Crafts were also the uneasiest part of the JCC program for Paul Schwartz.

Jewish children, traditionally, are more facile with, and interested in, words than with or in plastic materials. I had never heard that particular cultural characteristic even mentioned, much less described, before the summer of 1956, and I'm not totally convinced that I believe it even now. By the third or fourth time some well-meaning parent had tossed it as an aside into otherwise normal after-camp-hours conversations, however, I began to embrace it as the summer's most welcome generalization. I was far more facile with, and interested in, words than things, too, believe me, and mightily reassured to find myself among children of a similar turn of mind. Within a week, we had settled down, then, especially the older kids and I, to talking our way together through luxurious, metaphor-rich hours in that cool, removed, constantly shifting space of paint-spattered walls and wobbly tables.

The first operative consequence of a word-oriented approach to crafts is, of course, that once things are talked about with any precision and thoughtfulness, even the gaudiest of them tends to slip, to some greater or lesser degree, from being the means of craft into becoming a form of art. I don't mean to suggest that hours of raffia knotting or straw weaving or coil basketry or spatter painting or reverse etching or any of the dozens of other things the children and I did together that summer produced hangings or spattergrams or water goblets of great beauty. They most assuredly did not (although I do think that even the most stringent critic would have commended two or three pieces of the children's work as more than passingly fine).

If, however, "art" in the plastic media may be taken to mean a process as well as a product, then those kids almost all did art. By that definition, the engagement and exposure of the essence of a material in the course of its presentation and/or its rearrangement is art. It is also precisely what they so joyfully and brilliantly did. The only problem was that their execution was often lacking—ironically enough—in craft, the very thing their amateur instructor was ill-equipped to help them remedy. Nobody except me seemed frustrated by my deficiencies, however, and I have never felt any more loved or supported or approved in my life than I did in those classroom hours among those children . . . which undoubtedly is part of why I first found the Crafts Room to be so cushioning and secure as a place.

In the quiet after each day's camp was over and after the young voices had all slipped into another day's memories, I would spend my afternoon there, cleaning up the debris of the morning, inventing new ways to display a day's work and thereby to delight its creators, dreaming new projects that could naturally follow and extend a day's discoveries and, after that, in scouring the supply closets to see if the requisite materials were on hand. Sometimes, of course, I had to determine whether or not I could even guide such a project, most often by sitting down and actually doing it myself right there and then.

The truth also is that had I been using my off-duty time as I was supposed to do, that is, in cleaning up and in planning instead of in shooting obstreperous arrows into often impenetrable targets, I would have indeed been finished with my workday by two o'clock each afternoon. Since I was not about to give up archery for cleaning up anything, it followed that from two to three or so each day there were honest chores to be done. After three or three-thirty, though, any excuse based on professional necessity was a bit more tenuous, and so, too, was any more housekeeping activity. Thus it happened that sometime near the end of June I gave up on both my excuses and my busyness, and began instead to accept the fact that in some way too subtle for me to analyze, the JCC and its Crafts Room were kind to me, that they were in fact good places for me to be.

I started bringing a bag of books with me to work each morning. After my chores were done and before catching the bus home, I would sit an hour or two in front of the big windows in the afternoons, reading some novel or other. Mostly it was Anthony Trollope that summer, unless my memory misleads me; but whether it was Trollope or Austen or Lloyd Douglas or Taylor Caldwell doesn't matter much now. What matters is that, as is so often my way when I am reading for pleasure, my attention began to drift away from the page more and more frequently.

At first I simply wandered on into rumination. Within just a few afternoons, however, I realized that I had begun more to listen than to either wander or daydream. Originally, I think, I was just listening to the replay in my head of the things the children had said to each other and to me as we had worked together earlier in the day. Increasingly, though, I found I was replaying snatches of the adult conversations I had overheard among my fellow counselors at lunch and around the pool. I was replaying especially those bits and pieces of their conversations that had assumed a network of connections I half-recognized but couldn't quite render into its parts. I found myself listening as well to replays of the impersonal but very forthright and usually accurate critiquing of each other that took place constantly among both the staff and the children; and I found myself listening even more intently to the faintly foreign, faintly familiar habits of personality that seemed everywhere to pervade the people who were the Center.

Discovering oneself to be different from other people is not necessarily an uncomfortable thing. There are many people whom most of us go to considerable lengths to be different from, and think ourselves justified in the endeavor. To be different to the point of singularity is almost always uncomfortable, however; or it was for me anyway, as I began the process of perceiving it. To discover oneself to be singularly different and then to realize shortly thereafter that at some level or other one's singularity is that of near, but not identical, kin is even more unsettling.

"Damn it," I thought one afternoon in mid-July, "Paul Schwartz should have asked me if I were Jewish!" And the minute I thought it, the whole Crafts Room began to chortle around me.

I am being quite serious here and only partially facetious. To this day I would take at least half an oath that that room chortled. Then, as surely as if rooms could have voices of their own, it said, "Ah-ha!" and chuckled again. The only disconcerting thing about all this was that the "Ah-ha!" I heard was remarkably similar in timbre and attitude to an "Ahhh!" I had heard not too many months before. To be precise, it was first cousin or half-brother to one I had heard in my mother's dining room chiding me over covetousness and wedding gifts.

46.

By the rivers of Babylon, there we sat down, yea we wept, when we
  remembered Zion.
We hanged our harps upon the willows in the midst thereof.
For there they that carried us away captive required of us a song; and
  they that wasted us required of us mirth, saying, Sing us one of the
  songs of Zion.
How shall we sing the Lord's song in a strange land?
If I forget thee, O Jerusalem, let my right hand forget her cunning.
If I do not remember thee, let my tongue cleave to the roof of my mouth;
  if I prefer not Jerusalem above my chief joy.

THE WORDS are those of the 137th Psalm as they are rendered in the
King James Version of the Bible. They are also some of the most beautiful
ones in the English language. I cannot read them without having a sweet,
soft sorrow wash across me with all the stillness of a dying love song. I can
almost never recite them for an audience without the wrench in my upper
chest that makes an audible break in my voice. They are the love song of the
Jew for his or her God. They are also the love song of the Christian for his
or hers. They are the place in poetry where Judaism and Christianity lie
down together in peace. The only difference is that being a people in historic and actual exile, Jews in the West have lived the poetry more consistently and self-consciously than have Christians in the West. I just simply
had never made, much less appreciated, that distinction before 1956.

I had known the words of "Old One-thirty-seven," as it is most usually called, long before 1956, had known them by heart, in fact. I was,
moreover, religiously aware enough to perceive that the 137th was different from all its fellows not in its sentiments perhaps so much as in the perfection by which it conveyed them. In truth, had anyone asked me, I think
I would have said that there was in those words something very near to
magic or holy esoterica, some formula or construction of words that burrowed a hole into the extra-human and the frightening. In the days of my
youth, however, I also walked around the 137th with a shyness that be-

comes a child in another man's temple, feeling somehow that such richness of yearning could never be mine, could never be bought by a coward or inherited without agonies of loss I would never sustain.

One of the most consequential changes in American religion during the closing decades of the twentieth century was the dramatic growth in rapprochement between Judaism and Christianity. Exactly where and how that coming together began no one is quite sure, though most of us working professionally in religion writing each have our own favorites among the various theories. I go with the one which holds that the diminishment in mutual animosity and the commencement of mutual accommodation began at effective levels with the influx in the late 1930s and early 1940s of European Jews who were escaping Hitler and who, by their coming, brought to a grateful America some of the most brilliant minds and scholarly achievements in Western history. Whether that be the whole answer or not, it is certainly a substantial part of it, and it also explains why the Crafts Room laughed at me and then had the audacity to whisper "Ah-ha!" as well.

Nothing happens in isolation, at least nothing human does. If Jack Hornaday persuaded me of anything, he persuaded me of that; and later scholarship has confirmed his position. We speak to each other by means of a lacework of context that swings and vibrates like a spider's web touched. What happens on one part of that gossamer surface undulates across the whole, taking its messages with it. As surely as the notes of a violin's playing cannot be severed from the violin's strings, so just as surely the ways of our living cannot be severed from the web's elastic strands. What I had heard in the Crafts Room or even in my mother's dining room, in other words, had not been so much heard as it had been received. Some would say received out of thin air. I would say received out of the thoughts and motions that, played upon a mesh of immutables, are always and everywhere at large in the air and that we all—even the least imaginative of us—acquire and process extra-verbally.

The danger in this kind of discussion just here in my story is not so much that it will take us too far afield, but that it will blur with too many words the wonder of discovery that occupied the rest of my July and early August at the JCC. Since I had no way of knowing what I was tunneling my way toward that summer, I had all the true explorer's pleased astonishment to give me new energy as well as new clues every day. The truth also is that despite my giddy sense of derring-do, I was actually little more than an infant learning to toddle. It's just that I was most assuredly a very happy one.

What, near the end of August, I actually left the Center possessed of was, in quantity, nothing to what I have learned and discerned in the years since. In quality, that would not be true, however, for what I found at the JCC opened the way to all that I have found since. The thing that did matter enormously then and that has continued to matter is that my previous way of looking at Christianity was abruptly and irreparably changed in that place. I was given in its stead a new perspective that has informed and shaped my confessional life for all the years since (though one would hope that as a point of view, what was given in 1956 has matured and broadened along with the rest of me).

I do not wish to presume, and I certainly do not wish to generalize to my own embarrassment, but those things that I began first to hear and then to analyze in the Crafts Room of the Memphis JCC are very integral to Judaism, at least when viewed, as it was then and still is now, from my vantage point as an outsider. I am not so foolhardy as to think that I apprehend Judaism, either the religion or the ethos, intimately or even adequately. I never will. I do think, however, that over the years of my life since 1956, I have visited many of the places in doctrine, ethos, and practice where Judaism shares common ground with Christianity. I know for a fact that a goodly number of those places were, in 1956, largely unclaimed parts within the religious birthright of most American Christians. They most certainly were unclaimed parts of mine.

Labels are important, as we all know. They are also handy as a shirt pocket just because they are about as obvious as one. The first thing I fell to doing in the afternoons after my "Ah-ha!" experience, then, was considering the significance of labels. Almost immediately I had to admit to myself that saying "I'm Christian" is as different from saying "I'm Jewish" as saying "I'm American" is from saying "I'm Southern." Both of the latter instantly define one as part of a subculture; and life in a subculture is always more self-aware. It is also more intrinsically motivated to exaggerations of conduct. Sometimes, of course, those exaggerations are fierce, driven efforts to obliterate the evidences of differentness. More commonly, though, they are nobler, more socially useful things. Most commonly, they become the protectors and conservators of a community of the different which, while it engages the larger culture, finds itself most complete and realized within itself.

"How shall we sing the Lord's song in a strange land?" sang the people of the exile, and a psalmist recorded their words. It is the eternal question of Judaism that since the Edict of Toleration in 313 C.E. has not even been much of a question, much less an essential one, in Western Christianity. Until 1956, I had truly regarded Constantine's policy of accommodation as a great, divine beneficence to my faith. I had thought that because I had been taught to think that. The longer I sat in the Crafts Room, the more I began to think otherwise. It was not that I came to value slaughter and hideous centuries of genocide, but that I began to perceive for the first time in my life that religion cheaply bought is cheaply valued.

"Come ye out and be a separate people" began to roll around in my head in a most unsettling way. Separate not for the sake of separateness, I understood, but because a faith lived will inevitably eventuate in separateness. I found this conclusion to be as frightening and threatening as it was convincing.

Paul Schwartz's kind of forthrightness was almost as obvious as labels around the JCC, and it became for me the second clear expression of the difference between me and my fellows at the Center. If the man's directness in dealing with me had disconcerted—probably even offended—me in early June, it was no longer doing so by July. Much to my surprise, I had begun to appreciate—almost even to depend upon—it in the same way that one appreciates and depends upon a coach or spotter in tennis. In and of itself, this was a teasing bit of self-discovery, I thought.

When someone—a counselor or a Center staff member or even a child, it didn't matter—purposed something to Paul, you could almost see the man sorting his way, as rapidly as a riverboat gambler with his cards, through the right and the wrong of what had just been handed him. His instinct for what didn't quite ring true or wasn't quite logical was impeccable. It was his responses, however, that fascinated me. He usually began with the "Hmmm . . ." that he had used on me, but it was always followed with something like, "Why do you think this will work with the rest of what you just said?" or "Did you research that idea?" or "Where's your support for that?"

Such questions began to seem less and less like rude challenges to me not only as I watched Paul more objectively, but especially as I began to observe the same sort of approach in the children, both toward each other and toward me. "That won't work," one youngster would say gratuitously to another, and nine times out of ten the second child would answer not peevishly with "Nobody asked you," as would have been true in my classroom at Messick, but with "Why not?" "Are you sure?" or "Have you done it before?"

I would say to a struggling child something like, "Turn it this way and take the yarn in from the back," and the child would look up at me and say, with total sincerity, "Why will that work?" and there was no use in my answering "Because it just will," or even "Try it and you'll see." Until the question of validation had been addressed, nothing else was going to happen. The only thing more acceptable than explanation, in fact, was for me to answer with, "I'm not sure it will, but it ought to because of thus and so." A processing of what I had said usually was followed by "Okay," and without another word the work would be turned so that the yarn could be inserted from the back. I could also be sure I would get a report on the results every single time: "See, it did work," or "Nope, it won't work from the back," or just as neutrally, "Turning it is wrong. You can't see where you're going that way. Look, see, if you go in from the back like you said, only without turning, it works."

Amazing, I thought, followed by the logical next thought of why . . . why the difference and why is it so without offense among them? Once I had begun to observe instead of react, the answer to both those two was fairly clear. Paul, the children, and everybody in between were part and parcel of each other. Their questioning of things was nearer to the kind of evaluating process we all go through inside our own heads when we assess something than it was to overt social process. The intelligence of each party to an event or activity was supposed to be brought to bear for the sake of the whole. It was a process that was almost egoless, in fact, and the very humility of that began to gnaw on me as well.

It had been prophesied of the Christ that he would be a man of sorrows and acquainted with grief, having no comeliness that we should desire him and that "he shall not cry out, nor lift up, nor cause his voice to be heard in the street. A bruised reed shall he not break, and the smoking flax shall he not quench: he shall bring forth judgment into truth." The bulk of what Jesus of Nazareth actually was in his physical life, on the other hand, and/or of what he was remembered as having been is recorded for us, orthodoxly speaking, in the four Gospels of the New Testament.

Those books do indeed chronicle a peasant life without comeliness and a biography of inestimable sorrow. But if the Gospels reveal anything at all about the character, the disposition, the personality of the man himself, they most assuredly reveal his directness: "Why do you call me good? No one is good save God alone." "Who do men say that I, the Son of man, am? Who do you think I am?" "Get thee behind me, Satan!" "How is it that you have so little faith?" "The baptism of John, whence was it? from Heaven or from men?" "What think ye of Christ? whose son is he? . . . How does David in spirit call him Lord, saying, 'The Lord said unto my Lord, Sit thou on my right hand, till I make thine enemies thy footstool'? If David then call him Lord, how is he his son?" "How can Satan cast out Satan?" In short, Jesus of Nazareth was frequently rude or, to be a bit more cautious, he was certainly less than socially polished much of the time, at least by the usual standards of courtesy.

I had always seen these two threads of tradition—the humility and the directness—as contradictory of one another. For me, when I had first perceived them as an adolescent, they had constituted a kind of *de facto* schizophrenia that one had to accept to be Christian and that one was better off spiritually to leave alone. I was now being forced in adulthood to rethink that position. Were directness and great humility wedded in the personas of those choosing and chosen of God? Apparently so, I concluded. I certainly seemed to be walking around every day in the living proof of that enigma.

It took me much longer than the summer of 1956, of course, to finally comprehend at any working level that like most holy paradoxes, this one is more apparent than real. Loving and believing oneself beloved of God makes one a citizen in a country apart. It confines and blesses one with both loyalties and responsibilities that are unlike those of one's secularly-enfranchised neighbors. As a piece of political truth, that one has been both the bane and the glory of Judaism from its beginnings. The thing about Judaism, of course, is that over the centuries it has stood firm—if not always as a theocracy, then in whatever circumstances—as a physical as well as a spiritual community for those who are in temporary removal from the presence of the Beloved. Every religious community does the same thing. Judaism has just done it in a larger, more portable, and much more structured way than most.

The joy of community for the otherwise disenfranchised human being is that he or she is no longer an earthly plebiscite of one. The curse of it is that when a community of the like-minded is contained within a larger community of the not-so-persuaded, there's trouble every time, trouble that may abate, but that rarely is assuaged for long. As a besieged organism of the persuaded in exile, the religious community requires at least two things for survival: first, the absolute humility of every member before each other and before the God to whom all allegiance is owed; and second, the ability of every member to look out for every other member, lest any part stumble either spiritually or temporally and thereby threaten the worshiping and affianced whole.

When I speak in such detail of this particular matter, I do so with emotional and/or spiritual, not intellectual amazement. Nothing I have said is the subject of intellectual amazement. Most of it, in fact, is as obvious as the significance of labels. The amazement is not even that I had never thought about any of these things before I was twenty-two years old and a married woman. The amazement, rather, is that of retrospection. My absorption, that absorption first excited in me by the JCC, that absorption with religious community and its implications as well as its manifestations was to become the roof beam of my life. From it, everything else was to, in one way or another, depend.

It would lead me to seek out and find in the liturgy of my faith the invisible communion of the saints across both time and space. And I mean here not so much in the liturgy of Sabbath and fast or feast day services as in the liturgy of everyday worship—in the liturgy of the hours, the observance of fixed-hour prayer, the keeping of the offices. Called by whatever name one will, that blessed discipline is the entrance four, five, six, or seven times a day of the lover and his or her companions into the presence of the Beloved. Without those divine hours, there would be no story to be told here.

My absorption would lead me as well to the more visible and tangible communion of fellow Christians, most particularly to the religious and laity who live in vowed community as the Community of Jesus in Orleans, Massachusetts. Though we do not live among them, Sam and I have for almost a decade now passed in and out of their mercy on a regular and frequent basis. Theirs is another story, a story about the sharing of life and one that, God willing, I shall tell before I pass beyond my need of stories.

All of that having been said, however, my summer at the JCC began my instruction in something much nearer to the health of my soul than the costs and value of religion or even the purposes and conduct of spiritual community. On those long-ago afternoons when I first began to look at Jesus of Nazareth in terms of the faith and concomitant ethnicity of a discrete group of people who had become my friends, I began as well to look at him for the first time as a Jew. Viewed that way, much more than his directness began not only to make sense as reasonable to me, but also to seduce me into a love affair with him that would otherwise never have been possible. Up until then or up until some time shortly after then, I cannot now be sure, I had pasted a suit of Euro-American expectations on an irregular rabbi; and the rattle of his paper clothes, the dissonance of his deflected voice, had kept me at a distance that invited politeness, but not passion. As "the Word among us" Jesus made no sense to me and had no appeal. As Torah among us, he was breathtaking.

God of the snake, God of the cross, how shall we sing your song in a strange land?

PART EIGHT

No Man's Land

47.

WHILE I HAD BEEN in hospital the previous fall, a much more personable obstetrical and gynecological specialist had replaced my former one as the attending. Over the months of my recovery, I had continued to make routine visits to his office, of course, just as I had to those of so many other doctors; but during the course of those visits, Orin Davidson had subtly shifted from being "a" doctor to being "my" doctor, at least in my mind and, presumably, in his.

Nobody has ever adequately defined the cables of connection that bind the truly sick to their physicians, nor has anyone ever analyzed credibly the signals, like those of courtship, that persuade both parties to their dance of mutual trust. For decades now I have watched patients pass in and out of Sam's professional life and, over that time, have learned to recognize, almost immediately, those whom he has chosen and/or been chosen by *in perpetuum*. That palpable union of healer and patient is the platonic face of a love that any attentive spouse can see, but which none can touch, even in the marriage bed. It was also the bond between Orin Davidson and me.

He was not a handsome man. Rather, he was a memorable one. He had the biggest pop eyes I have ever seen in anybody who did not have chronic thyroid disease. He also had the only voice I have ever, ever thought could honestly be called gravelly. It rolled, modulated, and cracked out of all control every time the man opened his mouth, even to cough. Long after he had left the practice of medicine, I am told Dr. Davidson still spent a third of his conversational energies in clearing his throat as if there were yet some small hope of clarifying the sounds coming out of it.

That voice was his signature for the world in general. For me, and undoubtedly because of personal history, the signature was his office coats. It mattered not what time in his professional day—morning or late at night—nor in what place—office or hospital—Orin Davidson was always going to have on a long white coat so stiffly starched that he appeared not to be wearing it so much as he was occupying it in the way one occupies a house or a child playing horsey occupies a cardboard box. How he achieved this effect I have never known, for I have still never found the laundry that can produce it; but the crackle of those coats so perfectly matched the crackle of his voice that I cannot recall one apart from the other.

It was to this man, then, that I turned on Monday of the fourth week in August. I had had the miscarriage late on the previous Thursday, the day before camp was to be over; but this time there had been no heroics, no scurrying about. I had lain in a quiet room of the quiet house on East Norhall Circle and let my body finish its work. So, too, had my self; for this time there had been more than loss and pain. This time, there had been first the ice-cold waves of dread and, after them, the battering ones of shame. I could not do what I was designed to do. My body was in some way flawed not in form, but in function; and like an impotent man, I was less than I had been before knowing that, less than other women were, less than Woman.

Neither Sam nor I had said anything beyond the necessities to each other over the weekend lest we stumble by some verbal misstep into areas where there was too much to say. Neither of us—husband or wife, father or mother—had had the strength for such during and after those few hours of passage.

"Habitual aborter," the gravel voice said into the papers spread out on his desk, "habitual aborter," shaking the bald head . . . and the world finally stopped spinning on a Monday afternoon.

Lest there be any kind of confusion just here in my story, let me say that "habitual aborter" is the medical term—or it was in 1956—for a woman who cannot carry a fetus to term, one whose body chronically rejects its own child. It was, and still is even as I write it here, the ugliest phrase in the lexicon of medicine, the most unforgiving and graceless, a coupling as uneuphonious to the heart as to the ear. "Habitual aborter."

"Ever hear of it?" he said.

"No," I said, but I lied. I knew very well what it meant. I also knew that Orin Davidson had just set me in the place of anguish Sam and I had been walking around for almost four days, knew that with two words he had drop-kicked me into the possible future we had hoped by our silence to contain. Now the words were out of the box we had built and sitting across a desk staring at me. The truth is—and I think I knew it even on that Monday afternoon—that they would never entirely be out of my life again. Like Pandora's horrors they, too, could not be shoved back into a box.

"Do you know what I am telling you?" Dr. Davidson was looking at me so intently that there was no lying. A blind man could have seen by my face that I knew exactly what he was telling me. "Good," he said. "Now let's talk about this thing."

I nodded, I imagine. Certainly I could not have spoken, for I was already too far into another country for my voice to have carried out to him.

"You're young," he said, "in good health and in good shape. Nothing is wrong, except that your body doesn't like being pregnant for some reason, or it hasn't so far. Now we can either do nothing and let it keep on miscarrying until it gets the habit so completely that it will never go to term, or we can get you pregnant deliberately and try to fool it into accepting a baby before it even knows one is on the way."

It was a colorful way to put things, I thought, so infantile and mechanical that just for a minute one could almost believe this man could fix what he had just admitted he himself didn't understand.

"How?" I said, because I could think of no other response.

"You go home and throw away all that stuff you two have been using and then, just for a change, you try to get pregnant. The minute you think you are and/or the minute you're even one day late, you call me. We'll put you to bed and rock you through it, at least until the pregnancy is secure."

"I can't do that," I said, and knew I was crying now. "We have no money, and I have to work in order for Sam to finish."

Dr. Davidson pushed back his chair a bit and addressed me sideways as if, I think now, my face were too painful for him to look at or perhaps just out of some human kindness that did not want to intrude too directly on my despair. He was always and ever a gentle man.

"I don't know your folks," he said to the wall behind me, "but I don't know a single man anywhere who, given the choice, would not rather have grandchildren than not have grandchildren, if there's a thing in the world he can do about it. You go home and talk to Sam, and if the two of you have got any gumption at all or any love for them, you'll pick up that phone tonight and call somebody . . . your parents, his parents, both sets of parents . . . and you'll give them the chance to make this decision with you. How much do you make?"

"Two hundred and twenty-five dollars a month."

"Good Lord," he said, "call home."

48.

ORIN DAVIDSON was to be my doctor for over two decades, and he would deliver six of our seven children. The missing member in that generous progression happened only because we lived in South Carolina for four years, having gone there with a Davidson infant and having returned from there not only with that almost-five-year-old, but with our non-Davidson toddler and an at-term pregnancy that he did deliver.

That's all cheery enough to report now, especially when one reports it in such a jocular way. The problem is, as we all know, that flipness in reportage almost always veils the truth, assuming it does not outright destroy it. In this case the most obvious thing that my flipness obscures is how many more failed pregnancies Dr. Davidson would have to carry me through to get us those four little girls and three little boys. Five, six, seven? I don't even remember the number myself. After a while we all just stopped counting. The other thing that my flipness obscures is how the threat and the processes of repeated miscarriage would drive a stake through my life, one that runs from the primordial rock of female experience straight up to the roof beam of community. I would, in other words, pitch my small tent in the kingdom of God over the cross frame of these two things, and beneath their fixity I have lived it out.

In the life of an habitual aborter, the number of miscarriages does not matter, which is why I have long since lost any sense of accurate tally. What matters is the losing and the definitions assigned to that which has been lost. About the losing and the definitions, believe me: They matter profoundly.

The definitions for "that which has been lost" are multiple in our culture, and their very multiplicity creates for American politics an almost indecipherable cacophony. It also creates enormous, almost indescribable pain for millions of women—for those who miscarry habitually as I did, for those who miscarry only once or twice as so many women do, even for many of those who miscarry as a result of their own intention. Society, if by that one means the company of one's neighbors and associates, never quite knows what to say after a miscarriage of any sort. "How are you feeling now?" is the usual greeting.

"Well, the truth is my heart is breaking," is what I always wanted to answer, but I learned early on in the years of my fertility to never respond so candidly. The few times I tried it, the answer was "Why?" or "I know." The "Why?" was isolating and the "I know" infuriating. To the "I know" I wanted to scream, "No, you don't know! You have no idea! You can't know!" But just as illogically I wanted to screech back at the "Why?" with, "You fool, why don't you know why!" It doesn't take many such encounters before one learns to treat the question of "How are you feeling?" as pro forma and capable of receiving only the pro forma response of "Fine, thanks."

Eventually—that is, by about the time I was forty and a bit more sanguine about things in general—I came to forgive the system in which we were all trapped, (though I do have a great deal of trouble forgiving the fact that thirty years later we are still trapped in it). The truth is that society doesn't tell us what to say to one another about "that which has been lost," because society to this day hasn't quite figured out what really is lost in a miscarriage, be it spontaneous or otherwise. Part of the reason society fumbles, of course, is that medicine has a name for the whole thing, and as names go, it's too repugnant to be of any social use.

The first and only time Orin Davidson ever offended me was on that Monday afternoon in August of 1956 when he forced me to face the fact that I had had three miscarriages in a row and I then stumbled over my words in trying to talk about what I had had to flush away the previous weekend.

"Medical detritus," he offered, and let the offense of his words slap into me. "Medical detritus," he said again, lest I might have failed to hear him. And then looking at me as purposefully as he ever would in all our years together, he added, "Think of it that way, or you'll never survive. It's body waste, and that's all it is."

He was right and he was wrong. He knew that just as well as I did. He also knew about the spiritual as well as the psychological loneliness whose presence I had only begun to perceive. He knew, as I had not yet discovered, what happens when there are no rites of passage, no services of burial, no daily prayers of repose because one's dead are intangible, because the subject of one's mourning can never be either shrouded or interred. He understood as well the second death that is implicit in such a denial. Orin Davidson understood, in other words, that "that which had been lost" is medical detritus not only to medicine but also to religion.

There is, however, another way of knowing not so much beyond the institutions and systems by which our culture defines and runs itself as behind or prior to them, a kind of old country of the evolving spirit. Like the physical places of our immigrant pasts, this one stands nearer to the sharp edges of life than most of us ever want to be; but it is to this awareness without priests that women take their unborn dead . . . or perhaps once more I should say only that it is where I have each time taken mine. Like the immediacy of pain, there is in that gender-specific place an immediacy of being that needs no mediation. There is also a profound, active silence that first invades the soul and then persuades it into a new configuration . . . or it did so to mine.

Compassion is not a coveted spiritual virtue in the Christian religion. Christianity slices and dices virtues with all the same sense of nicety and exquisite seriousness as any other organized faith, of course; but it simply does not celebrate compassion's primacy among them in the life of grace. Instead, the learned of the Church from Ambrose to Aquinas to the present have consistently numbered her central virtues at seven and then subdivided those into the four cardinal or natural virtues of prudence, temperance, fortitude, and justice followed or, more properly, capped by the three theological virtues of faith, hope, and charity. I am a washout at all seven.

I don't mean that I lack the seven. Presumably I have at least a modicum of all of them—less of fortitude and more of faith, probably, with an about average allotment of the others. What I have in abundance, however, is compassion. It was given to me in the space where I took my grief for burial and where I learned, however slowly, to exchange even my mourning and my shame for the soft, low sorrow that, like a half-remembered melody, still informs my prayers and my active life. On that tortured Monday afternoon in August 1956, Orin Davidson may have torn without mercy through all my barriers, but that does not change the fact that he was merciless only, as the poet says, that he might in time be merciful;

and I have lived most of the years since as a debtor to his brusque wisdom. Certainly Sam and I together have lived all of them as debtors to his equally brusque astuteness as a physician. We called home.

49.

SAM THREW UP in the bathroom sink one December morning when he was shaving. Aside from that, it was a pregnancy almost without incident. It was, in fact, almost perversely normal.

My father had listened for less than thirty seconds in August before he had interrupted our call home with the words, "Do it! I'll send the first check tomorrow."

"No," I had said, surprised at how much planning I had already subconsciously done. "No, I don't want to do it that way. I can't leave Mr. Counce without a Latin teacher right here at the start of school. I'll go in tomorrow or the next day, explain what has happened, and tell him that I'll stay through September or until he can find a replacement, whichever comes first. They were too good to us last winter for me to just walk away now."

"You're right," my father said, "but be sure Shelby understands you mean it."

"I will." And I did.

Shelby Counce was a good schoolman who, as tended to be the way with Messick's principals, would become superintendent of the Memphis City Schools within a few years. He was also, as is the way with most good schoolmen, a very even-handed believer in the principle that institutions, or at least his institutions, were an act of kindness and a promise of hope to children and therefore were of inviolate worth. I liked him in no small part because I always knew where I stood with him and because the rules of the game were always as clear with him as they were to him.

He looked at me across his desk the morning of my appointment, sized up what I had just said for a second, and then nodded his head. "Thank you for dealing with the problem this way. I appreciate your candor," was what he said in that formal manner of his, and then as something of an addendum, "If you need to leave before the end of next month, let me know. And I will let you know if I can find a replacement before then."

I nodded in return, and that had been that. We both stood up, we shook hands, I said thank you again and turned to leave. Just as I got to his door, however, he said, "Mrs. Tickle, one last thing."

"Yes, sir?"

"Mrs. Tickle, if you should ever need a reference again, I'd be pleased to be asked." It was as near as Shelby Counce ever came to saying anything personal, but I have treasured it ever since as proof of a remarkable sensitivity as well as of a remarkable generosity.

As things turned out, I taught through September and almost the whole of October. I was quite definitely pregnant, but I was also quite definitely as happy as I could be and still bear my own company. At a more practical or relevant level, I was feeling healthier and far more energetic than I had in months. Dr. Davidson hovered and cautioned and acquiesced until finally one afternoon when I was in his office and tired, he came down emphatically on the side of "plain, old horse sense, and everything else be damned," to use a Davidson expression.

I came home midmorning the next day after my replacement had arrived, went to bed, took a long nap, listened to soap operas for the first time in my adult life, ignored cooking supper, and concluded I had died and gone to heaven. I previously had had no idea life could be lived in such an indulgent manner. By the time November came, I had turned into a monomaniacal brood hen, full of clucking and self-congratulation. I spent November mostly on the cot daybed that was our living room sofa or on our actual bed, my chief activities being sleeping and eating and sleeping and taking fistfuls of expensive vitamins, pretty much in that order. I bled a time or two, but by December even that had stopped. By December we could all say "pregnant," "baby," and "June," all in the same sentence and with a big, secure smile.

By Christmas I was as big not as a house, as the saying goes, but as big almost as our house, which is an important distinction. "Good Lord," was my father's reaction the first time he saw me. "It's either twins or inactivity, I can't tell which yet," was Dr. Davidson's. Sam's was to move all the loose chairs, foot stools, and baskets of newspapers back against the walls out of my way and insist that I turn on the lights before I tried to walk to the bathroom at night. He also, on the evenings he was home, took to cooking everything in sight as if his child depended on it. For all I know, she may have. Meanwhile, I was loving it. I was also deep into discovery that stretched beyond love.

I don't know who in the late twentieth century decided to take the traditional trichotomy of body versus mind versus spirit and popularize it into the unified buzz phrase of "Body, Mind, and Spirit," but I do know it was definitely a woman and definitely a woman who had been pregnant . . . either that or, as with Lazarus and death, I have had a whole string of aberrant pregnancies in my life. To generalize mightily from my own experience, I can say without hesitation that there is no more an interruption between mind and body than there is a line of demarcation between spirit and body, not so long as there are hormones around anyway. I was awash in them. Too euphoric to pray, I gave myself over to hours of vivid half-naps and to dozing afternoons of saying over and over again, "Thank You. Thank You. Thank You," until the monotony of the whole thing must have bored even Heaven itself.

There is no way now that I can accurately name, much less describe, either the all-encompassing continuum of my gratitude or what it was that I was so thankful for, though goodness only knows I have tried time and time again to capture both those things. Apparently, the great truth about ebullience in pregnancy is that one has to be in that state not only to feel it, but to retain it. There can be no reconstruction after the fact. Once that high tide of biochemicals washes back out to sea, while it may leave behind considerable evidence of their having come, it nonetheless takes away with it every means of recalling their grandeur. I have been in gestational euphoria enough times by now, however, to know that whatever it is about, it is not about the coming child per se.

Joy, even deep joy like Sam's and mine, over the promised coming of a child is an emotion, an invigorating emotion admittedly, but also a very describable one. The degree of fusion among body, mind, and spirit early in midpregnancy is not an emotion; it is a translation. It is, in fact, a translation into an ecstatic way of being that is more like existing within the aura of a great radiance than anything else I can think of now, though as a metaphor even that one is hardly proximate.

I know as well that the thanks being given—that the thanks that early in each midpregnancy I have given—are not to God as He/She is routinely conceptualized when one is outside of those brief, gravid weeks. The prayers of early to midpregnancy rise instead to some Completeness, to some Magnificence which, like the circumstances of my compassion, is beyond and prior to God as we usually employ that name—which is as beyond and prior, I think, in fact, as the "I Am" of Sinai or the Voice in Job's whirlwind or the Light in the Jerusalem of the Apocalypse are to the Lord of Eli's priesthood or the "God of My Father, David" in Solomon's Temple prayers or the Holy One of Israel in King Cyrus's politics.

Understandably enough, I had never known this until the late autumn and early winter of 1956. I had had no reason to discover it personally, and I had never heard other women speak of it. The nearest I had gotten to being prepared for it was the old folk cliché which holds that women "glow" when they are pregnant. Well, of course they glow! Anybody would glow who has been looking into radiance for four or five straight weeks with no interruptions! That seemed so logical to me at the time and yet so far beyond any hope of explaining that I can remember becoming quite impatient, before everything was said and done, over how many times family and visiting friends would say to me, "My dear, you are positively radiant." Especially I became irritated with my father (in and of itself a rare experience), because he would not only say, "You are positively radiant today," but follow it with, "You know, my father always said Mama was like that when she was expecting," or "I can remember when brother John D.'s wife would glow like that. That's how we always knew she was in the family way again, even before they'd tell us."

Before the words were even out of his mouth, I would find myself thinking first, and savagely, "Quit looking at me!" and then thinking, though less angrily, "If you recognize what's happening to me, then why can't you just shut up and let it be. This one time I don't want your words between me and what's happening to me."

I didn't say those things, of course, nor did my father ever, I hope, have any idea that he was disturbing me. Rather, I think, he was himself disturbed by this outward evidence in me of some inner thing that was obviously good but ineffable and that he could neither name nor ever parse. So close had been our relationship over the years, however, that he, more than Mother or even Sam, perceived I was visiting this time in lands where he had always, as a broadly traveled man, wanted to go, and he was as much fearful of my leaving him for them as he was envious of the trip.

It is a strange thing to know about one's father, but I recall it every single time I hear somebody discuss with heat the orthodoxy of ordaining women to the priesthood. The proscriptions invoked in such discussions are, I suspect, rooted deeply in the thing my father sensed, envied, probed so repeatedly, and ultimately feared; and while I know that those proscriptions are foolishness, I also know like him that a respectful fear for the ecstasy from which they arise is not.

50.

NORHALL CIRCLE is not a circle at all, but a horseshoe. As horseshoes go, it was also considerably rustier at its two ends in the 1950s than in the arcs of its curve. Boyer Avenue, which is a bit rusty itself nowadays, was once the commercial and eastern margin of Messick's neighborhood as well as the north-south artery that connected it to Memphis. Three-quarters of a mile to the west and slightly more than a mile to the south of the spot where Boyer peters off and ends, Porter Road broadens out and truly may be said to begin.

Before World War II, Porter had been a central north-south artery for the small communities of southern West Tennessee and northern Mississippi. As cotton land had been converted to housing, however, and as more and more human traffic had turned north toward Memphis, some civil engineer, or maybe just some frustrated Street Department supervisor, had paved a road of sorts to connect the two, giving to the resulting dog leg the incongruously elevated name of Crider Road. It was this short space of curbless asphalt that Norhall Circle swung in and then back out the south side of, East Norhall being on the Boyer side of Crider's shalom, and West Norhall being on the Porter side.

The impoverished and sometimes just the ill-prepared of a rural South in transit—or at least small clots of it—tended to get caught in such places fairly routinely in those days. It was almost as if pushing on around one more twist in a jerry-rigged road had suddenly become too daunting for their already spent wills, and they had simply given up while still standing in place. Certainly several such families had not made it the near-mile northeast up Crider to Boyer. Instead, they had settled as and where they could on the north side of Crider or in the first few houses of East and West Norhall Circle where they remained as isolated from their city neighbors as they had been by their lack of rural ones.

I had first come to Norhall Circle, not in 1956, but in September of 1955 when, three weeks into my first year of teaching, I had begun the round of home visits that were encouraged, if not actually demanded, back then. I had gone, on one afternoon, from the neat and slightly overfurnished home of a widow whose daughter was an "A" student by sheer force of maternal will to the home of a tantalizingly bright girl who for some reason couldn't stay awake in my afternoon homeroom without nodding off.

Norhall's houses, lined up in two unimaginatively even rows, face each other across the equally curbless and sidewalkless lane that is the road in and out of Crider. The houses on the legs of the horseshoe sit on identically sized lots and more or less stare directly into each other all day long. The houses on the southern or curved end of the horseshoe are spared this aesthetic indignity only because those on the outer sweep of the rim have lots that, while narrow in front, flare out in back. Those on the inner rim or side of the horseshoe's arc sit on lots that, while they funnel back to nothing, have, relatively speaking, very adequate front lawns. In 1955, however, the lot shape and positioning of the houses on the curve were the only noticeable variations in Norhall's general appearance. Every fourth or fifth house simply repeated a previous floor plan and offered only minor modifications of its exterior. It had been something of an explanation, as well as a heartbreak then, when on that September afternoon I had walked three or four houses down from the widow's house to the human realities of my sleeper's house.

The concrete steps had been broken off of the front stoop in some way or other and then left in pieces in the front yard, three cinder blocks having been stacked upon each other as their replacement. The woman who met me at the edge of the stoop never asked me in. She had simply pushed some dirty clothes and a baseball bat off one of the two unmatched chairs that crowded it and, signaling me to sit down, had sat down herself.

"I'm Mrs. Tickle," I had begun, "Jennie's homeroom teacher."

"I know who you are, right enough" she had interrupted, and had then barreled ahead before I could react to her evident lack of goodwill.

"I know who you are, and I almost called up that school last week about you, so's it's just as well you come by today . . . save yourself some embarrassment and me from having to get shut of a nickel calling over there!

"The thing is I'm not having you or anybody else over there giving that girl any more crazy ideas than what she's already got about books and going to school after she turns sixteen next fall. She don't need books to do what the Good Lord aims for her to do in this life, and there's no good to come of you or any of those others in that school making her think any other way than straight about that one. Besides, I need her here. She has to tend the brats most afternoons while I go up the road to do the wash, and she sure can't be fooling with books at night while the babies is back there with her trying to sleep. She's been rowling them up enough here lately getting up at the crack of dawn with those books just to please the lot of you. Ain't no good going to come of it, I tell you, and I want it stopped afore it makes us all sick, her, me, her daddy and the babies."

And that had been the end of that. It also had been my introduction to Norhall Circle.

There had been no way to fix the world for Jennie. Chronic absenteeism had finally gotten her expelled while I was ill, and by the time Sam and I had moved into 1075 some twelve or thirteen houses farther south and across the lane on the inside rim of the curve, Jennie and her family were gone. Their house had obviously passed to more ambitious owners. Over the almost two and a half years we lived on East Norhall, they gradually healed the house's more visible wounds and, before we left, had even begun bit by bit to add shutters and shrubbery as they were able. I was happy for them, but very aware as well that one of the houses between them and the widow had begun its own slow slide into despair even as they were resuscitating Jennie's. It was the way of Norhall. As such, it was also the way of the neighborhood in which I found myself on those cold late January and early February days when I slowly began to drift back from the ecstatic stages of pregnancy and into the deep contentment of an advancing one.

51.

SAM TICKLE is hardly a taciturn man. I have, on the other hand, seen him laugh uncontrollably only twice in my life. Once he had a dream so wondrously funny to him that he woke me up with his thrashing about, and he was still laughing and thrashing for days thereafter. He tried to explain the plot line and nuances to me, but a dream is a dream and as idiosyncratic as experience can be. Consequently, I never quite grasped the humor of his dream, let alone why it was so compelling. The other time I almost lost him to laughter was on East Norhall Circle just after supper on the last Friday night in December 1956. This time I could not only be transfixed by the totality of his laughter, I could even appreciate it.

Not many people in this life go around reading Aristophanes, though that may be something of a loss to our national sense of proportion. Certainly I had never bothered to do much with Greek comedy even when I had been working in classical languages with Dr. T. Our tutorials had all been the serious stuff, Plato, Homer, Aristotle. From time to time, however, Dr. T. would make some kind of offhand reference to *The Clouds* as being as light as their title or to *The Frogs* as being of more use to the world as an undergraduate rowing chant than as a piece of drama. This kind of aside was always followed by some contrasting mention of the *Lysistrata*, as in "It was in the *Lysistrata* that he hit his stride," or "Such a pity Bostonian censorship won't allow the *Lysistrata* to be published in this country."

In the late-Victorian days of the 1950s, few things were more assured of fixing adolescent attention than the words "Bostonian censorship." I have no idea how poor Boston managed to be assigned all the blame for keeping America's bookshelves morally pristine in the twentieth century, but every youngster knew that whatever was banned in Boston was what we wanted. Apparently we also did not outgrow our prurient interests as we matured either, because a friend from Shorter—one, actually, whom I had never really chummed with much—had been in England studying for a year, had bought several copies of the *Lysistrata* while she was there, and had sent me one for Christmas, somewhat to my surprise . . . my surprise, that is, until I read the thing. As usual, Dr. T. was right.

The plot is simple, the idea as powerful as Aristophanes' presentation of it is masterful, not to mention ribald. Greece is at war in a conflict that shows every sign of destroying both sides, including everybody and everything around them. The warriors and statesmen on the two sides of the argument—Sparta and Athens, basically—refuse to give an inch, despite a patently impending doom. The women of both cities, however, become increasingly convinced that it is not issues but male pride and male stupidity that are in the way of making peace. They decide as well that the only way to control male anything is with sex. Having reestablished those ancient truisms to their satisfaction, they then strike their own truce amongst themselves, Spartan women with Athenian women, and contract to withhold all sex in both cities until the men of both sit down and shut up. Simple, and already bawdy as well as bold.

The leader of the women is Lysistrata herself, thus the play's name. The farce for moderns, however, is not so much in Lysistrata's plotting as it is in how hard a time she has enforcing it. Most of the women, long before peace has been achieved, find that they are as miserable and crampy as their men are agitated and phallic, if not more so; they petition Lysistrata and even her council of advisers with every ploy and excuse imaginable for one—just one—exception to this awful ban or one—just one—night of relief from it. This was what Sam Tickle was reading when he fell off the living room daybed on Norhall Circle and without missing a lick went right on reading and rolling back and forth on the hardwood floor until he had finished every word and started the thing again. I left him there and went to bed. He was too pathetic to deserve rescue.

Every time that delicious memory of the mighty physician out of control scrolls up in my consciousness, it brings with it not only a smile, for there is nothing sweeter than to see a lover laugh, but also a sobering, almost oppressive sense of how appropriate it was that we should have met the *Lysistrata* on Norhall Circle. Like Aristophanes' stage, ours was an arc without men. It was, in fact, the only place I have ever lived where men mattered so little and were reduced so completely to the invisibility of wage-earner and nuisance.

Part of my perception of Norhall Circle as a land without men was, without question, a result of Sam's absence from it. That is, number 1075 remains as the only house in our life together where I have been sole occupant and primary landlord for most of our residence. We had been together there, obviously, during the first few weeks of our settling in, but those are also the two or so months that were clouded by the vagueness of my receding illness. Almost as soon as I was beginning to experience life fully again, we were in the financial straits that drove Sam to his exhausting schedule of work in the Methodist Hospital Laboratories.

Even when he was not working all night, he was hardly present. He would come in after thirty-six hours of being awake, hang his tie on the refrigerator handle, toss his coat in the general direction of the washing machine, drop his shirt on the table in the dining room and his pants on the floor of the living room. His undershirt I always found, for some unknown reason, in the bathroom sink and his socks just inside the doorway to our bedroom. There, within less than four minutes of having parked the car, I would find the man himself, belly-side down, in his shorts and already snoring. As often as not, I would not see him again until he was dressing in the dark the next morning to go back to classes.

On the third evening of this unforgiving cycle, though we usually had supper together, he had three days of makeup cramming to do immediately thereafter. Most nights, as a result, supper was the last I saw of him until the next morning when he was once again dressing in the dark, this time to be gone for another thirty-six hours. Thus I spent nine months of our two years on Norhall as a kind of pregnant widow.

There can also be no question but that a large part of my remembrance of Norhall as a time without men has less to do with the actual paucity of maleness there than it does with the overwhelming presence in every part of my life of my own femaleness. All—and I mean such breadth of inclusion quite literally here—all the dominant experiences and compelling discoveries of Norhall for me were related to my self as gendered, not to those of a more balanced or normative existence.

Fortunately the course of instruction in gender-specific insights can be accomplished adequately in a year or two and fortunately one has to take it only once to have at least the essentials down pat. It does, however, probably have to be gone through, and Norhall Circle was where I received my education. That does not mean, however, that I was an unenthusiastic student. Actually, I was a deliriously happy and chronically amused one for half of it and an introspective but affirmed one for the other half. My two major instructors in the happy and amused first semester were Anne Lehr and Hilda Wright.

Anne lived next door, just to the west of us, removed by the breadth of our driveway, their driveway, and the four-foot strip of grass that is a side yard on Norhall. She was as rotund, dark blond, and white-skinned as Bob, her husband, was skinny, black-headed, and eternally suntanned. She hated the outdoors and refused to do more than pass through it to her car. His need for removal from domestic intimacy, on the other hand, was so great that he could tolerate only the outdoors and watching TV in a minuscule den of sorts that he had built for himself off the living room. Since there was precious little outdoors within his property lines or anybody else's on Norhall Circle, Bob had to annoy every plant and blade of grass he could find in order to satisfy the outside part of his restlessness. The television part was simpler, although he did that largely alone as well.

Anne's idea of entertainment was to hostess a well-attended Tupperware party for us in the neighborhood; his was to slip the dog a beer or two before three o'clock on Saturday and then watch her antics for the rest of the afternoon. They were Roman Catholic and both observant; but it was the only characteristic they held in common, and even that one was hardly a source of unanimity. Anne parceled out their sex life in terms of Roman rules. She had had one difficult pregnancy and been told she would not survive another. While he complained, she remained traditionally religious; and their life together was diminished in the quarrel of their differences.

Now if all of that sounds like little more than a recaricaturing of Jack Sprat and his wife, it's not, for two reasons. First, it is the truth; second, caricature immediately implies scorn or disaffection or sometimes even cruelty, and nothing could be further from the truth than that. I can't say I ever really knew Bob, for he remains for me the shadow in a flower bed or the white object caught in the glow of a flickering light, but I adored Anne.

Anne Lehr was the first woman I had ever met who was a woman professionally—that is, who took on her apron and her vacuum cleaner as the uniform and the principal tool respectively of a totally absorbing career. Her house was managed with the precision of an office and her affairs with the deliberation of a corporation. Every aspect of a thing was considered, and only then was a decision made. She expected Bob to provide without question the funds for effecting those decisions, but she expected with equal discipline that she herself would decide only within the parameters of his ability to do so. She preferred him outside or with his TV, but she was very aware she needed him or somebody like him if she were to be a wife. She also cooked like an Italian angel.

The one child of the house, Anna Marie, was mothered with the same skill as the house was kept, and Parent-Teacher Association meetings at the parish school were far, far more significant than, for instance, East Germany or, more locally, than the fallout from Boss Crump's dissolving empire. It was this last thing, this worldview deliberately held to the size of her own reach, that was the key to Anne Lehr's success in housewifery; it was also what, in the end, taught me more as a negative rather than as a positive example. In the beginning, however, from the days of late January when I was at last moving about until the days of mid-June when Nora was born and the constitution of my interior chemistry began to shift back to its nonpregnant state . . . in those almost five months, narrow focus was the quality I most admired in her and most wished I could attain.

Hilda Wright, on the other hand . . . oh, mercy. I cannot think about Hilda Wright without laughing. Hilda Wright had three strapping boys in a two-bedroom house when we moved to Norhall Circle, and by Christmas she had another of each—boys and bedrooms, that is—on the way. Few bonds among women are stronger than those of a shared pregnancy, and Hilda was my sister in that process almost from conception to termination.

One did not admire Hilda, one enjoyed her. She, too, was rotund, but in an ungirdled kind of way that looked friendly rather than unkempt. Her eyes were as black as the asphalt in Norhall Lane and merrier than Santa Claus's are purported to be. She laughed constantly, usually about sex and how strangely compliant men became just over the mere possibility of it. She claimed to dangle it in front of Bob—she, too, was married to a Bob— just for the entertainment of the thing when she was bored and seriously when she needed a third bedroom like the one he was busy every night and Saturday of that winter building for her. I would describe Hilda's Bob if I could, but to tell the truth, I don't remember ever seeing him often enough to remember what he looked like, undoubtedly because of the enormity of Hilda's earthy skills. Regardless of the time of day or night I was at Hilda's, Bob was either at work or "out there hammering away on my new bedroom."

While Anne truly had little time in her life for sitting down to chat, she always would stop when I came knocking. She would offer me a cigarette and a chair, and then tell me about Anna Marie's latest accomplishments or ask me about some detail or other of her current sewing projects. Hilda, on the other hand, always had time for company because there was always something in her disarray that company could do—fold the clean sheets, stack those breakfast dishes in the sink, sew on those two buttons, whatever. The amusing thing usually was that while I was folding, stacking, and/or sewing, Hilda usually was sitting down "just for a second until I can catch my breath." (Though I cannot remember Bob Wright, I can remember thinking more than once that, with or without sex, the man probably never had a prayer of controlling his own destiny.)

The Wright house was almost precisely across the street from ours, the "almost" being a result of their occupying the side of Norhall's arc that flared out as it went toward its back property line while we occupied the inside part of the arc that gave us such gracious footage in front but room only for the clothesline and a garbage can in back. I couldn't see Hilda's house, however, not only because of the slight lack of truing in the positions of our opposing houses, but also because between us there were actually trees . . . or what passes for trees in instant slums.

Nothing grows faster than kudzu in the South unless it is mimosa trees in the South. Right behind mimosas are pine trees and willow trees. Somehow we had been spared the pines, but the southern curve of Norhall certainly had its fair share of mimosas and willows, especially in Hilda's small front yard and our generous one. In the winter I could see through my mimosas, but I could never see through her willows. As a result and because one didn't use phones lest a serious, gestational nap be disturbed, if I wanted conversation and Anne's car was gone, I had to walk across the lane to see if Hilda were home. She, on the other hand, would send one of her boys when she wanted to know if I were home. Actually, Hilda, by her own admission, was more interested in whether or not Sam was home. Sam didn't quite approve of Hilda . . . or he was not persuaded, shall we say, that overmuch exposure to her methods was entirely desirable from his own point of view.

Usually when one of the Wright boys came for me, it was because

Hilda was craving barbecued beans—not just any barbecued beans, but the ones from Leonard's Barbecue. Bob Wright had long since given up the battle about pregnant women's cravings and/or what they could do to the household budget, but he had somehow held the line on where Hilda could go alone, especially after dark. Leonard's was not in the best section of town, to say the least, but it was not so far down the scale of possibilities as to be either unsafe or improper for two women together.

I liked barbecued beans well enough in those days, but in those days I didn't so much crave them as I craved anything in sight. As a result, if Hilda wanted Leonard's beans and had the money to buy them for us, that was good enough for me . . . or it was right up until the night she told me with the greatest regret in her voice that both our babies were going to be marked somewhere on their bodies with three or four tiny, bean-shaped discolorations. She plainly believed what she had just said every bit as sincerely as she had just said it, and briefly an abyss opened up in front of me. It shut immediately and stayed shut until the next summer when, as with Anne Lehr, I had to begin to define my understanding of Woman and Woman-ways by opposing my self-understanding to theirs. And though I chose perspectives and intentions that went a hundred and eighty degrees away from Anne and Hilda's, I could not have had two more candid or unpretentious markers against which to draw my bead, nor could I ever have had two more generous ones.

52.

COLLEGES—or residential institutions of advanced instruction, which for most of us means colleges almost never sit in the memory as physical neighborhoods despite the fact that we usually live in them for extended periods. They often do not sit in our memories as the property of other people's lives either. Instead, we tend to describe them idiosyncratically and by time, as in "Oh, yes, I finished in 1996," or "I didn't finish there, but I always think of myself as part of the class of '75 anyway," or "Now Cornell, when I was there in 1963–67, would never have . . ." We tend as well to remember our colleges with an uncommon intensity.

In life, that which is defined primarily by time almost always is defined as well by a fixed set of activities and enjoys a more or less fixed purpose. Such is, of course, one of the justifications as well as benefits that underlie the governance of time in human affairs. In effect, fixed time and its employment foreshorten the space between our attention and our activities, granting us not only a heightening of our memory but also and consequentially, an exaggeration in our retention of it. We literally can process and feed ourselves for whole lifetimes from such memories.

I have remembered Norhall Circle all these years in just such terms and with just such utility. I was resident in a place of instruction from April 1956 until September 1958. The only irony to the whole thing, as I have said, was that as a married woman I passed that time in something nearer to a girls' dormitory than a co-ed campus; but then, such separation by gender was at the core of the curriculum anyway and more desirable than it was deleterious. The other thing worth noting, though I don't want to crush my metaphor with an overload of the obvious, is that like any good academic program, the time of my education on Norhall was divided into two more or less equal halves: Before Nora and After Nora.

Even after I was free of anxiety about the pregnancy and was moving about at will and even after I had passed through the weeks of ecstasy and into the more tranquil ones of deep content, I spent, proportionally speaking, only a small part of my days and evenings with either Hilda or Anne. I spent them instead reading and doing what Sam called "nesting." The reading was singular, the nesting was natural; both were part of my gender-specific course of study.

I read everything in sight and retained nothing, at least not as far as I could tell at the time. I had spent two whole days in absolute delight with a compendium of Ortega y Gassett when Sam came home one weekend to discover me at it. He was horrified, suggesting that Norhall Circle was not the place to even have such a book out in plain view, much less to be caught reading it. I can remember looking up at him and saying, "Why ever not?" to which he said, "Because he's a flaming Communist, you idiot, and we're living in a neighborhood that most definitely is not! If anybody ever figured out what you were reading, it would be all over for us around here," to which I responded, "Oh," and put Ortega y Gassett away in the bedroom closet. I was, however, more amused than disturbed at the time to realize that in two days I had not perceived aberrant politics in the man. In fact, I realized as I hid the book away, I couldn't remember having discovered much of anything at all about him in those two days. "Oh, well," I thought to myself, "he writes quite nicely, even in translation." That was that until After Nora when I chanced upon the book in the bedroom closet, read a page, and laughed my head off. Sam was right . . . but only After Nora.

Fortunately for the sake of my later life, my reading was confined pretty much to what was at hand. That is, there were no bookcases in most of the houses around us because there were few or no books in them to shelve. Certainly there were none to borrow or swap or chatter about. I was, as a result, forced to fall back upon what we already owned and/or the boxes I had brought from college with me.

There were occasional, pleasant exceptions to this, when Mother or some friend would mail in a book with a "Thinking of you" or "This one reminded me of you" kind of note. *Lysistrata* had come to us that way, of course, and I remember that someone—Mother, I think—had sent a brand-new copy of Millar Burrows' *The Dead Sea Scrolls*, with one of those "Reminds me of you" notes. I read the thing from cover to cover, which, given its heft, took a while. It entertained me for the better part of a week, in fact, but two days later I had less than no idea about what I had read, only a pleasant memory of having been for a while in the presence of something fairly remarkable. And so it went.

There were, of course, certain advantages to all of this. I could no longer solve any of Perry Mason's murders before he did, which made them even more entertaining. I was no longer concerned about Greek verbs, so I could read every drama Aeschylus and Sophocles ever wrote without any concern at all for historical presents or badly rendered preterites in their translating. That's a distinct advantage. I also never got bored. Francis Bacon would have been positively aghast at me, in fact, for once I had picked a book up, I was committed to finishing it, to some degree out of sheer inertia, but mainly out of a total inability to decide whether or not it was going anywhere either reasonable or worthy.

As for the nesting, it, too, was lovely, or so I thought at the time and so I have thought every time since. I got downright fussy in my tastes, that is to say, I began to like fussy things . . . ruffles and swooshy pillows and anything with little teddy bears on it, for example. I cleaned up the second bedroom, which, in essence, we had not occupied except as a dumping place, primarily because we had had nothing to occupy it with. I painted it a charming blue. We wanted a girl so badly that I didn't want a boy, should that be what we were having, to feel as if he had been undesired or unprepared for. (It's called Pregnant Logic and has an unusually long course description in most catalogs.)

My father, who with Mother drove back and forth across the state of Tennessee so often that year that he had to buy a new set of tires shortly after Memorial Day, my father had made before my birth what was called in those days a baby coop, primarily because it looked like one. It was as long as an adult bed and about half as wide, stood on four tall spindles, had four solid sides of screen wire, and a screen wire lid. I rebelled at the lid, but I was stuck with the rest. We had our baby bed.

The old mattress on which I had slept when I was in the coop was in fair shape, so I recovered it and made sheets to dress it—striped this time, so either sex would feel welcome. I took our wicker laundry basket and padded and beribboned it into an infant bed, finding the coop too over-whelming to even think of putting my newborn in it. Mary Ada, God bless her, brought us a baby pen that she had badgered away from some-body, God bless them . . . or I assumed they probably needed blessing. Most people did after Mary Ada got intentional with them. I made cur-tains of a sort out of burlap—opaque and cheap was the operative princi-ple on that one—and decorated them with cheery borders of scrap fabric.

Life on a tight budget can even have its unique gratifications to the pregnant. Because Sam wore lab coats instead of suit coats all day every day and because he was constantly in a world of germs and the paper products designed to prevent their spread, he never used pocket handkerchiefs. He nonetheless had a whole bureau drawer full of them, gifts every Christmas and birthday for years from every aunt and neighbor the man had ever had, I think, as well as from quite a few sisters-in-law. It occurred to me one day that not only were those handkerchiefs quite lovely, but that they also were almost all of a perfect weight for a baby's summer shirts. Within less than six weeks, Sam no longer had an excess of handkerchiefs. The baby-in-the-making, on the other hand, had a satisfactory plethora of both sleeveless and long-sleeved jackets with incredibly tiny buttons and deli-cate, loop closures. It was amazing, even to me. Somewhere along the way I had lost me in a flurry of domesticity without precedent.

Whether with or without precedent in my own past, however, those Before Nora months pretty much followed the standard curriculum for such courses of study. They and the times just like them that would punctuate my woman's life over the subsequent years have also been ones of great worth not just in the growth of our family, but in mine as an individual within that family. It is, I am convinced, much easier, much more natural, to accept and practice faith in the ordinary circumstances of time if one has spent sustained periods of well-being outside of them. There is a comfort in that and a security for which, even in old age, I am grateful and by which I still am helped.

53.

IN 1999 Loyola Press published a collection of what they called *Inspiration, Wit and Wisdom from the Mothers in Our Lives.* The idea was simple. They asked women of some prominence to recall the maternal adages, maxims, and favorite phrases that had inhabited and shaped their childhoods. At this exercise, I was once more a washout, not out of personal failing but because my mother was an absolute failure as a source. My mother's speech could be dotted with literary allusions, but it rarely dealt in aphorisms and maxims except in spoof. She would, in annoyance, sometimes say something like "Too many hands spoil the broth," and then with that wicked twinkle in her black eyes, add with the next breath, "But then one must remember that many hands make light work," which pretty much sums up her lifelong opinion of the usual flotsam and jetsam of human wit and wisdom.

Since I was a nonparticipant in the Loyola project because of my lack of original material, the collection's compilers went the next step and contacted each of our four daughters, asking them if they could recall something I had said consistently and memorably in the years of their growing up. They could. All four of them, unknown to each other, filed with Loyola the same remembered phrase. And thanks to them, there I sit on page twenty-four of the published volume, though the editors did have the courtesy to use my initials and not my full name. My remembered quotation? "Sssheeze, I hate babies!"

This should not be interpreted as meaning that I did not love our babies. I just liked them better after they turned into people. Turning into people meant for me when they could at last talk. Preverbal infants kept me wrapped around anxiety's wheel twenty-four hours a day. Postverbal children, on the other hand, were playing the game in my court, and I had some hope of coming out if not the winner, then at least a coparticipant.

Nora Katherine Tickle, named for Mamaw and my mother in that order, came in June, and my guess is that in her case I didn't say, "Sssheeze, I hate babies!" for at least four or five months, by which time she was well on her way to no longer being one. The thing that excused Nora from my frustration was pure distraction. Half the known world came to see her. The drop-bys like Minsky or Mary Ada or Cootsie would have been pleasures had the house not been a wreck—I never have understood how babies can do that so well—and had I had on something besides my night-gown every time they came—something else I still don't quite understand about babies. The back-breakers, however, were the come-down-and-stay-a-week ones. They looked a lot like grandparents to me in the beginning. By the end of July they were looking more like oh-no-not-agains, but what can one do? I soldiered on and wished fervently that I were Sam with a damned hospital to go to.

It was not that I didn't like having them all show up so frequently. I did; and besides affection on both sides of the equation, there was considerable need on our part. Half of those grandparent trips, I realized years later, were not so much to indulge their own desires as to augment our meager goods and supplies. After each set of parents would each time leave, I would find our kitchen cupboards a bit fuller than they had been, Nora's room with a few more baby sacques and receiving blankets than it had had, the living room decorated with a bit more infant equipment than it had been. Bit by bit and trip by trip, the four of them imported the necessities without ever once exercising the loss of face that would have come from writing yet another check. That having been said, however, and new young motherhood being what new young motherhood is, I was more given that summer to exhaustion than appreciation, more inclined to peevishness than to gratitude. The whole summer of 1957, in fact, was one of those times in life when everyone does what he or she has to do, but without much moral or emotional economy.

Near summer's end, more and more of the chaos at number 1075 had little to do with Nora. Sam Tickle was graduating, medical school was almost over and done with! Even in memory, the elation of those few weeks still brings a small rush of tears. Invitations had to be mailed, and accommodations once more arranged. Big meals out of a small kitchen and with a dearth of chairs had to be figured out. A suitable babysitter had to be found.

A week before the ceremony, the university doled out the appropriate academic garb to each candidate, and I spent hours crooning to Nora about her daddy while I fussed with the wrinkles in that wondrous black gown with its velvet sleeve stripes and its mighty, flowing arms. I spent more time steaming and resteaming the long hood, its University of Tennessee white and gold velvet radiating even at night like sunshine in the nursery where I had hung it for her to see. We costumed him for pictures and then, reconsidering, took more pictures in other poses and different attitudes, and so it went for days and days.

From the perspective of the years, such total, consuming abandon over an achievement could, perhaps, seem naïve, almost foolish, but it does not for us. In memory as in 1957, the completion of Sam's doctorate in medicine and the receipt of his license to practice with it were as real—as worthy of sustained, unreserved celebration—as marriage and parenthood. Though the truth also is that even when we were in the midst of our headiest celebrating, one or the other of us would stop from time to time to pick up our daughter and say, with a look or with words, that without her there would not have been such richness in our rejoicing, not such depth in its experiencing.

54.

IN 1957 fledgling doctors were expected, but not required, to serve an internship before they began to practice medicine privately. If, however, they wanted to enter a residency program in order to specialize, they had no choice; they had to do an internship. Sam wanted one for both reasons.

From our point of view and that of most of Sam's classmates, there were only two internships worth coveting in 1957—City of Memphis Hospitals and Bellevue in New York City. Sam applied for, and received, one to City of Memphis. The man was so pleased with himself that he would have become intolerable had the internship itself not started less than two weeks after he graduated—and had it not proved to be a trial-by-fire that reduced his pleasure to a mere parody of itself within the course of a very few days.

Though the Methodist Laboratory had been demanding, it was as nothing compared to the rigors of a mid-twentieth-century internship, especially of one in a large teaching system like City of Memphis. Where once Sam had worked only one night in every three, he now worked every other night . . . thirty-six hours on, twelve off, thirty-six hours on, twelve off. Where once he had gone from room to room visiting with patients as he collected specimens, he now was assigned for three months solely to the labor and delivery rooms of an obstetrical suite. Where once there had been few precipitant emergencies in the dark hours of a usual night's shift, there were now two, three, four babies birthing during a single tour of duty, and there was no repairing of one's errors here. Sometimes there was not even another physician to spot and stopgap one's simple lapses of weariness.

I had never worried about Sam before, never doubted his capacity to survive any and every thing. Now I did. I found myself not only worrying about him, but trying to shield him from anything bothersome and especially from anything that might disturb his sleeping. The ten hours he was home out of every forty-eight (two of his twelve were consumed in driving back and forth) were geared entirely toward him—toward rocking a baby or walking a baby or going visiting with a baby—anything that would guarantee she wouldn't be fretful or cry; toward cooking two or three things that might appeal and/or be easily digested high energy and/or be portable if time ran out, and then eating the leftovers myself the next day; toward paying bills and making decisions arbitrarily for him as well as us, even while knowing that there is always risk and inevitably some negative consequence in doing so; toward a dozen such activities that any physician's spouse could name as readily as I. As compensatory mechanisms, they are not good for anybody, and they can become habits as quickly and firmly as crab grass can become a lawn. They did for us in those twelve months, anyway, and the vestiges of that year reared their mean, little scruffy heads from time to time over all the years that Sam practiced medicine and we reared children.

The first months of Sam's internship cut two ways. If his being awake and gone for thirty-eight out of every forty-eight hours were a schedule almost without justification, it was nonetheless still a schedule, and one that brooked no variances. Moreover, it did not seem to be a bad thing for Nora. Being unaware that the rest of the world organized itself around twenty-four-hour pacing cycles, she had no acquired reservations about assuming the rhythms of forty-eight-hour ones; and our double days, hers and mine, soon settled into their own regimens and routines with little to distract us from their slow pleasures.

Hilda was as occupied with her new son as I was with Nora; and Anne was deep into the meetings and PTA committees of Anna Marie's new school year. Within no more than a week or two of Labor Day, Norhall Circle had become even quieter than it had been in the dead of the preceding winter. I can remember, in fact, only one interruption to our languor, and it didn't last long. In late September and just three or four houses west of Anne on the opposite side of the curve, we picked up a new family, the Winters. Jayne was tall and graceful, so proportioned that anyone, even those of us on Norhall Circle, would have called her statuesque—in fact, we did, over the course of many conversations. In pure physical beauty, though, Holt Winter outshone her. The man was so well-turned he was dramatic—big, broad shoulders; straight-as-an-arrow posture; trim, tight torso. His face was the open one of an intellectual, and his voice had the ring of authority when he said even so simple a thing as, "Hello, how are you today?" The problem was that he rarely seemed to be around to say it, even when they were still unloading the van and settling in.

There was a little girl, Christina, maybe two at the time, whom they called Crissy. Every morning Jayne and Crissy came out the door, both of them dressed to the nines, and went on their way, Jayne to work and Crissy, presumably, to her babysitter. Whatever Holt himself did, he had to do inside, alone, and at home; for we never saw him after that first week, and there was no other car in the drive by means of which he could leave us. After a few days, Jayne's car and her infinite range of expensive clothes got to be of more interest to most of us than Holt, however. Even if he in his Dionysian glory could fade out of the neighborhood's level of active interest, the presence on Norhall Circle of haute couture and a car as large and expensive as a Cadillac De Ville could not.

"I tell you," said Anne over and over again, "it's just not natural for people with that kind of money to live here. Why would they want to?

They plainly don't belong." Hilda's answer to that one, like almost all of Hilda's answers to people questions, was of a pragmatic bent. Holt was just too good-looking, she informed us, for any wife with sense to leave him out in public or among women who might appear to him as her equals. Anne always countered, when the conversation got just here, that that was the silliest explanation she had heard since the last time Hilda had said it, and plus which, there had to be some better one. Something in the Winters' past, perhaps? Maybe Holt and Jayne weren't really married? Maybe he was a gambler and only needed telephones to do his work? Maybe . . . ?

It went on like that for several days before the two of them gave the whole discussion up for lack of any new material with which to further their interest. For my own part, I thought Hilda and Anne might both be right to some greater or lesser degree, but I didn't bother to say so. What I really was thinking about more and more frequently by the end of September was not the Winters problem; what I was really thinking about was how, regardless of what his original reasons for coming may have been, Norhall Circle, like Circe's island, somehow managed to ingest and then consume any man who came within a block of her.

As the dusty, wearying heat of late September began to give way at last to the cleaner and crisper air of October, I began not to revive with the weather, but to wilt in spite of it. As I progressed farther and farther away from the delicious distortions of pregnancy, I became more and more morose about my loss of contact with a world larger than Norhall Circle. My brain was back—or that is, the one I remembered having trained for years and having taken to Messick with me in the mornings was back—and my books were becoming an increasingly lonesome exercise. What good to read if one can't talk afterward? And to whom was I to talk? I had no husband whom I could engage just then in much of anything beyond the most elemental necessities of sleep, food, and clean shirts. I had no job to go to and no colleagues with whom to greet and then dissect the world.

After we had moved to Norhall, as Sam's workload had increased and as pregnancy had limited my movements for a while, our church attendance had become more and more spotty. Now, with Sam's interning schedule, it was nonexistent, the animated exercise of Sunday morning give-and-takes having gone with it. I was, in short, trapped again. I was marching in place simply to pass through a block of time until the internship could be finished. Early October began to feel alarmingly like my last year at Shorter, and I wasn't ready to go into that particular slough again.

It was somewhere around mid- to late October that it dawned on me I wanted not only to talk, but that even more I wanted—I needed—to hear men as well as women talk. I needed to hear conversations once again that were at least spiced from time to time with a man's inventive reasoning, with a man's must-solve aggression, his global perspective, and—Oh, dear Lord, yes!—with his nondomestic points of reference.

"Hells bells," I thought to myself one depressed afternoon, "I just want to hear a man's voice saying something longer than two sentences and a grunt." And the minute I achieved that bit of self-understanding, I thought as well, "I'd give anything for one hour just listening to those men in the Pig Skin!" After that, I thought, "Hmmmm . . ."

There was no Pig Skin on Norhall Circle. There was not even a Pig Skin look-alike, so far as I knew, within miles of Norhall Circle. (The place really was Circe's and had long since eaten up all of a Pig Skin's potential customers, I thought to myself with some bitterness.) But if there were no bars nearby, there was a Walgreen's about a mile up Norhall, across Crider, and two blocks north on Boyer. More to the point, that Walgreen's had a soda fountain which, if my memory served me correctly, was almost always filled for an hour or so after lunch with old men drinking coffee. "Hmmmm . . ."

One of the more annoying benefits of grocery shopping in the 1950s and '60s was the giving and receiving of Green Stamps. Miserable little rectangles of unevenly gummed and incompletely perforated paper, they were as green as their name and, unfortunately for the impatient among us, they were worth something. In general one received one Green Stamp in exchange for every dime spent at checkout. One did, that is, unless a market were having a double-stamp day, in which case one got two stamps for every dime expended.

Sam Tickle, before internship and while he was still in thrall to his marketing obsessions, had been known to spend whole Wednesday nights with the evening paper and its Thursday grocery specials, calculating which would be the next day's better buy—green peas at seventeen cents a can and regular stamps at Store A or green peas at eighteen cents a can with double stamps at Store B. He usually decided in favor of the eighteen cents with doubles. As a result, by the time Nora had been firmly on the way and during the afternoons of my rampant domesticity, I had spent inordinate amounts of time getting all our caches of loose stamps stuck down into complete books and then calculating the sum of their worth against the list of our baby needs.

The acquisition process itself involved getting a catalog from the stamp company's showroom, matching the desired items against their price in stamps, and then, assuming one had enough stamps, paying for one's chosen goods with books of the pesky green things rather than with cash. As systems go, it would really have been quite a lovely one, had acquiring and processing the bloody stamps not been so exasperating. Before Nora, however, I was far less irascible about such tedium, and I had actually enjoyed spending the stamps on her necessities. My one bit of foolishness, Sam and I both had thought, was a plaid stroller that was surprisingly cheap.

Surprisingly cheap is usually just cheap in premium exchanges, I have found. It certainly was in this case. The thing was made of aluminum so light and thin that the frame itself could not have weighed in at a full pound. The whole stroller did not weigh in at two. The wheels were scarcely a half-inch wide and definitely not a quarter-inch thick. The sides and back of the contraption were of a plasticized, loosely woven plaid fabric neither Sam nor I could identify. The result was a kind of sling-on-wheels that had grown less and less appealing to my maternal instincts as I had become more and more of a mother and less and less of a mother-to-be. However, we did have a stroller. Hmmmm . . .

I got it out of the closet that restive October day, opened it up and checked such latches as there were, and set my four-month-old daughter in it. She responded by kicking, and the more she kicked, the more she swung, the sling keeping rhythm with her bouncing feet. She giggled. "All right," I thought, "we'll try it as far as Crider. No harm in that." We ended up at the Walgreen's soda fountain in record time. The bumpy asphalt of both our lane and Crider had proved even more enthralling than kicking, and Miss Nora's little bottom had swung from side to side all the way while she laughed and clapped her hands with appreciative enthusiasm.

Every time I see a high-tech stroller these days in an airport or on a city sidewalk, I think of that cheap plaid fabric and unimaginative aluminum frame. While I am very sure no federal regulatory code would allow Nora's stroller to be marketed now—it probably shouldn't be, in point of fact—I still have one of those unattractive moments of eulogizing the

Good Old Days when strollers were strollers and not miniature, padded tanks. I rarely have such moments about anything else and those I do have usually leave me as quickly as they come. The stroller ones always linger a bit longer, however, probably because of the soda fountain as much as the sway of the stroller itself.

We loved that soda fountain. It would be very hard to say who enjoyed it more over the ten months we trafficked there, but my guess is that Nora did. The minute I pushed her for the first time inside the chrome rails that marked the fountain area off from the rest of the store, she clapped her hands more or less together and pursed her mouth in unmitigated delight at all the smells and sounds. She stared raptly at the illuminated signs that, with genuine electrical flair, were advertising bubbly Cokes and incredibly colorful bacon and lettuce and tomato sandwiches. She was transfixed by the hustle and gyrations of the two soda jerks, watching them much of the time with something that looked for all the world like comprehension. She also was plainly addicted to the rush of public attention. Mercy, but did I have things to tell this girl-child as soon as she was old enough!

The truth is that from our very first day at Walgreen's, the after-lunch coffee cadre all came by. How could they not with her parked in the aisle between their tables and the cash register? They talked and jostled the stroller—certainly not a difficult trick—and pinched her toes until she withdrew them only so she could thrust her foot back and ask for more. Most afternoons and primarily out of an embarrassment not unlike that at the Pig Skin, I ordered a Coke and let her taste it. Giving her a sip or two of Coke legitimately extended our time, of course, but it also made us look as if we were a self-sufficient social unit; for by November I could already feel myself slipping into that other thing I had forgotten about the Pig Skin: I was once more beginning to think like a writer. I was once more becoming a watcher, in fact, more pleasured by riding in the cadences of these mostly male voices than desirous of engaging them. If Walgreen's were not the Pig Skin and coffee by the cup were not beer by the icy mug, they still accomplished much the same thing. Both were that third good place, and I was as much comforted by one as I had been by the other.

We didn't go to Walgreen's on the days when Sam was to be home. I usually was too busy fretting over attractive supper menus and creating a tranquil, restorative environment to allow for two hours away from it, despite the contradiction patent in that statement. Nor do I mean to suggest

that we went to Walgreen's every early afternoon when he was not to
come home. Obviously we could not do that either. There were rainy afternoons and chilly afternoons and, sometimes, just plain cross or busy afternoons; but we certainly went often enough so that the sight of the
stroller coming out of the closet was all it took for the smiles to begin. We
also went often enough for our soda fountain trips to give a pacing to all
of our days, whether spent at Walgreen's or not. By two-thirty or three,
especially as fall progressed into winter, the early-afternoon kibbitzers were
winding down their coffee drinking and starting to think about getting
home before the late afternoon cold could set in. Once they were gone,
the show was over, and Nora and I would leave as well.

By four o'clock we, too, were always home and warm again. Nora,
weary but content, would lie on her back in the playpen beside the daybed
in the living room, some times batting at the mobile above her head and
some times just watching whatever I was doing; and four o'clock gradually became a valley of peace in the landscape of our day together. The
house was still and clean; so, too, were both of us. Supper's prepreparations
were done, and it was much too early to begin the final ones. Nora didn't
want to be played with anymore for a while, and my need for company
was sated as well. A natural valley of quiet suspended between the morning's completed chores and the evening's approaching activities.

It began so unself-consciously, so without intention on my part, that I
am not even sure—have never since been sure—exactly when or how it
came to be; it just did. One afternoon long before mid-November and
hard winter, I was taking my four o'clock break on the daybed, just watching Nora and doing nothing. An afternoon or two later, I was taking my
four o'clock break sitting up on the daybed, watching Nora, and saying,
"Thank you," except that this time I knew to Whom I was saying it and
why. Things progressed from there.

They progressed from "Thank you" to "O God of mercy, protect her,
take care of her," to "Lord, bless us and keep us and teach us. Shape us and
form us after Your will," and straight on from there to the four o'clocks of
my mother's afternoons. Suddenly I was home and knew not by what
means I had arrived. I looked at my daughter and knew with all my heart,
soul, mind, and memory that I did indeed have things to teach this girl-
child and that they started now.

Thus it was that sometime before Thanksgiving 1957, four in the af-

ternoon became the appointed hour of prayer in my house as in my
mother's. Like early morning and the time just before retiring, four o'clock
became, and still is, the hour in which to offer the prayers that are of my
own making, the petitions of one life, the intercessions of one perspective
and one set of affections.

Within less than ten years of those Norhall afternoons, I would learn
as well to observe the Daily Offices. Using the ancient Psalms and the set
prayers and hymns that the Church has employed since the very first days
of her beginning. I would learn to keep the fixed-hour liturgy of the "little hours" of Terce, Sext, and Nones in accordance with their appointed
times of 9:00 A.M., noon, and 3:00 P.M.; but I would keep as well my
mother's hour and the freedom of my mother's words. In the course of the
intervening years, I have discovered from experience, as the Church already knew, that the commercial or business day breaks its afternoon quite
naturally at three o'clock. The domestic day, on the other hand, breaks its
afternoon more naturally at four o'clock, as my mother had known.
Always and in both instances, as surely as faith is informed by the wisdom
of our fathers, just so surely is its practice shaped by that of our mothers.
Or so I have thought in all the decades that I have lived in the hope of
someday becoming a worthy one.

55.

THE FIRST TIME was the Friday night after Thanksgiving. Sam was at
the hospital, and Nora and I had had an early evening. Supper had been
holiday leftovers, dressing for me, mashed potatoes and equally mashed
peas for her, with Daddy hopefully getting enough break to enjoy the
turkey leg he had taken with him that morning as he left us. Because there
had been little preparation needed for supper, there had been little cleanup
afterwards. Tired from the day before and with an unusually full tummy, I
fell asleep on the daybed and didn't rouse until sometime around ten-thirty
or eleven.

Once awake, I went into the bathroom, turned on the light, pulled the
blind as closed as a cheap venetian blind will ever really go, and had started

to undress when I heard it—the soft, half-scraping sound of something brushing against the base of the house below the bathroom window. "Cat," I thought to myself, and then thought, "Whoever heard of a cat walking into the side of a house! Raccoon, maybe." Nothing more happened, and I went to bed, losing my raccoon and my self in deep sleep.

Two nights later, on Sunday, I read late in the living room . . . later, I knew, than I should have with a baby who liked her mornings early and friendly. Turning on the hall light so I could see, I went back into the living room, switched off my reading lamp, and was back in the hall flipping on the bathroom light when I heard it again. This time it was a small "uumph," the kind we all make when we step up too high on a step, and it was coming from the other side of the bathroom wall.

There was silence after that, except for a slight scraping sound, like a sleeve or some other fabric rubbing briefly against the house's wooden siding. I clicked off the light behind me without taking my eyes off the window. Once the light was off and my eyes had adjusted, I could see just the roundness of the top of a head shadowed through the thin blind by the streetlight across the road. I slipped off my shoes and as silently and quickly as I could, crept to the kitchen and then fumbled in the dark until I found and retrieved both Sam's claw hammer and his heavy ballpeen one. When I got back to the bathroom, the half-dome shadow was gone and there was no noise outside at all, the silence being almost more threatening than the "uumph" had been.

Norhall Circle was the kind of neighborhood in which, whatever else the houses might lack, they all had burglar guards. Being far more afraid of fire than of people, I also thought that in a family of smokers being trapped inside a burning house with no egress was a much more likely horror than being robbed in a place where the houses were literally within a whisper's distance of one another. As a result, I had urged Sam on several occasions to remove ours, especially before Nora's birth. Arguing that bars would have to be in the windows before we could resell the house, he had refused. Now I was grateful; but I also knew because of our detailed discussion of the issue, that the only window in number 1075 without bars was the bathroom one. Apparently, the rationale behind omitting bars in the bath had been pure economy; like most bathroom windows, ours had been too high to climb into without a ladder—or it had been right up until the gas company had put its silvered and solid, two-foot-high meter directly below the window. I knew, in other words, what my "uumph" had come from. It had come from somebody's stepping two feet up on a gas meter.

I also knew that there was no way in to us except through that window, so I stood there in the dark, the claw hammer in my right hand and the ballpeen in my left. I calculated that I could rake the skin off whoever with the forked end of the claw hammer as he entered and perhaps even drive him away. The ballpeen hammer, if I could just transfer it without dropping it, would be the second surprise, I hoped the one with which I could incapacitate or kill him.

I stood in the bathtub pushed against the outside wall beside the window for thirty minutes before I decided he had gone . . . and before I realized what I had done. I had just armed myself with all I had at hand for the express purpose of maiming, possibly killing, another human being, and I had done as dispassionately, though perhaps not as aptly, as a seasoned murderer would have. Whatever he might do to me and whatever I might do to myself in the course of it, he was not getting in to that coop, he was not coming near my baby.

I don't know whether I was more shaken by fright or by my violent introduction to the dark side of motherhood, but I began to tremble. I trembled and then shook and finally chilled for the rest of the night, until Nora woke to a morning that was too friendly even for her. I held her in a death-grip for most of it.

At some time during the afternoon, I settled down enough to understand that I had probably had no more than a peeping tom, that if my visitor had truly wanted in, he could and would have come. I also looked up the number of the police department for the first time in my life and taped it to the underside of the hall phone. Because Sam must not have his attention at the hospital divided between his patients and us, I was determined to say nothing, just as I was determined not to call the police unless something else happened. Once a police car came on to Norhall Lane, everybody on both sides of the circle knew who had called and about what. I simply could not risk drawing that kind of attention down on us unless I had to.

After that, nothing happened. Sam, still innocent of what had transpired, did another thirty-six hour rotation without incident, and I forgot my fear enough to doze through the nights we were without him. I could not entirely shake off my disquietude about the rod of amoral, ahuman purpose I now knew sat near to the core of me. At the same time, however, I was also mature enough at nearly twenty-four to recognize that the steel of that rod was probably the oldest tool, as well as the cleanest evil, I had in my possession and that I was as incapable of regretting its presence as I was unable to expunge it. It was, all and all, a weary—almost exhausting—five days before I heard him again.

I had been undressing in the dark since the previous Sunday night, but I had without thinking continued the habit of pregnancy by flipping on the bathroom light when I used it during the night. I had hardly sat down before I heard a creak in the outside windowsill as if the grip of fingers or the press of an arm were depressing it slightly. I did not look up, but keeping myself as normal as possible, finished, turned out the light, and took the hammers from the towel closet where I had hidden them just in case. I waited, trying to decide whether or not to risk the police, when I saw the shadow of a full head move from one side of the window to the other and then disappear. I heard his footsteps as he crunched across the frozen grass and headed out toward our driveway.

The fourth time it happened, almost a week later, I had learned to use no lights, but he had also gotten bolder. This time the moon was full and I could see the outline of his head the second I entered the dark bathroom. I also could hear him breathing through the window, and that was what did it. Peeping tom or not, he was not going to go away. And peeping tom or not, he also had to know enough about us to know when and for how long Sam was gone, he had to be a familiar of the neighborhood.

I didn't call the police. If my two weeks of night visits had been filled with tension, introspection, and fear, they had also lent me some common sense as well. The reality of the situation was that even if I were to call for help, there would be nothing for the police to see once they had arrived. The minute my peeper heard a car or saw a flashing light, he would be gone, completely out of the officers' reach long before they could even get out of their patrol cars. Much worse, he could keep returning and I could keep calling and he could keep running away right up until the night—the night that would surely come—the night that the officers would decide not to hurry so, to take their time, to be a bit less eager to indulge a frightened woman . . . right up until the night, in other words, when I might truly need help. No, I decided, until my tom actually came over that windowsill and became my intruder, there was nothing the police could do. He was my problem and mine alone.

I took Nora the next day not to Walgreen's but two miles farther up Boyer to the variety store in the shopping center. She loved riding the bus and was charmed by all the minutiae of the five-and-dime. Because I was holding her, not strolling her, however, it took me almost an hour to locate and decide upon the toy automatic that looked real enough to be credible in the dark. It also took almost six dollars that I would have to cook around and without, but I did it and we went home.

The next night, I deliberately left the hall light on so that it shone through the half-opened door of the bath. About midnight, I went by intention into the bath, leaving the door and its light behind me to illuminate the outlines of my body and my gestures. I coughed sharply to make my presence known. The breathing was hard now, and he was careless enough to scrape one leg against the lower side of the house. Once he was up high enough for me to see his head and know I had his attention, I stood up, pulled the gun out of the folds of my gown where I had hidden it, and then turned so the light could catch the gleam but not the tawdriness of it.

"Holt," I said to the window, "I've got a gun and I will shoot you right where you are if you try to come through that window. And even if I don't kill you, Jayne will know what you've been up to."

I heard him hit the ground running, heard the faint curse when he banged into something, heard the silence after that of a neighborhood once more asleep. I had no way of knowing whether I had won or lost, whether I had named the threat or simply angered a man who would return to us bated as well as unstable.

Sam came home the next evening and, with him there, I slept like the proverbial dead, slept as if I were trying to get two night's worth of rest into one, in fact. When the phone rang in the hall the next morning just as the predawn light was creeping in around the bedroom shades, I couldn't quite understand what the noise was or where it was coming from. I finally roused enough to reach it just as it woke Nora. Above her stirrings and whimperings, I could hear Jayne Winter's gasps. "Is Sam there," she asked, "I think Holt's killed himself! Oh, God!" and the line went dead.

Sam was alert the minute I shook him. "It's Jayne Winter. She needs you. Holt's killed himself." He was in his trousers, stethoscope in hand, al-most before I had finished the words. Twenty minutes later the whirring lights and sirens were everywhere and the neighbors were all out in the lane, wrapped in blankets and calling to each other about what was wrong. From the kitchen window I could see Sam's figure skirting in behind them, making his way home as inconspicuously as possible. I opened the door as he got all the way into our driveway.

"Well?" I said.

"Totally rigid," he said. "He must have done it after she went to bed last night. Took the vacuum cleaner hose and taped it to the exhaust pipe, pulled the other end in the back window of her car, wedged towels around the difference, and turned the motor on."

"Any note?" I asked, my breath sounding tight even to me.

"None that I saw. I just pronounced him and released the body to the police. They'll send somebody over to the hospital later today so I can sign his paperwork. Damnedest thing, though, that man had a steel plate in the top of his head the size of a salad plate. I've never in my life seen one that big before. Beautiful repair from the surgery, however. I'd never have seen it if I hadn't been doing a routine check for trauma."

The obituary, when it ran two mornings later, was unusual primarily in that it ran a picture as well as a bio. There Holt was in a major's uni-form, as handsome as he had been when he was among us, though perhaps thinner. Korea, the paper said. A head wound, the paper also said, from which Major Winter had never fully recovered and which had left him de-spondent. Postinjury depression was believed to be the underlying cause of his suicide. No note had been found. There were the added details about Jayne (an investment consultant, as it turned out), the surviving daughter born after her father's injury, and the parents and relatives, all fairly promi-nent in Mississippi and Alabama. It also mentioned the Winters' having resided in two or three other towns since the major's leaving the service and where many friends would mourn his passing.

We were safely out of internship before I ever showed Sam the toy gun and told him its story. I did, however, say something to Anne one day in passing, just because I had to know. "You know," I said, "I thought maybe I saw Holt Winter looking in one of our windows one night. Can you imagine that!"

She looked at me, her head cocked to the side in that way she had when she was gauging something. I knew almost before she said it, what she was going to say. "You, too?"

"Yes."

"Good God, why didn't you say so? Bob would have chased him off for you, and he really would have loved to catch him. We chased somebody out of here the first week after they moved in, but we were never sure, you know? I mean, Bob thought so, but then nobody else ever said anything, so we thought maybe it was a onetime thing or something. And we didn't feel like we could afford to say anything to Jayne, of course."

"I suspect Jayne knew," I said.

"Look at the string of places she's taken him in the last three or four years," Anne said. "I just wonder if there's a bunch of women in every one of those towns who have let her know." Then she added, almost wearily, "I told you and Hilda there had to be a reason for them being here instead of somewhere else."

"Yes," I said, "you did."

Jayne moved quietly away two or three weeks later. We all stopped by to wish her well, but not to visit. There was nothing to visit about. She had made choices that I still am not sure I myself would not have made, yet I could not praise her for having made them. She had protected, but at our risk as well as hers, what she loved. She had, without question, protected it in sickness as faithfully as she would have in health. All of us who are married are pledged to do no less than that. She had dealt as best her ample resources and considerable intelligence would let her with an illness properly called, not traumatic dementia, but war; and the tax dollars and votes of every one of us on Norhall Circle had gone to support that process. To spend our resources otherwise would have been an unspeakable complicity on our part in the destruction of thousands of people, and probably of our own security as a nation not to mention as a system of government.

The Lehrs had suspected and kept quiet out of respect for Jayne's pain and Holt's obvious dignity, certainly; but they also had been silent because of their own, very real fear of being wrong in a social system that would have condemned them had they been and a legal system that could have held them liable as well as culpable. I had kept quiet out of need to protect what I loved and without a care for whether or not my silence might jeopardize anybody else. When I had acted, I had taken the safer, though not necessarily the better, of two courses: I had tried to drive the evil else-where rather than incur the risks involved in trying to contain it.

We had done those things, each of us; and as Jayne Holt drove out of our lives taking her daughter with her, we all knew that were the same thing to happen again on Norhall Circle, we would, each of us, including Jayne, exercise the very same decisions again in the very same way. We knew, but we dared not say so. Instead, we said nothing, and *Forgive us our trespasses as we forgive those who trespass against us* became for me the most frightening words of the Christian faith.

56.

THE FIRST POEM CAME, fully formed, in January. I had never had that happen before, the coming of the words complete in all their junc-tures and parts:

1
Norhall sleeps in summerland
Suburban to the city's sweep.
Where once the varied grasses grew,
Now her whitened houses stand
And asphalt paves the arteries of man.
Built to hold the working crew
For a human wealth she never knew,
Norhall waits in sullen heat
For her time to be complete,
And waiting where she stood,
She sang the magnitude of man.

Derivative in places, a pastiche of the chords and rhythms of others, but a coherent and well-behaved one; and I knew it.

2
I heard the song of Norhall in the morning hour
And saw the dawn arise in a verdant shower;

Smelled the grasses in their mingled sweetness
And bethought me in the moment's fleetness,
Of music played with stems for strings
And willows for an oboe's weeping.
All of Norhall, in quietness sleeping,
Sang of beauty while in newness steeping.

Although I would tinker with it a bit and tweak it in a place or two from time to time, refining a cadence here and adjusting a pause there, those were minor occupations, nearer to the care and dressing of a baby than to the process of producing one:

3
I heard the song of Norhall in the troubled noon,
Heard the barren thunder clang the drums of doom;
Saw hot heat, in febrile stillness pressing,
Wet the walk in a sweaty tressing;
Watched children dance the Congo's fevered beat
To the prism rhythm of a white-hot heat;
Saw love like flowers wilt away,
And beauty burned in the hellish May;
Sang of a land forever cursed,
Sang of Norhall always athirst.

And at the end of the poem as with the friends so briefly known:

4
I heard the song of Norhall ringing
Down a dusty, fenceless lane;
Heard the evening weep in sadness;
Heard the wind's upsurge of madness,
While all around in sacred orgy springing,
Wildly sang the priests of rain.
Men and women in sorrow bending,
Human souls, like human twilights, ending,
Sang the song of Norhall in their rending.

After that, there were more, and in a steady, reassuring flow, though few of the others would ever arrive so fully formed as *Norhall* had. I would never be a poet, as I have already said, but I had at last found poetry. I knew where it flowed and where its channels lay. Like a mighty tributary, it ran broad and deep; but now I could navigate its courses from its headwaters down to the wine-dark sea and back again. Holt and Nora had brought me that.

It was time for us to go. Sam and I both were finished here.

PART NINE

*The South
Carolina Piedmont*

57.

SAM'S GRANDFATHER and great-grandfather had both been physicians, which statement, while true, confuses almost as much as it explains. Great-grandpa Gammon, who was Mamaw's maternal grandfather, was apparently as able and well-trained a physician as the nineteenth century was capable of producing. He also, like many a physician before and after him, saw medicine as a vocation of religious obligation as well as of innate skill. In this, his reach was demonstrably as extensive as his craft was accomplished. He established, for several years practiced in, and for his whole life supported, the Gammon Institute, a medical facility for the indigent in central Brazil. That Institute, so far as I know, is still in operation and still bears witness to the man's dedication to his calling and to the honor in which he held it.

Great-grandpa, for some reason I have never been clear about but my guess would be health, returned to this country in the latter half of the nineteenth century and began a new and equally rural practice in the Appalachian hill country of northeastern Tennessee and southern Virginia where he had been born and reared. For a well-schooled and adept physician like George Gammon, rural practice in those days offered some inducements other than merely humanitarian ones. One of the more attractive of these was that if a man were proficient and his hands blessed, he could in time gain a reputation that would spread over sizable areas of sparsely settled country. The value of such a reputation was not to the ego, though that must play a part in any human endeavor of consequence, but to the intellectual curiosity and professional vigor of the physician. A reputation as a skilled healer drew to one's door a highly disproportionate number of challenging pathologies from which a good man could learn. It also, and for the same reason, brought to one's doors the best and the brightest young men who were themselves aspiring to a career in medicine.

For young men who had already had some formal schooling in medicine, teaching physicians like Great-grandpa Gammon offered the hands-on, clinical instruction of what was then called a preceptorship and what we would now probably regard as a protointernship. Young men who, because of financial or logistical difficulties, had not been able to receive formal instruction could surmount this impediment by first "reading medicine" with a teaching physician of reputation. Reading medicine was a kind of one-on-one tutorial education that could last for two, three, sometimes four years before both parties judged the candidate prepared enough to begin an actual preceptorship.

As a system of training, reading medicine with a country doctor and then going out on one's own to repeat and refine his processes on living flesh would seem to be not only primitive but potentially barbaric. The very thought of it leaves most of us cringing at the pain and debility that must have accrued to our predecessors who suffered and died under it— or we think that now because we are accustomed to massive medical installations and to heavily credentialed teaching centers. We like our medicine bustling with state-of-the-art equipment, not to mention state-of-the-instant research with which to inform and direct the use of that equipment. Within its own time, however, reading medicine and serving a preceptorship under a physician who had the gift—the terminology of the nineteenth century, not mine—speaks to a modus of healing that, for lack of science, was largely an art. Human health depended on the inspired acumen of its physicians and not on the scope of their equipment, of which there was precious little anyway. Great-grandpa Gammon was such a healer, and Grandpa Witcher became one.

Grandpa Witcher had, in his youth, been one of those aspiring young healers who had had no access to formal training in the use of his gift and who, as a result, had sought out the best preceptors whom he could find. That search led him to Great-grandpa. Great-grandpa was not the only Gammon to find Grandpa worthy of further study, however; and when the reading and the preceptorship were over, Rebecca Gammon became Rebecca Witcher. Within a few years thereafter she also became Mamaw's mother.

Grandpa Witcher was a farmer all of his life. He never stood for a license—in his day one did not have to—he simply practiced an adroit level of medicine on the side, while living as a farmer. Emergencies were more likely to find him down in the barn or over on the back field than in the house; but they never found him in an office, because there was none. He went when called and saw when asked and in general extended good health to his neighbors, his own retainers, and his family for decades. Sam can remember in crisp detail having himself been a patient within this last category.

When he had been not quite three, Sam had roughhoused one week-end with his big brothers and gotten hurt. For several days, he says, his left arm throbbed, but then the pain began to lessen. Shortly after that, he and his family went home for a Sunday visit with Grandpa on the farm. Sam remembers crawling out of the car, running toward his Grandpa Witcher, and having the old gentleman snatch him up in mid-rush, saying quite sternly, "Nora, this child's got a broken arm!" Sam remembers that, he says, because Grandpa's tone was very accusatory, and at not-quite-three, he was dumbfounded that anybody would dare find fault with his mother. He remembers as well that his grandfather took him into the house, set him on the kitchen table, felt up and down the broken forearm, reading it with his fingers before he said, "I'm going to hurt you, boy," and did. The instant it was over, though, the arm felt better, according to Sam; and Grandpa's splinting of the newly set bones held them firmly in alignment until they had healed into the strong, straight right arm that his grandson and I both appreciate to this very day.

All of which is not to indulge in either family memories for their own sake or in amateur disquisitions on early American medical practice. All of it is to say that these are Sam's stories. They have, from boyhood, been his dominant role models, his family's most honored hagiography, his received definitions of what a man with the gift should and must be. The fortunate among us, I think, are often defined by the presence of just such powerful and often ghostly mentors. Their heritage sets the bar and then demands we clear it whether we wish to or not. Without them, there is no bar to sight from, and we can lose ourselves in a forest of too many possibilities. With them, however, we are determined forward by a bequest that can neither be returned nor denied; and that was the case for Sam as 1957 be-gan to turn into 1958. He had completed formal instruction, he was serv-ing his preceptorship as an intern in the best there was. Now it would soon be time for him to test his mettle against the legends of those who had en-trusted it to him.

58.

SAM'S INTERNSHIP had barely slipped from the punishing every-other-night schedule of obstetrics to the more comfortable one of duty every third night in plastic surgery before he had become deeply engrossed in the questions of where we should go and what we should do next. The two of us spent hours over supper on his at-home nights talking about what he thought those next steps should be. He didn't articulate his aspirations in terms of his grandfathers, of course. Instead, he thought aloud in restless sentences that tended to circle back upon themselves.

"I have to get away from all this equipment to learn how to make do without it. It won't always be there, you know—not every time, anyway—and nobody's taught us to work without it, how to practice when it's not all right there at our fingertips." Or, "We've got to be near enough a big medical center, so if I do get in over my head, there's backup for the patients." But immediately thereafter, "I have to get out of cities, go somewhere where people can't doctor-hop and I can learn how to take care of the whole picture . . . what each one of them has to have personally to get on with it. You can't do that when they go one place for their gut and another for their arthritis." And, "Before I can specialize, I've got to know how to treat whole patients and not just pieces and parts of them."

A recurring subtheme in those evenings had been the almost plaintive, "I need to know my patients as people with families and lives before I go too much farther. This business of treating them on a ward and sending them home is just fixing them, and that's absolutely not what I want to do." There also was the other, closely related plaint of "So much of what I'm supposed to do with the new drugs I think might be done better with some of the older ones, if I could just have the patients long enough to adjust the dosages to them as discrete systems and not as averaged bodies." And like a leitmotif through the whole thing, "I'd like some patients for a while who knew my name without having to read my coat first!"

By March, the ghosts of the unacknowledged grandfathers were smiling. I could see them in the shadows of our evenings, nodding and sometimes even congratulating each other. They had their boy. By March also,

Sam had persuaded his best friend, former classmate, and fellow-intern, Max West, that whatever the two of them did after City of Memphis, they should do it together.

Max West was—still is—one of the most orderly, carefully attired men I have ever known. He somehow always managed even as a young man on a ferocious schedule to look as altogether and kempt as if he had just stepped out from a long shower and a professional manicure. Likewise, the space around him was always of the same state of orderliness within a minute or two of his arrival in it. The contrast between Max's discipline in such physical details and Sam's leave-it-where-it-falls lack thereof has always stood for me through the years as the quintessential example of opposites attracting, though the two of them had a fair number of less interesting differences as well. Max was short and thin, Sam of medium height and heavy. Max was even-tempered and Sam short of fuse. Max was an indifferent manager of money, Sam a very shrewd and careful one . . . the list could go on; but once all of it had been said and done, there would still be the shorter but more relevant list of their similarities and shared sensibilities.

Both men are precise in their thoughts and in their dedication to them. Both have wry senses of humor that thrive on extracting illogics from mighty conversations and then parading them around afterward in effigy. Both are iconoclasts, though in 1958 I suspect they came closer to being barely controlled anarchists in matters medical. Both were probably as tough and as matter-of-fact sensible as any two young men to leave the University of Tennessee's medical program in the 1950s. Both were passionate physicians; and both wanted to specialize, but only after three or four years of general practice. It was the list of their similarities, in other words, that had drawn them together as friends in the first place and that would weld them into medical partners for three and a half extraordinary years.

The dinner conversations about what Sam needed gave way briefly, then, in mid-March to late-night conversations with the Wests about what Max and Sam both needed; but the four of us discovered almost immediately that there was little difference between the two sets of criteria. Max came from a deeply devout family, and he had always assumed he would go into some form of service or indigent-care medicine. Sam's need to engage people at a one-on-one human level and to do it where the accou-

trements of affluence did not appertain meshed perfectly with the circumstances that usually characterize Max's kind of mission-driven career.

For most of April and all of May, the two of them, with June, Max's
wife, and me hanging over their shoulders, investigated every "Call for
Physician" classified ad in the *Journal of the American Medical Association*. By
early June they had winnowed the list to four possibilities and had begun
arranging all our schedules to allow one or the other of us to do a site visit
on each possibility. By the end of June, the four of us knew where we were
going come mid-September.

We were going to Pelzer, South Carolina, to a place that none of us
had even heard of before April and to a feudal paternalism that the rest of
America had either never had or else had laid aside almost a half century
earlier.

Sam would find in Pelzer everything he had wanted and asked for. His
skills would be honed there, his style of practice established for the rest of
his life; and everyone would know his name even when he wasn't wearing a white coat. More important for him, he would at last know the name
and particularities of every man, woman, or child whom he greeted in return. As for me, I went to Pelzer wanting nothing—anticipating nothing—
except the next step in our educations. We were preparing ourselves to
assume mature positions in life, and Pelzer was to help us while we
helped it.

That was all—the whole sum of the matter for me—in the late summer of 1958, but only because I had not yet heard of the holy paradoxes;
only because I had not yet read the koans of the great Eastern teachers or
the haikus of Japan; only because I did not yet know what Basho had once
written: "I looked into the eye of the newt and saw Fujiyama behind me."
Pelzer was to be my newt and its eye was to teach me something very clear
and particular, something that Basho suggests, but does not say: When
looking into the eye of the very specific, minuscule, and self-contained,
one cannot see Fujiyama until one has first located and then set off to the
side the reflection of one's self.

59.

SOUTH CAROLINA'S PART of the Appalachian Piedmont sits in the upper, western corner of the state, more or less contained by the borders of southern North Carolina and of northeastern Georgia. The mountains of the Blue Ridge formed it millennia ago as they eroded down into the rich, flat fields that are now central South Carolina, and eventually into the tidewater lands that today are the Carolina coast. South Carolinians, who hold the area in something like a mixed regard, refer to it more usually, not as the Piedmont, but as upstate. They do that, but they say the words as if they should be written uncapitalized and together—upstate—and as if they referenced a discreetly different world from the Low Country, which is always capitalized and separated. As is true with the distinctions of most native-born speakers, the South Carolinians are astute as well as correct in their manner of speaking.

Upstate is a study in contrasts. The high rim of it that runs just under the North Carolina line is, in places, possessed of an almost unspeakable, natural beauty. Even in 1958, one could discover thriving artists' colonies tucked away there or glimpse the summer homes of the nation's more affluent through the scrim of its old forest. From its cool highlands, moreover, to its hilly, almost untillable midlands and flattening southern reaches, upcountry is also and everywhere enriched by dozens of rapidly moving, easily harnessed waterways rushing pell-mell to the Atlantic. Yet when one South Carolinian refers to another as an upstate man, he or she usually is making reference not so much to a place of birth or residence as to a way of living; for upstate is textile country, and in 1958 many—perhaps even most—of its citizens were the victims alike of isolation and industrial greed. Having said that, however, let me also say that the upstate Pelzer to which Sam and I went in 1958 no longer exists.

The story of how Pelzer came to be, while unusual, is hardly without precedent in the annals of nineteenth-century America. Well before the outbreak of the Civil War, entrepreneurial textile manufacturers, concerned with increasing productivity and lowering costs and weary of the antiquated and overextended facilities in the Low Country, had decided that the future for South Carolina's cotton industry lay in the Piedmont where there was the same or better water power on cheaper real estate and with the possibility of importing more compliant, less costly labor. As a result, a few new mills had been opened and become operational upstate before the outbreak of war interrupted the process of further industrialization in the area.

Within fifteen years of the South's defeat, however, a group of Charleston industrialists—one of the principals being named Pelzer—decided that the time had come to try again. Understandably, there was far more entrepreneurial urgency behind their plans in 1880 than there had been earlier. Almost two decades had been lost, while at the same time demand for manufactured cotton had mushroomed. The most expeditious solution to their problems, therefore, seemed to be simply to build a new town, mills and all, from the ground up and as quickly as possible. The result was Pelzer, an instant and totally manufactured town.

In August 1880, Francis J. Pelzer, on behalf of his associates, began to buy up large, adjoining tracts along the Saluda River, the largest tributary in the northwestern section of the Piedmont. By February of the next year, the Pelzer Manufacturing Company was a legal entity, and by March work had begun on the village as well as on three new mills. In an area that by census had fewer than five hundred resident adults of working age, the village was pivotal to the success of the enterprise. The town of Pelzer was also, however—and here let the record be very clear—originally conceived of, and presented by its founders as, a modern utopia.

Every house in the new mill village had four rooms—the exact same four rooms as its neighbors, in fact; a front porch—of the exact same size and positioning as its neighbors so that all would be forever equal in appearance as well as appointments; and an outhouse, in which traditionally little variation is possible. Each cabin came equipped with a new, wood-burning stove, and—the *pièce de résistance*—an electric cord hanging down from the ceiling in each of the four rooms. Colonel Pelzer gambled that light upon demand, free of charge and without lamps that had to be filled, lit, and cleaned, would be the crowning inducement for the restless in the coastal cities like Charleston, just as he gambled that weatherproof housing would be the crowning inducement for the dirt farmers of the central plateau who had been left landless by Reconstruction. He was correct, and they came. All of the poor and the unemployed, the discontent and the disenchanted, who could find the means to do so went upstate, settling into new, company-owned houses in order to walk to work on company-maintained streets with the promise of company-supplied medical care and, for those who wished it, company-provided education for their children. Pelzer—the original Pelzer—was a nineteenth-century socialist's dream in wood and theoretical goodwill.

Pelzer, as Colonel Pelzer designed it and as it still was when we lived there, was less a single place than a geographic site on which two towns lived in ironic but symbiotic relationship to one another. There was the village, composed of the rows and rows of four-room houses, and there was Lebby Street, William Lebby having been another of the original investors. The village itself was circumscribed by a somewhat irregular triangle composed on the northwest by the state road that runs north to Greenville and the mountains beyond, on the southwest by Lebby Street and what was the Piedmont & Northern Railroad, and on the east by the three lower mills and the Saluda River. It is in understanding Lebby Street, however, that one first begins to understand Pelzer.

Lebby is Pelzer's main thoroughfare and therefore the central part of the town, but in 1958 it was in no way part of the village save to serve as one of its boundary lines. Lebby runs from the state highway south by southeast to the Saluda a little more than two miles away and, for all practical purposes, is divided into two somewhat unequal parts by the single track of the P&N. The lower or river end of Lebby is the commercial center of town where the grocery, the drugstore, a dry goods merchant, a barber shop and beauty parlor, a café, and the post office were when we lived there.

The upper or highway part of Lebby Street is lined on its south side by wooden and solidly white houses that are large and unremittingly utilitarian. The one exception to this lack of art is on the north side of the street and is the home of the mills' general manager. One of only two pieces of architecture in all of Pelzer, the general manager's house was originally the managing partner's home and was constructed not so much for his comfort as for its message. The visible and daily presence of a manor house affirms more humanely than can almost anything else the rules of the fiefdom and the role of the serfs within it.

Across Lebby from the general manager are the homes of the lesser lords and counselors. They were built to house the mills' senior management as well as the clergy, physicians, and pharmacists whom Colonel Pelzer had to attract and to whom some inducements greater than a four-room cabin with wires had to be offered. When Sam and I came to Pelzer, Lebby Street was still owned by the mills and was still being used to house its privileged. The transition, in other words, from paternalism to self-definition and autonomy was scarcely more than well-begun when we arrived, though the Kendall Corporation, which owned the mills in 1958, could hardly be blamed for the long delay in its coming.

The Kendall Corporation, which had purchased the mills only a few years earlier, was the industrial giant best known in those days for its Curity brand name and, in particular, for its Curity diapers and baby products. As a large, multinational company, Kendall had brought with it to Pelzer the enlightened labor and management policies that were the standard practices of modern industry. Too much enlightenment can be blinding, however, and as a result, vestiges of the old ways were constantly bumping into the principles and policies of new ones in 1958. By that time, for example, the mills had managed to divest themselves of almost all of the village houses by selling them to their occupants at very reasonable prices. The private ownership of one's own home, on the face of it, would seem to be progressive as well as long overdue; and ultimately it would come to be seen in that light. Getting to the "ultimately" can be a draining, disorienting process, however, especially for those who neither desired nor sought change in the first place. Owning one's own home, in other words, entails maintaining it; and the adjustment from being maintained to suddenly having to maintain is not nearly so simple or emotionally neutral as it sounds like it should be.

Pelzer, in 1958, was being encouraged to think of itself as an independent, civic-minded unit with civic governance and citizen events. Another, ultimately good, idea. To make it happen, however, most of the events still had to be underwritten to some greater or lesser extent by the mills; and the mayor who presided over them, as well as over all the town's meetings, was not yet an elected official. Instead, he was appointed by the mills from among its ranks of middle management.

Staying warm in the winter was regarded by 1958 as the legitimate responsibility of each head of house. To lessen the burden of transition, however, the mills still bought coal by the boxcar loads and then had the full cars brought in and parked on a spur line. The purpose of this was two-fold. Mill workers could go and buy at cost their coal in whatever quantity they chose and get home with it in whatever vessel or conveyance they might wish. The mill superintendents and the town's private but ancillary personnel (like doctors and clergymen, for example) were served in a more gratuitous way. The mills had an employee whose job it was to estimate exactly how much of each new load of coal each particular house should need, drive the projected amount to each house, dump it down the coal chute into the house's basement, and bill the householder, again at cost but without his or her ever having had any say in the process one way or another. The incongruities and disjunctions of this and similar arrangements seemed almost beyond counting to me at first.

Trained sociologists can have a field day with any society that is in flux, especially with one in Pelzer's kind of stereotypical, anachronistic flux; and the temptation to join the experts as an amateur dancer in their frolic is always seductively present. The problem with sociological dissections, however, is that they work at a remove. They may hold the newt close enough to describe its eye, but never close enough to peer in, lest such an extended focus blur the broad contours that are their proper study. What sociology can never discover, as a result, is the measure of its self—that, and just how searing the mere reflection of Fujiyama can be. It is the measuring and searing, in other words, and not the sociology of Pelzer that have been my proper study over the decades since we left there, and it is the measuring and searing whose marks I still bear in my soul.

60.

NUMBER 19 LEBBY sits directly across the street from the general manager's home and, other than the general manager's home, is the largest and most commanding of the houses on Lebby. It was certainly the most commanding as well as the most highly regarded house we were ever to live in . . . not that 19 was beautiful. Lord knows it was never beautiful, but it was the Doctor's House, with such capitalization once more intended. As the medical needs of Pelzer had grown to necessitate two doctors, a pleasant, one-storey, country cottage four lots up from 19 had also been allocated for physician use. Even with its greater charm, however, the cottage had never quite managed to shake off the stigma of being a second-class citizen and was, as often as not, referred to by the locals simply as "that other doctor's house." Regardless of what the Doctor's House may have lacked in aesthetics and imagination, in other words, it more than made up for in prestige. It was also good to us, during our years of living in it, not like an old shoe is comfortable and fits so much as like an institution is reassuring and always there.

In mid-June of 1958, Pelzer had been nothing to us except the site visit assigned to Sam. He had, therefore, approached Pelzer in his first visit there as an inspector or program director would have. His questions and concerns had been about the town's past history of physician services, its own medical facilities as well as other nearby ones, its human needs and professional opportunities, etc. In this he was looking as much for confirmation and detail as for broad information, primarily because we thought we already knew the answers to many of our questions. Part of Pelzer's initial appeal for us, in fact, had been the desperation of its circumstances and the benefits of its location.

The town had had no doctors for over a year, thus its desperation; and it was located, fortuitously enough, midway between a very good regional medical center and a smaller, but adequate municipal one. Greenville, only thirty miles up the state highway to the northeast, was and still is a major medical hub, though it was hardly accessible for either mill emergencies or mill workers in 1958. The problem in the first instance was the time it took to cover the distance; and in the second, the lack of a means to do so. To Pelzer's southeast and slightly farther away was Anderson, a gracious town almost on Georgia's eastern line, that had an ample, if less sophisticated, level of medical coverage but was likewise too far removed for immediate help or sustained treatment. Right from the outset, in other words, Pelzer had three of Max and Sam's criteria—a community in need, a patient base unlikely to engage in doctor-hopping, and nearby medical support centers of some sophistication.

The fourth thing that had first drawn our attention to Pelzer had been the fact it had a hospital, albeit still owned by the mills. Touted in Kendall's *Journal of the American Medical Association* advertisement as "a two-ward general hospital with emergency room," the hospital went rent-free and with utilities furnished to anybody who would agree to equip, staff, and run it at private expense. When Sam had returned from his June site inspection, he had had the pluck to admit that the hospital itself was a kind of three-dimensional euphemism, but that was a matter of no moment to him in June. Sam Tickle had seen the promised land; and by the time he had gotten himself back home to the Wests and me, he was ready to ford the Jordan River if it would not part for him by itself. (Eventually, he did slow down enough to note that life in Pelzer would be nicer if the rest of us were to decide to come along as well, but it took him several days to get there.)

Once Sam's/our decision had been made, however, everything began to fall in place. Much of July had been given over first to signing an agreement of mutual intent and stipulations with the mills and then to arranging the financing necessary for us to honor them. The four of us took out a loan for more money than I could imagine our ever repaying this side of death and life insurance. I assume the bank agreed, since they asked for the latter and urged us all to exercise due care in avoiding the former. Despite their show of courteous caution, however, banks in 1958 were distressingly eager to lend young physicians any amounts of money they needed for getting started, for it was the heyday of medicine when the operative perception, even among bankers was, "He's a doctor. He either is, or is about to be, very, very rich."

By August, the time had come for June and me to make a quick trip to Pelzer together so we could see what it was we had agreed to and what it was each of us had to prepare for. When June and I slowed and then turned into the cinder-paved driveway of 19, however, I almost lost my courage on the spot, signed agreements or no. It was twice—maybe three times—the size of East Norhall Circle, and it looked for all the world as if it were serious about being a House.

Nobody had told me I would have to grow up and run a "*House*" house, for goodness' sake. I didn't want this great box of a place; all I wanted was a home in, preferably, no more than four rooms and a bath. It wasn't, in other words, that I didn't love the Doctor enough at that moment, but I was scared to death of how much of me it was going to take to be the Doctor's Wife and run the Doctor's House in a manor-defined context. The world of mill workers and limitations I was prepared for. The other world I was going to have to simultaneously function in—the one Sam had neglected to mention, or probably hadn't even seen—was rigid with social strata and already had exhausted itself from sending hierarchical messages.

Number 19 sat back from the road at a gracious enough distance to have approximately a quarter acre of front lawn to be mowed and raked, something else I had not foreseen. As a partial relief to the austerity of its nineteenth-century, utilitarian origins, it also had a white-railed porch that ran the entire length of its front and should, I calculated, take no more than twenty minutes to sweep each morning. Other than that, the house seemed to offer no external surprises, and it did offer one pleasure. Two-storied with a full basement, 19 had been built into a small rise of sorts, so that its back door was at ground level while its front one was ten or twelve steps up. The result was that the house appeared to be settled into its piece of earth rather than simply sitting on top of it, as was the way of its neighbors on either side. Though that small bounty turned out to be the house's most sophisticated feature, it nonetheless became a sufficiency for me over the years of our tenure.

As soon as June and I had gotten home, the four of us began to carton up our Memphis lives with expedition. Our house sold as quickly as we had known it would; Sam's and Max's internships finally wound down to their welcome conclusion; and one bright Sunday morning in mid-September, the five of us headed east by southeast with an excitement far more adolescent than adult. Nora, June, and I were in the crammed-to-the-gills Bel Air, Max was driving the Wests' equally crammed Ford, and Sam was bringing up the rear in a U-Haul full of everybody's household goods. We looked, I suspect, a lot like a confused wagon train going the wrong way, but we got to Pelzer a little over twelve hours later. Sam set up our bed and Nora's, and then the three of us fell upon the two of them as if there were no lights to be turned off or baths that needed taking.

The next morning, I awoke, if not exhausted, then at the very least uncomfortably lacking in up-and-at-'em energy; but I was also the only mother in the place. When Miss Nora decided just after six that she, too, was sore from riding and cross from discovering her tired self in a new room if not a new coop, I was the one who heard her . . . or more correctly, I was the one whom Sam shoved out of bed when he heard her.

I was standing disoriented in the middle of a box-filled kitchen, baby on my hip, when I heard someone opening the outside door of the enclosed back porch that served as the house's laundry room. Having spent all of my life up to that point in towns of one variety or another, I took exceptional umbrage to this and went to ward off whoever or whatever, I suppose intending to use Nora as a cudgel. As I say, I was very tired. Just as I got to the back porch and its outer door, in came something which, upon closer inspection, turned out to be somebody.

She—there was a skirt—was gray and at first hardly distinguishable from the early light of the shaded porch. Part of this effect was because she had on gray, and the rest was that she was herself a kind of warm or brown gray. Like many another person in upstate, she had the high cheeks of a Native American; the melanin of an African-American; and across her nose and cheeks in bold parade, the freckles of a Caucasian. Other than the whites of her eyes and a trace of gray in her hair, the part of her most visible in the dusky light was the collar of her uniform and the cuffs on its short sleeves.

"Mornin'," she said, as she stepped around me toward the kitchen. "I'm Lan. I go with the house. Folks called up last night and said you was here." She pulled an apron out of the reticule in her hand, carried the reticule to the door that led to the basement, opened the door, hung the reticule on what was obviously its customary hook, closed the basement door, tied on the apron, came back toward me, asked, "What's her name?" and took Nora out of my arms, all while I was still standing speechless and in more or less the same position on the back porch.

"Nora," I said, "Nora Katherine."

"Oh. She on cup or just bottle still?"

"Cup."

"Good. Where is it?"

"In the sink. Who did you say you are?"

"Lan. I go with the house . . . always have."

And that was that. It was also as informative a conversation as any of the others I ever had with the woman in the entire almost-four years we shared space, children, and chores together. I finally gave up on trying to get a last name from her. Her answer stood as she had given it: She was Lan, she went with the house, she always had. Her going with the house, I discovered, did not mean, however, that she was another piece of industrial paternalism paid for by the mills. No, community custom and long-standing job assignment were her appointment, but I was to be her paymaster. Twenty dollars a week, Saturdays included, she informed me as she left that afternoon. She told me, actually, as she got out of the Bel Air, because being taken home in the afternoon was part of her package. She bought a ride to work from a neighbor, but the Doctor always furnished the ride home . . . which, as it turned out, was as sensible as everything else about Lan. The Doctor and the Doctor's Wife rarely got home at the same time any two days running, but who knew that on her first day of living in the Doctor's House?

61.

LAN WAS as overtly incapable as she was laconic. Knowing, as wives do, that I probably had no more than two days of grace at the most before Sam and his back would abandon me for the far more interesting chores of un-packing and setting up a hospital, I spent forty-eight whirlwind hours of deploying everything I could lift into its assigned position while nagging Sam into positioning the rest. Every time I looked up during this process, Lan was either sitting on the kitchen stool, swinging one leg up and down over the other one and impassively watching us while we worked and she smoked, or else she was standing with Nora on her hip while both of them impassively watched us while we worked. It was something of a surprise, therefore, that when I headed out the door late on Tuesday afternoon to drive Lan home, Nora set up a hue and cry of rather remarkable propor-tions; nor was it my leaving to which she was objecting.

Finally to make peace and get on with the evening still ahead, I took both of them four miles down the highway to Williamston, where Lan lived. As she got out, Lan turned to the car seat, took Nora's hand as if they were both adults, said, " 'Bye, baby, I'll see you in the morning," and got out without looking back. Nora never uttered another sound after that, appearing to accept this adult communication for what it was—a pledge and a set of marching orders about how she was to behave as a result of that pledge. I had never had a Lan before; I had never given my child over to someone else's care, much less to someone else's authority, before; I had, in other words, not yet passed through that rending and redefinition of self that come, clean and surgical, when some casual comment or action as innocent as Lan's had been, severs mother and child into two selves for the first time. I mourned all the way home and half of the night, but I also learned for the first time that mourning life is not only larger than mourning death, which is only part of life anyway, but is also a sweeter pain for the heart. It buys one into some small piece of real estate in the common soul.

Once Nora and I were back home, I opened the oven door, pulled out our supper, put the warm dishes down on the set table, called Sam, and had sat down myself before it dawned on me that I had now eaten six meals in this place and had cooked not a one of them myself. Evidently "incapable" was not quite the right word here. Lan was not incapable, but neither was she what could legitimately be called invisible . . . good heavens, she was always in plain sight by the back door, sitting on that stool, swinging that leg in unremitting nervousness. What Lan was, was just removed—that is, removed from Sam and me, though not, obviously, from Nora.

Pelzer, like any town of any stripe, had its own bank of sacred texts in 1958, stories based in fact, but elaborated into inviolate myths. In that cache of tales, only two were held in universal and unanimous regard by the citizenry, and the two were always told as one story having two parts.

In addition to the Lower Mills, Pelzer has a fourth mill called, appropriately enough, the Upper Mill. Colonel Pelzer built it in 1895, fifteen years after the three Lower Mills and almost three miles away from them. Rather than construct another mill on the Saluda itself, Colonel Pelzer decided to situate his new mill just above the northwest corner of the village where it would have more efficient and cheaper access to the state highway and inland transportation routes. The colonel and his partners accomplished this bit of industrial derring-do by stringing electric cables for two and a half miles from the Saluda Dam up to the Number Four mill. Thus in 1895 the Pelzer Mills became the first American manufacturing company ever to operate one of its plants at a remove from its source of power, and the Upper Mill's two and a half miles of electric wire became the longest such cable in the world.

The compelling—or more correctly, the revealing—part of the story, however, lies elsewhere. Thomas Edison, who was a rabid proponent of direct as opposed to alternating current anyway, was so sure the lines to Number Four would never transmit enough power to run the mill that he publicly pronounced their construction to be tomfoolery. When the lines did work and the first electricity was successfully transmitted, Edison was indignant, rather than gratified, and again publicly. While Edison sputtered, however, dozens of Pelzer's unschooled peasants stood under the cables for hours, wash tubs and milk buckets in hand, trying to catch any escaping electricity and carry it home to their four light cords.

. . . And in that apparent, but actual lack of, contrast between the mighty Edison's loss of face and her impoverished citizens' feudal naïveté lay the terrible humor that by 1958 had come to sit center of Pelzer's disposition as a social construct: In most matters, those above you in station and those beneath you in station are usually dumb about the same things, but just in different ways; if you're smart, therefore, you may watch both of them when you're bored, but you won't mess with either of them ever. Period.

Lan might have lived in Williamston, but she existed by the code of Pelzer. What I had to learn, what she began to teach me from that Tuesday night on, was first to see the code and then to accept it. Nora could come in, because Nora did not have self-conscious station yet; but I neither could nor ever would come in, because I did. Lan and I, most of Pelzer and I outside of hospital hours, would never engage each other in the charity of a personal engagement. She couldn't afford such a risk, nor would she have had the tools by which to dare it, had she ever wished to. For my part, I not only had no tools, but I lacked the spiritual energy, if not the intellect, by which to realize such an accomplishment.

It is this same principle of removal, of course, which, in the larger world, so often relegates the remarkably wealthy to the role of being donors rather than participants and which then, for their trouble, gets them accused of having acted out of self-aggrandizement or an impersonal morality. There is a kind of benison buried under all the messiness of learning this through direct experience rather than from a sociological tract, however . . . or there has been for me. My four years of living as a mem-

ber of the unimaginably privileged have, over all the years since, most certainly softened my indignation as an American when, from time to time, I
am forced to listen to the rant and bear the condemnation of those whose
own citizenship conveys less or no privilege.

Beyond such small mercy, however, there has been for me since Pelzer
the unrelieved awareness that I am indeed privileged, something I had
never considered, much less seen, before Pelzer showed it to me. Like most
members of the fourth estate and/or the American middle class, I am in
fact deeply and broadly privileged. Like Christians of any estate or class,
though, I am living under the disciplines of a faith that warns against privilege. My encumbrance is that I live, as well, as one who has never quite
found the courage, the wisdom, or the skills to be divested of privilege
while keeping faith with the obligations and responsibilities inherent in it.
"Cast not your pearls" has gone at loggerheads with the widow's mite almost every day of my life since 1958.

All of which is to say that for me as a former Pelzerite, the sacred text,
the tale told and turned and retold in my prayer time ever since, is as familiar almost as the stories of Christmas and Easter, even among non-
Christians:

*And behold one came and said unto him, Good Master, what good thing shall
I do that I may be saved? . . . Jesus said unto him, If thou wilt be perfect, go and
sell that which thou hast, and give to the poor, and thou shalt have treasure in
heaven: and come and follow me. But when the young man heard that saying, he
went away sorrowful: for he had great possessions. Then Jesus said unto his disciples, Verily I say unto you, That a rich man shall hardly enter into the Kingdom
of Heaven. 'When his disciples heard it, they were exceedingly amazed, saying,
Who then can be saved? But Jesus beheld them, and said unto them, With men
this is impossible; but with God all things are possible.*

62.

MY SENSE of how long I could keep my husband at home and in tow
turned out to be distressingly accurate. By midmorning Wednesday, he was
nowhere to be seen, but as Lan observed in one of her few intimate moments, "Comes a time when getting shed of a man is more help than

havin' him under foot." She must have been right in her sense of timing. We spent the rest of that day without him and still accomplished a surprising amount of sorting and storing, especially given the fact that Lan never left that kitchen stool, at least not that I saw, though I did notice that someone had done our first three loads of wash and gotten it put away before lunchtime came around.

I spent Thursday and Friday as Sam-less as I had Wednesday, but just as effectively. June, who had managed to complete her own unpacking on Wednesday, had joined the men on Thursday and Friday at the hospital. About three o'clock Friday, she called and said the three of them wanted to cook hamburgers in the Wests' backyard in honor of our first weekend in Pelzer. Did I think that was a good idea and, if so, when could Nora and I take Lan home and be ready to start the party? The question tugged at my preoccupations and busyness the second it fell out of June's lips.

June West was a tall—almost five inches taller than Max, in fact—loosely built woman of an attractive trimness. She had the only eyes I have ever seen that honestly were cornflower blue, and they had a light in them that never, even in her moments of greatest pain, went completely out. She and Max had met while he was in medical school and she in nursing school. The attraction had been their shared vision of medicine and medical service as a mission more than a profession. In the end it would not be enough to hold them together, and the tensions that would eventually wreck them as a couple were already present among us. The incompatibilities and distresses were still veiled a bit, or maybe just tempered, by the fact that Max and June had been unable to have a child in their almost two years of trying. Though they would in time have two little girls, it would be too late; by then, the bitterness would have gone too deep.

In 1958 there was a certain irony in all of this which June was perfectly capable of laughing about—the irony that she couldn't get pregnant, I could scarcely prevent it, and the lives of all four of us were more or less chronically preoccupied with the two extremes. Laughing did not change the ubiquitousness of her grief, however. She had finished unpacking first because she did not have a child and therefore had less to unpack along with more focused energy with which to do so. She also had finished first because she had been assigned the much smaller doctor's cottage. She had the smaller house, however, because she had no child to put in it and also because, lacking a child, she and Max were much less of a family in Pelzer's mind. Her life went round and round in a never-ending circle of insults that, like a country dog, was always biting on its own tail.

The final indignity in all of this was that while I truly found little real excitement in caring for babies, June thrived on it. Almost from Nora's birth, June had watched her, played with her, taken her places with no complaints about the horrors of car seats and the drudgery of diaper bags. So when the question came about how soon Nora and I could take Lan home and get back to a party, I understood that the question was not about timing. The question was not even a question. It was a plea mixed with a directive: Please, please, don't ask Lan to stay late so you can leave Nora with her!

I took Lan home so early that, just for once, I came close to surprising her, but she recovered herself just before she actually asked why I was doing so. In a moment of inspired grace that proved I was at least learning, I managed to tell her where Nora and I were going and why by explaining both to Nora while that young princess was riding high and happy in Lan's arms.

As soon as Nora and I got back from Williamston, we parked the car in our driveway and walked down the wide, uncultivated, unfenced acreage that was the shared alleyway and backyard for all of us on the south side of Lebby. June threw down her oven gloves, swooped Nora up, and disappeared on a tour of the house, ostensibly to show Nora where Aunt June had placed each of their favorite chairs and Nora's favorite Aunt June toys. Max's eyes followed them, and as he leaned over to pick the mitts up off the grass, I caught in his face the mixture of guilt and empathy and displeasure that said the future was already written. We had only to pass through it.

I had never watched a divorce before . . . or more accurately, the dissolving of a marriage that finds its final expression in divorce . . . but the disestablishment of this marriage was, I am convinced, made so exquisitely painful by the fact that June and Max worked together every day, seven days a week, for two years and almost that closely for two more. There was no way to escape each other and no way to gain enough distance for any chance at perspective. Through it all, June's only joy seemed to be in Nora;

and even as a schoolgirl years after the divorce, Nora would occasionally mention her aunt June with homesickness, just as she could recall the bitterness in which she still remembers having been caught.

63.

THE PELZER HOSPITAL, on Saturday morning when I finally got there to help set it up, was a far spiffier place than the one I had first seen in August. That does not mean, however, that it would not have filled our bankers with huge angst had they been able to see, rather than read about, its appointments.

Because it was part of the commercial but essential part of the town, the Pelzer Mills had built the hospital on Lebby Street, but on the south side and—the mark of favoritism—just east of the P&N track, making the hospital and its lot a bridge of sorts between the homes of the hierarchy and the business of the village. A one-storey rambling affair, the hospital was like everything else in Pelzer, white and wooden. It did, just as promised, have two wards. Each, with careful positioning, could hold two single beds in intimate but still screenable contact. There were also two bathrooms, although neither had a shower, making them half-baths or, as June said, nearly a whole bath when put together. There was a surgery, or at least a cheery cavern of a sunlit room that claimed to be a surgery and that, the best I could tell, had eaten up without a burp thousands of dollars of equipment that I would be expected to spend the rest of my life paying for. There was a delivery room whose high ceiling and focused Cassel lights made me feel as if we were on a movie set rather than a hospital every time we delivered a baby in it.

There was an X-ray room that, while probably a bit shy by contemporary standards on lead shielding, did have lead aprons hanging on its outer door. The machine itself, a leftover from some previous doctor, reminded me of the washing machine on East Norhall. It looked, in other words, as if Roentgen himself had probably used it as an early test model, but it still took very decent pictures upon demand. There was a small kitchen, about twelve by twenty feet, that was also the hospital laboratory. It, too, had come equipped. There was an autoclave for June to use in sterilizing syringes and bandages; a refrigerator that was supposed to serve equally as a repository for drugs or specimens or food, according to the needs of the moment; an electric coffeepot for our reassurance; and a hot plate for preparing patient meals, though how anybody thought that might actually be done I never quite ascertained.

More or less in the architectural center of all this was a kind of room without definitions. That is, it was a cleared space about thirty by twelve feet that had no walls of its own, just the doors and hallways of the outside walls of other rooms. More nearly than anything else, it stood in relation to the hospital as a roundtable stands to a rail yard. Everything emptied into it, everything had to pass through it, and everything in it was there only so it could get somewhere else. Other than that, its one claim to significance was that the side door of the building—the one with an honest-to-goodness ramp up it and an "Emergency Room" sign about it—opened into it. By the time I arrived to help on Saturday, June had appropriated a cabinet hanging on the outside wall of the X-ray room, dragged an over-painted and very chipped metal desk under the cabinet, found herself a chair with rollers, and dubbed the whole thing as the Nursing Station. Ah, rhetoric. It is always and finally all in the rhetoric.

To the front of the hospital part of the Pelzer Hospital were two doctors' offices, each with an examining room next to it. Between them and looking out onto Lebby was the waiting room. The largest room in the building, it was more rural-intriguing than urban-attractive. Its walls were of ceiling or bead board that had been white-washed and then dotted in places with faded announcements of permanent importance, like the seven food groups or the days of the month when the state Healthmobile would be in town to administer free inoculations and newborn shots. The furniture itself was all chairs. No tables, just chairs—seven or eight folding chairs, a variety of cast-off rockers, some actually quite comfortable, and an unmatched straight-back chair or two. In the middle of the waiting room's back wall were the desk and two filing cabinets that constituted the hospital office and reception area; though one was hard put to discover where the waiting room ceased and the hospital office began, there being no line of demarcation between the two.

From the beginning, the plan had been for June to serve as the hospital's nursing staff and me as its administrator, at least for a while. What this meant, first and foremost, was that we had to have her license as an R.N.

and my presence as nonmedical support to satisfy South Carolina's prereq-uisites for opening a licensed hospital. What we all hoped it meant was that June and I would soon be excused to other duties. That time was not to ever entirely come for June who, though she eventually was not on call twenty-four hours a day seven days a week, still retained some sense of ownership and oversight responsibility for the nursing program right up until the day we left.

I was less vested in my job than June was, however. That is to say that as frequently as possible, I was back on her turf in the hospital part of our operation, having discovered from the very first that maintaining the pa-perwork and financial records of a hospital and/or two medical practices is even more tedious than babies. Going back to June's nursing station for me, however, was not just an escape from unending minutiae of legal and fiscal import, but also an addiction to the drama that was constantly rush-ing in, out, and through that part of the hospital. The only day I can re-member when this was not true was the Tuesday on which we opened, the unusualness of this choice of weekdays being simply that our license to operate as a hospital became valid on Tuesday.

On that Tuesday of our second week in Pelzer, we hung out the "Open" sign, turned on all the lights, and pretty much sat there. A few people opened the door, nodded at me, and went on. Herman Taylor, the mill general manager, was kind enough to drop by and express his personal and corporate appreciation for our presence. Nelle Deanhardt, the town's really gracious grand lady and the wife of the pharmacist, came by with a bowl of fall flowers from her Lebby Street yard. Other than that, as I have said, Tuesday was a really quiet day in Pelzer. On Wednesday at lunch, the mayor's wife shot herself, however, and we were off and running.

64.

IF I REMEMBER our first Tuesday as the only quiet day we ever had in Pelzer, I remember that first Wednesday of Mary Ann Patrick's suicide as the prototypical one. It was as matter-of-fact and dramatic as everything else in that town was in 1958.

Life in a mill town is governed by the mill whistle. In Colonel Pelzer's day, the whistle had blown at five to wake the town, at five-thirty to tell the women that breakfast should be on the table, at five-fifty to tell the workers of either sex or any age to leave their houses, at five-fifty-five to tell them to be at their machines, and at six o'clock to say that the supervisors were about to turn on the power. Happily, one of the principles of more enlightened times was that the mills had, long before our coming, accepted the notion that people bright enough to operate dangerous machinery were probably bright enough to figure out when to eat breakfast and when to leave their own homes without the direction of five whistles in one hour. By 1958, we were down in the mornings to just the five-of-six whistle that said (and meant) "Be there!"

Because the mills had not been working three shifts a day in 1880, there mercifully were no whistles for organizing the lives of the second and third shifts. There was still, however, a noon whistle for which, in 1880, everything had been supposed to stop. By 1958 the only things that still stopped for it were the town's businesses and the mills' upper management. Most of the stores slowed down or just plain shut down; and the managers and supervisors went home for lunch, leaving the foremen and lesser management in charge for an hour. Henry Patrick was a supervisor paid in part to be the mayor, but working as a supervisor as well.

When the noon whistle blew on Wednesday, Henry drove home right on schedule, went in his house, kissed his wife, picked up his six-week-old baby daughter, sat down to a perfectly normal, home-cooked lunch, and nodded at his wife when she excused herself from the table for a moment to wash her hands. Thirty seconds later he heard the gun go off.

She had waited, her note said, until Henry would be home to see to the baby and until the new doctors were here so that if the baby or Henry needed anything, there would be help, because God knows she had needed it. She had also jerked, so that the .44 in her mouth shot out the top of her head and not the essential brainstem that sits lower. She lived for almost seven hours.

When the call came in to us, it was Henry himself, and he said only, "This is the mayor. My wife has just shot herself, and I think she's dying. Please send a doctor." It never occurred to me to ask for an address, and I used up a minute or two looking for the Patricks in the phone book while

Sam grabbed up his emergency bag and waited at the back door for me to call it out to him. An hour and a half later he called in from the Anderson Hospital. Mary Ann Patrick was not going to survive—there had never been any question about that—but he had managed to keep her alive long enough to make it to Anderson with her in the back of the mortuary's hearse, and he would stay with the family until it was over.

At eleven o'clock that night, an exhausted and emotionally drained young physician came in my back door, but he had seen it through. He had for ten hours been about the business of being doctor and healer to broken people who could not just be repaired and then sent on their way, to people whom he would see the next day and the day after that and the day after that, to people for whom he was to become the trusted source of informed comfort. We had come home in Pelzer.

65.

PELZER IN 1958 was a twenty-four-hour town, not like a bustling city but like a highly routinized mill village. First shift went on at six in the morning, second shift at two in the afternoon, third shift at ten in the evening, first shift at six in the morning, second shift at . . . it was unrelenting, but it was at least all-incorporating and steady.

Cars went and came on Lebby without pattern, there being no hour more rushed than any other, nor any less so. As Sam was to tell me many times during our four years, the washing machines in the public laundry were as busy at three o'clock in the morning as they were at three in the afternoon. The carousing of too much liquor mixed with too little other diversion was as likely to break out at high noon as at midnight. Pelzer was a study in three parts, all of them going simultaneously, like a folk song constantly being sung in round, but with considerably less concern about harmonizing.

For the practice of medicine, this civic attitude or pattern of being had uncomfortable implications. The first time Sam was waked at one in the morning because a baby had rampant diaper rash, he was more bumfuzzled than angry. After he hung up the phone, he just kept sitting there in the dark. His stillness roused me more than the phone had.

"What was it?"

"Damnedest thing I ever heard of."

"What?" I was honestly curious, for Sam is not much given to studied moments, even in the middle of the night.

"That woman . . . she did her wash after shift and just got home. The neighbor's let the baby get galled and it's got a bad case of diaper rash."

"What are you supposed to do about that over the phone?"

"Why am I supposed to do anything about it anywhere at all at one o'clock in the morning?"

"Oh," I said and, having no answer, went back to sleep.

Such tranquillity of reaction on both our parts was short-lived. The deal breaker happened at four forty-five one morning. The phone rang. A man needed a doctor because of his heart. A woman's voice gave the address, Sam wrote it down, dressed and drove off. It could not have been twenty minutes before I heard him back in the driveway, or more than twenty-two before he was back upstairs undressing and seething, though one of those is hard to do in the dark. I raised my head, always a mistake in cases of seething, as any doctor's spouse knows painfully well.

"That old coot! You know what he wanted? He wanted me to take his blood pressure!"

"Huh?" Seething is not always unjustified.

"I said, when I got there, all he wanted was his blood pressure taken. At five o'clock in the morning he wants a house call to get his blood pressure taken!"

"Why?"

"Oh," Sam said, "because he has a bad heart, just like he said, and because—and I quote—'the last doc said I should get my pressure took quick as a new doc come in, and this here was the first chance I got to call you.' "

It was a problem of innocence, albeit a maddening one, and we never did quite solve it. The mills had a sound but very basic health insurance program that included every millhand and his or her dependents as part of each employment package. On the face of it, this, too, was a good thing, but with an unfortunate side. The policy paid for house calls, no questions asked. Having had to call a doctor was considered sufficient proof of need to validate the charge—three dollars, to be specific—for payment. The ability to ring up a doctor without having to get in line and sit two hours in a waiting room was just too attractive. All the arguments in the world about how sustained medical care requires equipment, laboratory work, and support staff never quite triumphed over the convenience of that free, three-dollar house call. We learned, of course, to be more probing before the fact about who needed help and why; but the human heart is devious, and lying for personal convenience is comfortably at home within it, regardless of place or circumstance.

The mill insurance not only paid for house calls, but unlike many industrial policies, it also paid for routine office visits—a dollar and fifty cents, to be specific about that as well. The problem was with the charges that are sometimes attendant to an office visit but which the mill insurance would not yet cover. I say "yet" because these were usually for newer procedures and more recently perfected drugs, the discrepancy in coverage being as much a matter of time lag as reluctance to ante up. While Sam and Max tried to balance the use of noncovered procedures and drugs against the needs of the patient, every day there was at least one case in which charges exceeded what the mill insurance would allow.

We hadn't been in Pelzer a full month, nor I at my job as receptionist/bookkeeper/administrator for a full three weeks, before one of the older millhands, an elegant old man in freshly ironed coveralls, came out of Sam's office with his charge slip in his hand and headed toward my desk to pay. He passed the charge slip over to me and then, reaching in his pocket, pulled out a check book and handed it to me as well.

"You fill out what I owe Doc myself, please."

I filled in the hospital's name, wrote in the three dollars and a quarter he owed above his insurance, and handed the check back to him. "No," he said, handing it back to me again. "You forgot to sign my name."

"I can't sign your name," I said.

"Well, I don't know why not, young lady. Everybody else in town does." He seemed close to offended, and I was still too slow of wit to understand.

"Everybody signs your name on your check?"

"Yes," he said, and pointed to the bottom line of the check as if he thought the problem might be my not knowing where to sign.

The check was drawn on the Bank of Williamston, which was at least near enough home so I thought I might be able to explain my way out of forgery and theft charges, especially for as little as three dollars and a quarter. I looked at his name on Sam's charge slip and dutifully wrote it on the check's signatory line. The old gentleman took the check from me, squinted at it a minute before he said "Yep," and took a carpenter's pencil from his bib pocket. Laying the check down on my desk, he carefully drew an "X" beside his name, scooted the check back to me, said "Thank you, ma'am" and left.

I had never seen an "X" before, primarily because I had never seen an illiterate before. I don't know what, up until that point, I had thought an illiterate looked like, but it certainly would not have been an immaculately turned out old gentleman who was as straight in his carriage as a soldier and as courteous as a schoolteacher. I looked first at his retreating back and then at the check. The "X" beside where I had written "Alford G. Payton" was up to the left and high of the "A." Its lower left arm was shorter than the other three, and there was a jerk or kind of hesitation mark on the upper right one. Within another week or two, I had filled out and processed enough "X's" to perceive in a wonder that was very close to a small glory that each was consistent with its owner and distinct from all the others; that somewhere in the Bank of Williamston there was a teller or cashier who knew how to read the runes of "X" like I knew how to read the slashes and curves of A, B, and C; and that there was no effective difference between the two . . . none, that is, except the conventions of the larger culture and my own preconceptions.

Not all of Pelzer's illiterates were from Mr. Payton's cut of cloth. Many were as unkempt as working folks often are at the end of a hard day; some few even matched with great exactitude the probable stereotype of my original assumptions. Regardless of their variation in physical appearance, however, they all had the same bank of stories to tell . . . stories about having gone into the mills when they were six or seven because there was not enough food at home otherwise, about how a special bell would ring in the mills every time a federal inspector or some well-intended do-gooder would come on the grounds, about how there were special rooms in each mill where the children had to run and hide until the bell rang the all-clear again, about how as children they had loved for the bell to ring because it meant they could rest, and more importantly, because the mills kept toys in the hiding rooms to keep them occupied and quiet until the all-clear was sounded, about how those were the only toys they had ever had, about how much they had loved them all . . .

Pelzer could break your heart sometimes.

66.

UPSTATE, or at least our part of it, purportedly had the highest murder rate in the country in 1958. It was another one of those facts that the Kendall Corporation had not mentioned in their *Journal* advertisement and that Sam had failed to inquire about, not that anybody in his right mind ever would have thought to. In the halcyon days of America's 1950s, sensible folks who were considering a move to some new location assumed the presence of a safe community and spent their time inquiring about more significant variables, things like an area's politics, its economic base, and its educational facilities. Questions about the quality of life—itself a term unheard of in the 1950s—were usually couched as queries about a place's cultural opportunities, which, as a rule, meant the number of well-established social and civic events a community held in an average year and whether or not there was at least one carnival, fair, and/or circus each fall. The customary questions simply were not designed to be probes of local statistics on murder and mayhem.

Our ignorance about the rural Piedmont's claim to national stature was, as Sam managed to mention on several occasions, as much our own fault as anybody else's, however, which was a point fairly taken. Erskine Caldwell was regarded, in the 1950s, as a kind of Southern or poor man's John Steinbeck. His books, constantly on the bestseller lists, had the two added advantages of being not yet encumbered with the label of "classic literature" and of being more explicitly scandalous than Mr. Steinbeck's had ever thought of being. All four of us, by our own admission, had read all or part of Caldwell's *Tobacco Road* and *God's Little Acre*. We had also, by our own admission, thoroughly enjoyed them, itself a scandalous confession at the time. What we had not done was perceive that the "Erskine" in "Erskine Caldwell" came from the same "Erskine" as the one in Erskine, South Carolina, a little town just down the road and over a few miles from Pelzer. Nor had we made a connection between Caldwell's Georgia Piedmont and Pelzer's South Carolina Piedmont, for goodness' sake! And it most certainly had never once occurred to us to associate Caldwell's plot lines with observed reality, much less with *théâtre vérité*.

We had not been in Pelzer quite two weeks, however, before our gulli-
bility began to be diminished by our circumstances. It was a little before
nine one evening when we received our first lesson in upstate statistics.
Sam and I were still sitting at the table with the remains of supper scattered
around us. He was on call that night, so there was nothing unusual in having the hospital emergency line ring in the kitchen. I answered and had
barely delivered my "Hello," when a woman's voice interrupted me.

"Mrs. Tickle, this is Mrs. Welburn, Chief Welburn's wife. They's been
a shootout up in front of the roadhouse on the highway, and they's just left
two of 'em dead in the street. Chief's gone on up there, but he said tell
Doc to come on up quick as he could. He can't move 'em without Doc
or the coroner, and the coroner's drunk, but one of the bodies is blocking
traffic."

Since, as I was to discover, the coroner was always drunk, Mrs.
Welburn and I came to be very good friends after that night, though on a
telephone-only basis. I cannot remember ever actually seeing her, and I
know I never had more than "Mrs. Welburn" or "Chief Welburn's wife"
as a name for her. Not knowing the woman on a face-to-face basis did not
mean, however, that she was not a friend in the sense of being a trusted associate and respected colleague, because she was, and not just for me. Mrs.
Welburn was as essential to the community's safety as Chief Welburn was,
if not more so. She worked the phones and radio twenty-four hours a day
without relief and dispatched her husband as much on the basis of her own
judgment and knowledge of people as on the facts as reported. She saved
Sam's life at least one time that I know of.

The time I know about and for which I have ever since held her name
in honor happened in our second year in town when we were far more
aware of the area's ways than once we had been. It was a Thursday night
and third shift had already gone on when Sam got a call that Ernest was
out of hand again. Ernest Arg, who worked first shift in the Spinning
Room at the Lower Mill, was the meanest of the village's chronic alcoholics. He never went to work drunk, but every week on his day off, he
threw a bender, sometimes small and inconsequential, but sometimes large
and of reportable proportions. Thursday was Ernest's day off, as almost
everybody in the village could tell you; and the bender in progress, which
he had been working on for almost ten hours by that time, was already way
beyond being a small one.

I had answered the call when it came and had heard Ernest's voice in the background. "You tell old four-eyes I want him up here now, God-dammit! You tell him I'm sicker 'n I've ever been. You tell him I mean it, too!"

Ernest never called Sam "four-eyes" unless he was in, or approaching, really bad shape, and I could hear the anguish in Virgie Arg's voice. "Please," she whispered into the phone, "please."

"Have you called the cops?"

"I can't," she whispered back, just as I heard something crash and then heard Ernest's voice again, this time telling her to hang up the phone.

Sam checked the supply of injectable tranquilizer in his bag and went out the door. He hadn't been gone twenty minutes before the line rang again—Mrs. Welburn this time, and her voice was concerned.

"Mrs. Tickle, did Doc go up to the Args' a little while back?"

"Yes, not quite a half hour ago, I'd say."

"And he's not back yet?"

"No, but it usually takes an hour at least to get Ernest to sleep. Why?"

"I just got a call from the neighbors up above 'em, wanting the Chief to come take care of some kind of disturbance in Args' front yard. Ain't like Ernest to be out in the yard when he's drinking. Something's going on that ought not be." Then she added as an afterthought, "I'm going to ra-dio the Chief to get himself a couple of deputies afore he goes up there. You call me soon as Doc gets back, if he does. Okay?"

"Yes, I will." My stomach clutched and every system went into over-drive.

When the phone rang again, she said, "Doc didn't show up yet?"

"No. What's happening?"

"I just got a call that Ernest's holding somebody up there at gunpoint."

"Sam?"

"That'd be my guess right now. Chief's still trying to rustle up another deputy or two, but they'll be up to Args' quick as they can." She never told me not to worry nor did she waste her breath and time in platitudes. All she said was, "It'll be a help that they're all out front where the Chief can see 'em," and I understood the truth as well as the kindness of her observation.

After that, there was nothing. No cars outside on Lebby, no tires grind-ing the cinders in the driveway, no whimper from the nursery, no whistle from the mills. I have never been so quiet or so alone in my life before or since. I prayed a mantra without content, "Oh, God. Oh, God. Oh, God . . ." until the phone finally rang. "Doc show up yet?"

"No."

"He will. Chief's got Ernest in the car now. Doc gave him a couple of shots, so he won't be any more grief for a while. The judge is going to throw the book at him this time, though."

"Mrs. Welburn," I interrupted her and then could not find quite the words I had thought I had. Instead, I just said, "Mrs. Welburn . . . Mrs. Welburn, thank you."

She hesitated the length of one good breath before she answered. "He scared me to death this time," she said, "and I hope Ernest Arg rots in Hell. We could've both been widows tonight . . . and you're more 'n welcome for whatever little bit I did."

We didn't say good-bye. She just hung up; and so far as I can recall now, neither of us ever discussed Ernest Arg with one another again. Sam got home, and I cried while he slammed a cupboard door or two because he didn't know what else to do and because he was out of emotional reserve himself. After that we went to bed, too exhausted to process any of what had happened alone, much less together. It was the next night at supper before Sam said, almost as a non sequitur to the conversation, "You know what that was all about last night?"

"Yes," I said with all my pent-up anger, "I know exactly what it was all about. It was about a damned alcoholic who should be shot so as to put his family and the rest of us out of our misery."

"Virgie Arg's pregnant. Did you know that?"

Another non sequitur, but I said, "No."

"It's Ernest's baby, according to Virgie, but Ernest insists it's his brother's. That's what it was all about. He wanted me to tell him the baby was going to be his brother's so he could kill him."

"Who? His brother or the baby?"

"His brother." He was thoughtful for a moment or two before he said, "Ernest was going to hold me there until I told him he was right."

"But there's not a way on earth that you can know that without Virgie Arg's saying so herself." (This because indeed there was no way to make a close-kin paternity determination in the days before DNA testing.)

"Ernest doesn't believe that. He thinks I can, and he also thinks that pregnant women always tell their doctor who a baby's father is. But what he knows for sure is that Virgie's been talking to his brother a lot after church lately. Then he says he saw her kiss him behind the church last Sunday after Sunday school and before services, and he's not going to have 'no Judas brother sniffin' around my woman.' That would, according to Ernest, be shame enough to damn even a God-fearing man to Hell forever."

"And by killing his brother he's going to avoid Hell and make everything right again? Come on. Even drunk, Ernest doesn't believe that."

"Yes," Sam said very quietly, "Ernest does believe that. So do most of the people who were standing in the middle of Lyman Street last night watching him point that gun at me, and you know it as well as I do. An eye for an eye, a tooth for a tooth, the blood of the sinner for his sin—it's the world's oldest religion and it's still the code here. A man who can't be proud can't be acceptable to God or himself, and a family that doesn't value its own sanctity enough to kill for it can't be either."

I honestly don't know what Christianity had been to me before Pelzer. I wish sometimes that I could go back inside the child who learned to pray from her mother by example rather than from need, or back inside the girl who refined that art in the bathroom of an abandoned dormitory suite. I would like to capture in some kind of spiritual freeze-frame just how it was that I integrated what I was doing with what I was claiming at the communion rail, for my guess now is that there was an innocent but effectual disjuncture between the two.

I know for a fact that I was worshiping the God of the Hebrews in the words of the Hebrews all those years, but I was just as naturally accessing the place that is prayer through the name of Jesus, the Christ, not of Moses and the Prophets. I know that I was willingly submissive to Christian principles of conduct and an earnest, if rather self-taught, student of Christian doctrine. I know that I found, like the blast of a mighty shofar, an Immanuel at the Jewish Community Center who fired my heart where it had never been fired before. What I had not yet done . . . or else had done so incompletely as to not perceive it in myself . . . was make, much less accept, the demeaning but required connection between my Jesus crucified and the code, between the Son of God and the Son of man, between the relief of looking up and the risk of looking eye-to-eye. If that be true, and I think it is, then it is also true that it was in Pelzer where my soul first began to become Christian.

67.

LIVING ON LEBBY STREET meant that, simply by virtue of an address, one could never have much experience with the rather tempestuous social and cultural life of the village. Instead, one had a life that was almost entirely a matter of social convention. Lebby Street was, in fact, the most completely mannered existence Sam and I were ever to participate in. When from time to time the two of us happen to mention it in those "Do you remember . . . ?" conversations that old married people have from time to time, I always hear the strains of a Viennese waltz playing in the background and, in my imagination, see swirls of well-gowned dancers moving with fixed smiles in fixed sets. That persistent image is truer to the intent, of course, than to the content, of what we or anybody else on Lebby Street ever did. For the Lebby Street set, socializing was as removed from clavichords and baroque ostentation as bridge clubs, the annual New Year's afternoon tea, and American Protestantism could be.

The tea was always given by the general manager and his wife. In our Pelzer years, that meant by Herman and Marian Taylor. Marian was as gracious and accomplished a hostess as any large, white house anywhere ever enjoyed. Within five years of our leaving Pelzer, the nation was to have her twin in Lady Bird Johnson. (Oddly enough, Herman looked and acted remarkably like a red-headed edition of LBJ, a similarity I found less sympathetic than was that between Marian and Lady Bird.)

The bridge clubs were actually singular, but they were also interminable, a fact that made the thing feel plural whether it was or not. It met, I believe, every Tuesday night; and the fact that I am forced to say "I believe" instead of "I know" exposes the true depth of the problem. Even more telling is the fact that Sam cannot remember the frequency or appointed night either. We both just recall that it met and met and met.

Until Pelzer, I had always rather enjoyed bridge. We had played a good deal as a courting couple and had continued to do so even in medical school. An evening of cards is an inexpensive and pleasurable a mode of diversion as humanity ever invented, in fact, right up to the point where it becomes a command performance. The Lebby Street bridge evenings were command performances. One did not decline an evening of cards unless there were serious illness, and one went "just to watch" even if one's mate were justifiably absent doing something like healing the sick or raising the dead.

Having said all of this, I must immediately soften my arch tone with a large mix of ambivalence and confession. Those evening gatherings were not entirely unwelcome at the time and, I suspect, not nearly as unappealing in reality as they have become in memory. No small part of their attraction at the time was the dearth of any other, competing attractions. Bridge nights were the only diversion in town. More to the point, while there was nothing either optional or democratic about those nights, they were also my only direct window onto the politics of the mills and the relative, but constantly shifting, status of our neighbors. People being people, there was also always gossip, often veiled, but nonetheless conveyed, and absolutely unavailable in any other venue. As I have said, a Viennese waltz complete with fans and flirtations.

If bridge and a certain amount of circumspect naughtiness were expected of those of us on Lebby Street, church and proper doctrine were ten times more so. Private faith was not required, or at least it was not regarded as anybody else's business, but individual participation was, and one's visibility in the performance thereof was absolutely regarded as everybody's business.

Religion in Pelzer was culturally Christian and in its praxis Protestant, a simplification that was more a result of isolation and circumstances than of externally imposed policy. The public exercise of religion and the institutional means for sustaining it, however, had been matters of concern and policy to the mills even before the opening of Pelzer as an artificially constructed town. Part of the appeal as well as part of the strength of Colonel Pelzer's utopia in the first place had been its pledge to its worker-citizens of a clean, safe place to live; and for many a well-intentioned nineteenth-century industrialist, including Colonel Pelzer, the Christian Church and a prohibition on all forms of liquor were the surest way to deliver on that promise. Accordingly, a meeting hall was furnished at mill expense and liquor was forbidden.

As the town had begun to settle down and mature, however, the need for churches more doctrinally specific and diverse than a meeting hall had grown as well; and by the turn of the century the mills had erected or helped erect six churches. Only one was on Lebby Street, the Presbyterian. Captain Smyth, who had been one of the original investors in Pelzer, had been the mills' first general manager; had built the manor house as a statement of that position; had been the only one of the mills' investors to ever live in Pelzer; had been not only a proud man but a staunch and deeply convicted Presbyterian as well. Besides the general manager's house, in other words, the other of the two pieces of architecture in Pelzer is Captain Smyth's Presbyterian church. As a building, it is, even today and after numerous modifications, as near to a perfect gem of nineteenth-century, rural American sacred space as I ever hope to see, complete with a Jardine organ and complete, during the Captain's life, with its own organ tuner brought over every other year from Austria to see to that instrument's ongoing health.

Just off Lebby Street, but so slightly off as to appear to be on it, is the Methodist church. Whether such near proximity or simply such a shared sensibility in doctrine qualified the Methodist church as a Lebby Street church I never quite knew, but it did qualify. All of which means, again simplistically, that by 1958, if one lived on Lebby Street, one was either a Methodist or a Presbyterian with the occasional exception of an errant Baptist or two. Additionally, if one were a Presbyterian or a Methodist, it was very probable that one either lived on Lebby Street, did not work in the mills, and/or was in middle or lower management.

There is great danger in discussing religion as a thing, as a sociological phenomenon. I have spent a goodly portion of my mature life doing just that very thing professionally, and yet I have never, in all those years, managed to surmount completely my own sense of spiritual and religious anxiety while doing so. Looking at the presentations of faith—one's own or anybody else's—through the lens of social, economic, and ethnic constructs is as false and as valid as looking at birds in terms of their aerodynamic structure and mating patterns. Neither form of study gets to the vitality of its subject, and both run the risk of obscuring the beauty of what they seek to analyze; but both are, I believe, requisite to a full appreciation of either birds or faith. The human animal learns by analyzing, by disassembling and then reconstructing either literally or in theory. While Pelzer had nothing to say to me about birds and bird-watching, it did have a lot to say to me about religion- and congregation-watching.

Pelzer, with its history of strong secular involvement in religious formation, was an exaggeration of all the characteristics of religion that are most easily parodied or scorned. By the time we got to Pelzer, there probably was not a town in the whole country whose corporate worship and affiliations were any more clearly divided along class lines than were Pelzer's. Certainly very few communities have ever defined upper-class obligation to the civic and common good in terms of religion more overtly than Pelzer did. And I have never, even in my professional life, seen a town that more naïvely forswore the spirituality of religion for its utility—that is, for the morality, conservatory function, and cultural conventions that are all natural components of established religion anywhere.

Over the years, the result of having lived and worshiped within so contrived a system has been, first and foremost, to use it as a cautionary tale. The disconnect between secularly instituted and supported religion and a scarcely controlled murder rate has always informed my judgment about the proper relationship between religion and the public and/or secular institutions of life. The desired aims and proper functions of both seem to me to be always and everywhere diminished by such affiliations, which is a strong statement even for one as given as I to strong and sometimes regrettable statements. This one, however, I have never wavered from; and every time I feel myself softening or pausing to reopen the issue with myself, I remember Pelzer and how many times Mrs. Welburn called me during our four years in upstate and among the polity of secularly inaugurated religion.

The most obvious result of our having lived and worshiped within an artificially created and sustained system is my own professional career. I shall go to my grave persuaded that had there been no Pelzer years to plant the first skills of analysis and the first need for analyzing, there would have been no lifetime of continuing to do so. The more covert, but far more gracious result for me, on the other hand, has been a strong distaste for and suspicion about the easy labels of hypocrisy and spiritual quackery. It takes little intellectual energy to read a worshiping sinner as a pretender or simply as a conformist answering to external expectation. It takes time and study to lift off those very real layers and see what lies beneath and what often is more valid, as well as far more apparent, to the individuals being studied than are the layers.

But enough. Suffice it to say that Sam and I were Presbyterians for four more years, this time not by choice but for lack of any other option except Methodism, which did not have as charming a sanctuary and which had a much humbler organ. The saving grace of our last stint as Presbyterians was, in other words, not so much the body of Presbyterian belief, but the body of people who practiced it. I am convinced that Nelle Deanhardt, lovely and generous lady that she was, rarely did a thing or said a word that was not to some greater or lesser extent filtered first through her deep faith in God and the Calvinist way of engaging and understanding Him. Nelle was a studious Christian who gave time to questions and pursuing their answers, but who never got too well-informed or too sophisticated theologically to forget that the church bathroom needed scrubbing every Saturday night. Deanie, Nelle's pharmacist husband, was willing to depend on her for the choice of questions to be asked and for the configurations of their corporate worship, but his kindness verged on love at every turn. I have no idea how many times during just our years in Pelzer, Deanie got up at three and four in the morning to open up for some second-shift millhand who had run out of medicine or some third-shift foreman who was in distress, nor did anybody except Nelle know how many of his fellow citizens he was carrying on the store's books at the time he died.

When Sam and I think of the other personal giants of that congregation we always think of Jessie and Willard Gosnell. He was the town postmaster and probably its most handsome citizen, and she the heart and soul of Boy Scouts and enlightened town spirit. Jessie even volunteered two afternoons a week to babysit what was loosely referred to as the town library, a one-room frame cabin that, so far as I know, never had an adult visitor and had scarcely more books than users. The theory, however, was important, Jessie said, as was the fact that children did peek in the door sometimes, just to look.

When we were few in number, as we usually were on summer Sundays, Jessie could belt out the old hymns with enough gusto to make up for ten of the vacationing faithful. The gift in all of this, however, was that she had a very good voice which, when there were thirty or so of us present on winter Sundays, she could just as readily turn into a sedate, modulated enrichment of the group's singing. It used to fascinate me to watch her make that distinction in function and then pursue it to our corporate benefit, though I was never quite sure whether the shift were deliberate or just simply instinctive on Jessie's part. Even with Jessie and Willard and Nelle and Deanie, however, the best part of Sunday each week was simply surviving another one through to twelve o'clock and the right to go home for a nap.

68.

MARY WAS BORN in October of 1959. It had not been so idyllic a pregnancy as I had enjoyed when Nora was in the making, and I had spent almost all of it either in bed or on light activity. Jessie and Willard had known from the start that there was trouble, and good heart that she was, Jessie began to come into the hospital office for a day or two to cover for me when I was having difficulty. Within two or three weeks, she was there more than she was not; and within two or three weeks after that, she was there more than I was. Finally, we all realized—including Jessie—that she was working for the Pelzer Hospital and needed to be put on the payroll.

Jessie was funny. She couldn't help herself. At least a third of what came out of her mouth on any given day was built out of a droll humor and a slightly skewed way of looking at the world. She held Pelzer in the deepest affection, her civic spirit being not something she worked at, but something she experienced as personally pleasurable. The fact that most of her affection was for the village rather than Lebby Street and that half her tales played off of the aberrations and singularities that were the village's stock in trade bothered her not at all. She laid claim to every one of those aberrations and singularities as hallmarks of a unique environment she was privileged to live in and be part of. There was, in other words, enormous humanity in the woman, as well as a highly developed appreciation for the charm that often lies at the center of the absurd.

As my pregnancy and the months of enforced inactivity had moved along, both Jessie and Sam had increased their effort to amuse me as well as to reassure me, subtly but effectively, that I was still part of the life of the Pelzer Hospital. Sam would come upstairs to our bedroom every afternoon before supper and tell me whom he had seen that day, what unusual pathology he had treated or suspected he was going to have to treat if his diagnosis were correct, which accounts had been cleared by insurance, where we were in our debt payment, and so forth. I loved those afternoon hours in that huge, almost empty but fully windowed bedroom when my husband sat for a time and reviewed his day like a reporter covering a beat. I loved them for his attention as much as for the facts they conveyed; but truth told, it was Jess who gave out the real skinny. The phone could ring at any hour of the day, and there would be Jessie on the other end of the line, laughing her head off.

"You remember Mary Beth Garner?"

It would be hard not to remember Mary Beth, for her story wrapped itself around the woman in me. She was having her eleventh child soon, and she was having it, for the first time in her life, in a hospital and with a doctor. Mary Beth had decided she trusted Sam because he had cured her ten-year-old's mouth sores a year earlier with buttermilk and frequent gargles of peroxide and hot water. Whether it was the simplicity and economy of these prescriptions or the immediacy of their relief, we had never been sure; but Mary Beth had become a believer. Having Mary Beth decide to give up the granny woman for a man in green pajamas looking at her privates remains as one of the highest compliments ever paid to Sam Tickle, and one that I more than understood, both then and now.

In January, Sam had calculated, as a physician has to, Mary Beth's expected date of delivery and told her when to expect the new baby. She had been impressed at the time that he could tell exactly when a baby was coming, and she said so. Sam just failed to hear what she meant. When Jessie called, she was still chuckling. Thirty minutes earlier, Mary Beth had walked into the waiting room, her suitcase in her hand.

"It be passing strange," she had told Jessie, "how folk today kin tell about sich things, fer I got me nary a pain yet with this babe, but I'm shore here and ready, if Doc be."

After all, Jessie told me, it was August 8, and August 8 was the day God masquerading as Dr. Tickle had told Mary Beth her baby was going to come. The funny part though, Jessie said, had been watching Sam scramble to keep his divine status while still managing to get Mary Beth to take her suitcase and go home.

"Ask him about Mary Beth Garner tonight when he gets home," Jessie said, and then added, "and be sure to call me tomorrow with what he says"

Jeff Stovall owned and was the sole employee of the West Pelzer Garage. His specialty was repairing old tires, but he did a tolerably good job at yanking a motor or on the more routine business of radiator and brake replacement.

Jessie called me one morning about ten o'clock, chortling in the deep-throated, satisfied way she had when she had a really good one to tell. "I'm calling you from the back phone," she said, "so nobody'll hear me laughing, but ask Sam tonight about Martha Stovall's diaphragm."

"What?"

"Just do what I say. Ask him."

As it turned out, Mrs. Stovall's mission that morning had been to be fitted for and receive a new diaphragm. The reason for this, she had told Sam, was that Jeff said he couldn't patch the old one another single time. She had then proceeded to pull the old diaphragm out of her purse and show it to Sam to prove her point.

Even when Sam was telling me about it late that afternoon, he started laughing again. "What did you say to her?" I asked.

"Nothing. I couldn't. I just took it like I was going to do something with it and beat my way out of there as fast as I could. I made it as far as the kitchen before I just lost it and laughed 'til I cried. There wasn't a quarter inch of that thing that didn't have a tire patch on it. Must have almost killed both of them, but Jeff was sure right about not being able to fix it again. Vulcan himself couldn't have got another patch to hold on there."

Sometimes Jessie's updates were not so much funny as just interesting, and sometimes they were even tinged with her admiration. "You know those little Scottie dog magnets you have in your desk drawer?" she called and asked me late one afternoon.

Yes, I knew those dogs. There was a pair of them, one black and one white. Each was less than an inch long and a half inch high, and both had tiny, rectangular magnets glued to their bases. The point was to put a sheet of paper between the two and move the dog on top by manipulating the dog on the underside of the paper. Children loved them, and some kindly intended patient with no sense about two-year-olds and small objects had given a set to Nora. I had persuaded her that such a fine toy needed to be in Mama's desk for safekeeping. True to my end of the bargain, I had let her play with the dogs on her afternoon visits to the hospital with Lan when I could watch her, but I had deliberately left them in my desk at the hospital when I had had to come home.

"Well," Jessie said, "the most remarkable thing I ever saw Sam do."

"What?"

"Big Jim Murray brought Little Jim in here about an hour ago, and that kid was screaming bloody corruption. I could hear him all the way from the parking lot before they even got in the back door. Little Jim had put a BB in his ear on a dare and couldn't get it out. Neither could Linda Sue. I don't think the kid was hurting so much as he was terrified Big Jim was going to whip him when he got him home.

"Anyway, turns out Linda Sue had tried to dig the BB out with a hairpin and had got it wedged in all the way down onto the drum where Sam was afraid to try to go for it with his loop. So he took them all three back to surgery and tried to wash it loose with a syringe. Then he and June tried to loosen it with warm oil. The kid was yelling, Big Jim was yelling, Linda Sue was crying one minute and threatening them both the next. Everybody in the waiting room was getting edgy from the screaming. It was a carnival. And you know what Sam Tickle did? He came in here and got one of those dogs out of your desk, pried that little magnet off its bottom, stuck it into the eraser end on one of my pencils, went back in there and stuck the whole thing into Little Jim's ear and pulled the BB out clean as a whistle."

"I'm impressed," I said.

"Yeah, but don't tell Nora Katherine until I can glue her dog back together . . . and for goodness' sake, don't mention any of it tonight to Sam."

"Why not?"

"Big Jim refused to pay us. He told Sam if he'd known it was that simple, he'd have done it himself."

So even if my second pregnancy were not as uneventful physically as my first had been, it was not without its own social occasions and amusements. Nor was it without its rewards. Mary Gammon Tickle checked in at ten pounds and twenty-three and a half inches. Two days later, Mamaw took one look at her and said, without thinking, "That's the poorest looking baby I ever saw!" Once again, it was pure Mamaw, and once again she was absolutely correct. Ten pounds of weight spread over almost two feet of baby makes a thin, near-to-emaciated-looking newborn.

It didn't take Miss Mary long, however, to discover how to correct that problem. We had not been home from the Greenville Hospital a full day before Nora announced to all and sundry that the baby was eating her mama up. After that observation, things remained tense between the two of them for some time . . . several years, in fact . . . and there were whole weeks in their adolescence when I thought Nora's early animosity and Mary's necessary counteroffensives might remain with both us and them for life.

Other than that small irritation, however, there were no problems. Mary continued to thrive, and by Christmas was a much plumper, if still unusually long, baby with ringlets that bordered already on being curls and the easiest disposition I have ever seen in a newborn. From Santa Claus, Nora got a bright red Wonder Horse that was all she saw, thought about, or wanted for the rest of the holidays. With her thus diverted and Mary beginning to bloom out into a black-haired, brown-eyed beauty, things on Lebby Street settled down into that small gully of suspended time that connects Christmas to New Year's and the resumption of life as usual. Hundreds of miles away, Camelot was being planned and shaped, but in Pelzer everything was at rest and content with itself.

69.

DECEMBER 28 fell on a Thursday. At six forty-five that morning, the weather was as cold as the old stoker furnace in our basement could ever hope to pull against. Much too cold to get out from under the covers in a holiday week. Much too cold, as well, to answer the persistent, deadly beating on the door downstairs, the insistent faintness of "Doc! Doc!" coming up the stairwell. Sam rolled out and into his robe from one side of the bed and I out from the other. Through the ice coating on the window sashes, the stores and buildings below the P&N track were a postcard etching in desperation gray; and beyond the village and the mill, clouds were already churning in the low cold of a coming snow.

"Doc! Doc!" Too quiet, much too quiet, a voice. Even the hand beating on the front door was too steady. Why wasn't he using the doorbell? Or better yet, why hadn't he gone around to the hospital and used the emergency number? Sam headed down the steps while I slipped in to cover Mary and close Nora's door against the muffled beating, more like the rhythm of a man's heartbeat, I thought, than like an earnest caller in the morning twilight.

I was halfway down the stairs when Sam opened the front door. Jeb Martin stood there, his hand still raised against the memory of the door. No more than nineteen, he worked in Carding where the cotton was processed for its trip through the spinning machines and looms that would turn it into cloth. Woolies, the other millhands called the carders, and Jeb still had on his black hair a dusting of white lint from his last shift. Otherwise there was no expression on his face, no tone to his body or his voice.

"You gotta help her, Doc."

No other sound rose from the outside cold. Not a horn or a whistle or even a sparrow stirring in the warm leaves around the house. Everywhere the earth was winter quiet.

Behind Jeb and two feet back stood Tina, older than Jeb, twenty-two or three perhaps, and drab. She had delivered their second child only some six or seven weeks earlier, but she was already back at work in the Weaving Room. Hard work, too hard for her kind of thinness, her kind of blond pallor. She had thrown an old army blanket around herself, and I could see that she was holding the baby against herself under its warmth. Jeb stepped sideways and nodded to her. She walked in and, while we watched in silence, went past Sam to the black lacquered bench that sat beneath the stairwell in our entrance hall. She settled down on the hard bench, shrugged off the blanket, and began to cuddle the baby. From my place halfway up the staircase I looked down on her and the child. It was rigid, fingers crooked and skin waxy like a plastic doll that had gotten too hot in shipping and run a bit. Sam looked at Jeb. "It were like that when we got up this morning. She didn't hear it cry and I knowed afore she went and looked."

Jeb turned and closed the door between himself and us. We watched through the glass as he went to stand soundless and motionless, leaning against the support railing of the front porch, waiting for her as if in all of time only his waiting mattered.

Tina kissed the child and began to rock it. A tuneless, primal hum like the soft wind under the eaves in November came up from the bench below me. I started down the steps when Sam motioned me to stay where I was. I slipped quietly down onto the stair tread to wait. He disappeared into the kitchen and I could hear him moving back through the kitchen to the back porch and then I heard him open and close the dryer. In a few minutes he came back. He had found my vegetable basket with the bailing wire handle and had padded it with some clean rags from the kitchen. Over the rags he had spread a freshly washed baby blanket. The little blue and yellow rocking horses that rode across it were faded but still baby pretty. Tina looked up only once as he sat the basket down on the bench beside her. The crooning sound soon shifted, deeper in her throat now, less soft, more craggy.

For almost an hour we watched, I on the stairs and Sam from a chair in the living room. The wordless haunt of Tina's requiem broke at last, dying into silence as effortlessly as it had begun. She rocked on without sound or weariness until, midway of an arc, she abruptly stopped. She lifted the baby into the basket and covered it, face as well as body. Saying nothing to either of us, she stood up, wrapped the old blanket around herself, opened the front door, and walked out. Jeb trailed quietly behind her down our front walkway to the street and then right, down the slope, toward the village and home.

Sam set the basket on top of the washing machine on the back porch. In a little while the gray panel truck from the mortuary drove into the driveway. Joe White knocked as he came through the door. Stepping in, he picked up the basket and called into the kitchen. "This it, Doc?" Sam nodded. "We'll send you the post and the paperwork as soon as we get them," and he was gone, as simply as he had come, back into the hush of the beginning snow.

Because there was indeed no way to know yet what had happened and because we had two small children of our own, we began the long process of washing down the front entrance hall and the furniture, our bodies and our clothes. Whether contagion or poverty or sleep apnea, it would be days before we would know and much too dangerous to wait. Lan took

Mary and Nora to Nelle Deanhardt and then came back to help us. The three of us disinfected and scrubbed and then disinfected again with a fury that with each wring of a rag and each slosh of a bucket had less and less to do with washing away contagion and more and more to do with drowning out the noise that would not wash away. Millions of lives away from us Camelot might indeed be rousing, but in Pelzer there was only the sound of Rachel weeping for her children; and we could not be comforted, for they were not.

70.

I HAVE AN ASSOCIATE considerably younger than I but already well established in the writing craft, with whom I enjoy occasional bouts of repartée. Despite his age, most of our conversations are war stories being told by two old veterans, neither of us lying, but both of us elaborating just beyond the far reaches of actuality. Both the victories and the insults are painted large and held up either for sympathy or for the sweet reassurance of giving and receiving insider humor.

As is proper professional decorum in such conversations, we never hang up the phone until each of us has inquired about the progress of the other's current manuscript. The answers given by either of us to those queries will be not war stories, however, but honest reports of exactly where in its pilgrimage from idea to page a particular project is. When, therefore, Jay tells me that a current manuscript is "seasoning in the disk," I always chuckle at his witticism and understand perfectly what he is saying.

There is an interruption in the fashioning of anything when all the pieces being brought together to compose it must be given a time apart, time to meet and meld with each other, time free of external manipulation. No artist or writer, no baker or farmer, no vintner nor any other craftsman one can name knows exactly what that process is. None of us knows in precise detail what the composing elements are doing in a piece of clay as it rests, wrapped in damp rags, on the potter's wheel; in a manuscript as it sits in the drawer or, indeed, on a disk, while it seasons; in the dough waiting in a bowl, its processes and mysteries hidden beneath the covering of a damp cloth; in the plowed and furrowed field that, though barren to the eye one day will in three be green from the wheat that rests just now beneath it; in the grape juice that, only if undisturbed, will become the wine.

None of us knows these things. We only know that life, too, is an act of composing; and whether we would have things be so or not, the rules of art will have their way with life and the souls it is forming. The first six months of 1960 were my time of melding and fermenting; and when they were done with me, I would emerge aware of a mind that was no longer lord of the interior, but simply servant and lackey to it. It was in those months that, as I at first nursed and then, near to their end, began to wean Mary, I was free to read again as I had not been since our coming to Pelzer.

Albert Camus would die that year, but he would exit the spring of 1960 as an immortal for me. Like hundreds of thousands of other forming adults, I might never understand empathetically either his angst or that of Jean-Paul Sartre; but all of us, me included, could perceive in their work the intellectual legacy of a troubled half-century and one, if not the core, question of our approaching passage into maturity. *The Glass Bead Game* and other works by Hesse were now appearing in English, and the lush mysteries of Hesse's world, so long whispered by those who were fluent in German, were now loosed and roaring through America's bookstores and book clubs, roaring even in South Carolina's upstate. My father wrote with a tantalizing concern about Tillich's *The Courage to Be* which he had just discovered. I immediately had to order myself a new copy in from Greenville. He was right, of course, my father, that is, in his concern, and so was Tillich in much of what he had to say about the conflicts of an unresolved generation, conflicts that were gift and imperative to my own emerging one. As one bit of reading led to yet another that I absolutely had to pursue, Dietrich Bonhoeffer came up hard against Alan Watts and both of them with equal ferocity against my religious insouciance.

In late March, doing so simple a thing as looking in our upstairs bookcases for a reference book that Sam wanted and had somehow mislaid, I came across Millar Burrows' *The Dead Sea Scrolls*. I had unpacked it months before, set it randomly on the shelf, and thought no more about it. This time, however, as I shifted the volume's position, I saw the two letters I had secreted in it. One was from me, a copy of a letter I had written to Mr. Burrows shortly after Nora was born, and the other was his response. Mine was the awkward, stiff, self-conscious work of an eager but intimidated child, and dealt with an obscure point in the book. Burrows had treated, as if it were faintly curious, the *Scrolls'* use in a place or two of rock eagles as a symbol or metaphor for Roman tyranny. Perhaps, I had written, there was a connection between the people of the Qumran community and the citizens of Crete, for I thought I remembered having read in one or two Roman historians that the Cretans, an unpleasant lot at best, denigrated the mighty Roman eagle by referring to it in their native tongue as a rock eagle.

The audacity of so fractured and inept an approach appalled me as I reread the copy of my letter, but the graciousness of Burrows' response abruptly moved me to tears. One of the routine paradoxes of domestic life, or at least of mine, is that all too frequently I lose what I treasure most by the conservatory process of putting it somewhere where it will be safe from loss. That has happened to those two letters. I have turned books and drawers over time and time again over the years looking, in particular, for Professor Burrows' letter to me, but to no avail. Both are simply gone as objective artifacts. As subjective ones, however, they live on, impervious to loss so long as I myself remain impervious to death. Thus it is that I remember, if not the words, then most certainly the generosity of Burrows' response. In effect what he said was that the significance of my letter for him was not rock eagles (though he would chase those references down), but that I had cared enough to write. He suggested that possibly such interest should be of significance to me as well, that I perhaps should consider doing formal work in matters of religious import like the discovery of the scrolls, that even amateur scholarship can be of use to the culture.

I wept, but within a few days thereafter, I knew. I knew that I could not go back to my desk at the hospital. Not to its funny stories, its dramatic events, its poignant depths. Not to its administrative tedium. They had all been addictive to me, even the tedium, for it at least had offered me the satisfaction of chores and tasks that could be brought to resolution within the space of a day or two. Nor would I go back to working side by side with my husband. That union of our days as well as of our nights had been the dearest part for me, the part most difficult to lay aside; but the time had come to turn my face to the wind and not its shelter.

Sam and I, from the very first days of our courting, had always had the understanding between us that we would interleaf our educations. I would finish undergraduate and get him through medical school and internship. He would work and get me through a master's degree. I would work and get him through residency and subspecialty training. He would work and get me through a doctoral program. We had, however, always assumed that that plan would mean our moving for my sake from Memphis to a university town for two years between internship and residency. One of Pelzer's original attractions for us, therefore, had been its proximity to Greenville. Not only was Greenville a medical center, but it was also home to Furman University.

Among the premier schools in the South, Furman had been one of the three colleges I was considering as an undergraduate when Shorter had proffered the package I could not afford to refuse. Now Furman might once again be a possibility. Mary was old enough to leave and goodness only knows we had Lan, ready or not. Nora was in love with Nelle Deanhardt as well as Aunt June. Jessie was willing, and Lord knows she was able. Only Sam was anxious at first about whether or not we could swing graduate school and debt repayment both on dollar-fifty office visits and three-dollar house calls.

We solved that one the way we and half the people I know always solve it. I said let's don't decide. Let's just take this thing in stages. He said all right. I said let's just apply and see what Furman says. He said all right. I said that Furman says I need to come in for an interview and schedule the entrance exams. He said all right. I said the scores were acceptable and Furman would like a check of deposit that is small and refundable if we change our minds. He said all right. In June I entered graduate school.

71.

FURMAN DID NOT HAVE a graduate program in classical languages in 1960, so I bought time for deciding what I wanted to do by taking the un-avoidable—orientation to graduate studies, methods of basic research, statistics—none of them as dreadful as it sounds, despite the fact that statistics did just about do me in. I chose the English poets of the sixteenth and seventeenth century for reasons that are beyond me now. I know that, left to my own devices, I would never have chosen to spend months of my life with Edmund Spenser or John Milton, much less with any of their assorted contemporaries. By some act of grace, then—some predestined act, for I think it must have been so—I ended up being assigned to Professor James Stewart who was not only fond of Spenser and Milton, but downright intimate with them. He was also chair of the department.

If Dr. Thompson were ever to meet her equal in the after-life, his name would be James Stewart. He saw the same language-made world as she and had her uncanny ability to expose, for better or worse, its architectonics. He also had her brilliance and her passion for teaching. He lacked her idiosyncracies, but he exceeded her by light-years in political enterprise. Jim Stewart knew, as few of my acquaintances ever have, how to effect a program of study so it would address the question being asked instead of the other way around.

While he ostensibly was teaching five or six of us Spenser and Milton, he really was continuing my education in the psychology that undergirds Old Testament grandeur, the machinations of poetry as theology, and the tricks of sound and semantics by which the shaman works. I have no idea what insights he was giving to my fellows at the same time; but I would be incredulous if someone told me each of them were not looking at Milton and Spenser through equally customized perspectives. The man was amazing. The man also knew why grammar was one of the seven basic studies of humankind.

Noam Chomsky had published his *Syntactical Structures* only three years earlier. In places a very difficult discourse on how we come to speak, the book had nonetheless shaken the academic world. Like Dr. T. almost a decade earlier, Professor Chomsky was suggesting the presence in us of an innate facility for language that was purely biological and that was present in the human family, even across the presumed divisions of tribe and race. His arguments that there were principles common to all human speech and that those principles constitute a universal grammar were the products of intense and highly original scholarship, and the questions he raised have since commanded entire careers of study by gifted minds employing sophisticated research facilities and opportunities. No one other than a keenly trained bio-, psycho-, or sociolinguist was going to follow, contest, and/or affirm Chomsky's data and, by extension, his conclusions. That was not the point. The point was that even if one were not prepared to track along behind the intricacies of Professor Chomsky's proofs, it did not take either much genius or much prior instruction to perceive that many of his conclusions were valid and therefore immediately usable. As a result, in 1960, when nobody yet knew the Age of Enlightenment was in its death throes, the allure of playing with the implications of language as biological was pure and unencumbered frolic. It was especially so if one were a student of poetry. All of which is by way of trying to explain why and how my master's degree program became as peculiar a cobbling together of pieces and parts as the final construction of my Shorter transcript had been.

Dr. Stewart had a colleague, Professor David Pulley, who was head of Education. Between the two of them, they had by summer's end contrived a course of study that had me doing everything from translating John Milton's original poesy text out of Latin into English to writing a thesis on philosophies of education to teaching undergraduate courses in human growth and development. They also had, on behalf of Furman, offered me the position of Fellow of the University. The provision for such a post had been in the university's by-laws for over a century, but it had never been exercised before; the receipt of it remains as the greatest academic compliment ever paid me.

Serving as fellow meant, among other things, that my tuition was provided, that I was in addition paid for my teaching, and that I had faculty privileges in the library. I also had a carrel in the library, a charming, warm space tucked up against a massive window and secured on its other sides by oak walls and a substantial bookcase desk. It became my first office, and I loved it as a child loves a hidey-hole. I could slip into that high-vaulted and narrow space, be shielded by the professional decorum that forbids the interruption of a scholar at work, and follow in intense concentration the arguments of my own mind as it explored one thought possibility after another. I could also, for the first time in five years, offer noon prayers without fear of interruption—a hidey-hole for the spirit as well as the intellect.

It would have been hard in 1960 to find anybody in the world who was less prepared to lecture on human growth and development than I. I knew—anybody who has ever watched a child knows—that we begin speaking in sing-song, rhyming, multitoned, rhythmic, repetitious verbalizations that are, by definition, the compounding elements from which formal poetry is made. I knew that as children, we lay aside poetry, or at least rhyme, very reluctantly. Most of us, in fact, hold on ferociously to rhyming books and refraining stories well into our school years, just as most of us continue to rhyme, accent, and refrain our playground games or, as we mature, our adolescent raps and taunts. Why? Why does the self speak most naturally in poetry? What is happening in the body that requires, and/or must eventuate in, poetry constructs? Where does the child slip from random sounds that simply feel good in their making into sounds that mimic and from there over into audible analogy and association?

I did not know, primarily because nobody else knew either; but the first, small, requisite step in addressing those questions was to become familiar as quickly as possible with just what scholars and scientists did know about how the physical body grows and matures. Given that need, David Pulley concluded, as has many another teacher, that the best way to arrive expeditiously at a working grasp of a body of alien and obscure facts is to teach them every day to somebody else. He was right, and I did. What the undergraduates learned, the good Lord only knows. What I learned was material that would settle down over the years ahead into being a good basement for the rest of my life. In it I have stored all the rarely used but occasionally necessary tools for thinking about not only professional and academic questions, but also about the most fundamental question of all for those of us who claim the theology of the Judeo-Christian tradition: If God formed us in His image, what can we learn from the study of ourselves about what it is we image?

72.

IN THE YEAR when Sam and I married, an essentially unknown black preacher named Martin Luther King, Jr., had begun a protest in Montgomery, Alabama which, by 1956, had broken its regional bounds and become the first, full battle cry of the American war for human equality. In the summer of 1960, the Democratic Party, meeting in national convention, had nominated Jack Kennedy as its chief standard bearer, and for the second time a Roman Catholic was making the race for the American presidency. In January 1961, the country inaugurated Kennedy and assumed the promises of Montgomery and Camelot as our national reality.

Even in my snug carrel, it was impossible to escape the trills of heightened alertness around me. Like hunting dogs in autumn, everyone I knew at Furman was, either metaphorically or literally, sniffing the air, savoring the scent of change, catching the odors of national greatness ahead. We all knew it was there. Somewhere just over the next hill, America was waiting for us in a blaze of glory as we pushed beyond the lost frontier into the final realization of our founders' political visions and dreams.

For me, things were a bit more schizophrenic. The environment of the university may have been so heady as to make one hypoxic on some days, but the environment of Pelzer remained constant, unperturbed by anything external to its own borders except the price of cotton on the domestic market, and even that intruded only into the conversations on Lebby Street. At the hospital, June and Emma and Jessie had christened what they called "Jessie's Rule," which said, much to Sam's annoyance, "If she's young, nervous, and wants Dr. Tickle, you can just stick a green label on her folder to start with, because she's pregnant." What annoyed him, I think, was not the fact that Jessie's Rule was almost never an inaccurate prognosticator, but that there was very little about childbearing in Pelzer that was funny and absolutely nothing that should be considered as such before the fact.

A hydatidiform mole is a disease of the placenta, or after-birth, that always consumes the fetus and that in addition can become aggressively malignant. In that event, the delivered woman almost always dies a horrible death. More than anything else, a hydatidiform mole looks like an eight-pound cross between a Portuguese man-of-war and a cluster of distended grapes, except there can be hundreds, rather than dozens, of polyps hanging from it. One of the great stories in the history of medicine and religion is of the English queen who was delivered of an hydatidiform and then insisted upon having each of the polyps baptized. There were, if my memory serves me correctly, some four hundred twenty-odd of them so baptized. Hydatidiforms are also rare enough so that that bit of charming esoterica is as close as most physicians ever get to one.

Lutie Mae Cantrell was pregnant with her third child in February 1961. By the time she was four months along in January, Sam had begun first to fret and then to be alarmed. He could not feel movement, although Lutie Mae insisted she did; he could not detect a heartbeat; and he knew without even examining her that she was much, much too enlarged for a woman only four months pregnant. Then early one cold Saturday morning when Max and June were gone for a weekend break, the phone rang. Lutie Mae was in labor—hard labor. We left the girls with Lan and made it the two blocks down Lebby just as Lutie Mae and her husband pulled into the parking lot.

Sam got her into delivery and on the table, telling me to pull the delivery cart over from the wall. Just as I turned back toward him, Lutie Mae delivered a hydatidiform. "My God!" I said, one of the few times—and certainly the most appropriate time—in which I have ever raised that expression in common speech.

"I never saw one before!" I said.

"Shut up!" Sam murmured out of the corner of his mouth, and I realized Lutie Mae was, of course, not anesthetized. "Lutie Mae," he said to her as gently as if the specter of death were not watching us, "I'm going to give you an injection now so you can go to sleep and rest while we take care of things here."

She nodded knowing already, without his saying so, that there would be no baby out of so early a labor. He assembled tools, monitored her, and issued instructions to me all at the same time. "Call Greenville General," he said, "and tell whoever's on OB call what we've got. I'm going to scrape her here, tell them. It's too dangerous to wait. But God willing, she'll be to them in three or four hours. Then call Gray's and get the ambulance standing by in the parking lot."

And he did exactly what he said he was going to do. He scraped the uterus, working for a good hour or so, until he had swabbed out every bit of placenta he could suspect, much less detect, and he got her to Greenville, and Lutie Mae lived. She never fully understood what had happened to her, but the medical community in Greenville knew exactly what had happened. A young doctor with the gift had done the improbable under circumstances that were impossible, and he had done it in Pelzer.

In April, a young president with the gift brought us through the improbable, too, though some would say he had created this disaster himself. The Bay of Pigs invasion failed on the seventeenth of April, my father's birthday. This time the resulting tension pierced through Pelzer's insularity. Even upstate, South Carolina was too close to the coast and to Cuba for comfort. I stocked the basement with dried and canned foods, filling all the jars we had with fresh water and placing Clorox beside them. Sam laughed at me, and still does, but half of Lebby Street was doing the same thing.

Receiving a direct hit was of no concern to any of us; it was being on the fringe of a direct hit that one needed to prepare for, especially given the fact that we were sitting right in the area of fringe between the coast and the Atomic Energy Commission's facilities at Oak Ridge. Sam kept saying, "You can't put enough stuff down there to save a whole town," and I kept saying, "I have to try." He also observed that since 19 Lebby was built into a small hillock, half our basement was to all intents and purposes aboveground and therefore not shielded from radiation. His logic, however, could not override my need to do something, however futile it might prove to be.

Part of my need to respond in some physical way to the Cuban crisis may have been exaggerated by maternal instinct and the subrational drive to protect even to the point of the ridiculous. Part of it may have been my own disposition, which prefers always to act rather than impotently wait. Most of it, I think, however, was a reenactment of my mother's activities during World War II when, during air raid drills, she would cut all our lights, put me under the dining room table with blankets to cover me, and then would fetch and set beside me the boxes of water, matches, candles, crackers, and dried fruit she kept ready in the cupboard. I remember her quiet, emotionless efficiency in accomplishing all of this as being among her most maternal moments. She became in the dark and with the sirens wailing around us a protectress whom I recognized in some primitive but grand way as more present even than my father.

My other response to the giddy promises of Kennedy's presidency, to the gathering signs of domestic upheaval, and to the rattling sabers of international rupture was far less physical than stockpiling a basement with water and medical supplies. It was not even of my own doing. Most certainly it was not born of my own intention, though there can be no question that it took its form from the work in which I was so immersed.

The poetry came to me in my carrel, in the car on the way back and forth to the university, in the kitchen where the force of its coming would sometimes arrest me in midtask and drive me upstairs for paper. It never came fully formed, it always required work, and it was never complete. Rather, the lines were pieces of some larger whole that I could not grasp save to recognize that each concerned itself in some way with the prophetic traditions of ancient Israel. Those first stanzas of lament and those early pieces of lyric praise were to be joined over the next ten or twelve years by others of like kind until, as with the disparate parts of an elegant equation, they one summer fell softly into place beneath my hands. The result was a liturgical drama that retells the life of the prophet Jeremiah.

It would be the autumn of 1974 before I finally finished the writing of the play, and 1975 before Sam and I first saw it produced in sacred space; but to this day, it is not the performances of that drama which move me so much as the process to which its very existence as a completed opus bears witness. It was in Pelzer that I first learned to trust and record without requiring a prior understanding or a logical cohesion. Whatever else that may mean or imply, it means first and primarily that my mind and will had at last been honed enough to recognize and engage the commerce of the interior life; it means that mind and will alike had learned to barter and tithe, buy and sell, the goods of the spirit as readily as they had learned to trade in the goods of the body; it means that mind and will were at last selecting for themselves which merchants in the spirit's world were to be trusted and in which stores I was to shop. It means also that youth was almost done.

In June I received my master's. The university extended me an invitation to join the faculty for the summer, and I accepted with appreciation and considerable gratitude. Sam wanted another year or eighteen months of practice in Pelzer; I wanted a few more months of access to Dr. Stewart, Dr. Pulley, and the university library; and we both wanted another child; it looked as if all those things were possible. I would teach through the summer. After that, we would try to make it successfully through one more pregnancy while Sam was still working and before it would be my turn to support us again. By then, it would be time for us to begin laying plans to sell the practice and move on to his residency. For the first time since we had married, we could see the near-future as well as the distant one, and we liked what we saw. It was orderly, remarkably ordinary, and fiscally reassuring. . . . Woe betide any man or woman foolish enough to think such thoughts as those!

73.

WHETHER AS A RESULT of divine largesse or evil misfortune they never could decide, but for better or for worse, when we went to Pelzer in 1958 the Methodists were the only established faith in town who owned their own parsonage. The clergy of the others lived in parsonages owned by the mill. Given the politics of things, it was entirely reasonable, therefore, that in 1960 the new Presbyterian minister and his wife should be housed next door to the doctor and his family, although I cannot recall anyone's ever calling 23 Lebby a manse as such. It was just the Preacher's House, something of a misnomer in and of itself.

Earl King was a retired missionary. He and Mrs. King had served for over thirty-five years in Africa in what was then called the Belgium Congo, she as a registered nurse and he as a civil engineer. A graduate of Virginia Polytech, Mr. King knew about as much about preaching as I did about constructing water systems and laying roadbeds. He was, hands-down, the worse speaker, let alone preacher, I have ever had to endure on any routinized basis. When he was done with us on most Sunday mornings, even the unflappable Jessie had no idea about what he had just said, much less about why he had just said it.

There were two saving graces to the whole thing. First, he was as miserable as we, which usually made for truncated as well as fractured homilies; and second, he was a singularly attractive man to look at, even in his sixties. One of the limitations of mid-twentieth-century Presbyterian worship for me was its lack of poetry, both visual and verbal; but looking at Mr. King in the pulpit of the Pelzer Presbyterian Church, especially on a bright day when the light coming in through the stained glass played over him, was almost a liturgical experience all by itself. He had the deeply textured skin of a man who had worked outside all his life, but the broad, high forehead of an intellectual and the steadiest eyes God ever gave any human being.

I never once saw those eyes flick away from what they were addressing, nor can I remember their ever seeming to roam the surfaces of what they were attending to. They were soft brown and they just simply looked without offending or intruding. But what one saw when one looked at Mr. King—and this was the part of him that the window light most loved— was his hair. It was not only as thick as a young man's and as wavy as an actor's, but it was of the purest and most brilliant white I have ever seen. The result was that though he might be dull of message, the physical presence of the man conveyed a kind of stereotypical sanctity. He looked, quite literally, like a holy man. Jessie and I used to say, probably irreverently, that Sundays would be much godlier if Mr. King would just stand there without saying a word and let us look at him for twenty minutes.

There was, I suppose, a third saving grace in all of this as well, namely that the Kings and Lebby Street at least had each other; and we all knew that with was better than without. Pelzer was not a clerical appointment that anybody much wanted to receive in those days. I don't know about the politics of Presbyterianism, but I do know that Methodist clergy in the South Carolina Conference used to say being sent to Pelzer was the price one paid for having crossed or offended the bishop. I assume that Presbyterian clergy, though they lacked assigning bishops, were pretty much of the same opinion. So not only did Mr. King serve as an ordained presence among us, but he also brought the added benison of being neither a misfit, a malcontent, nor an ecclesial incorrigible. He was just a retiree with no money and a sick wife.

Mrs. King's health had failed in Africa, and probably because of it. At first, she had stopped working, and they had lived in the Congo on his salary. As her heart had deteriorated, however, they had found themselves spending more and more time back in this country on medical furlough. Eventually they had had to face the reality of her situation and come home to stay, but home was an economy they were ill-prepared to survive in financially. The Church, as a way of providing for them, had placed him in Pelzer where the workload was light, the living cheap, and the stipend, though modest, predictable and always paid on time.

The Kings had come to Pelzer after I began graduate school, so ours

had, in the main, been a Sunday acquaintance until the early autumn of
1961. We spoke, of course, in the friendliest of ways as we chanced to see
each other going in and out to our cars, but that itself was a fairly rare occurrence, given my long days and Sam's erratic hours. Nora, in effect, had
been the only personal connection between our lives and theirs. She
adored Mrs. King, which I to this day still cannot quite explain.

It was not that Celia King was unattractive or unkind, she was just matter-of-fact and without texture. Her hair was white, but no whiter or
thicker or better set than the hair of any other sixty-year-old woman. She
was of average height and average weight, though not stooped in her
shoulders as many older women are. But then, she was not particularly
erect either, and she certainly was not commanding in her posture. If she
ever modulated her voice to attract a child's ear or to speak an endearment,
I did not catch her at it. She had—and I asked Nora this on several occasions—no secret cupboard of cookies or snacks in her kitchen, either, and
never exhibited any other effort to entice or please that I saw. She apparently was just comfortable to be around. There was no question that she
held Mr. King's heart in her hands. I never saw them embrace or kiss, but
he held doors for her and lifted packages for her and introduced her and
in general attended her with a sincerity that matched the steadiness of his
eyes. There were also two daughters, both married and living elsewhere,
who came for visits often enough so I understood they were drawn by affection not duty. Aside from Nora, Mr. King, and the daughters, however,
there was very little traffic in and out of 23, presumably because of Mrs.
King's health.

Because of the lack of informal contact between us and because of the
deadliness of his sermons, I had assumed without giving any thought to it
that Earl King was a dull man as well as a dull homilist. That was not a condemnation on my part, just an assessment. He was certainly not the first
bright person I had ever known who lacked any apparent desire to exist
outside of his or her own mental and emotional environment. Social
amenities are a sufficiency in such cases, as they had been between the
Kings and us until I found myself once more pregnant and on limited activity.

Mary was almost two and Nora a sassy four. Like all children, they preferred the outdoors to Heaven. Even in Pelzer, however, Mary was too

small to be allowed out of doors without an adult. Nora, with the superiority of age, was allowed to go back and forth to the Kings' if someone were watching her from the kitchen window. If Lan or I were outside, she could run up and down the cleared land that was everybody's backyard as far as the house beyond the Kings', which meant she could not go to Nelle's alone at all, but she could get close enough to Aunt June's to holler for June or Max to come grant her the rights of further passage.

It did not take me long that fall to realize that sitting down and even lying down are as easily done out of doors on a lounge chair as indoors on a daybed, especially when the weather is autumnal and sunny. As a matter of fact, I soon realized that both are much more easily and satisfactorily done out of doors if one has a two-year-old and a four-year-old constantly circling one's daybed wanting to know precisely when and how soon they can go out. I gave in and moved my base of gestation to the backyard and its webbed, aluminum lounger.

I cannot now remember exactly when in the course of that late September or early October Mr. King quit waving to me in passing and began to walk over to where I was resting to inquire about how I was feeling, but he did. Then he took to pulling one of the yard chairs over and sitting down for a few minutes. Then, without my realizing it at first, he was talking to me.

The man was not dull, nor did he lack personality. He was just what, for lack of a better term, I would call culture-bound and experience-isolated. Almost four decades in Africa had set his life to rhythms and perceptions that were so alien to American rhythms and perceptions that he could no longer find a bridge back and forth between what he had become and what the rest of us were. He had lost the common ground that sustains conversation, and beyond that, he had no idea of who we were anymore. He did not say these things at first, although he did come eventually to talk about what he called having been "disoriented" when he and Mrs. King had first returned.

Even before he grew familiar enough and comfortable enough to claim his own sense of frustration, however, the content of his conversation betrayed him. I had never before had an occasion to realize just how separated we become when we have no one with whom to share our stories . . . which opportunity was really all Mr. King needed in order to metamorphose from poor homilist to perceptive raconteur and deft revealer of truth.

What we talked about was spirituality, or that is the label most people would use now to describe the content of our conversations. I suspect most people today might even add an adjective and say that what we talked about was New Age spirituality; but I do not wish to suggest either heterodoxy or ecumenism, for neither was present in Earl King. He was a straight-line Calvinist, just one who had seen strange things.

When I say we talked, I flatter myself. At first, he talked. Eventually we got to the place I asked; but it would be a presumption to say I was ever really partner to the conversation. He began very tentatively with small, largely secular references to the Congo. Did I know racism existed in the Congo and was what we would call tribalism? Was it not debilitating to dignify our own tribalism with the more acceptable term of racism? Did I know that the Congolese women never cut the umbilical cord? They chose a spot along its length which they then rolled back and forth between their fingers until it clotted, wore thin, and finally severed by itself. Did I know that Congolese artists painted with outdoor enamels because they had little or no access to oils? Would I like to see some of the canvases he and Celia had managed to get out of the country with and bring back home?

Oh, mercy, yes, I would like to see those! And we had our first real connection. He fetched out a canvas, and for the first time I did not believe him. "I thought you meant house paint," I said.

"I do mean house paint. Turn it over. This one is not only just house enamels, but it's done on a piece of sheeting as well. I know because I gave him the paint and the sheeting from the mission station."

I turned the frame over, and Mr. King was right. It was sheeting, gessoed and heavy, but sheeting nonetheless; and though the medium was an oil-based paint, it was not oil as we normally think of it. The scene was of a high forest and of a trail wandering through it. A figure was coming from the back of the forest toward the foreground, a basket on his or her head . . . an ordinary scene, I am sure, in the Congo. What was not ordinary was the light. How anyone can capture such light and hold it to canvas I do not know; how it was done with the crude tools of house paint and sheeting no Western observer, amateur or professional, would ever know. What the painter had lacked in tools, he had compensated for many times over with intimacy and passion. The forest breathed before me.

"It's the color I miss most," Mr. King said that afternoon, and I perceived immediately that he had just stepped over the abyss and told me something personal. "More here, of course, than in Roanoke."

"Well, of course, you do!," I said. "There's no color here."

"I didn't know whether you knew that or not," he said.

"I didn't, until you said it just now. That's what's missing here, isn't it? What I've been missing all this time?"

"Yes. Everything here except the church windows is a variation on gray or ready-made."

He was right again; and just having him name the beast was like having him lay warm hands on a small ache. I just had not known until then what was wrong or how to lift the burden from me.

"When we leave here, Sam and I are going to become Episcopalians," I said, which may read like a non sequitur, but which did not feel like one at the time nor appear to him to be one.

"Of course you are," he said. "The theology is too loose, but the color is there. Better for the soul that it have color." Then he took the painting I was holding back in the house and, one at a time, fetched out another three or four that he and Mrs. King had hanging in the house.

Mr. King and I did not talk every afternoon, but we did not miss many that October and early November. There was never any set agenda, or at least none that I discerned, though he may have had things he thought needed saying. I remember particularly one afternoon when we had the roiling sky that precedes a thunderstorm but is preternatural when it comes in autumn. I had already sent the girls in to Lan when a shard of lightning flashed from one bank of clouds over to another.

"Weirdest stuff," I said, making conversation until we, too, would have to go in. "Have you ever seen it hit anybody?"

"Have you?" he asked instead of answering.

"Last summer," I said. "I saw it last summer for the first time. I was standing at the kitchen sink with my hands in the water, washing some canning jars, and Lan was sitting in the stool by the door watching me when this storm suddenly came up. I mean, I saw it rolling in from the west through the window, but it didn't look like much until suddenly it was just there, if you know what I mean, with thunder and lightning, the whole works.

"I've always loved a storm, so I was standing there watching when Lan made some kind of noise, and I turned around to look at her. Just as I turned, this light—this two-inch-tall sheet of light—ran in from somewhere outside, along the metal edge of our drainboard, and then jumped off onto Lan. It picked her up and threw her into the stove so hard a pot fell off into the floor. I was sure she was dead, but just as I stooped down to touch her, she half-hollered 'No!' and told me to get back away from her. A minute or so after that, she got up by herself. She wouldn't let me get her anything or call Sam. She said it happened all the time like that to her. I doubt I'll ever see lightning the same way again."

"You mean you're afraid of it now?"

"No, not really. More than anything else, it's more beautiful now that I've seen it so close up."

Mr. King chuckled. "You'd be a good Congolese," he said, "except you'd need to listen to Lan more if you were going to survive for long." The rain began falling, and we said our good-byes.

The next day was cool but sunny, so we three put on sweaters and went outside for a while. Within a few minutes, Mr. King came out in his sweater and sat down beside me. "Did I ever tell you about what engineers like me had to do first when we went into a new village or started a new project near one?"

"No."

"Well, the first thing we had to do after talking with the head man of the village was spend a day or two in one of the village's guest huts. If the hut we were in were struck by lightning, it would burn, and we might or might not burn with it, but either way the village would know that we were evil and our project not good."

"Not a very pleasing form of discernment," I quipped.

"No, actually, a very good one. What you do is wait until after dark each night and then look all through the thatching along the outside perimeter of the roof and up the inside spines of it. If you find a copper wire or a strip of sheet metal buried there, you know somebody in that village doesn't want you, and you have to rethink what you'll do next."

"That's how juju works?" I was more astonished than curious, actually.

"That's how fake juju works, but not the real thing. Every faith's got its charlatans, but the real witch doctors scorn such conniving. A real witch doctor kills by the spirit, not tricks."

There was the longest pause on record just there. I looked at the previously dull man, and he looked back as naturally and unflinchingly as if he had just announced they were having pot roast at his house for dinner that night. He believed what he had just said. "That's not true," I said. "There's no such thing as killing by thinking about it or willing it or hexing or whatever!"

"Why not?"

"Because there's just not."

"Not in this country," he said, "or maybe just not in your part of it because you don't believe it can be done. I've seen too many Congolese die, however, to think for one minute that it can't be done."

"How?"

"I don't know how to answer that for you. There are strings of communication between all living things that the Congolese sees and uses. The fact that you can't doesn't mean they're not there. And it doesn't mean they can't affect you. They can and do, but you'll just find some explanation other than them for what happens."

It was the most frightening three minutes I have ever spent with a clergyman. He was talking about what Jack Hornaday had been trying to capture; but where it had been titillating to toy with Mr. Hornaday's possibilities, it was paralyzing to face Mr. King's. "It's why you can't move mountains," he said, and then left it at that.

As the weather began to grow chillier, I moved our outside time up earlier and earlier in the afternoon. Because of Mrs. King's health, Mr. King did most of the housekeeping chores and cooking. He would see us—probably, given my girls, hear us—come out, and in a minute his back screen would bang and here would be Mr. King still in his lunchtime apron and drying his hands on a dish towel as he came. By then we were talking about everything. He kept wanting me to understand about Vietnam, a country I could scarcely find on the map and whose erstwhile conflict with France I could not have cared less about. "Pray about it," he would say to me with something as close to urgency as he ever got. "Pray about it for the sake of your own children, if not theirs." All of which went right by me. Even six weeks later when Jack Kennedy sent U.S. troops into that strange country as military advisers, it went right by me.

"What do you think really happens when we pray?" I asked him one day.

"Happens?" he repeated. "I guess the best answer is 'What was the Mount of Transfiguration?' "

"You mean we are transformed?"

"Good heavens, no, that's not at all what I meant!" He seemed almost ready to withdraw again, discomforted for the first time in weeks by having been so misunderstood. He looked off a minute as if thinking about whether or not to go on. Then, apparently deciding to risk the effort, he said, "What I mean is that prayer is a place, and Peter and James and John just happened to catch Jesus while he was in it."

Just, I thought, like I caught Dr. Thompson once and my mother several times.

"But," he added, before I could say anything, "you can't go there as long as you don't recognize that the spirit works, because it's made of spirit."

There were not many more conversations after that. There were "Hey, how are you's" across the driveway and "Can't wait for spring and some more backyard time togethers," but no real contact. Mrs. King's health declined a bit more, the weather was cold, and I was confined a great deal of the time. In April, just as the weather was becoming outdoor-perfect, Mrs. King died. One of the married daughters was there at the time, and we heard the other one drive in before midnight that night. The next morning, they all had breakfast together and spent the morning over the details of how he wanted things done. The church and neighbors brought in food, and at lunch everyone more grazed than ate in the kitchen. Then excusing himself for a nap, Mr. King got up from the table, went to the kitchen door, rested his hand against the jamb, smiled one more time at his daughters, and sank dead to the floor, less than twenty-four hours after his Celia.

The Spirit, if one chooses to see it.

PART TEN

Home

74.

IN THOSE WARM FIRST DAYS of summer when the world is large and cordial, the chubby caterpillar crawls upon some log or limb or walkway each morning for little reason other than that the courses of the log or limb or walkway are there and that crawling is innately the business of caterpillars. The greening earth provides food at every turn of each day's paths, and the infant butterfly eats at will and by opportunity, innocent of its coming purposes.

In those warm first days of summer when the world is large and cordial, the chubby child crawls upon some floor or playpen or bit of grassy earth each morning for little reason other than that the courses of the floor or playpen or bit of grassy earth are there and that crawling is innately the business of babies. The tending mother and welcoming father provide food at every turn of each day's paths, and the infant adult eats at will and by opportunity, innocent of its coming purposes, innocent of its self.

By the very virtue of such doing and being, caterpillars and babies are of earnest, if transitory, interest to young children, puppy dogs, and introspective writers. Little boys particularly are given to prodding caterpillars with twigs and dirty fingers just as little girls particularly are given to stroking the softness of babies. Each gender seems equally persuaded, though, that there is something most curious locked up and out of sight within both babies and caterpillars, some creature other than that which presently meets the eye.

Puppy dogs, who likewise are great observers of the world, are less susceptible to wonderment and caution than are children. They are given to nuzzling and licking babies and caterpillars rather indiscriminately. Introspective writers, of whom autobiographers presumably are the extreme example, alternate between the two, between the child's puzzlement about hidden processes and a puppy's probing, sometimes incautious and dangerous, engagement with the subject of its passing attention. That is why in caterpillars and babies, introspective writers find the most obvious examples of the patterns and mystery that we all perceive to be the stuff, as well as the story, of our selves and that novelists and autobiographers, like errant puppy dogs, feel constantly compelled to probe.

The baby is proof of a givenness to life, of a beginning not of the self's own choosing. A baby is a body, a spirit, and an intelligence that, while present, have not yet begun to converse with one another in any kind of balanced dialogue, much less in terms of the soul that they are by way of becoming. A baby is what will first be made by circumstance and then turn, in its maturity, to create circumstance, that pivot being for us and our kind as the bursting of the chrysalis is for the butterfly and its kind.

If Pelzer had been the last and thickest layer of my cocoon, as indeed it was, then Earl King's death was its rupture, the pivotal, thin tear through which I would move out into the world of my own mature identity. He had loved as I wished to love, and he had seen as I wished to see—the Spirit at large in the world and ever at the ready, the soul as life's inescapable result, the self as the dear, enticing, mortal construct that our order of creatures must lay aside in time.

We left South Carolina that year. Max and June went to the Menninger Institute, where he had been awarded a residency in psychiatry and June was to do postgraduate work in psychiatric nursing. Sam and I came back to City of Memphis where he had been awarded a so-much-desired residency in internal medicine and where I had received an almost equally coveted position as lecturer at Rhodes College. We would never leave West Tennessee again, the places of our maturity ever afterward being ones of the spirit or simply those we passed through as visitors on either business or holiday.

Two years later, Sam would become chief resident in medicine and then go on to another three years of advanced specialization in pulmonary medicine before entering private practice. I would go from lecturer at Rhodes to academic dean of a sister institution, the Memphis College of Art, before I finally set aside the life of the academy for the life of a writer and publisher. We would have five more children during those years. One of them, our small son Philip Wade Alexander Tickle, would die in that time of fecundity and grief, and we would bury him in Memphis. Such a planting forever roots the heart as well as its affections.

Camelot would be shattered in the sunshine of a cold autumn day scarcely more than a year after Earl King had slipped quietly down a doorjamb toward joy. Vietnam would become the grinding, maiming machine of his prophecy, and Martin Luther King, Jr., would by his own death galvanize the forces and agencies of just cause. The nations of the First World, like the builders of Babel's Tower, would strive to escape the earth's hold, the difference being that, unlike their predecessors, they would succeed. The Berlin Wall would fall and, in time, Communism itself would follow. The moral issues of the twentieth century would spare none of us; and religion, increasingly my chosen field of study, would be democratized and then reformed by an expanding media, an increasing literacy, and a more populist, as well as more accomplished, scholarship.

Sam and I would complete the process we had begun so long before. We would take instruction in the Episcopal Church and receive the rite of confirmation at last as the Anglo-Catholic Christians we have continued to be in all the years since. After Laura's birth and weaning, I would chance . . . though I doubt that verb more now than ever . . . I would chance one late October morning upon a pile of old books abandoned to the floor in the back corner of an antiquarian book dealer's moldering shop. Idly sorting through that unlikely heap, I would find my first breviary; and in that finding, the final piece of what I was to be would fall into place.

My mind had for some time known about and understood, at least in principle, the ancient monotheistic tradition of fixed-hour prayer and the spiritual discipline for laity of living, like Benedictines, under its rule. My hands now held its means; and at three o'clock that afternoon, at the appointed Christian hour of nones, my spirit began the practice that has been its vocation ever since. These and more are all stories about the living of a life, however, not its shaping, and as such, they must wait for another place and time. The stories I have chosen here are instead prior tales, most of them fondly remembered and all of them gratefully recorded.

There is, I have learned, as much spiritual and emotional labor as mental and physical fatigue inherent in the business of remembering; and being a wiser woman than once I was, I know now that those who enter into the process of recall and self-discovery are never permitted to serve as their own guides. Rather, they are first confronted and then directed by the inexorable truth of what they themselves have been. They are instructed as well; for in the vast, intricate lacework of being within which we are and each of us is, there is a generosity of freedom and a rigidity of boundaries that forever lie in unresolvable tension.

Being but recently returned from my own time of wrestling with that conundrum and of being instructed by it, I have arrived now not just at the end of my stories, but also and predictably at that ancient epilogue within which faith and reason have for millennia met: Blessed be the Name of the Lord, and blessed be His kingdom now and forever . . . words that, like stories, are the juncture of a faith that is sure knowledge and of a reason that believes at last that in blessing God, we most bless ourselves and one another.

Even so, come, Lord Jesus.

© PETER MURPHY

PHYLLIS TICKLE is Contributing Editor in Religion for *Publishers Weekly*. One of America's most respected authorities on religion, she is frequently interviewed for both print and electronic media and is a regular guest on PBS's *Religion & Ethics Newsweekly*. The author of more than two dozen books, including the recently published *The Divine Hours,* she lives in Lucy, Tennessee.